CAPITALISM AND DEMOCRACY

ECONOMISTS OF THE TWENTIETH CENTURY

General Editors: David Colander, *Christian A. Johnson Distinguished Professor of Economics, Middlebury College, Vermont, USA* and Mark Blaug, *Professor Emeritus, University of London, UK, Professor Emeritus, University of Buckingham, UK, Visiting Professor, University of Amsterdam, The Netherlands and Visiting Professor, Erasmus University of Rotterdam, The Netherlands*

This innovative series comprises specially invited collections of articles and papers by economists whose work has made an important contribution to economics in the late twentieth century.

The proliferation of new journals and the ever-increasing number of new articles make it difficult for even the most assiduous economist to keep track of all the important recent advances. By focusing on those economists whose work is generally recognized to be at the forefront of the discipline, the series will be an essential reference point for the different specialisms included. Wherever possible, the articles in these volumes have been reproduced as originally published using facsimile reproduction, inclusive of footnotes and pagination to facilitate ease of reference.

A list of published and future titles in this series is printed at the end of this volume.

Capitalism and Democracy

Challenges and Responses in an Increasingly Interdependent World

Dennis C. Mueller

Professor of Economics, University of Vienna, Austria

ECONOMISTS OF THE TWENTIETH CENTURY

Edward Elgar

Cheltenham, UK • Northampton, MA, USA

Published by
Edward Elgar Publishing Limited
Glensanda House
Montpellier Parade
Cheltenham
Glos GL50 1UA
UK

Edward Elgar Publishing, Inc.
136 West Street
Suite 202
Northampton
Massachusetts 01060
USA

A catalogue record for this book
is available from the British Library

ISBN 1 84064 810 4

Printed and bound in Great Britain by MPG Books Ltd, Bodmin, Cornwall

Contents

PART III TAX AND SUBSIDY RESPONSES

PART IV COMPETITION POLICY RESPONSES

Acknowledgements

The publishers wish to thank the following who have kindly given permission for the use of copyright material:

Cambridge University Press for excerpt: 'Public Subsidies for Private Firms in a Federalist Democracy', in *Competition and Structure: The Political Economy of Collective Decisions: Essays in Honour of Albert Breton* (eds. Gialuigi Galeotti, Pierre Salmon and Ronald Wintrobe), Cambridge, UK and New York, USA: Cambridge University Press, 2000, pp. 339–63.

The Cegla Institute for Comparative and Private International Law and the Buchmann Faculty of Law, Telaviv University for article: 'Defining Citizenship', *Theoretical Inquiries in Law*, **3** (1), January 2002, pp. 151–66.

Department of Public Finance, National Chengchi University, Taipei for article: 'Capitalism and Democracy in Northeast Asia: Present and Prospects', *Public Economics Review*, **1** (2), December 1996, pp. 1–32.

Elsevier Science for article: 'Lessons from the United States' Antitrust History', *International Journal of Industrial Organization*, **14** (4), June 1996, pp. 415–45.

Kluwer Academic Publishers for articles and excerpts: 'Fundamental Issues in Constitutional Reform: With Special Reference to Latin America and the United States', *Constitutional Political Economy*, **10** (2), June 1999, pp. 119–48; 'Constitutional Constraints on Governments in a Global Economy', *Constitutional Political Economy*, **9** (3), September 1998, pp. 171–86, reprinted in *Concorrenza Fiscale in Un'Economia Internazionale Integrata* (eds. Massimo Bordignon and Domenico da Emploi), Milan: Franco Angeli, 1999, pp. 11–33; 'Centralism, Federalism, and the Nature of Individual Preferences', *Constitutional Political Economy*, **12** (2), June 2001, pp. 161–72; 'Federalism and the European Union: A Constitutional Perspective', *Public Choice*, **90**, 1997, pp. 255–80, reprinted in *Constitutional Political Economy in a Public Choice Perspective* (ed. C.K. Rowley), Dordrecht: Kluwer; 'Merger Policy in the United States: A Reconsideration', *Review of Industrial Organization*, **12** (5–6), December 1997, pp. 655–85.

Routledge for excerpt: 'Constitutional Issues Regarding European Union Expansion', in *Widening the European Union: The Politics of Institutional Change and Reform* (ed. B. Steunenberg), London: Routledge, 2002, pp. 41–57.

Springer-Verlag for article and excerpt: 'Capitalism, Democracy and Rational Individual Behavior', *Journal of Evolutionary Economics*, **10** (1–2), 2000, pp. 67–82; 'A Global

Competition Policy for a Global Economy', in *Merits and Limits of Markets* (ed. H. Giersch), Berlin/Heidelberg: Springer, 1998, pp. 211–35.

Every effort has been made to trace all the copyright holders but if any have been inadvertently overlooked the publishers will be pleased to make the necessary arrangements at the first opportunity.

Introduction

The latter third of the twentieth century was a time of great economic and political change. On the political front three main sets of developments can be identified: (1) The increasing political integration of Western Europe through a series of treaties that have transformed a loose confederation of nation states into a hybrid structure that lies somewhere between a confederation of independent states and a federation of sub-states. The expanding size and scope of this aptly named European Union as more and more countries are brought into it. (2) The collapse of Communism in Eastern Europe and the Soviet Union with – at least initially – the appearance of democratic institutions in virtually all of the former Communist countries. (3) The widespread displacement of dictatorial regimes by democratic ones in Latin America, Asia and other parts of the world.

Dramatic changes have been equally apparent on the economic front, although these have not been as unidirectional as have the political changes. The collapse of Communism symbolized, of course, a great triumph for the institutions of capitalism. Add to this the deregulation and privatization movement that spread from North America to Europe and then across the rest of the world, and one has a tremendous shift over the last quarter of a century toward greater reliance on the free play of markets to allocate all sorts of goods and services, the allocation of which would formerly have been partially, if not solely, the responsibility of the state.

Although these broad trends all seem to go in one direction, undercurrents were also visible over the last third of the twentieth century that suggested significant structural weaknesses in the economies of some countries. Over the 1970s and 1980s, corporations in the United States lost market shares in one industry after another to foreign competition – particularly to Asian companies. This apparent loss in competitiveness was frequently attributed to managerial failures. The Anglo-Saxon corporate governance structure was thought to be inferior to the bank-based systems in Japan and Germany.

The 1970s, 1980s and much of the 1990s were, however, not decades characterized by spectacular economic performance in Europe either. Productivity lagged, unemployment grew. The German and Swedish miracles came visibly to an end. Considerable concern was expressed in the waning stages of the millennium about the competitiveness of the European economies.

The faltering economic performance in North America and Europe over much of the last three decades stood in stark contrast to the continual spectacular performance of the Asian tigers over the same period. Indeed, when China was factored in, many crystal ball gazers began to proclaim that the twenty-first century would belong to Asia. The 'Asian crisis' that struck in 1997 has placed this projection in doubt, however. The economies of most of the Asian tigers still have not fully recovered from the crisis. The Japanese economy has been sputtering for more than a decade now. Thus, capitalism's triumph over socialism does not imply that all is well in each capitalist economy. Many challenges remain to be tackled.

Part I of this book discusses some of these challenges. The opening essay asks why democracy and capitalism in the former Communist countries have not been a greater success up until now. The emphasis is particularly on the failings of democracy in these countries, and upon whether these can be attributed to the fact that individuals do not behave as rationally as our economic models predict they will.

The varied economic performance of countries in North America, Europe and Asia over the last three decades raises the question of why it is that some nations rise economically and some decline. The economic literature on growth contains many hypotheses to explain the rise of nations. Why once successful nations decline is more of a puzzle. Most of the second essay deals with this puzzle.

Although both the United States and Europe experienced sub-par economic performance over much of the 1970s and 1980s, the performance of the US economy over much of the 1990s far surpassed that of Western Europe. This difference has been so striking that it has elicited much discussion in Europe about the relative roles of the market and the state, and how they differ on the two sides of the Atlantic. The third essay tries to account for some of these differences and discusses their implications.

Where capitalism has been tried in East Asia its performance has been little short of spectacular. The same cannot be said for democracy. Indeed, some of Asia's economically most successful capitalist countries have yet to try introducing democratic institutions. The closing essay in Part I discusses why this might be so and makes some suggestions for what these institutions might look like.

All of the essays in Part II discuss constitutional institutions that might be introduced to improve the performance of an existing democracy or to create a new one. The first essay in Part II (Chapter 5) discusses the properties of a full range of constitutional institutions. It represents a drastically abridged version of my book, *Constitutional Democracy* (Oxford University Press, 1996). The essay was written for presentation to the constitutional convention that took place in Equador at the beginning of 1999, and thus examines specifically the problems that arise in presidential systems as they exist in North and South America.

One of the alleged dangers of globalization is increasing tax competition across countries. This tax competition is claimed to be bad because it forces states to cut needed expenditures and transfers. This claim is challenged in several essays in this book, the first one being Chapter 6. It is argued that tax competition does require institutional changes, but that these institutional changes will in fact be welfare enhancing not welfare reducing in contradiction to the claims of opponents of tax competition.

The increasing economic and political integration that globalization fosters places increasing decision-making burdens upon the individual *qua* consumer, worker, investor and citizen. The increasing mobility of individuals raises issues of when citizens should lose their citizenship after they have left one political jurisdiction and when they should be able to obtain citizenship in another jurisdiction. Chapter 7 takes up the issue of defining citizenship in an increasingly complex and mobile world.

One of the challenges that we face in our increasingly interdependent and mobile world is how to design the institutions of democracy so that individuals can control their own collective destinies. Federalist institutions are particularly attractive in this regard because they can both 'bring government down' to the level of the individual citizen and, where need be, allow it to expand upward as far as needed to satisfy the collective wants of individuals for public goods with very broad spillovers. Chapters 8 and 9 deal with the design of federalist institutions. The first discusses the advantages and disadvantages of federalist and centralist forms of government, and relates them to differences in the degrees of heterogeneity of individual preferences. The issue of preference heterogeneity is also of importance in Chapter 9, where the issue of European federalism is taken up. Whether or not a federalist or a confederalist European Union would be optimal should depend on whether European-wide public goods exist, and whether individual preference for these goods are homogeneous within the existing nation states or not.

The final chapter in Part II discusses the constitutional issues surrounding the admission of new members to the European Union.

The conventional wisdom in much of the economics profession is that subsidies to private firms are bad and that tax competition is bad. These shibboleths are challenged in Chapters 12 and 13. There it is shown that neither subsidies to private firms nor tax competition need be feared, if they arise in a polity with a federalist structure in which the beneficiaries from collective actions also bear their costs.

Where Parts II and III deal mostly with the design of political institutions, Part IV is concerned entirely with the functioning of the economy. In particular, it seeks to describe the kinds of competition policies that are needed as we begin the twenty-first century. Chapter 14 seeks to determine what lessons we can learn from the experience of the United States over the last century. After reviewing this history, it offers some suggestions for an improved set of competition policies.

Chapter 15 does the same, but concentrates entirely on merger policy. The final chapter of the book explores the issues raised in trying to establish a global competition policy.

Although the arguments and recommendations made in this book are, of course, based on the author's knowledge of the past, they are much more future oriented than is true of most contributions to economics or public choice – including those of the author. What should a new democracy's constitution look like? Should the European Union be organized as a federation? What should a global competition policy consist of? These are broad and difficult questions and no one – certainly not this author – can claim to have definitive answers to them. But in posing these questions and offering at least partial answers to them, I hope to succeed in at least provoking the reader to come up with better answers.

PART I

CHALLENGES

J Evol Econ (2000) 10: 67–82

Journal of
Evolutionary
Economics

Capitalism, democracy and rational individual behavior*

Dennis C. Mueller

Institut für Wirtschaftswissenschaften, Universität Wien,
Brünner Straße 72, A-1210 Wien, Austria

The collapse of communism in Eastern Europe and the Soviet Union beginning in 1989 to many observers seemed to signal the triumph of the capitalistic and democratic institutions of the West over the socialist and totalitarian institutions that had been the hallmark of communism.

In the nearly ten years that have elapsed since "the great transition" was launched, neither the West's capitalist nor its democratic institutions have been fully and successfully transplanted in the former communist countries. Nor have the benefits these countries have received from the transplants lived up to their, or most Westerners', expectations.

Given the magnitude of the transition process, and the depths to which the communist countries had fallen, the lack of "instant success" in transition is perhaps, with the help of hindsight, not so surprising. Nevertheless, the fact that the opening up of markets has not led to more visible improvements in living standards in the former communist countries must be judged as a contradiction of sorts to the predictions of standard neoclassical economics. Why have individuals in the former communist countries not responded more aggressively to the incentives for profits and self-gain that the opening up of markets has produced? Why has the unleashing of market forces not led to greater and more consistent improvements in welfare?

There are, of course, many possible answers to these questions, and no single answer is likely to come close to being correct. But a part of the answer may certainly be that the expectation that the opening up of markets would work wonders was unrealistic, as unrealistic as the assumptions

Paper presented at the 1998 World Conference of the International Joseph A. Schumpeter Society, Vienna, June 13–16, 1998.

*This paper has received financial support from the Hochschuljubiläumsstiftung of the City of Vienna.

regarding individual behavior that underlie the neoclassical models of competitive markets that engender such expectations.

The key behavioral assumption of neoclassical economics is, of course, that all individuals are rational egoists. This behavioral assumption is perhaps the most conspicuous methodological difference between economics and its sister social sciences.[1] It lies at both the *positive* and the *normative* hearts of the discipline. It is used by economists to explain *how* the competitive process allocates resources, and *why* this allocation is socially optimal. It has also been employed by practitioners of public choice to explain the behavior of political actors, and to proclaim the inherent irrationality of the democratic process.

Both the rationality and the egoistic components of the rational egoism assumption have been heavily criticized. These criticisms call into question both the positive and the normative predictions of economics regarding the workings of the market, and at least the predictive side of public choice. These criticisms may also help to explain the faltering start of capitalism and democracy in the aftermath of communism.

In this essay I do not belabor the criticisms of the rational egoism postulate that have been made. Instead, I accept many of them as valid, and offer an alternative "behavioralist" assumption about human behavior in its place. In certain contexts this behavioralist assumption leads to similar predictions as the rational egoism postulate, and thus can reinforce both the positive and normative claims of neoclassical economics. In other contexts it undermines these claims. With respect to political behavior, however, the implications are almost uniformly negative. Positing more realistic individual behavior undermines some of the positive analysis of public choice without necessarily overturning its pessimistic normative implications.

Having explored the implications of the more realistic behavioral assumption offered in this paper, I return to the question of the future of capitalism and democracy in both the former communistic countries, and in other countries that have yet to embrace one or both of these sets of institutions. I shall argue that the potential for capitalism and democracy to take hold does indeed depend on a limited degree of rational egoism on the part of the individuals living in these countries.

I The formation of habits and economic behavior

Rational agent models in their purest forms assume that individuals are forward looking optimizers correctly calculating which strategy promises the highest payoffs in each situation. When making a decision, each actor contemplates only the *future* payoffs from each possible action. Past payoffs are relevant only to the extent that they help the forward-looking rational agent to accurately predict the future. One implication is that in a one-shot prisoners' dilemma, each rational player chooses the noncooperative strategy with probability one.

[1] This statement is, however, less true today than say 25 years ago.

In the typical one-shot prisoners' dilemma experiment, however, the participants routinely violate this most basic prediction of rational actor models. For example, in public goods experiments participants normally voluntarily contribute in the neighborhood of 50 percent of the jointly optimal amount, when a contribution near zero would be individually optimal.[2] Such seemingly irrational actions can be readily explained with models of man that are *backward* looking, and that view human behavior as *adaptive*. Individuals are generally rewarded in every day life for cooperating in prisoners' dilemma situations, and when someone correctly perceives that she is in such a situation her response conforms to those that have been previously rewarded.

Consistent with this behavioralist psychology interpretation, we find that participants in PD-experiments are quickly conditioned to defect by the half-hearted cooperation of the other players. After a few repetitions of the game, the noncooperative Nash equilibrium predicted by rational choice does emerge. Only following *many* repetitions do the cooperative outcomes described in the supergame literature begin to be observed, if at all.[3] All of these experimental results are much more consistent with a theory of adaptive behavior than with rational choice theory. Indeed, the celebrated tit-for-tat strategy that most reliably generates the cooperative supergame outcome is nothing more than a formula for conditioning the other player to cooperate by rewarding past cooperation and punishing defections.

Anyone who has trained a dog to sit and roll over has successfully applied the principles of behavioral psychology, as has every parent. By applying the principles of operant conditioning parents develop good, and sometimes not so good, habits in their children. As children grow older, people outside of the home and the institutional environment play an ever increasing role in rewarding and punishing their actions.

Behavioral psychology's account of human action is fully consistent with the *egoistic* portion of the rational egoism postulate. Human behavior, as that of all other animals, is hedonistic. Humans respond unconsciously and almost unwillingly to various stimuli, and the recollections of past rewards and punishments that they arouse.

Despite the significant differences in assumptions about human behavior that underlie behavioral psychology and neoclassical economics, they can lead to similar predictions for *experienced* agents. A behavioral psychology account of the law of demand would run as follows. Each week the consumer spends a $100 on groceries at the supermarket. In those weeks when the consumer chooses items marked "on sale," he finds that his basket contains more items. Looking for and buying items on sale or with newly reduced prices is reinforced. The experienced (well-conditioned) shopper behaves *as if* he were consciously maximizing a utility function subject to a budget constraint. Psychologists have been able to confirm the law of

---

[2] The seminal contributions are by Marwell and Ames (1979, 1980, 1981). For a short summary of the major findings, see Hoffman (1997, pp. 415–419).

[3] See Isaac, McCue, and Plott (1985), and again Hoffman (1997, pp. 415–419).

demand and other predictions of economics in the laboratory (Staddon, 1983). The thirsty rat, like his human cousin, has a negative sloped demand schedule for water.

Thus, because of the egoistic dimension that behavioral psychology and rational actor models share, both lead to much the same predictions with respect to the repeat actions of individuals in an unchanging environment. Behavioral psychology has the advantage over rational actor models of also being consistent with the seemingly "irrational" behavior of individuals in unusual situations, as for example the failure of people who have not been flood victims to purchase insurance against floods even when it is offered at less than its actuarial value (Kunreuther et al., 1978). In the absence of past rewards and punishments, all actions are essentially random events and there is no reason to expect them to conform to a rational actor model.

If one is willing to substitute the sort of hedonism assumed by the behavioral psychologist for the economist's utilitarianism, then behavioral psychology's description of human behavior can also be used in a *normative* defense of competitive markets. The market process conditions search on the part of consumers and innovation and efficiency on the part of firms. Consumers are rewarded with greater consumer's surplus for each dollar spent, firms with greater profits. In an unchanging environment market competition tends to maximize the rewards to consumers.

II Collective conditioning mechanisms

Every society contains institutions that reward behavior that benefits the community, and punishes socially harmful behavior. Customs and taboos play this role in primitive societies, state enforced laws in advanced societies. All religions have commandments forbidding various types of antisocial behavior. All religions have their "golden rules" that prescribe cooperative behavior in prisoners' dilemma situations.

The existence of these sorts of institutions can be explained in either behavioralist or Darwinian terms. A random act of punishing theft reduces the frequency of theft and thereby benefits all members of the community. Over time the collective habit of punishing theft evolves. Tribes which happen to develop taboos against incest produce healthier and more intelligent members, and win out in the evolutionary struggle against tribes which condone incest.

III "Irrational behavior"

Habits develop as a result of a rather crude causal association in a person's mind or subconscious. An event following an action is interpreted as being caused by it. Correlation often does not imply causality, as we all know, and thus individuals often mistakenly infer causality. Out of such mistakes arise habits that are afunctional or even dysfunctional. The football player accidently dons different colored socks on a day when he scores three goals, and consciously begins to wear nonmatching socks on days when there is a game.

For actions that are often repeated, the failure of the chance sequencing of events to reoccur generally leads to a reduction in frequency. But for some actions, reinforcement may occur often enough to maintain a habit once formed. Events loosely match those predicted by the day's horoscope with enough frequency that the individual continues to check the morning newspaper to see what the stars have in store for her today.

The importance of chance sequencing can also account for the variety of "collective habits" that we observe across cultures, and their differing mores and traditions. The tribe has unusually good luck hunting on a day when a pair of bald eagles is spotted, and it begins to pray to the eagle. Good luck by a full moon leads to prayers to the moon.

All religions reinforce habits of compliance with rewards and punishments. Most supplement immediate rewards and punishments with promises of much greater ones in the hereafter. Not being verifiable, these constitute a particularly effective way to sustain modes of behavior that would otherwise disappear.

Thus, the behavior of most individuals is a mixture of "good" habits that lead directly to improvements in the welfare of the individual; actions with no substantive consequences that are sustained by chance reinforcement in the past, and a certain number of dysfunctional "bad" habits that arose in the same way. The same sort of triumvirate of social institutions – functional, afunctional and dysfunctional – can be identified.

It should be stressed that dysfunctional behavior need not be restricted to primitive societies or to those of low IQ. Thomas Kuhn's (1970) discussion of scientific paradigms fits behavioral psychology well. The young scholar follows the structures of the reigning paradigm and is rewarded by the accolades of her peers. By middle age, the scientific habits of this paradigm are so thoroughly conditioned that she can adopt no other, even though her research under the old paradigm produces many falsified predictions, and is now frequently criticized by the young. Old scientists, like old dogs, cannot learn new methodological tricks. It is the young who must be conditioned to adopt the new paradigm.

IV Political behavior

One of the most famous and venerable results in the public choice literature is the Hotelling-Downs prediction that two parties competing over a single dimensional issue space converge on the same, central position. This prediction is not born out in the course of a single election, but does seem to emerge over time. Candidates perceived to be far to the left or right of the median of the ideological spectrum, as Barry Goldwater and George McGovern were, suffer humiliating defeats. Tony Blair brought the Labour Party back into power by abandoning the most extreme of its traditional ideological positions, and Bill Clinton – dubbed "Republican Lite" by his opponent in the last election – has survived in the face of a Republican Renaissance by occupying the center of the American ideological spectrum.

The tendency for extremist candidates to lose to centralist candidates, and thus the dominance of middle-of-the-road politicians in two-party systems can be interpreted in either Darwinian or Skinnerian terms. Those candidates who take positions far from the center and stick to them, tend not to survive in a two-party system. Those candidates who experiment with different positions find that movement toward the center is rewarded with increases in votes, movements away from the center are punished with fewer votes. Under either interpretation, one expects the Downsian prediction of candidates locating near the center to emerge. Candidates are not the only people whose behavior is conditioned by election outcomes, however.

When the sportsfan's attendance at a game is rewarded by the home team's victory, the probability that the fan attends another game increases. Winning teams have higher attendance figures than losing teams. A party or candidate's victory in an election rewards its supporters, while punishing the actions of the loser's backers.[4] In a two-party electoral system, some 40 percent or more of the electorate is disappointed by the election's outcome. In contrast, under proportional representation virtually all competing parties win some seats, and thus all party supporters are rewarded by at least the partial victory of their party. One predicts greater voter turnouts in PR-systems, and that is what one observes (Powell, 1982).

Of course, the voter's only reward or punishment from an election is not the victory or defeat of her party. The policy outcomes that flow from the election results should also affect the voter's behavior. Here, however, the link between action and reward or punishment is attenuated. First of all, the consequences of the election enfold over several years, which tends to break the subconscious causal chain. Second, the government's policies are likely to contain some elements that improve the voter's welfare and some that do not. Third, the voter may not recognize that a given change in her welfare was in fact a consequence of the election. Thus, both the act of voting and the choice of candidate or party are likely to be weakly rewarded or punished in a democratic system. For this reason, a large proportion of the rewards and punishments a voter experiences through participation in the democratic process come through the reactions of her peers rather than from the outcomes of the election itself.

This behavioralist interpretation of voting matches well what we know about voters. Those individuals who do vote, do so not because they expect their vote to be decisive and the victory of their preferred candidate to have a significant impact on their future welfare, as the rational choice literature postulates, but out of a sense of civic duty.[5] Good citizens are conditioned to do a lot of seemingly irrational things like contributing to charities, not littering, and queueing at bus stops. The rewards for these actions are typically the approbation of one's neighbors. With time these rewards become *internalized*, the voter's reward for voting is simply avoiding the guilty conscience she would have, if she did not vote.

---

[4] Brennan and Buchanan (1984) draw an analogy between voting and cheering for a sports team.

[5] The literature on voting is vast. For surveys, see Mueller (1989, Ch.17), and Aldrich (1997).

The choices voters make at the polls also conform to the predictions of behavioral psychology. The best account of voter choices is provided by the theory of *retrospective* voting.[6] When making a party choice the voter looks *backward* at her past choices, and the past performance of the party in office. Most empirical studies of voter behavior also find that voters have short memories. It is only the recent performance of a party that influences voter choices.[7]

Thus, the picture of the voter which emerges from the empirical literature is quite different from that underlying rational choice theories. Individuals are creatures of habit when they vote, as when they work and play. They vote for the same party in the present election as in the last one, unless that decision is perceived to have been unrewarded or punished. Unlike in market transactions, however, the rewards and punishments that follow voting are neither immediate nor often clearly linked to the act of voting. Thus, rational or irrational political beliefs and behavior – like beliefs in the prognostic powers of constellations of stars – are likely to persist even in individuals whose everyday behavior in the market place conforms well to that predicted by rational actor models.

Despite the potential for irrational political behavior, one can imagine a democratic system evolving in which citizens actively participate, punish governments which provide bad policies and reward those providing good ones. Parties are conditioned to provide good policies and the political participation of individual citizens is rewarded by these policies. The strength of the country's democratic institutions increases over time, as the good performance of governments and the responsible actions of citizens reinforce one another.

One can also readily imagine less happy democratic scenarios, however. The bad luck or bad policies of a government produce unhappiness in a large fraction of the population. Politicians and parties step forward with a variety of proposals to improve the situation. Having no experience with any of the parties, voters are ill-equipped to choose from among the options offered to them. They punish the existing government and replace it with a new one. Should they fail to elect a government that can significantly improve matters, it too is likely to be replaced. If fundamental reforms are required to improve outcomes, and a lag exists between implementing any reforms and their beneficial effects, no government may be able to survive long enough to correct matters. The country shifts from one government to another, sometimes returning a previous party to power without ever hitting upon a party or a set of policies that voters judge to have benefitted them. Citizens perceive meagre benefits from democracy, and do not defend it when it comes under attack from a demagogic politician or general.

Such attacks on democracy cannot succeed, of course, without the support of some elements of the population. Such support is made possible, even for the most ruthless dictator with the most improbable ideology, by the irrationality inherent in politics. Having been punished by the present

---

[6] See Fiorina (1981, 1997) and Hibbs (1987).

[7] See Paldam (1997, p. 346).

government, citizens are willing to try a new one. Should this one fail too, its failure may not be linked to its improbable ideology or the actions of its leaders. With time the memory of a government's failures fades and is displaced by experience with the most recent government. Thus, failed parties with improbable ideologies survive to govern again.

V The dilemma of democracy

Philosophers have been well aware of dilemmas arising out of social interaction and have propounded one logical argument after another to convince themselves, and indirectly we nonphilosophers, of the wisdom and morality of behaving cooperatively. An Immanuel Kant can readily recognize that mankind's only real choice is between a world in which everyone cooperates and one in which no one does, and from this observation conclude that it is in every rational individual's self-interest to cooperate. Few people seem to follow this chain of reasoning, however. While under the Kantian logic, cooperation is rational in *all* prisoners' dilemma situations, we tend to observe it only where individuals have been conditioned to cooperate. Cooperation is strongest in the family, followed by groups with ethnic, religious or similar cultural ties. Large cities have always had a reputation for greater crime than their surrounding countrysides, as one anticipates given the changing identities and greater numbers of participants in the many prisoners' dilemmas that are enacted in a large city each day. Crime is no where more rampant today than in the teaming megapolises of the developing world, filled with their recent migrants from the countryside. When informal rewards and punishment do not suffice to induce cooperative behavior, society resorts to the state to mete out punishment. Here, as in many other areas, the United States has become the world leader with its ever escalating penalties for crime, and its ever expanding number of overcrowded prisons.

These developments have disturbing implications for the performance of democratic institutions, as individual participation in the democratic process is itself a sort of prisoners' dilemma. Joseph Schumpeter (1950, pp. 250–264) was perhaps the first to emphasize the irrationality of active and informed participation in the democratic process, and Anthony Downs's (1957) expression "rational ignorance" has joined "free rider" and a handful of other terms coined by economists in the layman's vocabulary. Despite the blatant irrationality of the act of voting, apparent to all economists, millions of citizens – and even a few economists – have persistently participated in the democratic process. Behavioral psychology can again come to the rescue and account for this anomaly. In the small New England or Swiss village, townspeople gather at the polling place on election day. Each citizen knows the other, and the absence of any one of them is readily observed. Where direct democracy is still practiced in Switzerland, the day on which the townspeople meet to exercise their rights as citizens is a local holiday in which citizens don their traditional customs and socialize with their neighbors.

But the small towns of New England and Switzerland, like small towns in all other industrialized parts of the world, have seen their young people move to the cities, and many who now live in them commute to the cities. Ties to community have weakened, and consequently the habit-reinforcing effects of peer group pressure have also weakened. Citizen participation in the democratic process is declining in every mature democracy in the world.

The social response to noncooperative behavior of other forms is to pass laws, impose penalties and hire police, that is to invoke the power of the state. But behind the *democratic* state is the *demos*. The essence of democracy is that the citizens rule. But if the citizens choose independently not to rule, the citizens collectively are not going to be able to compel them to do so, or at least not very easily. One can, of course, fine or bribe people to vote, and some countries do this. But one cannot fine people who choose to remain uninformed. Rational ignorance remains a challenge to democracy even if voter participation can be somehow compelled and sustained. Indeed, it becomes more of a problem, since the additional participation induced by compulsory voting is of the least well-informed members of the community. Their participation seems more likely to worsen the outcomes from democracy than to improve them.

VI The viability of market and democratic institutions

A. Market institutions

The rewards from trade are apparent to every pair of children when they first exchange a piece of candy for a piece of gum. Each exchange rewards both buyer and seller and reinforces their loyalty to the exchange process. Thus, the opening up of markets to unrestricted exchange as occurred in Eastern Europe and the Soviet Union following 1989 and 1991 could and has won quick converts to the merits of markets.

The benefits from spot market transactions are immediate and apparent, and thus this form of behavior is readily learned. The benefits from saving and investment are less immediate. The pain of reduced consumption is immediate, but the reward of additional consumption comes later and is more uncertain. Thus, both individuals and governments find it more difficult to acquire the habit of saving than that of spending. It is similarly difficult to establish institutions that encourage saving, investing, innovating and risktaking. Although the former Communist countries have by and large become *free market* economies, in the sense that much exchange taking place is at market determined prices, they have not succeeded nearly so well in becoming *capitalist* countries with institutions that secure property rights, enforce long-run contracts and encourage investment, innovation and risktaking.

This failure has resulted in the former Communist countries experiencing less investment and growth than they otherwise could have, of course. But it has had another perhaps even more unfortunate consequence. Market competition creates winners and losers. Many regard this aspect of a market/capitalist system as its most unfortunate characteristic. When the profits of the winners are obtained from innovations and investment, however, they can be defended by pointing to the new products, jobs, and overall increase in social welfare that accompanied them. Bill Gates' immense wealth can be tolerated, if not celebrated, by all, because it has come from the spectacular growth of a company whose success is due to a continual stream of product improvements.

Many of the nouveau riche in the post-communist countries, however, have earned their fortunes through arbitraging differences in spot market prices in the West and East, or by acquiring existing assets owned by the state at bargain prices. Although arbitrage can enhance social welfare, arbitragers do not create assets, jobs and wealth, and thus their conspicuously displayed riches are more difficult to defend.

If asked to explain the collapse of Communism, most Western economists would probably begin by talking about the virtues of markets, invisible hands, and the like. Most would, and this would certainly be true of members of the Schumpeter Society, go on, however, to discuss the failure of Communism to generate the product and process innovations that a dynamically competitive capitalist economy produces. Communism's singular failure was not its pricing and allocation of *existing products*, but its failure to develop new ones.[8] The post-Communist countries have also failed, relative to their potential, by not adopting institutions that facilitate the capital investment and innovation of a dynamically competitive capitalist economy. Introducing such institutions would require, however, the kind of forward looking, farsighted behavior on the part of citizens and politicians that our rational actor models typically assume exists, and psychological experiments seldom confirm.

B. Democratic institutions

When Communism collapsed, both those living in the Communist countries and those in the West expected these countries to adopt both the capitalist and the democratic institutions of the West. These institutions were conceptually conjoined. Capitalism and democracy in tandem would increase economic and social welfare. In no former Communist country has this prediction been realized to the degree that many thought would occur.

Our behavioralist discussion of human action helps us to understand why this has been so. Democracy, unlike market exchange, yields few immediate benefits. A free press allows the citizen to learn more about her government and those in it, but what she learns does not always make her happy. The right to vote allows her to express her preferences for public policies, but majoritarian democracy ensures that nearly half of the population fails to have its preferences satisfied. Where market exchange produces only winners, democratic action inevitably produces winners and losers. The benefits from democracy are both less immediate and less apparent. The frustrated citizen/voter can well wonder whether another party, or another set of institutions might not yield better outcomes. The

[8] Murrell (1990).

demagogue's promises of immediate prosperity can easily captivate someone who perceives little gain from democracy's outcomes. Democratic institutions, like the basic institutions of capitalism, can increase the welfare of society only over the long run. For this to happen, forward looking, farsighted behavior on the part of citizens and politicians is again required.

VII The future of capitalism and democracy

Behavioral psychology gives a good description of how humans learn, and can account for many of their actions, particularly at the early stages of their development. But as humans pass from childhood into adulthood, many seem to "breakout" of their conditioned behavior patterns. Many begin to question why it is that they should behave in this way or that. Many begin to think and act in at least some areas, as our rational actor models predict.

The same process seems to take place occasionally at the societal level. The behavior of members of a primitive society, heavily constrained by customs, traditions and superstitions, seems to conform to what one would expect from behavioral psychology. The same might be said of the rather static, slowly evolving societies of the Dark and Middle Ages. But during the first half of the present millennium Western Society, like many a bright adolescent, began to break out of its intellectual constraints. The advances in science, mathematics and philosophy that the European Renaissance unleashed suggest that the human mind possesses the capacity to engage in rational thought at the highest levels.

Probably no single sentence in all of philosophy is better known than Descartes' "I think therefore I am." In placing the individual and his thought process at the center of the search for a proof of God's existence, Descartes embraced the revolutionary idea that evidence of God's existence was not to be found in declarations of the Church, or the King, nor by consulting a holy book or a holy man, but in the reasoning process of the individual contemplating God's existence before his fireplace in the solitude of his study. If a thinking man could construct an argument for God's existence that convinced himself, then God existed. No higher authority was needed than the rational logic of an individual's own mind.

Descartes helped to advance the transformation in Western thought that began in the Renaissance and culminated in the Enlightenment, a transformation that saw the individual move to center stage in social and philosophical analysis, and which placed increasing faith in the individual's powers of reason. Democracy was also rediscovered during Europe's intellectual reawakening in Renaissance Italy. It was the thinking of the Enlightenment, however, with its optimistic faith in human reasoning that provided democracy its intellectual raison d'être. The optimism of the Enlightenment is reflected in Adam Smith's *Wealth of Nations* (1776), with its faith in the invisible hand of market competition, and in the U.S. Declaration of Independence with its faith in man's capacity for self-government.

The thinking of the Enlightenment can also be discerned in the U.S. Constitution. In putting this thinking into practice, however, the Founding Fathers exhibited considerable concern about democracy's potential excesses, and accordingly considerable caution. The popularly elected House of Representatives was to be held in check by both the Senate and the President, neither of whom was to be popularly elected. Considerable caution was also apparent in the original constitutions of the individual states, which often set the term of office of a governor at one year. Perhaps, no aspect of the early phases of American democracy reveals the Founders' ambivalence over democracy's potential better than the requirements each state placed on participation in the democratic process, requirements that limited participation to a tiny fraction of the population.

Writing almost a century after the signing of the Declaration of Independence, John Stuart Mill (1861, p. 114) would also express deep concern about the potential of democratic government.

The natural tendency of representative government, as of modern civilization, is toward collective mediocrity; and this tendency is increased by all reductions and extensions of the franchise, their effect being to place the principal power in the hands of classes more and more below the highest level of instruction in the community.

John Stuart Mill was arguably the greatest mind of the 19th century, and one of its most liberal thinkers. The quoted lines come from a treatise in which Mill proclaimed the newly invented proportional representation system to be "one of the greatest improvements yet made in the theory and practice of government." Mill believed, based "on principles of equal justice," that "every minority in the whole nation [was] entitled to a representative" (Mill, 1861, p. 111). Yet he also believed that the demands placed upon the citizen by a system of self-government were so great that participation in such a system had to be limited to those of "the highest level of instruction in the community."

Anyone today who even suggests that the privilege of voting be limited to those who can read and write, or to those possessing a modicum of knowledge about the institutions of government, is immediately labeled an arch conservative – or much worse. Yet we have seen that the rationale underlying democracy rests on the premise that the individual participant possesses a certain capacity to reason, a capacity to recognize the cooperative nature of the democratic game, and to perceive the long run benefits from playing this game cooperatively, despite being rewarded only intermittently and indirectly for such behavior. The history of democratic government, most of which has been written over the last 200 years, gives ample evidence of the fragility of democracy. This history offers no grounds for assuming that democratic government can thrive or even merely survive regardless of the cultural environment in which it is planted, or the inputs it receives from the citizens.

In a few places it has survived. Switzerland, the United Kingdom, and the United States have all enjoyed long, uninterrupted histories of democratic rule with only occasional threats to their democratic institutions as during the Civil War in the United States and World War II in the United

Kingdom. All of the Western Europe countries seem likely to continue being democracies into the indefinite future. Even if citizen participation in the democratic process continues to wane in the West, a total collapse of democracy does not seem imminent.

The notion that humans possess the intelligence and self-restraint to govern themselves democratically is distinctly of Western origin. It is among the ancient Greeks that concepts like individualism and humanism first appear, and perhaps no society has ever proclaimed and trusted man's capacity to reason more than the Greeks. That the Greeks would invent democracy seems almost natural in this respect. Yet even among their most formidable thinkers, like Plato, grave doubts were expressed about the *average* citizen's capabilities, and thus about the desirability of democratic government.

Democracy is Western in origin, and where it exists today, it is almost exclusively a Western transplant. It has its firmest roots where Western influence is the strongest. All of the democracies of the New World have Western origins. In Asia's oldest democracies, India, Japan, and the Philippines, a departing Western occupier either provided the model for the country's democratic institutions, or dictated their form. Africa's strongest democracy is arguably South Africa, its most Western country. Democracy has taken tenuous hold in only a few countries in the Middle East – Israel, Turkey, Egypt perhaps – and these too are the most Western-oriented of the Middle Eastern countries. No country has adopted democratic institutions that are not modeled on those of the West. Until only very recently, the origin of every democratic country's institutions could be traced directly back to Europe.

Samuel Hunington (1996) has recently emphasized how unique Western culture is among the world's civilizations with respect to the emphasis it places on individualism, humanism, rational behavior, and the like. Hunington goes so far as to predict a sometimes violent "*clash*" between Western civilization and its many rivals. Even if the differences between the West and the rest are not so great as to lead to major, armed confrontations, they are great enough to suggest that democracy may not take firm root in many non-Western countries, and may indeed never be tried in some.

Strong tribal alliances lead naturally to the kind of redistributive coalitions and winner-take-all approach to politics that so often produces violence and the overthrow of democracy. Tribal traditions can engender habits of obedience to leadership that make dictatorship seem like the natural form of government.

When tribal and ethnic loyalties do not stand in the way of democracy, religion often can. The only notable difference between the Northern Irish is that some are Catholic others Protestant, yet this difference has sufficed to make normal civil and democratic society impossible. Past conditioning has generated strong patterns of hatred, which are reinforced by occasional new acts of violence. Although Catholics and Protestants in Northern Ireland have been locked into a series of prisoners' dilemma supergames, they have continued to play the noncooperative strategies. It is difficult to reconcile day-to-day events in Northern Ireland over the 20th century with the postulate of rational, self-interested individual behavior.

The same can be said for Israel. Only an extreme optimist could envisage Jews and Moslems in Israel meeting to write a constitution that would advance their common interests, in the way that scholars in constitutional political economy assume that rational actors write constitutions.[9]

Where Descartes began his celebrated demonstration of God's existence with the words "I think," the Apostles' Creed begins with the words "I believe." In religion belief substitutes for thought, and most organized religions demand an unquestioning obedience to God. Religion can foster authoritarian modes of behavior that are easily transferred to a political leader, particularly when he dons the robes of the state's religion, or claims the support of the church for his rule. Why consult the citizens regarding which actions the state should undertake, when there are those in the society who can consult with and speak for God? The rise of fundamentalist religious movements in many parts of the world bodes ill for the future of democracy in these areas – and that is true also for the United States. One often hears Americans complain about the dearth in quality of the candidates for public office today in comparison with previous eras. Yet, if that quintessential man of the Enlightenment, Thomas Jefferson, where alive today, his agnosticism alone, not to mention his other liberal and radical views, would preclude his being elected President. Is it the quality of the candidates or the quality of the electorate that has declined in America compared with previous eras?

The claim is sometimes made – by political leaders in Asia – that their conformist, collectivist culture is better suited to nondemocratic forms of government. Support for this position might be gleaned from the public choice literature. If the purpose of democratic participation is to reveal differing individual preferences in a heterogeneous society, then there may be less need for such participation in a society whose members share "common values." Whether Asian societies are all that homogeneous, and whether they will remain so with increasing exposure to not only Western culture, but also the other cultures of the world, is debatable. Less debatable is the fact that Asia's few democracies have tended to be dominated by a single party throughout their short histories.

Thus, as one looks into the 21st century, it is difficult to foresee capitalist and democratic institutions spreading hand and hand around the globe. Of the two, it is certainly capitalism that will march forward more triumphantly. Its rewards are more immediate and apparent. Its institutions and modes of thought can be directly transplanted through the spread of multinationals in ways that are not possible for democracy.

Capitalism has already taken firm root in Asia and Latin America, of course. Indeed, to the extent a conformist, collectivist characterization of Asian culture is accurate, Asia may be a more hospitable soil for capitalism than that of the West – at least for the kind of *corporate capitalism* that is dominant at the close of the 20th century. Conformity to the corporate cultures of large hierarchical organizations may be easier for workers and managers who share the common values of the East, than for those in the West who fancy themselves to be individualists.

---

9 For example, Buchanan and Tullock (1962) and Mueller (1996).

Even capitalism's triumph is unlikely to be complete, however. The many failed experiments in sub-Saharan Africa suggest that its soil provides a fertile bed for neither capitalism nor democracy with South Africa again the possible lone exception. The same can be said of the sands of the Middle East. Were it not for the impressive economic growth of Indonesia, one would be tempted to hypothesize that Islam and capitalism are somehow antithetical. And recent developments suggest that even Indonesia's economic success may prove to be transitory.

And what of democracy's triumphs? These certainly will be fewer and even less secure. After some 50 or 70 years of repression, one might have expected democracy to take strong hold following Communism's collapse. But it has not done so, or at least not in most cases. Perhaps, this is because the revolutions that ended Communism were too short and too bloodless. No centuries long struggle to wrest power from the crown took place as that which led to democracy's triumph in Great Britain. No armed struggle to wrest power from the crown took place as that which led to democracy's triumph in the United States. As a result, there has been neither the occasion nor the necessity for a John Locke, a John Paine, or a James Madison to make the case for liberty and democracy, and design the institutions to ensure their continued existence. The former Communist countries quickly donned the democratic institutions of their West European neighbors, as a less fortunate family might don the well-worn clothes of its rich neighbors, without pausing to consider how well they fit, or whether new clothes, better tailored to their needs, might not be worth considering. In some cases these borrowed clothes barely concealed the fact that the same persons were governing in much the same way after Communism's fall as before. But even in the most democratic of the former Communist countries, politics lacks the enthusiasm and idealism one might have expected following so many years of dictatorship. Instead, democratic politics in the former Communist countries, where it exists, mirrors politics in the West with all of its rent seeking, corruption and zero-sum game orientation.

Thus, one should not be surprised if democracy succumbs to dictatorship in many of the former Communist countries, as it has with great regularity in Africa, and all too frequently in Latin America. The same is likely to be true in those parts of Asia where democracy is tried. In this essay I have tried to explain why this occurs. Most of us most of the time are creatures of habit responding to the rewards and punishments of the recent past. Democracy in practice means *majoritarian* democracy. Majoritarian democracy tends to reward about as many persons as it punishes with defeat. Many of the benefits that citizens derive from democracy do not arise out of the electoral process as such, but from the institutions that evolve along with free elections – an independent and impartial judiciary, a free press, and the like. Only the most farsighted and forward looking of a country's citizens are likely to appreciate the causal linkages between the existence of these democratic institutions and the quality of their lives.

In practice democracy often does not seem to sustain the habits and loyalty that induce citizens and politicians to behave responsibly. In the most extreme cases, democracy fails to sustain sufficient loyalty to its basic institutions to motivate citizens and politicians to rise to democracy's defense when it is endangered. Thus, although the behavior of many persons in a democracy may not be well *explained* by the rational actor paradigm, a *normative* defense of democracy generally requires that we assume the kind of farsighted, cooperative behavior that only the most sophisticated of rational actors would exhibit. Moreover, without this sophisticated, farsighted behavior on the part of individual citizens, democracy may be unable to survive the many short run challenges it faces. And this may be the most paradoxical of democracy's many paradoxes.

References

Aldrich JH (1997) When is it rational to vote. In: Mueller DC (1997), pp 373–390
Brennan G, Buchanan JM (1984) Voter choice: evaluating political alternatives. American Behavioral Scientist 28: 185–201
Buchanan JM, Tullock G (1962) The calculus of consent. University of Michigan Press, Ann Arbor
Downs A (1957) An economic theory of democracy. Harper and Row, New York
Fiorina MP (1981) Retrospective voting in American national elections. Yale University Press, New Haven
Fiorina MP (1997) Voting behavior. In: Mueller DC (1997), pp 391–414
Hibbs DA Jr (1987) American political economy. Harvard University Press, Cambridge, MA
Hoffman E (1997) Public choice experiments. In: Mueller DC (1997), pp 415–426
Hunington SP (1996) The clash of civilizations and the remaking of world order. Simon & Schuster, New York
Isaac RM, McCue K, Plott CR (1985) Public goods provision in an experimental environment. Journal of Public Economics 26: 51–74
Kuhn TS (1970) The structure of scientific revolutions. 2nd edn. University of Chicago Press, Chicago
Kunreuther H, Ginsberg R, Miller R, Sagi P, Slovic P, Borkan B, Katz, N (1978) Disaster insurance protection. Wiley, New York
Marwell G, Ames RE (1979) Experiments on the provision of public goods. I. Resources, interest, group size, and the free rider problem. American Journal of Sociology 84: 335–360
Marwell G, Ames RE (1980) Experiments on the provision of public goods. II. Provision points, stakes, experience, and the free rider problem, American Journal of Sociology 85: 926–937
Marwell G, Ames RE (1981) Economists free ride: does anyone else? Journal of Public Economics. 15: 295–310
Mill JS (1958) Considerations on representative government. Bobbs-Merrill, New York (first publication, 1861)
Mueller DC (1989) Public choice II. Cambridge University Press, Cambridge
Mueller DC (1996) Constitutional democracy. Oxford University Press, Oxford
Mueller DC (ed) (1997) Perspectives on public choice. Cambridge University Press, Cambridge
Murrell P (1990) The nature of socialism, Princeton University Press, Princeton
Paldam M (1997) Political business cycles. In: Mueller DC pp 342–370
Powell G (1982) Contemporary democracies. Harvard University Press, Cambridge, MA
Schumpeter JA (1950) Capitalism, socialism and democracy, 3rd edn. Harper and Row, New York
Smith A The wealth of nations. The Modern Library, New York (first published 1776)
Staddon JER (1983) Adaptive behavior and learning. Cambridge University Press, Cambridge

[2]

1. On the economic rise and decline of nations

Dennis C. Mueller

The idea that nations rise and decline calls to mind the grander hypotheses that civilizations or cultures rise and decline as put forward by Oswald Spengler (1922, 1923) and Arnold Toynbee (1946, 1957). The rise and decline of the great civilizations and empires is to a considerable degree a history of military conquest and then defeat. As Paul Kennedy (1987) has demonstrated for the last half of the millennium, a military rise and decline is inevitably also a story of economic rise and decline, but there is clearly much more involved than economics. Moreover, in some cases, as with the Ottoman Empire, the story seems to be largely one of military superiority and inferiority, of governmental efficiency in running a military state, with economic prowess clearly taking a back seat (Fernández-Armesto, 1995, pp. 239–41, 379–80).

Other factors beyond economic and military strength may also have played important roles in the fortunes of past empires. Toynbee (1946, 1957) emphasized the contribution of religious zeal and religious decay, Spengler (1922, 1923) described a process of general cultural decline. I am an economist, and my comparative advantage in the study of history does not fall in the areas of military, cultural and religious history. Indeed, most historians would probably argue that economists are particularly ill-trained and ill-suited to the study of culture and religion. I shall therefore mostly confine myself to the question of economic rise and decline, and to more recent history, where these factors have been salient. This narrow focus is perhaps even more justified if one looks forward and tries to envisage the history of the future. With the United States now having a near monopoly of effective nuclear military power, it is difficult to imagine another nation rolling over its neighbours as Rome did two millennia ago, and as Germany briefly did a half century ago, without precipitating a violent and decisive counteract. Thus, so long as the United States is willing to play world cop, and until its decline leaves it unable to carry out this role, one can probably look forward to a Pax

Americana, in which future rise and decline histories are likely to be largely accounts of economic success and failure.

The causes behind economic advancement in recent history have been well described by several writers. I shall, therefore, only briefly recount these explanations in the following section. The reasons why a leading economic power falls into decline are more difficult to explain (Section 1.2). I shall, therefore, concentrate upon these, offering first an analogy with the rise and decline of firms (Sections 1.3 and 1.4). In Section 1.5 I present five main causes for economic decline within modern capitalism. In Section 1.6, I speculate on whether these causes of decline can be offset, and a nation can enjoy perpetual growth. The concluding section speculates on whether such an optimistic scenario seems likely for today's three leading economic powers, Japan, the United States and Europe.

1.1 THE CAUSES OF ECONOMIC SUCCESS

1.1.1 The Development of Market Institutions

The idea that there are 'gains from trade' is, of course, fundamental to the discipline of economics. Indeed, Adam Smith's (1776) theory of *The Causes and Consequences of the Wealth of Nations* is largely an account of the many ways in which all members of a nation, and all nations can prosper through trade. Adam Smith's explanation for growth has been most systematically developed and documented in the work of Douglass North (1990; North and Thomas, 1973). North has emphasized the important role played by the development of property rights, markets and other institutions of capitalism in the rise of both Great Britain and the Netherlands. Our first explanation for the economic rise of nations lies, therefore, in the development of the economic institutions of capitalism, particularly as they pertain to market transactions.

1.1.2 The Development of the Modern Corporation

While Douglass North has emphasized the importance of the evolution of market institutions in Great Britain and the Netherlands during the industrial revolution in the 18th and 19th centuries, Alfred Chandler (1990, Chapters 2 and 3) has stressed the importance of the evolution of the modern corporation, particularly in Germany and the United States, over the period between 1880 and World War II. According to Chandler and Oliver Williamson (1985), the large corporations that came into existence over this period were the major source of the innovations in production, distribution and organization in these countries. The 'economies of scale and scope' that these 'giant enterprises' achieved led to the rise of the German and United States' economies to world leadership in the second half of the twentieth century. If, following Coase (1937) and Williamson (1975), we think of firms as institutions for solving 'market failures', that is hierarchical organizations that can produce and distribute certain goods and services more efficiently than the market can, then the Chandler/Williamson view of capitalism complements that of North. Successful economic growth follows the development of 'the institutions of capitalism' in both a market and a nonmarket form.

1.1.3 Other Explanations of Growth

In addition to the general theories of growth of North and Chandler, there exists a variety of narrower hypotheses that might explain the growth of a particular country, or a particular kind of growth. For example, Great Britain's economy may have benefited from its imperialism over the 18th and 19th centuries, America's during the 19th century from the development of its frontier. One of the intuitively most plausible, and empirically best supported hypotheses as to why 'follower' nations grow more slowly than leading nations is the 'catch-up' hypothesis. The technological leaders must invent new technologies to lower their costs and improve their products. Followers can achieve these gains by simply copying the technologies and designs of the leaders.[1] Although each of these hypotheses probably does account for some of the success of the countries to which it is applicable, being country or situation specific, they are obviously less appealing than the more general alternative hypotheses discussed above. All of these explanations for the economic rise in nations are similar, however, in their inability to shed light on the complementary question of why leading nations tend to decline.

1.2 THE PUZZLE

No nation can decline, unless it has first risen. Thus, an obvious place to begin an inquiry into the decline of nations is by examining their rise. The simplest of all explanations for why some nations decline might be that the factors which led to their rise are reversed. The same causal process is at work, only the signs on the inputs are changed.

The most spectacular recent example of a nation which has risen and then fallen is, of course, Great Britain. One is hard pressed, however, to adapt Douglass North's explanation for Great Britain's rise to obtain an explanation of its decline. Most observers would probably argue that Britain's decline set in toward the end of the last century. But, one searches in vain for evidence that property rights, markets and the other important institutions of capitalism were fundamentally weakened or destroyed in Great Britain at that point in time.

Similar difficulties arise when using other explanations for why nations rise to explain their decline. What events in the last generation have occurred to convert the economies of scale and scope that led to Germany and the United States' rise into diseconomies, and thus set these economies into decline? Great Britain's economy may have benefited from its imperialism, America's from the development of the frontier, and the start of Britain's decline did roughly coincide with the close of the age of imperialism. But America's frontier was closed long before the end of the 1960s, and important parts of Britain's empire, like the United States, were lost long before Britain's decline began. Other causal factors seem needed to explain the decline of nations than those that explain their rise.

Mancur Olson (1982) has offered one such causal explanation. Economic growth is strangled by the rentseeking avarice of interest groups. I think Olson has identified an important determinant of economic decline, and will come back to it. But I do not think that it is the *sole* explanation for Great Britain's sustained slide, and America's and Europe's more recent troubles. If the activities of interest groups alone could reduce a country's growth in income per capita from 2 or 3 per cent per year, to zero or 1 per cent, all members of society could benefit from emasculating the interest groups, and somehow compensating them in other ways. To some extent, that was part of the Reagan and Thatcher revolutions, with their emphasis on deregulation, privatization and attacks on organized labour, and to some extent they succeeded. But they have not fully succeeded, and I shall argue that more is needed to return these and other mature economies to permanently higher levels of economic growth.[2]

The 'catch-up' hypothesis has, as noted, received considerable empirical support.[3] But this hypothesis predicts that followers *catch-up* to the leaders, not that they zoom right by them. As a follower catches a leader, it must take over the costly activity of developing new products and technologies, and its growth should slow down. To explain how a one-time leader falls behind other countries, one needs more than the catch-up hypothesis. Indeed, the question of why leaders become followers becomes even more perplexing, once one takes into account the considerable advantages of being the leader.

The industrial organization literature contains several hypotheses as to the advantages of first movers, and considerable empirical evidence regarding the longevity of market leadership positions.[4] The learning-by-doing hypothesis, for example, predicts falling costs over time with increasing output. While one might expect the *rate of decline* in costs to slow down after a point, there is no reason to expect it to reverse. There is no reason to expect *forgetting-by-doing* to set in after a while. Indeed, so strong are the first-mover advantages at the micro level, that a micro-based theory might predict that the leading nation would simply 'take over the world' economically.[5] Thus, the task of explaining how and why a nation which is once a leading economic power loses this position, is not an easy one. I am a microeconomist, and shall begin to try to answer this question by examining the rise and decline of leading firms.

1.3 THE RISE AND DECLINE OF FIRMS

If nations rise and decline this suggests that they go through a sort of life cycle and, to a microeconomist, this in turn calls to mind a life cycle of firms. The classic discussion of firm and product life cycles is undoubtedly that of Joseph Schumpeter (1934). Schumpeter saw firms coming into existence due to an innovative idea of their entrepreneurial founder. When this innovation was a radical departure from existing products or technologies it led to the founding of a new market. Innovation was followed by imitation by other producers until the initial market advantage of the innovator was eliminated, above normal profits disappeared, and competitive equilibrium returned.

1.3.1 Motivation

Entrepreneurs

The typical entrepreneur's ideas are not such as to launch an industry, and lead to no flood of imitators. The typical new-born firm dies within a few years of its birth (Dunne, Roberts and Samuelson, 1988; Geroski, 1991, Chapter 2). Given the high probabilities of failure, one wonders what it is that motivates some individuals to take the entrepreneurial leap, to bet their time and probably all of their money on the belief that they can do something so different or so much better than every other firm that they can succeed, where most fail? Schumpeter described the entrepreneur's motives as follows:

> First of all, there is a dream and the will to found a private kingdom, usually, though not necessarily, also a dynasty. The modern world really does not know any such positions, but what may be attained by industrial or commercial success is still the nearest approach to medieval lordship possible to modern man. Its fascination is specially strong for people who have no other chance of achieving social distinction. The sensation of power and independence loses nothing by the fact that both are largely illusions. Closer analysis would lead to discovering an endless variety within this group of motives, from spiritual ambition down to mere snobbery. But this need not detain us. Let it suffice to point out that motives of this kind, although they stand nearer to consumers' satisfaction, do not coincide with it.
>
> Then there is the will to conquer: the impulse to fight, to prove oneself superior to others, to succeed for the sake, not of the fruits of success, but of success itself. From this aspect, economic action becomes akin to sport – there are financial races, or rather boxing-matches. The financial result is a secondary consideration, or, at all events, mainly valued as an index of success and as a symptom of victory, the displaying of which very often is more important as a motive of large expenditure than the wish for the consumers' goods themselves. Again we should find countless nuances, some of which, like social ambition, shade into the first group of motives. And again we are faced with a motivation characteristically different from that of 'satisfaction of wants' in the sense defined above, or from, to put the same thing into other words, 'hedonistic adaption.'
>
> Finally, there is the joy of creating, of getting things done, or simply of exercising one's energy and ingenuity. This is akin to a ubiquitous motive, but nowhere else does it stand out as an independent factor of behaviour with anything like the clearness with which it obtrudes itself in our case. Our type seeks out difficulties, changes in order to change, delights in ventures. This group of motives is the most distinctly anti-hedonist of the three. (Schumpeter, 1934, pp. 93–4)

Thus, Schumpeter did not simply repeat the assumption about entrepreneurial motivation that was already standard when he wrote, 'the entrepreneur maximizes the profits of the firm.' Schumpeter, observing entrepreneurs at the beginning of the 20th century, saw reincarnated medieval knights striving to build empires and to found dynasties.

Over 50 years ago, Tibor Scitovsky (1943) demonstrated that even the familiar profits maximization assumption, if single mindedly pursued, implied that the owner entrepreneur was a rather unusual fellow who was ever ready to take on a fair gamble, a workaholic who would never consume additional leisure, no matter how wealthy he became.[6] Frank Knight (1965, p. 319) saw the businessman motivated to 'produce wealth to be used in producing more wealth with no view to any use beyond the increase of wealth itself.'

Each of these descriptions sees industry's captains driven to achieve goals beyond the reach and desires of normal persons. When placed alongside the actual behaviour of the Krupps and Fords and Maritoes, they do not seem like exaggerations. The entrepreneurial founders of the industrial giants in Germany, the United States and Japan were empire-builders of extraordinary talent and drive.

Managers

Many people have observed, what Thomas Mann so brilliantly depicted in *Buddenbrooks*, that the third generation dissipates the fortune and destroys the business that the grandfather founded. Like all such observations it is not always accurate, but it is true enough often enough to indicate a danger all family businesses face. Not only are they threatened by the forces of competition from without, they are threatened by decay from within. For this reason, perhaps, most business empires come at some point in time to be governed not by members of the family that started them, but by professional managers, technocrats with no emotional attachments to the firm, and often with little financial stake in it.

Robin Marris (1964, Chapter 2) demonstrated that the pecuniary and nonpecuniary rewards of managers tend to be tied to the growth of their firms, and thus that professional managers also tend to be empire builders of sorts, more concerned with their company's growth rate than its profitability. Where the owner-manager wishes to see the firm survive and prosper indefinitely, the professional manager's horizons extend only to his expected retirement or departure to another firm. What is important is not the course of the empire over the next generation, but its course over the next five years. For this reason empire building in the managerially controlled firm frequently takes the form of mergers. Mergers are the quickest and surest way to grow, and the most popular route among professional managers (Mueller, 1969, 1972).

1.3.2 The Life Cycle of the Managerial Corporation

Although most new firms do not survive, and many that do remain small, family enterprises, in the exceptional case of a truly radical and important innovation, something like the Schumpeterian scenario does take place (Mueller and Tilton, 1969; Gort and Klepper, 1982; Graddy and Klepper, 1990). The firm that grows to be large goes through an initial phase in which it is either an innovator or an early, successful imitator (Klepper and Simons, 1993). But, first-mover advantages, barriers to entry, government protection in the form of trade restraints or other regulations, often combine to reduce 'the perennial gale of creative destruction' to a gentle breeze. Thus, many firms earn persistently high profits and seem capable of surviving almost indefinitely (Mueller, 1986, 1990).

At some point in the large, successful firm's life, it comes to be managed by professionals who, when the opportunities arise, take actions to advance their interests over those of the company's owners. Very often these actions turn out to be mergers.[7] Thus, we find Borg-Warner responding in the 1950s to Ford's cancellation of its contract for automatic transmissions by undertaking 17 acquisitions over a period of a couple of years; *all* US tobacco companies responding in the 1960s to the first serious 'tobacco scare' that suggested falling future demand for their products with a raft of mergers that reduced their dependence on cigarettes for sales to less than 50 per cent; the petroleum companies responding in the 1970s to the windfall profit increases generated by the OPEC price increase by undertaking a series of disastrous mergers;[8] and most recently, defence firms responding to budget cuts following the collapse of the Soviet Union by engaging in a series of mergers.[9] More generally, *every* period of economic and stock market expansion in the United States over the past century, except during World War II, has been accompanied by a merger wave.[10]

Did the Surgeon General's report linking cigarette smoking to cancer suddenly reveal hidden talents that cigarette company managers had for managing assets in other industries, and thus induce a rash of mergers, or did it frighten these managers into believing that their firms would soon begin to decline and thereby induced them to avoid this decline through mergers? Did the OPEC price increases reveal hidden managerial talents in the petroleum industry, or did they simply provide petroleum firms with the cash to make both their shareholders and their managers significantly better off? Do managerial abilities to manage the assets of larger companies expand with stock prices, or just the resources and discretion to do so?[11]

If the only consequence of managerial pursuit of growth through merger was that some companies grew much larger, and their shareholders somewhat poorer, it would not be a topic of much interest, or at least not of much interest with respect to the question addressed in this paper. But, the pursuit of growth through merger in the mature phases of firm life cycles is one of the factors that contributes to the decline of nations.

1.4 THE LIFE CYCLE OF MANAGERIAL CAPITALISM

Joseph Schumpeter first described the goals of the entrepreneur and the dynamics of capitalist development at the beginning of the 20th century, when he was in Vienna. The empire-building entrepreneurs, whom he would have observed close at hand, would therefore have been those from Germany, Austria and perhaps other parts of continental Europe. As Chandler (1990) has documented, the German firms that grew to be large during the first part of the 20th century quickly shifted from being family controlled to being manager controlled. In this respect the development of German and American capitalism over the course of the 20th century has been very similar.

The end of the 19th and early part of the 20th centuries was a period in which technological change and the introduction of mass production techniques led to significant economies of scale and scope, to use Chandler's term. The firms that were able to shape their organizations and raise the capital needed to take advantage of these economies grew to giant size, while remaining in the confines of their core industrial strengths. The empire building proclivities of corporate managers could be satisfied through internal expansion and horizontal or vertical acquisitions. The result was a transformation of German and American industry from the end of the 19th century to the middle of the 20th from one characterized by small family firms to one dominated by large managerially controlled corporations. The cycle of innovation, growth and monopoly that Schumpeter used to describe the life of a single innovating firm, became a cycle of innovation, growth and oligopoly across the entire economies.

Great Britain's economic development over the half century following 1880 was different from that of both the United States and Germany. To a much greater extent British firms remained in the hands of their founding families. Professional managers were hired, but were not able to rise to the highest levels in the managerial hierarchy (Chandler, 1990, pp. 292–4). Thus, ironically, as the first century of corporate capitalism evolved, the Buddenbrook's scenario became repeated much more often in the United Kingdom than in Mann's Germany, and Britain's economic development looked much more like that of the family firm than of the modern corporation. Thus, if we accept Chandler's explanation for the relative performances of the US, German and British economies up until World War II, the superior performance of the former two countries would be attributable to the institutional innovation of the large, managerially controlled joint stock company.

By the end of the 1920s corporate growth in metals, machinery, transportation equipment, rubber, chemicals, petroleum – all of the major industries in which scale economies are significant – had reached a stage of some maturity. These major industries were oligopolies dominated by large, fairly mature corporations. Already a great merger wave had taken place in the United States at the end of the 1920s. Had major US firms tried to continue to grow as they had over the 50 previous years, they would have had to resort increasingly to growth through mergers. But the Depression came, and then World War II. Corporate growth in America was arrested, except for the war build up.

The result was that when World War II ended nearly a generation had gone by since US businesses were able to invest and grow under normal demand conditions. The depression and war had left a large, pent-up demand for consumer goods, and a large pent-up supply of would-be entrepreneurs hungry to get rich. Large mature firms were able to expand rapidly within their existing markets, and many new firms came into existence and began to grow large.

The end of World War II was followed by a period of extreme shortages in Germany as people began to rebuild their war torn cities and economy. Thus, the post-war boom in Germany got started later than in the United States and with even more pent-up consumer demand and entrepreneurial supply. The major corporate giants from before the war came back to life, and many small and medium-sized firms began to thrive. There were big profits to be earned in both the United States and Germany, and many talented people were drawn into businesses both large and small.

By the end of the 1960s, many firms in the United States found themselves in much the same position as they were at the end of the 1920s. The potential for continued high internal growth was limited. But profits were currently high and the stock market was booming. The result was the United States' third major merger wave. It differed from the first two only in so far as during this wave the antitrust authorities did not sit back and idly watch. They intervened to prevent all mergers that might possibly have resulted in a substantial increase in market power, erring usually on the side of caution. Thus the third merger wave, unlike its two predecessors, was dominated by conglomerate mergers, mergers with the smallest likelihood of increasing market power, and the smallest likelihood of increasing efficiency.

Not only did the mergers of the 1960s not increase the efficiency of the merging firms, they almost certainly reduced it. Considerable evidence exists indicating that the mergers of the 1960s reduced the profits of the merging firms, reduced the market shares of the acquired firms, reduced the productivity of the acquired firms, and reduced the wealth of the acquiring companies' shareholders.[12] Perhaps no better evidence exists of the inefficiencies caused by the merger wave of the 1960s than that it led to a spin-off wave in the 1970s, as firms tried to undo the damage.[13]

Most economists do not give much thought to mergers, and when they do, presume that they must be harmless if not beneficial for the economy. This belief stems from the fact that most economists assume that all managers maximize profits, and that all, or at least most, markets are fairly competitive. If managers maximize profits, then any merger that does not seem likely to increase market power must be presumed to increase efficiency. If managers do not maximize profits, then an efficient market for corporate control will remove them. Thus, the first reaction of many economists to the conglomerate merger wave of the 1960s was to assume that these mergers *must* be creating some sort of efficiency, and many articles appeared with new hypotheses as to what these efficiencies might be. A new word was even invented – synergy – to describe these efficiencies that had never before been known to exist.

In an efficient market for corporate control an EXXON Corporation will be acquired and its management replaced as soon as it deviates from shareholder-wealth-maximizing behaviour. But buying the EXXON Corporation and throwing its management out because they have made a bad merger is not as easy as filling up at one of its stations. This fact allows EXXON's managers to pursue their own goals, even when they do not enhance the profits of the firm, as when they undertake an unprofitable merger.

Mergers do more than just reshuffle corporate assets, and transfer wealth from the shareholders of acquiring companies to shareholders of the acquired companies. Many examples exist of mergers which have destroyed healthy, efficient companies.[14] On average the efficiency of the acquired companies is reduced. The energies of the managers of the acquiring companies are diverted from making investments that create assets to investments that merely transfer them. The cash flows of companies get used to buy existing plants rather than build new ones. A whole industry grows up of investment bankers, stock analysts, lawyers and even economists engaged in the process of transferring ownership of assets, rather than producing them.

The great merger waves of the 1920s and 1960s in the United States were followed by decades of poor economic performance. We know at the micro level that the mergers tended to reduce efficiency. Could the poor economic performance of the 1930s and 1970s be *in part* a consequence of the merger waves that preceded them? The United States and Great Britain have had, proportionate to the sizes of their economies, far more mergers than any other countries. They have also had the worst post-World War II economic performances among the highly developed countries. On average Japan has one merger for every 10 in the United States. Italy has one of the lowest merger rates and highest productivity levels of all European countries. Coincidences perhaps, but I think not. If we accept Chandler's argument that the economic rise of the United States and Germany through the first half of the 20th century was to an important extent due to the rise of the giant, managerially controlled corporation, we must at least allow for the possibility that their seeming decline over the last quarter or third of this century is due to a decline in the performance of these ageing organizations. Mergers are characteristic of corporations in the mature phase of their life cycle. They are both bellwethers for and important contributors to the economic decline of nations.

1.5 THE CAUSES OF ECONOMIC DECLINE

1.5.1 Life-Cycle Effects of Corporate Capitalism

We are now ready to list the main causes of economic decline. The first of these I have discussed at length, because it is fundamental to understanding why a highly developed capitalist nation might decline. Firms and corporations are the major sources of productive investments and innovative activity. If a nation enters into decline it must in part be because these institutions have entered into decline.

Lawrence Yun and I (1995) have recently tested this life-cycle hypothesis regarding capitalism using data on large US corporations. Table 1.1 reports results for regressions of annual changes in the market values of firms on their annual investments. The coefficient on investment

Table 1.1 Estimates of c *with δ and year-effects the same for all firms*

$$\frac{M_t - M_{t-1}}{M_{t-1}} = -\delta + c\,\frac{I_t}{M_{t-1}} + \mu_k$$

$c_o = c$ for old firms $c_y = c$ for young firms

Time period	$-\delta$	c_o	c_y	n	$\bar{R}^2$
1951–1960	–0.0004	1.15	1.00	1493	0.420
	0.04	28.08	7.42		
1961–1970	–0.032	1.14	1.60	2403	0.370
	3.15	23.14	22.60		
1971–1980	–0.064	0.53	0.87	3692	0.396
	10.39	21.36	31.86		
1981–1990	–0.042	0.69	1.00	4008	0.661
	9.16	41.49	76.47		

Note: *t*-values below coefficients.

measures the ratio of the return on that year's investment to the firm's cost of capital.[15] A dollar invested at a return equal to the firm's cost of capital raises the market value of the firm by one dollar. Thus, if all firms invested in projects which on average had returns equal to their costs of capital, the coefficient on investment would be 1.0.

The data on firm investments and market value changes have been pooled by decade with separate coefficients estimated for old and young firms, with young firms defined as those that were incorporated after 1940. On average young firms earned significantly higher returns relative to their costs of capital than old ones in three of the four decades. In the 1950s and 1960s, American capitalism's golden age, investment opportunities were sufficiently attractive that even mature companies could on average earn returns greater than their costs of capital. Neither group had an average return on investment in the 1970s that equalled its costs of capital, with the typical mature firm earning a return only slightly greater than one half of its costs of capital.

The economic rebound of the 1980s raised the returns on investment of the by now somewhat mature young firms back to equality with their costs of capital, but the returns of the mature companies remained significantly below their costs of capital. Each dollar invested by a large, mature firm in our sample produced only 69 cents of new assets during the 1980s. This figure is very close to what Elizabeth Reardon and I (1993) estimated for a much larger sample of firms (699) from the end of 1969 to the end of 1988. These 699 firms invested a total of \$3670 billion over this 19 year period. These investments produced only \$2587 billion in new assets, however. Thus, more than a trillion dollars in potential wealth was lost because large US corporations invested in projects which on average had rates of return significantly below their costs of capital.

The life-cycle problems of corporate capitalism reflect the principal/agent relationship that exists between managers and shareholders. Shareholders would like to see managers invest in only those projects that promise returns greater than the cost of capital. Managers wish to see the firm grow faster (or decline more slowly) than this investment policy implies. Note that a form of rentseeking, or rent dissipation is involved here. In a perfectly competitive world, managers could not invest in projects with returns less than the cost of capital. Some markets – the product market, capital market, market for corporate control – would prevent such investments. But when the market process creates large economic rents, as it often does, those individuals who gain control over those rents are free to use them or dissipate them as their interests dictate.

1.5.2 Motivation

At the end of the 1960s I undertook several case studies of how companies grow. I looked at marketing innovations, technological innovations and mergers. For my case study of a technological innovation I chose the Xerox company.

Xerox was a classic example of a Schumpeterian firm. In 1950 it was a small photographic paper manufacturer in Rochester, New York struggling to survive competition with its giant neighbour Kodak. Its managers decided they would need to develop a new product. The director of research read an article describing some early experiments with a photocopying process, and he convinced the President of the company to buy up the patents on the process and start to develop it. To bring out the first machine in 1960, the management had literally 'to bet the company', a phrase I often heard used at Xerox. To finance the R&D the top managers invested all of their savings, took out additional mortgages on their homes and the like. Needless to say they were handsomely rewarded for the risks they took.

I was particularly impressed by some remarks of Chester Carlson, the photocopying process inventor, during my interview of him. He had graduated in physics from the California Institute of Technology in 1930, but could not get a job as a physicist during the Great Depression. He worked as a sort of errand boy in a patent office, and had the idea that it would be useful if there were a box that you could stick a document into and out would come clean copies, rather than have to make the many messy carbon copies that law firms required. He spent his evenings and weekends in a garage trying to construct such a box. Thirty years after he graduated from Caltech, the first commercially successful photocopier was produced, and Carlson began to reap the rewards from his perseverance. By the time I interviewed him in the late 1960s. he had earned more than $20 million in royalties and stock appreciation. What I remember most from the interview, however, was Carlson's observation that he would undoubtedly *not* have pursued his invention, if he had graduated from Caltech in the late 1960s. At that point in time there were plenty of good paying jobs for physicists and he would simply have taken a job with a large firm and been content to earn his regular salary.

Carlson was driven to invest the time and take the risks to invent a photocopying process by the economic hardships in the Depression. The managers of Haloid, who developed the process to commercial success, were driven by the hardship of having to try to compete with a progressive first mover like Kodak. Under less difficult circumstances neither might have been willing to undertake the risks. Indeed, Carlson approached over 20 large firms including Kodak and IBM and tried to interest them in picking up the development of his process before he agreed to give it to Haloid. They were less desperate for a new product, however, and refused to take up the opportunity.[16]

Although difficult to quantify, motivation is of central importance in the innovation and development process. According to Chandler (1990) corporate capitalism's development was more successful in the United States and Germany from 1880 to the end of World War II than it was in Great Britain, because the rising corporations in the first two countries were led by professional managers, while leadership in major UK corporations remained in the hands of members of the firms' founding families. This difference is important not only because it allowed US and German firms to recruit more competent managers, but it also meant corporate leadership in these countries continually went to those individuals who were most strongly driven to get to the top of the corporate ladder, who were hungriest for success. In Great Britain corporations were run by descendants of the founders, 'gentleman' who were less concerned with the growth of their firms than were their professional counterparts in Germany and the US (Chandler, 1990, pp. 291–4). Professional managers in the UK were prevented by a 'glass ceiling' from moving into the highest management ranks. Top managers in the UK did not have to work to get to the top, they inherited their positions.

In a low income family parents pressure their children to study hard, get an education and choose a job that pays well. Those children that seek a better life style than their parents follow their advice. In a well-to-do family, children do not necessarily seek a better life style than their parents. The pressure 'to get ahead' is less intense. Education and career choices take on the form more of consumption goods than of investment goods, with smaller consequent payoffs for society. In the UK careers in business were of low status relative to those in government, science or even academia throughout the last century.[17] The most talented individuals were simply not drawn into business (Chandler, 1990; Porter, 1990, pp. 115–22, 409).

In contrast business occupations have been of relatively high status in the US and Germany for the past century, and became so in Japan immediately after World War II. Akio Morito (1988, pp. 64–5), cofounder of the SONY Corporation, has succinctly expressed the motivation of entrepreneurs in post-World War II Japan. 'We were engineers and we had a big dream of success. We thought that in making a unique product we would surely make a fortune.'

To take great risks one must be truly driven to 'make a fortune', or found a dynasty. Such hunger is less likely in those born to a fortune, to those who are *n*th in the line of an existing dynasty. It is most likely in those who inherit neither wealth nor status, or in some other way are outsiders. The importance of motivation is also illustrated in the disproportionate role immigrants and members of religious or ethnic minorities have played in starting new firms. Many major UK companies were founded by entrepreneurs, who were *not* university graduates (Porter, 1990, pp. 496–8). Bill Gates, the founder of Microsoft, is one of Harvard's most celebrated dropouts.[18] On a much grander scale, Toynbee (1946, pp. 48–163, 209–16, 276) has emphasized the necessity of the proper 'challenge' to launch a civilization's rise, and the crucial role certain individuals and minorities play in leading a civilization's response to these challenges.

Thus, one reason that successful nations decline is that their very success, and the wealth it produces, dulls the incentives of the population to create new wealth, and to make the investments and take the risks that new wealth creation requires.[19]

Before discussing an additional reason for decline, it is perhaps worth pausing to contrast the argument presented here with those recently put forward by Manfred Neumann (1991).

Neumann seeks to explain not the secular decline of nations, but the kinds of cyclic variations first observed by Kondratieff. Neumann argues that the prosperity generated by long economic upswings changes individual rates of time preference thereby resulting in a fall in the saving rate, decline in investment and an economic contraction. My argument is complementary to Neumann's, but somewhat different. It is not the relative attraction of present and future consumption that changes with prosperity that I am emphasizing, but the relative attraction of work and leisure, of different types of work, and of risktaking.

The difference is illustrated by the history of Akio Morito's (1988, Chapter 1) family firm, a history which by the way contradicts the third generation law of family firm decline. This firm's decline set in several centuries after its founding. Morito's great-grandfather and grandfather chose not to manage the firm themselves, but to hire managers and devote their own time and money to acquiring precious antiques. The hired managers behaved exactly as Adam Smith (1776, p. 700) and John Stuart Mill (1885, pp. 138–9) predicted that they would, and in two generations the firm was nearly bankrupt. Here the problem was not so much the consumption pattern of Morito's great-grandfather and grandfather, but their substitution of leisure/consumption for work. Indeed, since their consumption was a sort of investment, Morito's father was able to save the firm, by selling some of the antiques, firing the hired managers and resuming the managerial role himself.

1.5.3 Managerial Rentseeking

Chandler (1990) depicts the professional managers, who built the giant enterprises of Germany and the United States, as growth maximizers continually reinvesting their companies' cash flows to expand their empires. Hiroyuki Odagiri (1982, 1991) has argued that since World War II Japanese managers have also behaved like Marris-growth-maximizers, and that this behaviour helps explain the Japanese miracle. Porter (1990, p. 471) claims that Korean firms, whose managers exhibit an 'awesome willingness to take risk, ... are [also] managed less for profitability than for growth.'

When Schumpeter first described the motives of the entrepreneur at the start of this century, it was only possible to rule an industrial empire, if one founded and created one. The same was true in Japan after World War II had destroyed the *zaibatsu* (Morito, 1988, p. 149), and today in Korea. It is not true today in North America and much of Western Europe. Someone set on ruling a corporate empire can do so either by creating one, or by rising to the top of an existing empire. For many the latter alternative must seem the most attractive. Very few people will be able to start a company and build it into a Coca Cola or Daimler-Benz in their lifetime. If they try and fail, they may find after 20 years that they are no richer than when they began. If one tries instead to reach the top of the managerial ladder at a giant firm, one does so with the knowledge that *some* of one's peer group will certainly succeed, and even if you do not reach the very top, you are almost certainly not going to find yourself no wealthier after 20 years than when you began the climb.

If the highest paid CEO in the United States in 1994, Charles Locke of Morton International,[20] is asked whether he has earned his $25.9 million compensation and other perks associated with his position, he could respond in the affirmative by pointing out that he attained this lofty position by beating out a hundred or more rivals that entered the CEO tournament at the same time that he did, and that due in part to his efforts Morton Salt, the company's most famous product, for yet another year remained the country's leading brand of table salt. No mean feats, but arguably the value of his efforts to society would have been better if he had helped launch a new firm and created a new market.

When corporate empires already exist, any rents tied to them go to those who gain control of the empire. The tournaments that ultimately select these individuals are classic rentseeking contests that award the prize to the person who has made the highest bid, in this case the bids taking the form of investments in effort, in human capital accumulation, etc. to get to the top of the managerial hierarchy. Such rentseeking contests are prone to generate aggregate investments that exceed the value of the prize won. Of course, the profits that large corporations make are not pure rents in the sense that they are forthcoming regardless of the efforts and talents of the managers. But there is a rent element to them, and to the extent there is, the familiar costs of rentseeking exist.

1.5.4 The Welfare State

The poor are more apt to enter risky occupations, and buy little insurance. The rich buy most of the insurance sold. The same is true of societies. The welfare state is the ultimate form of this sort of collective luxury good, an attempt to protect the individual against every sort of economic risk.

The institutions of the welfare state first began to be introduced in Europe at the end of the 19th century. At that time, taxation levels in the United Kingdom, France and Germany were low and roughly comparable to those in the United States.[21] By the mid-1920s taxes in the UK and France were more than double the figure for the US, almost triple in Germany.[22] Since then the institutions of the welfare state have grown on both sides of the Atlantic, but the government sector remains anywhere from 50 per cent to 100 per cent larger in European countries than in the United States, with the important exception of Switzerland.

The welfare state grew large in virtually all European countries, of course. But because of the great potential gains from rebuilding after the war, or the potential gains from 'catch-up', or the gains from introducing the Common Market, or the salutary effects of corporatism, most other European countries seemed to be more engaged in positive-sum-game activities than the UK, at least during the first generation after World War II. Their economies have only fairly recently exhibited signs of the 'British disease'.

One reason why the harmful effects on growth of the welfare state have only recently become significant is that its disincentive effects evolve slowly over time (Lindbeck, 1995a,b). Habits of upbringing and peer group pressures initially deter individuals from abusing the system. But the example of some individuals taking advantage of its generous benefits leads others to do the same, and eventually peer group pressure against abusing the system disappears – or perhaps reverses. Only 'a sucker' fails to take all of his sick leave, quickly finds a new job, and retires at the maximum age. Of particular importance to the growth of the economy are the welfare state's effects on individual savings rates and willingness to take risks. We return to the latter point in Subsection 1.5.6.

Recent papers by Alesina and Rodrik (1994) and Persson and Tabellini (1994) have modelled and estimated the effect of vertical redistribution on macro growth. They reason that the pressures on government to redistribute will be greater, the greater is the exogenous inequality of income. When redistributive taxes affect savings and investment, governmental vertical redistribution will reduce growth. Both studies find an inverse relationship between the extent of income inequality at the beginning of a time period and the growth of the economy during the period. Persson and Tabellini find that the inverse relationship only holds in democracies, and link the effect to governmental transfers. Alesina and Rodrik find that it holds in all countries regardless of form of government.

1.5.5 Collective Rentseeking

The existence of wealth provides an incentive to redistribute it, not only to those who are poor, but to any group in a position to use the government to their advantage. Mancur Olson (1982) argues that the ability of interest groups to organize and effectively engage in rentseeking develops slowly. Thus, as with the detrimental effects of the welfare state, the adverse effects of interest group rentseeking appear only after long periods of stability and prosperity.

Olson is careful *not* to merge his interest-group-decline thesis with a government-size-decline hypothesis. Peter Murrell and I (1986), however, have found that the number of interest groups in a country *is positively,* and it would seem causally, linked to the size of government. Interest group rentseeking through government activities should be a central part of the Olsonian thesis, also.[23]

The classic zero/negative sum activity of government is, of course, war. Defence expenditures are also the quintessential pure public good. Although a country may be significantly better off making large defence expenditures and experiencing zero economic growth than to make zero defence expenditures and be defeated in war, still better would be to make zero (low) defence expenditures, invest the money that would be spent on defence on growth, and not to be defeated in war. The relatively slow growth of the United States since World War II must be attributed in part to the wasteful dissipation on defence of potentially productive government outlays on other public goods. Particularly costly for economic growth has been the large diversion of scientific personnel and research and development activity to defence. Conversely, the growth of Japan and European countries has been helped by their opportunity to free ride on US defence expenditures, and thereby to avoid this wasteful diversion of resources.[24]

1.5.6 Interactions

Unfortunately, some of the causes of decline listed above reinforce one another thereby strengthening their adverse effects on growth. The growth of the giant corporation and the control over its rents that the principal/agent problem gives managers, converts managers into a rentseeking interest group. A possibly effective constraint on managerial discretion is the threat of take-over and expulsion. When this constraint began to be invoked in the United States in the late 1980s, managers approached the legislatures of the states in which they were incorporated and pressured them to pass legislation to protect them from hostile takeovers (Roe, 1993). When President Bush made his ill-fated trip to Japan to promote American economic interests, it was the managers of the giant, mature uninnovative companies who were most heavily represented in his entourage. When the United States risked a costly trade war with Japan in 1995, it was to advance the fortunes of its declining automobile industry.

The goal of the welfare state is to protect individuals from economic risks. Economic success and failure are no longer viewed as the responsibility of the individual, but become the responsibility of the state. State initiatives replace individual initiative (Taylor, 1987). Social solidarity reinforces social conformity. The social culture becomes increasingly hostile to the kinds of risk-taking, nonconformist attitudes that characterize innovators and entrepreneurs. No employee benefits are more generous in the welfare state than those of the government employee. No employee's life is more secure. As the state grows so too does the number of talented people drawn into government. Why take a chance building one's own empire, when one is asked to help run the nation's biggest one. Not surprisingly, new firm starts are proportionately much higher in the United States and Japan than in Sweden, Germany and the UK (Porter, 1990, pp. 327, 351, 413, 504). Within Europe, new firm start-ups are much greater in Italy with its individualistic, independent, risk-taking culture, than in its Teutonic neighbours (Porter, 1990, pp. 445–7).

1.6 THE POSSIBILITY OF PERPETUAL GROWTH

Schumpeter's (1934) description of capitalistic economic development at the beginning of this century suggested the possibility of perpetual growth. Entrepreneurial innovations would create profits and consumers' surplus. Imitation and the 'gale of perennial destruction' would eliminate these profits and reconstitute incentives to innovate. But the rise of large, managerially controlled corporations, and the growth of democratic governments bent on redistribution made obsolete Schumpeter's image of entrepreneurial capitalism.

Despite these events, Schumpeter (1950), writing at the middle of the 20th century, somewhat surprisingly was still able to paint a rather cheerful picture of economic development. Innovations would now pour forth from the R&D laboratory of the large corporation, and the whole process could be sufficiently routinized to be taken over by the state, when democracy's egalitarian tendencies eventually led to socialism's triumph. Once launched, capitalistic economies might innovate and grow indefinitely, even if transformed into some form of democratic socialism.

It is difficult from a post-1989 vantage point to give Schumpeter high marks for the predictive content of his last major work. Small firms have accounted for a disproportionate share of major innovations throughout the 20th century (Jewkes, Sawyer and Stillerman, 1969; Pavit *et al.*, 1987). The most dramatic economic failure of the Communist economies was undoubtedly their inability to introduce innovations. Even the most successful of the quasi-socialistic economies, like Sweden, have been better at maintaining employment and productivity by shifting workers around between existing firms than by generating new ones (Porter, 1990, p. 351).

The best examples of Schumpeterian corporations have been the pharmaceuticals, which have continually reinvested profits from existing drugs to develop new ones. More typical, however, have been companies like Polaroid, which despite strenuous efforts to create innovative environments and heavy expenditures on R&D have failed to duplicate their initial success.[25] Most mature companies eventually give up trying to develop new major products and switch to mergers as their route to perpetual life. Even the largest pharmaceutical companies appear to have switched to this strategy in the last few years.

That no country has found the formula for perpetual growth so far does not mean of course that no country ever will or ever could. Since all citizens can be better off if a country's wealth grows, agreement on policies to achieve this end should in principle be possible. We have identified three categories of impediments to perpetual growth: rentseeking and dissipation in the private (corporate) sector, rentseeking through government and motivation.

The inefficiencies that arise because of the principal/agent problem between stockholders and managers can be reduced by strengthening the hand of shareholders. Requiring managers to provide shareholders with more information, so that they can monitor managers better; prohibiting managers from owning *voting* shares; and taxing undistributed profits are just some examples. To the extent that wealth destroying mergers are the managers most egregious use of discretion, they could be prevented simply by prohibiting all acquisitions by large firms, subject to an efficiency defence.[26]

A prohibition on large firm acquisitions would also mitigate the costs of managerial rentseeking by reducing the magnitudes of the rents sought. Both managerial compensation and the nonpecuniary advantages of management are related to company size. Smaller firms are also easier for shareholders to monitor and control. A vigorous competition policy will limit corporate rents and thus the competition to control them.

Most directly, tax, competition and regulation policies might be adopted to encourage the formation of new companies. For example in Italy, where small and medium-sized firms have been an important source of growth, small firms are exempted from certain taxes and regulations of employment practices.

The welfare state can be dismantled and rentseeking made more difficult. Reforms to prevent collective rentseeking would most likely be of a constitutional nature. Switzerland has the smallest governmental sector in Western Europe, because its decentralized federalist structure and heavy reliance on direct democracy allow its citizens to keep government in check. Swiss institutions can be copied and supplemented by requiring supramajorities to pass some (all) legislation in the parliament, constitutional constraints placed on the nature of issues that can be adopted, and the like (Mueller, 1996).

Although policies such as these can be conceptualized, they are obviously not easy to adopt. To the extent that economic decline is the result of rentseeking, those who currently receive the highest rents will resist the reforms. For example, the potential benefits from privatizing state-owned enterprises in Europe have been undermined by placing ownership shares in the hands of groups 'friendly' to incumbent managements (*Economist*, 15 July 1995, p. 14). More generally, in countries like Sweden the number of people employed by or directly dependent on the government has grown so large that measures to contract government are now almost politically impossible (Lindbeck, 1995a,b).

The most difficult of all of the causes of decline to avoid, however, is the motivational factor. Mancur Olson (1982, pp. 252–53, n.10) demonstrated the fallacy in the argument that Germany, Italy and Japan's economic success relative to that of the US and the UK was due to *an advantage* the two defeated countries had because their capital stocks had been destroyed by the war, by pointing out that the US and UK could and would then have improved their economic performance by destroying their industrial capital.

A similar point cannot be made, however, against the argument that prosperity reduces the incentives to start businesses, take risks and to innovate. Since the goal of these activities, and the desirability of economic growth in general, is that it produces prosperity, it would be self-defeating to *manufacture* scarcity to create prosperity. The challenge to perpetual growth is to induce a well-fed society to behave as if it was hungry, while remaining well fed.[27]

1.7 SPECULATIONS

Which if any of the leading economic powers in the world today will be able to meet this challenge? We close with some speculative thoughts regarding this question. Let us start with Japan. Although it is difficult to view Japan as a socialist economy, it does have a fairly egalitarian structure, and many might cite it as an example of managed innovation and growth of the type Schumpeter described in *Capitalism, Socialism and Democracy*, with Japan's giant industrial groups and MITI working hand in hand to sustain economic growth. Who is to say that this will not go on indefinitely?

Perhaps it will, but there is reason to think otherwise. Throughout the post-World-War-II era, Japan was governed by a single party. This helped prevent Japan from engaging in the kind of governmental rentseeking that more competitive politics and majority rule tend to produce. The result is that Japan has a much smaller governmental sector than any other country with a similar standard of living. Japan's politics seems to be becoming more competitive, however. One expects more efforts to use government to redistribute Japan's immense wealth, with the inevitable consequences for growth.

It also seems likely that Japan's military budget will grow dramatically, as it assumes the place in world politics that its economic status allows, and that this too will have negative consequences for Japan's economic growth. Although they continue to eschew domestic mergers, Japanese firms have begun to show signs of maturity in shifting to growth through (foreign) acquisitions.

Finally one must wonder whether Japanese families will continue to place great pressure on their children to succeed in school, and Japanese workers will continue to work longer hours and take shorter vacations than workers in other developed countries, now that they are the richest country in the world?

During its economic rise over the 19th and 20th centuries, the United States was a large, competitive market. Over much of this period the government sector was small and did not interfere with the private sector except to ensure the competitiveness of its markets. Wave upon wave of immigrants entered the labour market, started new firms, and contributed to the country's economic dynamism through their drive and ambition. New waves of immigrants now press to get in. Why cannot America's development strategy of the past be applied again in the future?

Again the answer is that it possibly can, but again there is also reason for doubt. The immigrants from Europe in the 19th and 20th centuries went in search of 'the American Dream'. They left their homelands for good, they forced their children to learn English, they *became* Americans, legally and psychologically. Many immigrants today do not seem willing to make the same commitments. Sometimes they come seeking only work, with their families remaining in their homelands. Often they wish not to adopt the language of their community, but to retain their native language and culture, and have the community accommodate this 'diversity'.[28] A danger exists today in the United States that the same kind of linguistic divisions will develop as exist in Canada and Belgium, and that they will produce the same type of economically costly frictions. Not surprisingly, the United States seems likely to adopt ever more restrictive policies against new immigrants, thereby mitigating one problem, but eliminating a historically important source of economic dynamism.[29] America's protectionist immigration policies might also easily spill over into protectionist economic policies. We gave recent examples of this above.

On the other hand, the individualist, antigovernment ideology of the Americans seems much more likely to allow them to rein in governmental rentseeking than the Europeans will be able to achieve with their sense of social solidarity and deference to the state. Despite the much smaller share of GNP going to government in the US than in all European Union countries, politicians from Ronald Reagan to Newt Gingrich have scored major political victories by promising to reduce significantly the scale of the US welfare state and government intervention more generally. In stark contrast, even the modest recent proposals to cut back welfare spending in France, Germany and Austria have met with public protests and strikes. The US deficit and inflation rates as of June 1997 would have qualified it for membership in the European Monetary Union. Among the Union's countries, only Luxembourg qualified. At the end of 1998, by which time the major EU powers had imposed harsh monetary and fiscal restraints to meet the Maastricht targets, electoral processes had brought to power new left-of-centre governments.

The integrative steps that began in 1992 might have initiated in Western Europe the kind of disruptions that Olson (1982) feels are necessary to overcome interest group power, and initiate economic growth. Add to these the events of 1989 and 1991 in East Europe and the Soviet Union, and one might have envisaged the birth of a new Europe, whose growth and prosperity would be facilitated by its large common market, and stimulated by both demand and supply side pressures from the east.[30]

Had such an era dawned one would have expected Europeans to have recognized the critical juncture in history at which they stood, and have responded by writing a constitution *for Europe* that would integrate Europe politically as well as economically, and introduced the kind of safeguards to individual rights and to the market process that are necessary in such a large, heterogeneous community; introduced a new European language that in the long run would facilitate communication and cooperation among its diverse peoples, without giving an existing linguistic group an advantage over any other; introduced a single currency to facilitate economic transactions, and so on.

Some of these measures, like the common currency, are coming to pass. But Europe seems much more interested in protecting its institutions and rents of the past than in creating new ones. Many European corporations today, like their American counterparts in the 1970s and 1980s, respond to the pressures from increased competition not by developing new or less costly products, but by merging. Instead of developing a new language that all Europeans would use, existing languages are defended by forcing their use on individuals, and prohibiting the use of competing languages. How symbolic an intersection of Spenglerian cultural decline and economic decline is the effort led by France to protect the European film industry by *forbidding* the showing of non-European, that is, American, films. Could one imagine Holland in the 17th century prohibiting foreign artists from competing with Rembrandt or Hals? Could one imagine even France as recently as a century ago forbidding the showing of Van Gogh in Paris for fear that then no one would buy Monet and Manet?

Mere mention of the term 'European Federalism' puts large numbers of Europeans in a state of apoplexy. Yet, some form of truly federalist structure seems to be needed, if the European Union is ever going to assume a role in world politics that matches its economic position (see Mueller, 1997). Symbolically, the biggest item in the European Union's budget is not defence or some other pan-European public good but, as it has always been, subsidies for its most important industry, from *before* the Industrial Revolution.

NOTES

1. For discussions of the catch-up hypothesis in the context of Olson's hypothesis about the decline of nations, see Abramowitz (1983) and Pryor (1983).
2. Part of the reason that the Reagan and Thatcher revolutions were only partially successful is that they did not take on all interest groups with equal zeal. Business group rentseeking was virtually ignored.
3. For discussions of the catch-up hypothesis in the context of Olson's hypothesis about the decline of nations, see Abramowitz (1983) and Pryor (1983).
4. On the historical side see Chandler (1990, pp. 34–6, 227–8, 597–605), on the empirical side, Shepherd (1975) and Mueller (1986).
5. Such was the fear of the United States in Europe at one point in time, as expressed by Jean-Jacques Servan-Shreiber (1968). Akio Morito (1988), a founder of Sony, seemed in similar awe of America early on in his career.
6. For profits maximization always to be equivalent to utility maximization regardless of the rate of transformation of effort into profits, the owner-entrepreneur must have a constant marginal utility of income.
7. For reviews of the evidence that mergers reduce shareholder wealth see Mueller (1987, 1995). Firth (1980) presents evidence directly linking growth through merger and above normal increases in managerial salaries.
8. Petroleum mergers dominated *Fortune Magazine's* list of the 'Decades Worst Mergers' (Fisher, 1984).
9. An important exception to this pattern was General Dynamics, which simply used its existing cash flows to buy up its own shares and thereby handsomely increased the wealth of its shareholders.
10. Merger activity and stock market prices have also been strongly correlated in the United Kingdom, see Nelson (1959, 1966) and Geroski (1984).
11. Not only do most mergers occur when stock prices are rising, but the companies who make the acquisitions significantly outperform the market on average *prior* to their making the acquisitions. These companies' managers are most likely to have the resources and discretion to undertake mergers, even when these mergers reduce the profits and efficiency of the merging firms (Magenheim and Mueller, 1987; Mueller, 1995).
12. See surveys by Caves (1989), Jensen and Ruback (1983), Mueller (1987, 1995).
13. See Ravenscraft and Scherer (1987, Chapters 5 and 6) and Porter (1987). Some individual examples are striking. Heublein acquired Theodore Hamm Brewing Co. in 1965 for \$62 million, and sold it in 1973 for \$6 million. Murray bought Easy Washer in the mid-1950s for \$9.4 million and sold it in 1963 for \$0.77 million (Mueller, 1986, p. 204). American Safety Razor had sales of \$27.3 million when Philip Morris acquired it in 1960, and sales of \$17.8 million when it was spun-off in 1977 (Ravenscraft and Scherer, 1987, Chapter 5).
14. Many examples are given by Davidson (1985).
15. Let I_t be a firm's investment in period t, C_{t+j} the cash flow this investment generates in $t + j$, and i_t the firm's discount rate in t, then the present value of this investment is

$$PV_t = \sum_{j=1}^{\infty} \frac{C_{t+j}}{(1+i_t)^j} \tag{1}$$

If we take PV_t from (1) and place it into (2), we can define for any i_t, a permanent return, r_t, on the investment I_t, which creates an equivalent present value to that defined by (1):

$$PV_t = \frac{I_t r_t}{i_t} \tag{2}$$

The market value of the firm at the end of period t can be defined as

$$M_t = M_{t-1} + PV_t - \delta_t M_{t-1} + \mu_t \qquad (3)$$

where PV_t is the present value of the investment made during t, δ_t the depreciation rate for the firm's total capital, and μ_t the market's error in evaluating M_t.

The assumption of capital market efficiency implies that the error term in (3) has the usual properties assumed in regression analysis. In a cross-section of firms of varying sizes, however, μ_t is likely to be heteroscedastic. To remove heteroscedasticity we deflate (3) by M_{t-1}. Replacing PV_t in (3) with $c_t I_t$, $c_t = r_t / i_t$

$$\frac{M_t - M_{t-1}}{M_{t-1}} = -\delta + c\frac{I_t}{M_{t-1}} + \frac{\mu_t}{M_{t-1}} \qquad (4)$$

and rearranging yields equation (4) under the assumption that δ_t and c_t are constant across firms and time.

16. Kenneth Arrow (1962) was the first to show formally that the possession of monopoly power can act as a deterrant to innovation.
17. The low status of business occupations relative to the military, was also an important contributing factor to the decline of the Ottoman Empire, once its military expansionism had reached its limits, and wealth could no longer be acquired through conquest.
18. Porter (1990, p. 114) stresses the role immigrants have played in developing new products in the US, UK and Switzerland.
19. On success breeding failure, see Toynbee (1946, pp. 307–10). Results of a recent survey of 18-year-old Austrians by an institute in Linz are typical for both Europe and the United States, today. When asked what their greatest concerns for the future were, less than half mentioned uncertainties about their careers or employment. Nor were environmental dangers or crime a cause for much concern. The question that troubled the largest fraction of Austrian youths was how they would best be able to use their future leisure and vacation time (*Der Standard*, 5/6 August 1995, p. 1).
20. As reported in *The Economist*, 3 June 1995, p. 77.
21. Seligman (1925, Chapter 1), also reported in Tanzi (1986, p. 5), and Mueller (1989, p. 323).
22. *Ibid.*
23. For an analysis of the 'British disease', that links rentseeking, majority rule and government activity together, see Samuel Brittan (1975).
24. 'Offensive' governmental outlays have been a popular means to growth throughout the ages. All empires built through military conquest have eventually perished by the sword, however. The heavy burden of continually having to support armies to fend off the barbarians and resolve leadership disputes appears to have contributed to the fall of the Roman Empire (Gibbon, 1985). Paul Kennedy (1987, p. 539) notes that a 'great power' must have both manufacturing and military strength, but that the high cost of the latter undermines the former.
25. Polaroid's average return on investment over the 1969–88 period was *negative* (Mueller and Reardon, 1993, p. 440).
26. For further discussion of these and other proposals, see Mueller (1993, 1995).
27. Neumann's (1991) thesis would allow for perpetual growth, albeit with periodic depressions to regenerate the incentives to save and invest, and in the context of my thesis to innovate and take risks.
28. In part this change may reflect a shift in the composition of the immigrant population in the United States. Since the mid-1960s changes in immigration laws, a far greater fraction of US immigrants have come from the Western Hemisphere, so that returning home has been a more realistic option than was returning to Europe in the 19th or early 20th centuries (Borjas, 1994). In part this change reflects changes in the actual and perceived rights of immigrants (Soysal, 1995).

29. The changing composition of the immigrant population also appears to have been accompanied by a decline in their education and skill levels compared to earlier immigants, so that even if the flow of immigrants is not cut off, immigrants may not be as important a source of entrepreneurial talent in the US in the future as they were in the past. See Borjas (1994), and references therein.
30. More pessimistically, one might interpret the Great Depression sandwiched between the two world wars as Europe's 'Time of Troubles', and the European Union as Europe's 'Universal State'. Following Toynbee's life-cycle scenario, creation of the Universal State would provide only an interregnum in Europe's decline, which would be followed by the complete disintegration of its civilization as it is invaded by barbarians (from east and south?). All that is missing from Toynbee's saga is a Universal Religion (consumerism?).

REFERENCES

Abramovitz, Moses (1983), 'Notes on International Differences in Growth Rates', in Dennis C. Mueller (ed.), *The Political Economy of Growth*, New Haven and London: Yale University Press, pp. 79–89.

Alesina, Alberto and Dani Rodrik (1994), 'Distributive politics and economic growth', *Quarterly Journal of Economics,* **109,** 465–90.

Arrow, Kenneth (1962), 'Economic Welfare and the Allocation of Resources for Invention', *NBER, The Rate and Direction of Inventive Activity,* Princeton: Princeton University Press, pp. 609–25.

Borjas, George J. (1994), 'The economics of immigration' , *Journal of Economic Literature,* **32,** 1667–718.

Brittan, Samuel (1975), 'The economic contradictions of democracy', *British Journal of Political Science,* **5,** 129–59.

Caves, Richard E. (1989), 'Mergers, takeovers and economic efficiency: foresight vs. hindsight', *International Journal of Industrial Organization,* **7**, 151–74.

Chandler, Alfred D. Jr (1990), *Scale and Scope,* Cambridge, MA: Belknap Press.

Coase, Ronald H. (1937), 'The nature of the firm', *Economica,* **4,** 233–61.

Davidson, Kenneth M. (1985), *Megamergers,* Cambridge, MA: Ballinger.

Der Standard, 5/6 August 1995, p. 1.

Dunne, Timothy, Mark Roberts and Larry Samuelson (1988), 'Patterns of firm entry and exit in U.S. manufacturing industries', *Rand Journal of Economics,* **19,** 495–515.

Fernández-Armesto, Felipe (1995), *Millennium,* New York and London: Scribner.

Firth, Michael (1980), 'Takeovers, shareholder returns, and the theory of the firm', *Quarterly Journal of Economics,* **94,** 315–47.

Fisher, Anne B. (1984), 'The decade's worst mergers', *Fortune,* 30 April, 262 ff.

Geroski, Paul A. (1984), 'On the relationship between aggregate merger activity and the stock market', *European Economic Review,* **25,** 223–33.

Geroski, Paul A. (1991), *Market Dynamics and Entry,* Oxford: Basil Blackwell.

Gibbon, Edward, (1985), *The Decline and Fall of the Roman Empire,* London: Penguin Classics (first published in 6 volumes from 1776 to 1788).

Gort, Michael and Steven Klepper (1982), 'Time paths in the diffusion of product innovations', *Economic Journal,* **92,** 630–53.

Graddy, Elizabeth and Steven Klepper (1990), 'The evolution of new industries and the determinants of market structure', *Rand Journal of Economics,* **21,** 27–44.

Jensen, Michael C. and Richard S. Ruback (1983), 'The market for corporate control', *Journal of Financial Economics,* **11,** 5–50.

Jewkes, John, John Sawyer and Richard Stillerman (1969), *The Sources of Invention,* 2nd edn, New York: Norton.

Kennedy, Paul (1987), *The Rise and Fall of the Great Powers,* New York: Random House.

Knight, Frank H. (1965), *Risk, Uncertainty and Profit,* New York: Harper and Row (first published in 1921).

Klepper, Steven and Kenneth L. Simons (1993), 'Technological change and industry shakeouts', mimeo, Carnegie Mellon University.

Lindbeck, Assar (1995a), 'Hazardous welfare-state dynamics', *American Economic Review,* **85,** 9–15.

Lindbeck, Assar (1995b), 'Welfare state disincentives with endogenous habits and norms', *Scandinavian Journal of Economics,* **97,** 477–94.

Magenheim, Ellen and Dennis C. Mueller (1987), 'On Measuring the Effect of Mergers on Acquiring Firm Shareholders', in Jack Coffee, Louis Lowenstein and Susan Rose-Ackerman (eds), *Knights, Raiders and Targets,* Oxford: Oxford University Press, pp. 171–93.

Marris, Robin (1964), *The Economic Theory of Managerial Capitalism,* Glencoe: Free Press.

Meeks, Geoffrey (1977), *Disappointing Marriage: A Study of the Gains from Merger,* Cambridge: Cambridge University Press.

Mill, John Stuart (1885), *Principles of Political Economy,* 9th edn, London: Longmans, Green & Co.

Morito, Akio, with Edwin M. Reingold and Mitsuko Shimomuna (1988), *Made in Japan*, New York: Signet.

Mueller, Dennis C. (1969), 'A theory of conglomerate mergers', *Quarterly Journal of Economics,* **LXXXIII,** 643–59, reprinted in G. Marchildon (ed.) (1991), *Mergers and Acquisitions*, Cheltenham: Edward Elgar.

Mueller, Dennis C. (1972), 'A life cycle theory of the firm' , *Journal of Industrial Economics,* **20,** 199–219.

Mueller, Dennis C. (1986), *Profits in the Long Run,* Cambridge: Cambridge University Press.

Mueller, Dennis C. (1987), *The Corporation: Growth, Diversification, and Mergers,* London: Harwood Academic Publishers.

Mueller, Dennis C. (1989), *Public Choice II,* Cambridge: Cambridge University Press.

Mueller, Dennis C. (1990), *The Dynamics of Company Profits* (editor and contributor), Cambridge: Cambridge University Press.

Mueller, Dennis C. (1993), 'U.S. merger policy and the 1992 merger guidelines', *Review of Industrial Organization,* **8,** 151–62.

Mueller, Dennis C. (1995), 'Mergers: Theory and Evidence', in Giuliano Mussatti (ed.), *Mergers, Markets, and Public Policy,* Dordrecht: Kluwer, pp. 9–43.

Mueller, Dennis C. (1996), *Constitutional Democracy*, New York: Oxford University Press.

Mueller, Dennis C. (1997), 'Federalism and the European Union: a constitutional perspective', *Public Choice,* **90,** 255–80.

Mueller, Dennis C. and Peter Murrell (1986), 'Interest groups and the size of government', *Public Choice,* **48**(2), 125–45.

Mueller, Dennis C. and Elizabeth Reardon (1993), 'Rates of return on investment', *Southern Economic Journal,* **60,** 430–53.
Mueller, Dennis C. and John E. Tilton (1969), 'Research and development costs as a barrier to entry', *Canadian Journal of Economics,* **II**(4), 570–79.
Mueller, Dennis C. and Lawrence Yun (1995), 'Rates of return over the firm's life cycle', mimeo, University of Vienna.
Nelson, Ralph L. (1959), *Merger Movements in American Industry 1895–1956,* Princeton: Princeton University Press.
Nelson, Ralph L. (1966), 'Business Cycle Factors in the Choice Between Internal and External Growth', in W. Alberts and J. Segall (eds), *The Corporate Merger,* Chicago: University of Chicago Press.
Neumann, Manfred (1991), 'Das Buddenbrook-Syndrom und lange Wellen in Wirtschaft und Politik', *Bayerische Akademie der Wissenschaften, Philosophisch–Historische Klasse,* **2,** 3–21.
North, Douglass C. (1990), *Institutions, Institutional Change, and Economic Performance,* Cambridge: Cambridge University Press.
North, Douglass C. and Robert P. Thomas (1973), *The Rise of the Western World: A New Economic History*, Cambridge: Cambridge University Press.
Odagiri, Hiroyuki (1982), 'Antineoclassical management motivation in a neoclassical economy: a model of economic growth and Japan's experience, *Kyklos,* **35,** 223–43.
Odagiri, Hiroyuki (1991), *Growth Through Competition, Competition Through Growth: Strategic Management and the Economy in Japan,* Oxford: Oxford University Press.
Olson, Mancur (1982), *The Rise and Decline of Nations,* New Haven: Yale University Press.
Pavit, K., M. Robson and J. Townsend (1987), 'The size distribution of innovating firms in the U.K.: 1945–1983', *Journal of Industrial Economics,* **35,** 297–316.
Persson, Torsten and Guido Tabellini (1994), 'Is inequality harmful for growth?', *American Economic Review,* **84,** 600–621.
Porter, Michael A. (1987), 'From competitive advantage to corporate strategy', *Harvard Business Review,* May–June, 43–59.
Porter, Michael A. (1990), *The Competitive Advantage of Nations,* New York: Free Press.
Pryor, Frederic L. (1983) , 'A Quasi-Test of Olson's Hypotheses' , in Dennis C. Mueller (ed.), *The Political Economy of Growth,* New Haven and London: Yale University Press, pp. 90–105.
Ravenscraft, David J. and F.M. Scherer (1987), *Mergers, Sell-Offs, & Economic Efficiency,* Washington, DC: Brookings Institution.
Roe, Mark J. (1993), 'Takeover Politics', in Margaret M. Blair (ed.), *The Deal Decade,* Washington, DC: Brookings Institution, pp. 321–33.
Schumpeter, Joseph A. (1934), *The Theory of Economic Development,* Cambridge, MA: Harvard University Press (first published in German, 1911).
Schumpeter, Joseph A. (1950), *Capitalism, Socialism and Democracy,* 3rd edn, New York: Harper and Row.
Scitovsky, T. (1943), 'A note on profit maximization and its implications', *Review of Economic Studies,* **11,** 57–60.
Seligman, E.R.A. (1925), *Studies in Public Finance,* New York: Macmillan.

Servan-Schreiber, Jean-Jacques (1968), *The American Challenge*, New York: Atheneum.
Shepherd, William G. (1975), *The Treatment of Market Power*, New York: Columbia University Press.
Smith, Adam (1937), *The Wealth of Nations*, New York: Random House (first published in 1776).
Soysal, Yasemin Nuhoglu (1995), *Limits of Citizenship: Migrants and Postnational Membership in Europe*, Chicago: University of Chicago Press.
Spengler, Oswald (1923), *Der Untergang des Abendlandes*, I, Munich: Oskar Beck.
Spengler, Oswald (1922), *Der Untergang des Abendlandes*, II, Munich: Oskar Beck.
Tanzi, Vito (1986), *The Growth of Government Expenditures in Industrial Countries: An International and Historical Perspective*, Washington DC: International Monetary Fund.
Taylor, Michael J. (1987), *Anarchy and Cooperation*, 2nd edn, Cambridge: Cambridge University Press.
The Economist, 3 June 1995, p. 77.
The Economist, 15 July 1995, p. 14.
Toynbee, Arnold J. (1946, 1957), *A Study of History* (D.C. Somervill, abridgement), 2 volumes, Oxford: Oxford University Press (unabridged version published in 10 volumes, 1933, 1939).
Williamson, Oliver (1975), *Markets and Hierarchies: Analysis and Antitrust Implications*, New York: Free Press.
Williamson, Oliver (1985), *The Economic Institutions of Capitalism*, New York: Free Press.

[3]

The United States and Europe at the turn of a century

There are, of course, a countless number of dimensions over which one might compare the United States and Europe. It is natural that I, as an economist, will concern myself mainly with these aspects of the comparison. But I am also interested in the differences between American and European political institutions. Having lived for lengthy periods on both sides of the Atlantic, I have often been struck by various differences in attitudes toward government and market competition between Americans and Europeans, and what one might call the American and European *Weltanschauungen*. Because these differences in *Weltanschauungen* underlie all other differences between Europe and the United States, I begin with these.

Differences between Americans and Europeans

All generalizations can be contradicted by counterexamples, and so it is surely with a comparison of "the typical American" and "the typical European." For every American who believes he has a constitutional right to carry a gun, there is an American who believes that this "right" should be restricted, indeed a majority of Americans hold the latter belief. Free market liberals can be found on both sides of the Atlantic. Nevertheless, important historical differences do exist in the way Americans and Europeans view government and their views concerning the individual's position vis-à-vis the government.

In any discussion in the United States over gun control, abortion, crime or almost any other public issue, the discussion will not get very far before the Constitution is brought in. Does the Constitution protect an individual's right to carry a gun, to have an abortion? What constraints does the Constitution place on the evidence that the state can use against a criminal, on the punishments it can administer? Perhaps no difference between the attitude to government of U.S. citizens and the attitude of Europeans is more important than the view of Americans that their Constitution erects a barrier between themselves and the Government, a barrier that protects their privacy and individual freedom from willful or capricious governmental encroachment.

The U.S. Constitution was written by men who had recently participated in a lengthy war to free themselves from a European government which was viewed as tyrannical, oppressive and arbitrary. They were particularly interested in erecting checks on the Government and in protecting the individual citizen from the Government. The result was an elaborate system of checks and balances built into the Government's procedural rules and a bill of rights that fenced off certain spheres of individual action from government interference. Over the course of the following two centuries individual citizens have appealed to these rights, and to those that were subsequently added, to protect them from various governmental measures. By and large the judicial system has acted to protect or even enlarge the domain of these rights. Consequently over the course of these two centuries the belief has arisen among all U.S. citizens that there are certain things that the state cannot do, and that each citizen has recourse to the courts to protect herself from the state should it cross over this protected boundary.

If you ask a citizen of the United States what it means to be an American, she will undoubtedly speak of freedom, democracy, and opportunity in answering. Americans view their citizenship in terms of civil and political rights, and the opportunity to get ahead, to get rich.

Conceptions of citizenship are more heterogeneous across Western Europe than in the United States, and so it is more difficult to predict how a European would reply to the question "What does it mean to be a European?". But, at least on the Continent, I would expect the answer to be couched more in terms of economic rights – the right to a job, an education, security against unemployment and poverty. What is decidedly European is the belief that the state will guarantee economic well-being and security.

When the effort was first made in the United States to introduce a federal income tax it was opposed on constitutional grounds, and the Supreme Court upheld this challenge. An income tax could only be implemented after the Constitution was amended to explicitly allow such a measure. Which European country has had to amend its Constitution to be able to introduce an income tax? The notion that such an amendment would be necessary would strike most Europeans as odd.

A fondness for taxation is common to all governments. Thus, one could well imagine a state legislature in the United States, or even the Congress, contemplating levying a tax upon those who watch television or listen to the radio. It would immediately anticipate, however, that any attempt to enforce such a tax obligation by sending tax collectors into homes to search for television and radio receivers would be challenged as an unconstitutional invasion of privacy. Even if they thought that such a challenge would eventually fail, the legislators probably would opt not to implement the tax out of fear that the citizens would perceive it as an unconstitutional infringement on their rights, and the legislators would themselves have a price to pay at the next election. Neither the German nor the Austrian parliaments have perceived such a danger, and the citizens of these countries either dutifully pay the state for the privilege of watching television or fear a knock on the door by the state tax inspector in search of evidence of tax evasion.

Americans have from the founding of their country viewed government with suspicion. Government was a necessary evil to be kept as small as possible. When problems arose the attitude in America was often that these should be resolved by the individual confronting the problem, or by the individual and his local community. If the weather turned dry and the crops failed, one pulled up stakes and moved West. If the landlord raised the rent, one moved out. If someone broke the law, one hung him from a nearby tree. This kind of individualistic, self-action, self-help attitude undoubtedly was fostered by the fact that the federal government is a long distance from a large part of the country, and during much of the nineteenth century even local governments might be far away or ineffective.

Many Europeans also distrust and resent their governments, and are perhaps even more apt than Americans to try to cheat them out of tax revenue. But they also seem more ready to turn to the Government to solve their personal as well as their collective problems. The result is the plethora of price controls, restrictions on entry, exit, shop opening hours, hiring and firing practices, and so on, familiar to all Europeans. The landlady wants to raise the rent – then get the Government to prevent her from doing so.

A consequence of this difference in the conceptions of the average American and European as to what their individual rights and responsibilities are is not only the greater extent of government regulation, as just mentioned, but also the greater overall size of the government sector in Europe. Every member country in the European Union has a higher percentage of its national income accounted for by the government sector than does the United States.

It is noteworthy that the Western European country with the smallest government sector is Switzerland, since its Constitution was patterned after that of the United States and plays a greater role in Swiss politics than the Constitution of any other European country. Indeed, it plays perhaps even a greater role in Swiss politics than does the U.S. Constitution in its politics. Switzerland has the strongest federalist system of any European country. As in the United States, Swiss federalism offers additional protection to citizens against the state. Most tellingly, to protect its form of government and the benefits it provides to its citizens, Switzerland has refrained from joining the political union which surrounds it.

A second, but related, difference between Americans and Europeans concerns their perspectives on life. Historically the United States has always looked upon itself, and has been regarded from outside, as the land of freedom and opportunity, the land of dreams. Everyone is free to pray in his own way, work in his own way, and live in his own way. Everyone has the opportunity to get rich in America. This dream induced millions of Europeans to migrate to the United States in the eighteenth, nineteenth and beginning part of the twentieth century. These immigrants brought not only their dreams but also their desires to work hard and "get ahead," and thereby helped in many cases to make the dreams become realities. The result was an optimistic outlook on life that seemed peculiarly American. Americans were doers, problem solvers, inventors and innovators.

I distinguish liberals from conservatives by their degrees of optimism. The optimist expects the best, the pessimist fears the worst. The economic liberal is an optimist in his beliefs about the capacity of consumers to make good decisions and favors free markets and minimal government regulation. The political liberal is similarly optimistic about the capacity of voters to make good decisions and believes that government officials are striving to maximize the social good. The political conservative questions the capacity and incentives voters have to make good decisions and is skeptical about the motives of those in government.[1] The liberal is optimistic about what the future will bring and welcomes change and innovation. The conservative is fearful of change and innovation, and longs for the past.

The success that each wave of immigrants to America had in adjusting to life in "the New World" and in moving up the economic ladder developed a kind of congenital optimism in Americans, a "can do" attitude toward life. No problem could not be solved, no enemy would not be defeated, each generation would be better off than its predecessor. Thus, with a continual flow of motivated laborers and ambitious would-be entrepreneurs from Europe, and a seemingly endless supply of free land, an optimistic outlook on life developed in the United States during the nineteenth and beginning part of the twentieth century, and a corresponding brand of liberalism. During much of the nineteenth century this liberalism was mostly associated with attitudes toward the market. Toward the end of that century, however, a new brand of political liberalism began to develop in the United States. The movement to introduce a personal income tax of 2 percent (see above) was part of this change. New parties, such as the Populists, appeared with the radical, and certainly optimistic, belief that a coalition of farmers and laborers would be able to redress the power of the railroads and Eastern banks to the farmers' and laborers' advantage. The Progressive Movement, which lasted into the twentieth century and attracted such talents as Theodore Roosevelt and Robert LaFollette, sought to strengthen democracy and place it more in the hands of individual citizens. It led to reforms like primary elections to determine the identities of the candidates on the final ballot and eventually to women's suffrage. It carried on the attack on big business and produced first the Interstate Commerce Commission to regulate the railroads and then the Sherman Antitrust Act (1890), which combined economic and political liberalism in calling upon government to protect the freedom of the market.

The Great Depression shattered beliefs in the efficacy of market processes, however, and led to the New Deal. Government would end the Depression, regulate markets and protect the individual from the economic insecurities that market competition engenders. Political liberalism displaced economic liberalism so thoroughly during the 1930s that even today the word "liberal" in the United States is used only in reference to people who favor government intervention to solve social problems.

European history is to a considerable degree an account of kings and queens and emperors leading their respective countries to glory or to ruin. For this reason, perhaps, Europeans seem to have expected the state to play an important role in their lives for a much longer time than have Americans. Indeed, to refer to government as "the state" is itself decidedly European, and personifies government with the accompanying connotation of an actor pursuing certain goals in a way which is quite different from the way in which most Americans think of government. Given this long-standing acceptance of the prominence of the state in their lives, it was comparatively easy for Europeans to adopt the liberal view of government as general benefactor and source of economic security. Here, as before, the Swiss prove to be the exception.

Why economic liberalism is so weak in Europe compared to the United States is less clear. Perhaps this is because during the nineteenth century the industrial revolution had a more jolting impact on the life-styles and psyches of people in labor-surplus Europe than it did on their former countrymen in labor-short America. Be that as it may, the economic liberalism that we associate with Adam Smith, Joseph Schumpeter and Friedrich Hayek has, ironically, been far more visible in word and deed in the twentieth-century United States than on their own continent. The next section illustrates this point.

Attitudes toward competition in Europe and the United States

In the United States, if one returns late from a long trip, say 3 o'clock in the morning, and wants something to eat, one can drive to the nearby all-night supermarket and purchase whatever one wants. If one returns late from a long trip in Austria, say 8 o'clock in the evening, and wants something to eat, one can go to the nearby restaurant but not to the nearby supermarket, for it, and all others, are closed by law. At 3 o'clock in the morning, one goes to bed hungry. Similar laws on shop hours exist in Germany, although they were liberalized a little bit in 1996. France, on the other hand, has introduced legislation restricting shop opening hours, regulating selected prices, and even restricting the opening of new supermarkets in an effort to protect its small shopkeepers (*Economist*, April 6, 1996).

Any American visiting Europe is immediately struck by "how expensive everything is." High food prices are a direct result of high protective tariffs, price floors and non tariff measures like the bans on genetically modified seeds and hormone-fed beef. Non-food products are also often protected by, for example, the liberal use of anti-dumping duties (*Economist*, May 22, 1999b).

Books, compact disks, tennis balls and a variety of other products often sell in Europe at prices that are two and three times the prices paid by Americans for exactly the same product – even when these products carry European brand names such as Deutsche Grammaphon and Dunlop.[2] In some cases, as with books in Germany, this is a result of formal resale price maintenance agreements; in others it is a result of informal resale price maintenance agreements; and in still others it is a result once again of government regulations, for example France's *loi Lang* (*Economist*, April 6, 1996, pp. 81–2). European Union competition policy, particularly in the area of vertical restraints, should of course work against such practices, and in the very visible automobile market it appears that the vertical territorial dealership restraints will eventually disappear. But in other areas, such as book retailing, the trend may be in the other direction, with several EU countries planning either new restrictive legislation or the strengthening of existing restrictions (*Economist*, April 6, 1996, p. 82).

Competition in the market for academicians is also far more apparent in the United States than in Europe. At my former university in the United States, the University of Maryland, the salary of the highest-paid full professor was double that of the lowest-paid full professor.[3] My impression is that such differentials are common to most research-oriented universities in the United States. They are much less common in Europe, and such differentials as do exist are more likely to be related to age than to research productivity, as they would be in the United States. The reason for this difference is that salaries in European countries are generally set by the Government, and are tied to the salaries of other government workers. In most countries, such as Austria, the purchaser of academic services is a pure monopsonist. In others, like Germany, an informal cartel often exists among the purchasers (*die Länder*). The result is less or no competition across universities for professors of high ability. The result is that research after one has obtained a professorship is less handsomely rewarded in Europe than in the United States, with the unsurprising additional consequence that European professors publish less and claim fewer international academic accolades than their American counterparts.[4]

The world deregulation movement began in the United States during the 1970s with the deregulation of the airline, railroad, and trucking industries. It has spread to Europe, but very slowly. The airline industry is still not completely deregulated in Europe. Several countries continue to protect their national airlines by forbidding airlines from a second European country from picking up passengers in the first country and taking them to a third; by forbidding European Union members from signing "open skies" agreements with the U.S. that would open all cities in the European country and the U.S. to the airlines of the two countries; and by continually subsidizing their uncompetitive national airlines. Competition between the major European carriers and small, new entrants is often eliminated by the majors purchasing large fractions of the small airlines' outstanding shares. Competition between the majors themselves is often eliminated through the formation of "alliances" between airlines, which compete on various routes. Deregulation in other areas, such as telecommunications and postal services, also creeps forward slowly (*Economist*, June 15, 1996, p. 27). The potential efficiency gains from privatization in Europe are often undermined by governments placing the shares of newly privatized companies into the hands of groups "friendly" to the incumbent managements (*Economist*, July 15, 1995). Job security in Europe extends to the very top of the corporate ladder.

Perhaps the most conspicuous and futile example of protectionism in Europe, however, is the effort to preserve various aspects of European culture by subsidizing the local product and prohibiting its foreign competitors. In France this effort has produced regulations on the percentages of songs played on the radio that can be of foreign (non-French) origin, prohibitions on the use of foreign words, and the like. To some extent led by France, the European Union has also taken to subsidizing European film production and recommending European content requirements for television.[5]

The classic argument for subsidies and protectionism is the infant industry argument. But language, music, films and television are not infant industries. Language and music are aspects of national culture that are as old as the culture itself. The film industry recently celebrated its one-hundredth anniversary. Commercial television programming began more than a half-century ago. The explanation for some European countries having undeveloped television programming capabilities lies not in the age of the industry but in the fact that the incentives to produce programs were for many years stifled by the state's monopolistic control of television broadcasting.

The main advantage of knowing a language is the ability to communicate with other people. If a person has business in ten countries in which ten languages different from her own are spoken, she must learn ten new languages. If the people with whom she does business have a common second language, she must learn only one language in addition to her native tongue. Languages are characterized by significant network externalities. Activities with significant network externalities, for example, telephones, software and credit cards, tend to evolve into "natural monopolies" (Katz and Shapiro, 1985, 1986). Such is the case with a second language. Having established a dominant position around the world as a second language, English seems inevitably destined to play this role. To resist this dominance through regulations and subsidies, as some Europeans are wont to do, is to place needless and wasteful costs and burdens on citizens.

Here again the contrast with the United States is revealing. Considerable concern has been expressed in some parts of the United States about the increase in the use of Spanish. Efforts have not been directed against the publication of newspapers and magazines in Spanish, nor against radio and television broadcasting in Spanish. Were such efforts made, they would no doubt be held to be unconstitutional. Rather, resistance has been offered by some Americans against Spanish becoming the first language in some areas of the country, or an officially sanctioned, co-equal second language. To my knowledge there have been no attempts made in Continental Europe to replace a local language with English as the official language.

Differences between Europe and the United States in attitudes toward an individual's responsibility for his own welfare and the state's responsibility for it combine with and reinforce differences in levels of state regulation and taxation to make European job and product markets much less mobile and flexible than in the United States. The movement of capital to low-wage countries and shifting patterns of demand for products have resulted in the loss of jobs in manufacturing and have placed pressure on the wages of low-skilled workers in both North America and Western Europe. American workers have tended to adjust to this development by shifting from manufacturing into services and by working longer hours, often by taking second jobs. European workers have responded by working fewer hours. Rather than switch from employment in manufacturing to employment in services, Europeans have chosen unemployment in manufacturing.[6] Rather than significantly cutting taxes on workers to give employers greater incentives to create new jobs, France has introduced the 35-hour work week in the hope of spreading around the existing number of jobs. The 35-hour work week has been discussed in Austria, and will undoubtedly be pressed by labor groups in other European countries. Chancellor Schroeder is being pressed to lower the age for retirement in Germany from 65 to 60 despite the need for reforms to the pension system to reduce outlays (Cohen, 1999). The effective retirement age in Austria is under 60.

The Continental European country most successful at reducing official unemployment has been Holland. Although the celebrated "Dutch model" has reduced the number of people in Holland who are classified as unemployed, a good part of this reduction is the result of Dutch workers taking part-time rather than full-time jobs, leaving the labor force before they have reached the retirement age because they have been classified as "disabled," and so on (*Economist*, May 22, 1999a).

Michael Porter (1990, pp. 327, 351, 413, 504) in his analysis of *The Competitive Advantage of Nations* notes the dramatically higher number of new firm start-ups in the United States than in Sweden, Germany and the United Kingdom. Interestingly and tellingly, Italy, with its more individualistic, independent and risk-taking culture, also has proportionally more new firm start-ups than its Germanic neighbors. The performance of its economy in recent years has also far surpassed that of these and the other corporatist economies.

Particularly revealing are the different developments in women's employment between the United States and Scandinavia. In both areas the number of women in the labor force has increased dramatically over the last generation. In Scandinavia this increase is particularly conspicuous in politics and in other government positions. All of the increase in employment in Sweden over the last thirty years has come from women entering the labor force and going to work for local governments (Rosen, 1996). Women in Scandinavia have been driven into the labor market partly by high tax rates, partly by bribes of generous subsidies for day care, financed leaves of absence to have children, and the like (*Economist*, June 8, 1996). Moreover, the work they do in government is largely the same as they were doing at home – taking care of children (running day care centers) and the elderly. Thus, government output and measured GNP have increased, but no real additional goods and services have been provided (Rosen, 1996).

In the United States, on the other hand, the biggest increases in female employment have come from women in the top family income brackets entering the labor force. Given the much lower income tax rates in the United States than in Europe, and the reductions in these rates over this period, it does not seem plausible that their entry has been precipitated by financial necessity. Moreover, many of these women have started their own businesses. "Businesses owned by women are among the fastest-growing sectors of the American economy, [and are estimated to employ now] one out of four American workers. Most of the businesses are small, often operated from home and usually in the service or retail sector" (*Economist*, June 8, 1996). An important advantage of working at home is, of course, that it allows women to combine a career with looking after their own children. Many American women, like many American men, prefer to provide for their own livelihood and raise their own children rather than trusting either of these to large bureaucracies or the state.

Attitudes toward competition policy in Europe and the United States

The "second industrial revolution," which first harnessed the power of steam and then that of the internal combustion engine, led, during the nineteenth and early twentieth centuries in both Europe and North America, to the rise of the giant enterprise, the trust, the modern corporation. The reactions to this development in the United States and Europe in terms of competition policies were, however, quite different. With the passage of the Sherman Antitrust Act in 1890, the United States chose to prevent the trusts from forming cartels and monopolies and from abusing that monopoly power which they already had. In Germany, on the other hand, the policy was one of condoning, if not encouraging, the cartelization of industry. This striking difference between the United States and Germany in the legal treatment of cartels had the important consequence of forcing American firms to merge to avoid competition, whereas German firms could accomplish the same goal while remaining separate legal entities (Chandler, 1990, p. 398).

It is interesting to speculate as to why these two future industrial powers chose such different responses to the growth of giant enterprises. A debate among economists ensued on both sides of the Atlantic between those who argued that unbridled competition would be destructive and drive prices below costs, forcing numerous firms into bankruptcy and thereby destroying jobs and aggravating business cycles, and those economists who defended the beliefs of Smith and Ricardo in the salutatory consequences of unfettered competition (Scherer, 1994, pp. 17–21).

It is tempting, and flattering to the economist's ego, to argue that the differences in policies observed between the United States and Germany are simply the outcome of different sides of the debate having carried the day on each side of the Atlantic. But the different outcomes may have been much more the result of differences in the political environments of Germany and the United States. The United States was a burgeoning democracy in the latter third of the nineteenth century with many new parties coming into existence. As already noted the antitrust laws followed the populist movement led by workers and farmers against big business at the end of the nineteenth century, and the argument has been made that the original intent of Congress in passing the Sherman Act was to protect competitors not the competitive process (Libecap, 1992). No such populist political forces were at work in Bismarkian Germany. If the Government was responding to pressure to protect competitors, it must have come from the large corporations, for it is they that the Government chose to protect.

Although laws against monopolies and cartels had existed in Great Britain since the seventeenth century, they went unenforced, and Britain's initial reaction to the emergence of giant enterprises was, like Germany's, to allow them to merge and cooperate (George, 1990, pp. 104–5). One suspects again that this was simply because the interests of big business had greater political influence in Victorian and Edwardian Britain than those of consumers and labor. But it is also true that government officials cited, and perhaps believed, that large companies and cartels could manage competition better than the competitive market's invisible hand (George, 1990, pp. 104–5).

Although government policies toward large firms and cartels were not always as explicitly supportive elsewhere in Europe as they were in the UK and Germany, in no European country was an attempt made to prohibit the formation of cartels or to prevent the growth of giant enterprises. Consequently, when World War II came to an end, the United States found itself in possession of a set of competition policies that had existed and been perfected over a period of more than a half of a century, while Europe found itself lacking a single example of a pro-competitive competition policy.

This situation soon changed. The occupying U.S. forces imposed a pro-competitive competition policy resembling its own antitrust laws on Germany in 1947, and the German Reichstag adopted its own, highly stringent set of competition policies in 1957 (Kantzenbach, 1990; Scherer, 1994, pp. 28–30; Schmidt and Binder, 1994, pp. 16–37). Great Britain's parliament passed the Monopoly and Restrictive Trade Practices Act in 1948, which created a Monopoly and Restrictive Trade Practices Commission to investigate monopolies and cartels (George, 1990, pp. 104–5). France joined the competition policy bandwagon in 1953 (Jenny, 1990, p. 148; Schmidt and Binder, 1994, pp. 53–65).

The speed with which the major European countries adopted competition policies after World War II would seem to imply a recognition of the efficacy of such policies in advancing the economic health of a nation, perhaps because of the obvious emergence of the United States as the world's leading economic power and its longstanding experience with antitrust policies. Such a recognition may have occurred and may have accounted for these legislative actions, but if it did, it was not always well articulated or effectively carried out. Britain's Monopoly and Restrictive Trade Practices Act merely charged the Commission to investigate whether a monopolist's or a cartel's actions were against the public interest, and no mention was made of the benefits from competition in defining the public interest (George, 1990, p. 105). France's 1953 antitrust statute was introduced as an anti-inflation measure in the belief that competition helps to keep prices down (Jenny, 1990, p. 148).

The end of World War II saw the United States enter the most vigorous era of antitrust law enforcement in its entire history (Mueller, 1996). In Europe, on the other hand, most countries continued with no competition policy at all, and those that had newly created policies – with the important exception of West Germany – enforced them hesitantly and inconsistently during the first few decades of their application. Both the United Kingdom and France, for example, went through periods after World War II during which their Governments followed policies of actively encouraging firms to merge in the belief that such mergers were in the social interest but were not being pursued actively enough by corporate managers (George, 1990, pp. 126–32; Jenny, 1990, p. 147). In neither country has the Government ever chosen to block more than a handful of the mergers which were eligible for action under existing statutes (Cosh and Hughes, 1996).

The first competition policy at the European Community level was contained in the Treaty of Rome, signed in 1957 (George and Jacquemin, 1990; Schmidt and Binder, 1994, pp. 66–95). Its Articles 85 and 86 resemble Sections 1 and 2 of the Sherman Antitrust Act in prohibiting both collusive agreements and abusive monopoly practices which harm competition. These and the other Articles dealing with competition policy in the Rome, and subsequent European Union, treaties constitute a set of competition policies at the European level that can be said to be equivalent in intent and application to those existing in the United States. Exceptions to this statement might be made with respect to the greater use of *per se* rules against certain practices in the United States than in the European Union, and with respect to merger policy. Although Article 86 could be, and occasionally was, used against mergers, an explicit policy against mergers cannot be said to have existed at the European level until 1989 when, after 17 years of wrangling, the members of the Council agreed to a regulation on mergers. This regulation, however, limits Commission action to mergers in which the combined sales of the merging firms sum to at least 5 billion ECU across the world and at least 250 million ECU within Europe (George and Jacquemin, 1990, p. 238; Schmidt and Binder, 1994, pp. 83–9). These size limits are so high that most mergers involving European firms fall under them, and only about one merger per year was blocked by the European Commission in the first ten years after the regulation went into effect. Mergers that fall through the regulation's screen are scrutinized by the competition policy authorities of the individual member countries. Since only Germany among the Union's members has had a consistent and vigorous antimerger policy, at present antimerger policy in Europe must be judged to be far less stringent and effective than the other dimensions of the Union's competition policy.

Conclusions

The European Union was born in Paris in 1951 and was named the European Coal and Steel Community (Hitiris, 1994, Ch. 2). This might strike most people as an odd name for an association of nations bent on achieving free trade. Indeed, anyone familiar with the history of the Community must smile at the irony of this choice of names, because these two industries have been at the forefront of those selected for exemption from the Community's competition policies, those allowed to behave as cartels. The original intent for the Community was to restore these industries to health after the War, and with them the rest of Europe. Moreover, by tying France and Germany together in this economic undertaking it was the hope of Jean Monnet (1978), "the Community's father," that these two perennial enemies would be induced to live peacefully together. Thus the avoidance of war rather than the achievement of economic prosperity was probably the most important reason for the Community's founding. Economic prosperity was seen as the means to the more important goal of peace in Europe, and even this means was to be achieved not through the mysterious magic of free competition in a full customs union but through the managed rehabilitation of the core industries of the Community's first members. The initial success of the Community at achieving economic prosperity led to further expansions of both the economic integration of its members and their number. To obtain and preserve the benefits from competition across borders, competition needed to be preserved within the borders of both the European Community and its individual members. The Community had to and did develop an effective competition policy.

Given the general acceptance in Europe of the desirability of competition policies, their widespread introduction and growth in effectiveness since World War II, and the resemblance in language and enforcement of competition policy at the European Union level to that in the United States, it would appear that both attitudes and policies toward competition in Europe and the United States have converged. F.M. Scherer (1994, 1996) has claimed that such a convergence has occurred and by and large I agree with him. Indeed, while Europe was pressing forward, strengthening the language and enforcement of its competition policies during the 1970s and 1980s, the United States antitrust authorities went into a full-scale retreat, abandoning ongoing cases against the leading cereals manufacturers and IBM, abandoning previously held positions regarding the *per se* illegality of certain vertical restraints, and significantly relaxing the criteria used to determine which mergers to challenge (Mueller, 1996). The first Secretary of Commerce under Ronald Reagan, echoing arguments often heard in Europe, even went so far as to recommend repeal of the Clayton Act's antimerger provisions so that U.S. firms could grow bigger, and thereby more efficient, so as better to meet the Japanese and European challenges. Although the antitrust pendulum swung back a little under the Clinton Administration, predicting whether Europe or the United States will have the more vigorous competition policy over the next twenty years is not as easy today as it would have seemed in, say, 1970.

While competition policy in Europe has pulled even with that in the United States, in other areas one still detects a greater resilience against competition in Europe, a greater proclivity to trust the state rather than the market to allocate resources. The development of an effective competition policy in Europe must be placed alongside a lingering affection for industrial policies (Hitiris, 1994, Ch. 12). Is output falling in the steel industry? Then restructuring is needed. How is this restructuring to come about? Why, through output quotas and cartel exemptions of course. Does Europe trail the United States in the production and sale of large commercial aircraft? Why, then massive government subsidies and joint ventures are needed to create a viable commercial airplane producer.

The opening chapter of every public finance or public choice book states that governments exist to provide public goods and to correct market failures. The classic example of a public good is defense. Defense is the biggest expenditure item in the U.S. federal budget. Subsidies for agriculture are today, as they have always been, the biggest item in the European Union's budget. The United States treats its farmers well also, of course, and Europeans pay for defense at the national level. But it is interesting and ironic, given that Monnet's goal in forming the Community was to prevent future wars, that Europeans have not been able to agree on policies and expenditures on defense and yet have been able to agree on policies that interfere with those markets which come closest to fulfilling the conditions necessary for perfect competition. Symbolically, ministers in Brussels have been able to find more common ground in a policy that redistributes Community incomes and lowers overall Community wealth than in one that would be designed to protect this wealth.

Despite the similarities in competition policies in Europe and the United States and the benefits both areas reap from their free trade policies, Europeans seem to retain a distrust of market forces, a greater tendency to protect that which exists rather than take risks to create that which does not. The economic policies of the Reagan Administration and Thatcher Government are dubbed "neo-liberalism" in Continental European countries, and are heavily criticized and opposed by most labor union and socialist party leaders (for example, Greif, Leitgeb and Wintersberger, 1999).

Earlier I asserted that the main advantage of knowing a language is to communicate with other people. More accurately, I might have said "to communicate with other *living* people." A second advantage of knowing a language is that one can also communicate with all of those dead people whose works are published in that language. The works of these dead people form an important component of what we call a nation's culture. Efforts to protect a language are usually coached in terms of protecting a culture, a culture that is to a significant degree locked in the works of its past writers.

Reading is a learned skill, a desire to read certain works is an acquired taste. Teaching children to read and exposing them to works that help to develop their tastes are proper functions of a nation's schools. But all children grow up and eventually leave school. As educated adults they are, or in a liberal society should be, free to choose what they read or whether they read at all. To force Jörg Schmidt of Frankfurt to read Schiller in German rather than Hume in English once he has left school is to treat him as a child. It is a policy which attacks the very foundation of a liberal society, just as barring him from traveling to England would. Policies which treat citizens as children by controlling their access to books, music, theater, films or any other dimensions of culture are antithetical to the principles of a liberal society.

Such policies in one form or another have existed and are being pressed anew in various parts of Europe. More generally, many European governments seem much more concerned with preserving the past than preparing their citizens for the future. The old general hospital in Vienna takes up several square blocks near the center of the city. The hospital has moved to modern quarters, the building left behind is an ugly monstrosity taking up prime property. A perfect opportunity to bring new economic activity and new architecture to the heart of a thriving city. But the opportunity was not seized. The building is preserved as a monument to seventeenth-century hospital construction and as a reminder of the depths to which architecture in Austria once sunk.

During the seventeenth century baroque architecture swept over Austria and other parts of Europe. Buildings in earlier styles were torn down to make room for buildings in the new style and existing buildings were done over in the new style. The new architecture was thought to be beautiful, and everything had to be new and beautiful. It is almost impossible to imagine such a development occurring again in Europe. Each city center, except for a few that were totally destroyed during World War II,[7] carefully preserves the architectures of the past. So set on the past are the custodians of European culture that no new architectural style, however beautiful or functional, has a chance against them. In stark contrast, the Cantonese are not restoring the old buildings in the center of Shanghai but instead are tearing them down to make room for modern structures. As a tourist I lament such a decision, and I might also lament it if I earned a high salary as a government worker in Shanghai. But if I were a young person living in Shanghai, whose economic future was dependent on Shanghai's ability to compete in the world economy of the twenty-first century, I would probably be cheered by the optimism and self-confidence such changes symbolize.

The growth industry of the last decade has been software. The biggest company in this industry is an American firm, Microsoft. The richest man in the world, Bill Gates, is its president. Seventy-five percent of the software industry is located in the United States. The international language of software is English. The second leading nation in the software industry is Japan. Then come the Europeans.[8]

One industry does not an economy make. But the software industry is not the only new industry that seems to thrive better outside of Europe. Joseph Schumpeter once described competition as "a process of creative destruction," and so it is. Monopolies get destroyed, profits get destroyed, jobs get destroyed, possibly even communities get destroyed. In a competitive world the inefficient gives way to the efficient, the obsolete gives way to the up to date. But all that is new is not better, and all that is old does not die. Chateau Latour was a world leader in wines a hundred and fifty years ago, and it remains so today. Coca-Cola was a world leader in soft drinks seventy-five years ago, and it remains so today. Microsoft may not survive the budding revolution in software caused by the Internet.

Much of what Europe has and makes is competitive on world markets. To keep competitive on world markets Europe must continue to do that which it does well and abandon that which it cannot do. The globalization of markets has shrunk the advantages first movers have and increased the gains from flexibility and adaptation. In this rapidly changing competitive environment Europe, with its aversion to competition, its premium on security, its reliance on state intervention, and its fondness for the past, seems less adapted to succeed than the United States with its more liberal, more individualistic, more future-oriented society. But here too convergence can be seen. The Vietnam War, Watergate, the economic collapse of the 1970s, the crime of the 1980s and 1990s, and September 11th, 2001 seem to have combined to undermine Americans' inherent optimism. Today many Americans, like many Europeans, are fearful of international competition and the influx of immigrants – historically an important source of entrepreneurial talent in America. Perhaps both Europe and its New World offspring will find it difficult to compete in the global economy of the twenty-first century and will choose instead to preserve and protect that which made them the economic and cultural leaders in the past.

Notes

1. Milton Friedman (1962) has described himself as a liberal, and by my definition he is, in the economic sphere. He also fits my definition of a political conservative.
2. Of course, carrying a European brand name does not necessarily imply that a product is manufactured in Europe, but even for products manufactured in LDCs one cannot account for such price differentials by transportation costs and tariffs.
3. Information on salaries at the University of Maryland was freely available to the public because of its status as a state university. The student newspaper periodically published a full list of the faculty with their salaries as a public service.
4. See Frey and Pommerehne (1988) and Frey and Eichenberg (1993). Great Britain has taken a step toward more competition in the academic market by tying departmental budgets to research productivity and freeing up salary structures, thereby giving departments an incentive to hire or retain at higher salaries research-productive scholars.
5. A proposal led by France to require that certain fractions of each station's programs be of European origin was defeated in the European Union's Council (*Economist*, June 15, 1996, p. 76).
6. For evidence and references to the literature in support of this point as far as Germany is concerned, see Giersch, et al. (1992), pp. 198–207, 214–21.
7. An important exception is occurring in Berlin where parts bombed out during World War II are now being rebuilt in new architectural styles.
8. See the special report, "The Software Industry," *Economist*, May 25, 1996.

Bibliography

Chandler, Alfred D. Jr., *Scale and Scope*, Cambridge, MA: Belknap Press, 1990.

Cohen, Roger, "Workers Jam Berlin to Assail Schroeder," *International Herald Tribune*, Oct. 20, 1999, pp. 1, 10.

Comanor, William S., et al., *Competition Policy in Europe and North America*, Chur, Switzerland: Harwood Academic Publishers, 1990.

Cosh, Andy and Alan Hughes, "International Merger Activity and the National Regulation of Mergers: A UK Perspective," *Empirica*, **23**(3), 1996, pp. 279–302.

Economist, July 15, 1995, p. 14; April 6, 1996, pp. 81–2; June 8, 1996, pp. 55–6; June 15, 1996, p. 27; May 22, 1999a, p. 97; May 22, 1999b, p. 97.

Frey, Bruno S. and Reiner Eichenberg, "American and European Economics and Economists," *Journal of Economic Perspectives*, **7**(4), Fall 1993, pp. 185–93.

Frey, Bruno S. and Werner W. Pommerehne, "The American Domination among Eminent Economists," *Scientometrics*, **14**(1–2), 1988, pp. 97–110.

Friedman, Milton, *Capitalism and Freedom*, Chicago: University of Chicago Press, 1962.

George, Ken, "UK Competition Policy: Issues and Answers," in Comanor (1990), pp. 104–45.

George, Ken and Alexis Jacquemin, "Competition Policy in the European Community," in Comanor (1990), pp. 206–45.

Giersch, Herbert, Karl-Heinz Pragué, and Holger Schmieding, *The Fading Miracle*, rev. edn, Cambridge: Cambridge University Press, 1992.

Greif, Wolfgang, Gerlinde Leitgeb, and Gerald Wintersberger (eds), *Alternativen zum Neoliberalismus*, Vienna: Verlag des ÖGB, 1999.

Hitiris, Theo, *European Community Economics*, 3rd edn, London: Harvester Wheatsheaf, 1994.

Jenny, F., "French Competition Policy in Perspective," in Comanor (1990), pp. 146–88.

Katz, Michael and Carl Shapiro, "Network Externalities, Competition and Compatibility," *American Economic Review*, **75**, 1985, pp. 424–40.

Katz, Michael and Carl Shapiro, "Technology Adoption in the Presence of Network Externalities," *Journal of Political Economy*, **94**, 1986, pp. 822–41.

Kantzenbach, Erhard, "Competition Policy in West Germany," in Comanor (1990), pp. 189–205.

Libecap, Gary D., "The Rise of the Chicago Packers and the Origins of Meat Inspection and Antitrust," *Economic Inquiry*, **30**, April 1992, pp. 242–62.

Monnet, Jean, *Memoirs*, trans. R. Mayne, New York: Doubleday, 1978.

Mueller, Dennis C., "Lessons from the United States's Antitrust History," *International Journal of Industrial Organization*, **14**(4), June 1996, pp. 415–45.

Porter, Michael E., *The Competitive Advantage of Nations*, New York: Free Press, 1990.

Rosen, Sherwin, "Public Employment and the Welfare State in Sweden", *Journal of Economic Literature*, **34**, June 1996, pp. 729–40.

Scherer, F.M., *Competition Policies for an Integrated World*, Washington, DC: Brookings Institution, 1994.

Scherer, F.M., "Competition Policy Convergence: Where Next?," paper presented at the conference, Global Issues in Competition Policy, Vienna, June 1996.

Schmidt, Ingo and Steffen Binder, *Wettbewerbspolitik im Internationalen Vergleich*, mimeo, Stuttgart: Universität Hohenheim, 1994.

[4]

Capitalism and Democracy in Northeast Asia: Present and Prospects

Dennis C. Mueller*

This paper seeks to assess the current state of economic and political development in Northeast Asia, its prospects for the future, and to offer some recommendations, particularly as they pertain to possible political development and institution building. We begin with the most positive side of the story, the current economic situation in Northeast Asian countries.

1. Capitalism in Northeast Asia

Everyone is familiar with the spectacular economic success of the Asian tigers. Depending on where the exchange rate stands on a given day, the Japanese are now the world's richest people, or very close to it. Growth rates in South Korea, Taiwan, Hong Kong, Malaysia and Singapore over the last generation have been nothing short of spectacular, when compared to those of North America and Western Europe.

There is both agreement and disagreement over the causes of this success. Most economists would agree that the following four factors help to explain the success of these Asian countries: (1) their ability to play the "catch-up" strategy of adopting the technologies of the technological leaders in North America and Europe, (2) their

*Professor of Economics, University of Vienna.

公共經濟評論 (*Public Economics Review*), 1:2 (1996), 1–32。
國立政治大學財政學系出版

high savings rates, (3) their higher numbers of hours worked by members of the labor force, and (4) their heavy investments in education. Less consensus exists over the extent to which the success of the Asian countries is attributable to industrial organizational factors like team production, interlocking corporate ownership, the J-form organization, and the like; and over the extent to which it is due to enlightened governmental industrial policies.

One can only play catch-up so long as one is behind. Japan has clearly caught up, and in many areas has taken over the lead. At the rate that they are going this will soon be true of the other Asian tigers. Japan's economy has stumbled of late. Although one expects its economy to recover in due time, the fact that it is now one of the world's leading economies, with high wages and a very strong currency implies that some of the economic factors that have favored Japan in the past will not do so in the future.

As the Japanese settle into their prosperity one wonders how long it will be before Japanese parents begin to ease up on their children, and no longer enroll them in special schools and pressure them to study so that they get into the best universities? How long will it be before Japanese children resist these pressures and, like their western peers, opt for guitar and ski lessons, opt to "drop out for a few years to find themselves?" How long will it be before Japanese workers use their prosperity to increase their consumption of leisure, and their weekly hours and vacation periods begin to match those of Europeans?

In addition to leisure, one of the luxury goods that people tend to consume is charity. Over the course of the 20th century, wealthy capitalist countries have all adopted various forms of collective charity that fall under the heading of "the welfare state." For a generation after World War II, the pent-up demand for goods generated by the Great Depression and that war, residual habits of working hard, and peer group pressures against shirking and cheating, served to maintain high levels of work and honesty, in spite of the incentives inherent in many welfare state programs to behave otherwise. The poorer of the capitalist countries were able to play catch-up against the rich, and Western capitalism enjoyed its "Golden Age" of prosperity.

In the last generation, however, people in Europe and North America have responded to the incentive effects of welfare programs in the predictable way. The costs of the welfare state have skyrocketed both in terms of direct outlays, but also in reduced effort and productivity. Although Sweden's economic collapse is the most spectacular example of the effects on economic performance of the welfare state, virtually all European economies are being dragged down by its adverse effects. Newt Gingrich and company's rise in the United States has been due in no small part to their promise to reign in the costs of welfare programs.

Among the highly developed capitalist countries Japan has, along with Switzerland and the United States, one of the smallest government sectors. Switzerland and the United States are conservative, federalist countries in which citizens have considerable power to restrain government. Japan has a centralized government. Will its citizens step forward to constrain the Japanese government from expanding should it choose to do so? Will Japan and the other Asian tigers not follow in the Western world's footsteps in choosing leisure and socialized security over hard work and economic growth?

Many of the largest corporations in the United States and Western Europe are 50, 75 or more than 100 years old. The markets that they are in are mature. The growth rates of these companies, if they confine themselves to their original markets, are limited to the often slow growth of these markets. Many Western managers are not satisfied merely to remain atop the slow growing markets in which they have long held dominant positions. When the stock market is high and/or their cash flows are high, they seize the opportunity to accelerate their growth through the acquisition of other firms.

A wealth of studies now exists that demonstrates that mergers have on average probably reduced the profitability of the merging companies, reduced or left unchanged the growth rates of the merging companies, reduced the market shares of the acquired companies, and reduced the wealth of the shareholders of the acquiring companies.[1] Alongside this mountain of studies at the micro level, we have the facts that the Great Depression of the 1930s and the Great Recession of the 1970s followed the major merger waves of the 1920s and 1960s. Was the poor performance of the United States and the United Kingdom during the 1930s and 1970s in part attributable to the many mergers that preceded them? It is probably impossible to tell. But we do know from the micro level studies that these mergers reduced the internal efficiency of the merging firms on average, and we know that in the United States, the merger wave of the 1960s was followed by a sell-off wave in the 1970s, as managers tried to undo their previous mistakes.

Observers from both sides of the Pacific have characterized Japanese and South Korean managers, like their counterparts in North America and Western Europe, as empire-builders more interested in expanding the size of their companies than in maximizing its profits (Odagiri, 1981, 1982; Porter, 1990). An important difference has existed between empire-building Asian managers, however, and their Western peers. Where many Western managers have chosen the quick route to growth of mergers and acquisitions, Asian managers have by-and-large restricted themselves to internal growth strategies. Research and development outlays, and new plant and equipment have been their preferred avenues of growth.

[1]For surveys see Mueller (1977, 1987, 1996a); Jensen and Ruback (1983); Caves (1989).

Thus, we find Japanese companies undertaking one merger for every ten undertaken by comparably sized U.S. and U.K. companies (Odagiri and Yamawaki, 1990, p.170).

If Japanese and South Korean managers pursue growth over profits by investing in R&D and capital investment projects promising rates of return below the firm's cost of capital, their shareholders' wealth is reduced just as surely as when a U.S. company makes a bad merger. But the Japanese economy is arguably better off if its managers choose an internal growth strategy over an external growth strategy. The former creates assets and jobs and contributes to the real growth of the economy. An external growth strategy of mergers and acquisitions expands size while leaving the size of the economy unchanged. Indeed, if mergers do reduce the internal efficiency of merging companies, growth through merger increases corporate size while at the same time *reducing the size of the economy.*

In recent years Bridgestone, Sony and other large Japanese companies have made large acquisitions, albeit outside of the borders of Japan. Evidence so far suggests that Japanese managers are no better at the merger and acquisition game than American and European managers. If the slowing of Japan's growth and the maturing of their main markets lead Japanese companies to pursue a strategy of external rather than internal growth in the future, we have another possible reason for concern about the future health of the Japanese economy.

For all these reasons, one suspects that the economic performance of Japan, and eventually of the other Asian tigers may not be as good over the next generation as it was during the past one. But this does not mean that the economic future of these countries looks bad. Indeed, when one compares it to that of Europe, America, Africa and the former Soviet Union, one quickly concludes that the first part of the 21st century will belong to the Asian countries. When one includes China in the picture, the mind boggles. What Western European or North American politician would not trade his country's likely growth rate over the next generation for the weighted average growth rate of China and its Northeast Asian neighbors?

Thus, although there are reasons for some concern, the economic future of the Northeast Asian countries looks positive, *assuming of course that the governments of these countries do not do anything to upset the picture.* The most uncertain element in the economic futures of Northeast Asian countries is undoubtedly the potentially adverse effects of political developments.

2. Capitalism and Democracy

Milton Friedman argues in *Capitalism and Freedom* (1962) that these two concepts are logically joined. The institutions of capitalism both require freedom and breed it. For capitalism to yield its potential benefits, markets must be free. Entry and exit must be unrestricted, buyers and sellers must be free to choose their trading partners. When governments try to control the spread of capitalism by regulating or closing markets, these markets merely sprout up again dressed in black in the underground economy.

As capitalism takes root it opens up markets, it opens up foreign trade, it opens up eyes. A highly developed capitalist economy must have a highly educated labor force from the board room down to the shop floor. But one cannot educate people in science and mathematics without opening up the world of literature and history, of economics and political science. Once the educated citizen enters these worlds, she is exposed to all of the ideas and great debates that have gone before her. Each citizen can weigh the pros and cons of capitalism and socialism, the benefits of democracy and its alternatives. Each citizen can decide for herself, if only in her own mind, what kind of economic and political system she would like to live under. Each citizen can ask herself, if I am free to choose which television set to buy, why can I not choose which program to watch on it? If I am free to choose the brand of car to drive, why can I not choose the quantity and quality of roads to be constructed? Why can I not at least choose the people who make these choices?

In a healthy capitalist economy, businessmen travel abroad to close deals, scientists travel abroad to exchange ideas, citizens travel abroad to obtain the full benefits of the higher incomes that capitalism has brought them. Once abroad they can observe first hand how people in other countries live. If they see aspects of life abroad that they think are better than exist at home, they naturally wish these features of life abroad to be established at home.

Communism collapsed in East Europe not because it was an economic failure in an absolute sense, the average East European enjoyed a higher standard of living than probably a majority of people in the world at that time. Communism collapsed because it was a *relative* failure. During the 1980s it became increasingly obvious to East Europeans that they were living worse than their western neighbors. The East German could watch West German television and observe a life style far different and seemingly better than his own. Many Pols, Czechs and Hungarians traveled to Western Europe and found there goods that they could not buy at home, and that they could not afford to buy in the West. Pressure for change mounted. This pressure could be relieved temporarily by allowing the most disgruntled East Europeans to leave. But these people were typically the most mobile, the young, the well educated, the highly skilled. Their departure only worsened the economic situation in the lands that they left. East Europe found itself caught in a downward spiral that ended in communism and totalitarianism's collapse.

One can imagine a capitalist dictatorship in which an omniscient dictator and an efficient state bureaucracy optimally supply those public goods and services that the citizens demand, so that capitalism survives happily without democracy. But one cannot imagine such a situation lasting for long. As John Hicks observed long ago, one of the benefits of monopoly is the luxury of a quiet life. The words "efficient" and "state bureaucracy" do not fit comfortably together. One expects even the brightest and noblest dictator, and the best organized state bureaucracy to make mistakes. Since these mistakes go unpunished under a dictatorship, there is little incentive not to make them. As they accumulate, dissatisfaction with the government grows.

Even when a dictator makes the "right" decision, he may create enemies. A road must be built either here or there. If it is built here, those who preferred the other location are unhappy. Under a dictatorship, there is an obvious person to blame. Under a well-functioning democracy, there is no *one person or agency* to blame. The citizen must blame the fact that her side was in the minority, and can console herself with the thought that on the next decision, she may be in the majority. In this way democracy can legitimize governmental decisions even in the eyes of those who lose by them. This legitimacy in turn can help perpetuate democracy's existence.

Thus, one does not expect to find a country in the highest echelons of the wealthy nations, which is both capitalistic and a dictatorship. Citizens of a wealthy nation will wish to import those goods, which they want, but do not have access to at home. One of those goods is likely to be democracy.

3. Democracy in Northeastasia

One surmises that the first Neanderthals made some decisions by a show of hands, and therefore that "democracy" in one form or another is probably as old as human society itself. The organization of civilized society by formal democratic procedures did not occur until about the sixth century B.C. in Ancient Greece, however. Indeed, the word *democracy* is of Greek origin, as are many others in our political lexicon, attesting to the innovative character of the Greeks first experiment with democratic institutions.

The Romans put this experiment to rest, and democracy remained in dormancy for more than a millennium until the Italians rediscovered and revived it during the Renaissance. Although the second set of experiments in the Italian city states also did not take hold, they were to be followed by still other experiments in Europe, and then again in North America by immigrants from Europe. Today, with ideological history at an end, one can count more countries with democratic political institutions than at any other time in history. Among those that are not genuinely democratic, several appear on their way to becoming so. Still more have majorities of their population, or substantial minorities who think that their countries *should* become democratic.

The remarkable fact that stands out when one looks at the list of past and current democracies is that from Ancient Athens down to the present *nearly all have been directly or indirectly of European origin.* Outside of Europe itself, the democracies of the Americas exist in countries settled by Europeans, as is true of Australia and New Zealand in the Far East. Post-World War II Japan's democracy was launched with a heavy helping hand from the United States, as was true of the Philippines. India's and Pakistan's commitments to democracy probably also are due in no small part to the influence of Great Britain's long occupation. South Korea and Taiwan may arguably become the first major Asian countries to establish full-fledged democracies independently of Euro-American occupation.

When one looks upon the history of democracy, one observes that it has not always taken firm root, even when planted on what would appear to have been fertile soil. Numerous European countries have gone from democratic regimes to fascist or communist dictatorships. Virtually all Latin American countries have gone from democracy to dictatorship and back again, some with almost routine rapidity.[2] Nor has democracy always produced impressive results. In the late 1920s Argentina's income per capita was comparable to that of many European countries. With its educated and cosmopolitan population and wealth of natural resources, it seemed destined to become one of the richest countries in the world. But its democratic government made a series of major mistakes in economic policy that brought an end to both democracy and the prospect of prosperity in Argentina (Snow and Wynia, 1990). Although they never attained the level of income relative to the rest of the world that Argentina did, Brazil, Chile and Venezuela have also not employed their natural advantages well, and thus have failed to realize their economic potentials. In each case periods of mismanagement by democratic regimes have contributed to these lost opportunities.[3] The most one can say for the majority of Latin American democratic regimes is that they did not perform worse than the dictatorships that displaced them.[4]

Thus, one cannot assume that a shift to democracy will be a permanent shift, or that such a shift will inevitably produce better

[2]The major exception is tiny Costa Rica which has been a democratic state for over a century and a half, outside of a couple of years in the late 1940s, when it had a dictatorship and a civil war.

[3]See, Ames (1987), Kline (1990), Lamounier (1990), Levy (1990), McDonald (1990), Roett and Sacks (1990), Sigmund (1990), Valenzuela (1990) and Frieden (1991).

[4]The most prominent recent exception to this generalization is the Pinochet government in Chile. It combined economic liberalism and sound fiscal policies with oppressive dictatorial rule and severely constrained political freedom. The consequence was that when democracy returned to Chile it had the luxury of starting off with a healthy and relatively prosperous economy.

results. A look at Asia's few experiments with democracy since World War II is not particularly reassuring. Throughout almost all of its democratic history, Japan has been governed by the same political party, a record for political uncompetitiveness in this century that only Sweden has matched. Among the wealthier OECD countries, Japan is without question the leader in political corruption. Only Italy's record comes close to Japan's in the scale of corruption and levels at which it takes place. Again like Italy, Japan's governments at times have mismanaged their affairs dramatically, as for example by running large governmental deficits, and grossly underfunding its public pension schemes (*Economist*, Sept. 9, 1995, p.88). Traffic congestion and pollution levels in the major cities also suggest a failure by the government to provide those public goods that are the government's raison d'être. Once again like Italy, the weakness of Japan' governmental performance stands in stark contrast to its impressive economic record.[5]

The United States' other democratic protégé, the Philippines, has had more than its fair share of political corruption and mismanagement also.[6] Unlike in the case of Japan, however, Filipinos have not been able to enjoy the fruits of rapid economic growth in compensation for the failings of their governments. Those Asian democracies that have a British heritage have done much worse economically than Japan and the Asian tigers, and this poor economic performance is directly attributable to governmental regulation, trade and redistribution policies. In India corruption pervades in every level of government to such a degree that it has become institutionalized. Each business owner or manager knows the "price"

[5]The parallels between Italy and Japan are striking. Both joined the industrial revolution three generations after other leading economic nations (Adelman, 1995, p.193). Both are long and narrow countries surrounded by water, both are mountainous with numerous volcanoes,· · ·.

[6]Political corruption is not completely unknown to South Korea either, one must add.

in terms of bribes and kickbacks that must be paid to get a building permit, import licence, etc.[7] Unlike Japan, India seems to suffer from almost too much political competition, with political opposition and disagreement often being expressed by acts of terrorism and violence.

None of the above should be taken to mean that democracy in Asia "has not worked," or cannot be made to work. India has introduced reforms to curb corruption and reduce regulation. Japan's era of one party government appears to have come to an end, and reforms have been introduced to eliminate corruption. Asia's limited experience does indicate, however, that democratic institutions are not like software, which one buys and installs and then it performs the same for all users. Thought must be given to the structure of political institutions that are installed.

4. Choosing the "Right" Political Institutions

The political institutions of a country are defined in its constitution. Most constitutions are written documents where one can look up what the political procedure is for doing such and such, or what the citizen's right to do such and such is. How a country's government functions is determined by the rules, procedures and rights contained in the constitution. Of course, how a country's government functions in practice depends on how various provisions of the constitution are interpreted, how closely government bodies and agents adhere to the rules and procedures in the constitution, and so on. But, certainly, the constitution is a good place to start to gain an understanding of how a country's government functions, and if one wants to have good government one should try to write a good constitution.

[7]See Mueller (1996, pp.32–3), and references therein.

Most new constitutions get written following a revolution, civil war, defeat in a war, or similar major political or social upheaval. At these momentous occasions, passions may continue to be spurred by the previous events, and other concerns, like rebuilding a war-torn economy, may seem more pressing. The result is that first constitutions are often hastily drafted. Not surprisingly, therefore, they later are often found to be lacking.

No better illustration of this point exists than recent experiences with constitution drafting in East Europe. The collapse of communism was so quick, so unexpected and so complete that no country was prepared for it. The fact that communism fell following a "velvet revolution" in most countries meant that an obvious group of new leaders, who would run the government and, perhaps, help define its institutions, did not exist. Where a natural leader did exist, as Poland's Lech Walesa, he did play a key role both within the government and in writing the constitution. The consequence was that Poland got a constitution with considerable executive authority, with, of course, Walesa being that executive. This is one of the most important lessons to be learned about constitution writing. Those who write constitutions write them, in part at least, to advance their own interests.[8]

Because their economies also collapsed as communism fell, leaders of the new capitalist countries had to devote considerable energy to rebuilding their economies and keeping them afloat while they did so. Little time or incentive existed to reflect on the long run consequences of this rule or of that one. Constitutions were hastily put together that were consciously adapted from Western European constitutions, often by borrowing pieces from different existing constitutions. Where agreement on a new constitution could not be

[8]See discussion and examples in Mueller (1996, ch. 21).

reached, or other matters were particularly pressing, the constitution that previously existed under communism was patched up and used in the post-communism period.

The consequence of all this is that in many of the post-communist countries little attention has been given to the question of whether a particular constitution is the best one for the country adopting it. In all countries the citizenry has essentially played no role at all in defining what goes into the constitution.

There are two possible dangers to this general neglect of the constitution drafting process: (1) A country adopts a constitution that is highly ill-suited to its needs, and thus does not advance the interests of its citizens as it could. (2) Its citizens, having had little input into the constitution's drafting and ratification, do not identify with it. They do not think of it as being *their* constitution. Should someone come into power during an economic or political crisis and choose to set the constitution aside, the citizens may not offer much resistance owing to this lack of commitment. A democracy, which is potentially viable and desirable in the long run, may expire because not enough citizens step forward to protect it during a temporary crisis.

The countries of Northeast Asia are in the unusual and enviable position of being able to draft new constitutions without undue time constraints, or the threat of economic or political collapse if they delay. Their prosperous economies and stable political environments allow them the luxury of widespread political participation and debate in the process of choosing a constitution.

As previously noted, the most important lesson to be learned from observing how previous constitutions have been written is that those writing the constitutions tend to include provisions that are expected to advance their long run interests (Mueller, 1996, ch. 21). This observation argues against having members of the existing government take a hand in writing the constitution that will define the rules for all future, democratic governments. While it may seem obvious to a strong leader that the country should have a strong executive, it may be better for the citizens in the long run if the chief executive has very little power. Such a constitution is much more likely to be drafted, if the current chief executive is not involved in its design.

Citizen involvement in the constitution writing and adoption process can take several forms. One possibility is for the citizens to elect directly delegates to a convention whose sole purpose is to draft a new constitution. Under this selection procedure, delegates to the convention should not be concerned with how their political careers or political power will be affected by its outcome, as will be the case when an existing parliament forms the convention, or its delegates are selected by the chief executive. In choosing delegates to the convention, the citizens in turn will wish to select individuals noted for their statesmanship and impartiality, individuals who might be able to place the interests of the country and future generations of citizens above their own personal stakes in the outcome. Retired politicians, jurists, and other community leaders, noted scholars and academicians are the kinds of people citizens might expect would be able to place the community's interests above their own. The only country, of which I am aware, that has followed this procedure is Costa Rica, twice, when it wrote its first constitution in 1812, and again when it wrote its second constitution in 1948 (Ameringer, 1982, p.37; Seligson, 1990, p.460). The fact that Costa Rica has had such a long and stable democratic history speaks well for this method of writing a constitution.

The United States has also had a long and reasonably stable history as a democracy. Its constitution was also drafted at a convention assembled solely for that task.[9] Its delegates were not

[9] In fact they were assembled to amend the existing constitution, the Articles of Confederation. Once assembled they decided to scrap the Articles and draft an entirely new constitution.

selected directly by the citizens, however, but were appointed by state legislators, or in one case by the state's chief executive. The delegates thus perceived of themselves as representing not the interests of all American citizens, but only those from their own state, as well, of course, perhaps their own personal interests. The result was that in some places the United States Constitution clearly is not the one which would best have advanced the interests of all (potential) citizens — most notably in its creation of a gerrymandered upper house of the legislature, and in its preservation of slavery.

A second, and more frequently employed, way in which citizens participate in the constitution adoption process is by ratifying the final product, arrived at by whatever means, in a referendum. Such referenda can play four important roles in the constitution adoption process: (1) Most obviously they allow the citizens to reject a constitution that they consider not to be in their best interests. Such rejections have been numerous. For example, Irish citizens on two occasions rejected attempts by the largest political party, Fiana Fail, to change the electoral rules to those which tend to over- representation of the largest party. They did so in spite of the fact that it would be the party favored by the largest number of citizens at the time that would have benefited most from the change.[10] When General Pinochet asked Chilean citizens to alter the constitution to make him dictator for life, they refused thereby forcing him out of office.

(2) Knowledge that the constitution must be approved by the citizens should force whomever it is who drafts the constitutions to leave out those proposals that seem too self-serving. The examples at the end of the previous paragraph suggest, however, that one should not underestimate the confidence of incumbent politicians in their own popularity, and thus their audacity in placing self-serving constitutional provisions before the people.

[10]See, Manning (1978).

(3) The necessity of the citizens ratifying the constitution requires that a public debate in the press and other media of the constitution's features must take place prior to the vote on it. Such a debate can either serve to expose a constitution's failings, and thus lead to its defeat and redrafting, or to highlight its advantages and lead to its ratification. In the latter case the knowledge of the constitution's positive features gained through public debate can serve to strengthen the citizens' commitment to it.

Both outcomes occurred as a result of the debate between the Federalists and the Antifederalists between the Constitutional Convention in Philadelphia, and the subsequent ratification of it by the individual states. On the one hand, the demand for an explicit statement of rights in the constitution pressed home by the Antifederalists led to the Bill of Rights being added in the ratification process. In addition, however, the defense of the constitution made by the Federalists, preserved for future generations in the *Federalist Papers*, became part of Americans' cultural heritage, which helps explain Americans' unusual respect for their Constitution.

(4) This commitment may be further strengthened simply by the fact that the citizens had to choose consciously whether or not to accept it. By voting to ratify the constitution, the citizens in a meaningful sense make it *theirs*.

5. Defining the "Right" Constitution

Having decided how to write the constitution, the next question is what to put into it. This is far too big of a question to be taken up adequately in this paper.[11] I shall, therefore, restrict myself to addressing a few key questions regarding the content of the constitution.

[11] See however, the treatment in my book (Mueller, 1996).

One fundamental issue is whether to establish a unitary governmental structure or a federalism. If the purpose of government is to provide pure public goods and correct other sorts of market failures, then the answer to this question will largely depend on the size of the country and the nature of the market failures it faces. Most public goods and externalities have a definite geographic component to them. The pollution in a river affects only those who use the river, and these people are likely to live near the river. In a fairly small country, nearly everyone may be affected by the pollution of a given river, nearly everyone may live in the capital city or visit it enough to make the elimination of crime in the capital city, a national public good. In a small country a single level of government may suffice.

In a large country, many citizens live a long way from the capital city. Its crime has no direct impact on large numbers of citizens, as is perhaps also true of the pollution in a given river. Information gathering costs may be reduced by dividing the country into different governmental units and assigning particular governmental functions to each unit. Police protection is provided by city and town governments, river pollution is corrected by a regional government, and defense against foreign invasion by the national government.

All citizens at any level of government must consume the same set of public services. Citizen benefits from government will be enhanced, therefore, if citizens have homogeneous preferences for the public goods provided. A federalist structure may be optimal even in a small country, if there are significant regional or local differences in the views of citizens over governmental outputs.

South Korea is a fairly small country by area, but its population is reasonably large. Seoul's population is about the same as Denmark's. It is also a land with strong regional differences. A federalist structure of government is quite likely to be optimal. Such a structure would also facilitate the absorption of North Korea should communism ever fall there, and the two Koreas followed the path of the two Germanies.

To determine what public goods should be provided information concerning the preferences of the citizens must be gathered and aggregated. There are two aspects to this process that must be specified in the constitution: how are citizens' preferences represented in the parliament, and what aggregation (voting) rule is used to determine parliamentary outcome?

The choice between methods of electing representatives reduces essentially to two, logically quite different sets of procedures. Under the one, the objective is to represent the preferences of *all* citizens, and to do so as accurately as possible. One way to achieve this is to allow as many parties to compete for votes as wish to compete, and allocate seats in the parliament to each party in proportion to the number of votes it receives, subject to the constraints imposed by the total number of seats in the parliament, and perhaps some minimum cut-off rule. Such *proportional representation* (PR) procedures tend to produce parliaments with several parties having nontrivial numbers of votes, and with often ten on more parties getting at least one seat in the parliament. Consequently, each voter is almost certainly represented in the parliament by a party for which she voted, and which takes positions on the issues that come fairly close to those she favors.

The most frequent criticism of PR is that it produces *unstable* governments (Hermens, 1941, 1951). The Fourth Republic of France, and Italy's 50 plus governments since 1948 are illustrations of this. With several parties having substantial numbers of seats in the parliament, no single party is likely to have a majority of the seats, and the simple majority rule is prone to cycles. No coalition of parties can agree on the composition of the cabinet for very long.

There are two important observations to be made about this criticism. First of all, multiparty parliaments are not inevitably unstable, and even when they are, the outcome is not always *bad government.* Austria, Switzerland, The Netherlands, Germany and the Scandinavian countries all have the electoral rules that tend to produce multiparty systems. Yet, no one thinks of these countries as being unstable democracies, nor are the mistakes their governments sometimes make obviously attributable to their PR structure. Indeed, since the 1930s Sweden, like Japan since the 1950s, has had a single party in the parliament with a majority of the seats for much of the time. The result has been the installation in Sweden of the most advanced welfare state in the world. The result of this is that Sweden is in advance of its European neighbors in its state of economic decline (Lindbeck, 1995).

The second point to be made about the instability critique of PR is that, to the extent it is valid, this instability comes about not because PR is a bad system of representing individual preferences, but because the parliament has been given *both* the legislative and executive functions. In virtually all countries with PR systems, the parliament chooses the cabinet out of its own membership.[12] To avoid the instability that this requirement can produce, the legislative functions of government should be separated from the executive functions, the parliament should be separated from the cabinet.[13]

Such a separation still leaves the possibility of parliamentary instability in the form of cycles in the selection of government policies, but this problem is much less serious than that of cabinet instability. There is no reason why *the same coalition* has to form to pass each bill that comes up for a vote. What is essential is that

[12]Two exceptions are France, where cabinet members need not be members of the parliament, and Switzerland, which effectively has no executive.

[13]De Gaulle's constitutional reforms ended France's political instability problems by creating a separately elected president with the authority to appoint the prime minister.

some coalition forms to pass that legislation that benefits the community. Society is not going to be obviously disadvantaged by one set of parties agreeing on defense appropriations, and a different set on environmental issues. Moreover, cycling on legislation need not occur at all. Under a PR system, the parliament does not have to, and I would argue should not, use the simple majority rule. If the parliament confines itself to the kinds of public goods issues that justify the government's existence, then substantial agreement, in the limit unanimity, is possible on parliamentary issues. If issues are of this type, the preferences of the representatives will be such that cycles can be avoided, even if only a two-thirds majority is required in the parliament.[14] Still other voting procedures, like voting by veto,[15] are available that both avoid cycles and have attractive normative properties in their own right. The rationale behind choosing a PR system is to represent individual citizen preferences on public issues as accurately as possible, when deciding those issues. Electoral rules that produce multiparty parliaments combined with the appropriate parliamentary voting rule can fulfill this goal.

The usual justification put forward for an executive branch separate from the legislative branch is to provide a *check* on the legislature to prevent it from making rash decisions. The United States' system comes to mind here with its separate election of the President and the Congress.

To provide an effective check on the legislature, the chief executive must be given joint or additional authority. This can take the form of authority to veto actions by the legislature, authority to disband the legislature and call new elections, authority to disband the legislature and rule by decree.

Although granting the chief executive these authorities can help prevent the legislature from making bad decisions, it can also prevent their making good decisions, or any decisions at all. In the

[14] In fact, a 64% majority suffices, see Caplin and Nalebuff (1988).
[15] See Mueller (1978; 1984; 1996, ch. 11), and Moulin (1981a, b).

United States the system of checks and balances has degenerated in the last 20 years into a tug of war between the President and the Congress. Ronald Reagan, George Bush and now Bill Clinton have all faced Congresses controlled by the opposite parties. The result has been deadlock and frustration as neither the President nor the Congress has been able to effectuate their programs. For the American people the result has been a generation of failed promises and ineffective government.

Governmental authority in the Weimar Republic of Germany was divided among the President, the Chancellor and the parliament. During the economic crisis of the late 1920s and early 1930s, when difficult governmental decisions had to be made, this division of powers also produced a paralysis of government. In this case it took the form of President Hindenburg's continual disbandment of parliament and calls for new elections. The German people became steadily disenchanted with the government and turned to more radical political parties until Hitler eventually took over, and brought democracy and the republic to an end.[16]

Many Latin American countries modeled their constitutions after that of their large, North American neighbor and included provisions that established strong presidencies. They did not adopt the single-member-per-district electoral rules that tend to produce fewer parties in the legislature, however. Instead, they chose European style PR formulae. The result has been that a strong president has often had to work with weak parliaments, and parliaments in which his party does not occupy a majority of the seats. Deadlocks and ineffectual government have often been the result, followed by military takeovers. As with the the Weimar Republic, the cause of this sort of democratic instability has not been the existence of

[16]See Eyck (1962, 1963), Lepsius (1978, pp.47–50), Carstairs (1980, pp.165–6), and Mueller (1996, pp.45–6).

PR per se, but its use combined with an independent and powerful presidency. The rationale for having a PR system is to have the preferences of the citizens represented accurately in the legislature. This system should be combined with a *separate and weak executive*.[17]

If the citizens want to form a government with a strong executive, electoral rules that produce a two-party system should be adopted and the executive should be formed within the parliament. If there are literally only two parties, then one of them must have a majority of the seats in the parliament. The appropriate parliamentary voting rule under a two-party system is the simple majority rule. In deciding which party to vote for, the voter compares the entire packages of policies that both parties offer, their abilities to govern, and so on. The election determines the best party/program. In office the winning party should be able to implement the program that it promised. If the parliament employs the simple majority rule, this will be the case.

The method typically employed to obtain a two-party system is to elect a single representative from each electoral district. This procedure generally produces *fewer* parties than under multi-member-per-district representation, but has produced literally only two parties only in the United States, and even there not all of the time (Rae, 1971; Lijphart, 1990).

When there are strong regional differences, single-member-per-district representation tends to produce two large parties in a given district, but need not produce but two parties in the national parliament. Australia, Canada, France, Great Britain, and New Zealand have had single-member-per-district representation for much, if not all of this century, and yet all of these countries typically have several parties represented in their parliaments with no single party

[17] See discussion and references in Mueller (1996, chs. 8, 10).

having a majority of the seats. Indeed, France employed a single-member-per-district representation system for much of the period in which it had multiparty parliaments and considerable instability. Even when single-member-per-district representation produces a single party with a majority of the seats in the parliament, that party often will not have received a majority of the votes cast, and may even be ranked second to some other party by a majority of the voters. No party holding a majority of seats in the British Parliament during this century has received a majority of the votes cast in the general election. To be sure that one party does hold a majority of the seats in the parliament, and that this party has also received a majority of the votes cast, some other procedure than single-member-per-district representation is required.

One such procedure would be to have all parties compete for votes across the entire nation on a first ballot, and allocate seats in the parliament just as under a PR-list system. If one party received a majority of the votes cast on this first ballot, it would obtain a majority of the seats in the parliament and could implement its program under the simple majority rule. No second ballot would be required. If no party received a majority of the votes cast on the first ballot, a run-off election between the two parties receiving the most votes on the first ballot would be held, with seats assigned to these parties in proportion to the number of votes that they received on the second ballot.[18]

These issues are important to consider when deciding the kinds of democratic institutions that would be best suited for the Asian countries. One of the political reforms that has been suggested in Japan is to replace its single-nontransferable-vote electoral rules (a kind of halfway house between single-member-per-district representation and multimember-per-district representation of the type that produces PR) with single-member-per-district representation. But

[18]See discussion in Mueller (1996, ch. 9).

as we have just seen this would neither guarantee the emergence of a two-party system nor that one party would receive a majority of the seats in the Diet.

When democratic institutions replace a dictatorship, a natural tendency will be to build a strong chief executive into the new structure. As we have seen, when a strong executive is combined with a separation of executive and legislative functions, the danger of deadlock and ineffective government is high. The possibility then arises that the citizens become disenchanted with their new democratic government, and dictatorship returns. If one wants to implement a stable and long-lived set of democratic institutions, one should avoid having strong chief executives separate from the parliament which purportedly represents the preferences of the people.

6. Democracy and Peace

War is the quintessential negative sum game. It is zero sum in its distribution of territory, and negative sum in the destruction of lives and property. Moreover, in most wars even the winners lose more than they gain because of war's destruction. These facts must be obvious to even the most casual student of history.

Nevertheless, from time to time some leader comes along with sufficient hubris to believe that history's lessons will not apply to him. His country can beat the odds and be a net gainer by starting a war. Except in monarchies, it often takes considerable talent and effort to become the leader of a country. There are many volunteers for the job, and by one means or another the eventual leader has to prove that he is better suited for it. A dictator is, therefore, likely to have obtained his position by defeating high odds. Such feats can instill the hubris needed to defy the high odds against winning a war.

Such hubris is unlikely to extend across the entire population of a country, or even to a majority of it. Thus, one does not expect, and does not find, democracies starting many wars.[19] Indeed, they are extremely reluctant to enter a war someone else started. Thus, Great Britain and France ceded Czechoslovakia to Hitler rather than risk a war with Nazi Germany; the United States remained on the sidelines during World War II until the Pearl Harbor attack's catalyzing effect on its citizens; and, despite overwhelming odds in their favor, the United States and the Western European democracies remained out of the Bosnian war until very recently.

An upward trend in the number of democracies in Asia might, therefore, have the welcomed side effect of reducing the probability of war in Asia. And then again it might not. The reluctance of democracies to go to war may make war more tempting to some dictator. A mixture of democratic and dictatorial states in Asia might prove to be an unstable combination.

The collapse of the Soviet Union has reduced dramatically the likelihood of a major, nuclear war. Ironically, it has increased the likelihood of local conflicts. Had Saddam Hussein attacked Kuwait during the era of bipolar nuclear stand-off, Iraq's ally, the Soviet Union, would have been immediately drawn into the affair, and the United States and Soviet Union would have been squared off against one another in the Middle East. Because the gains to the Soviet Union from a successful attack by Iraq on Kuwait would be small, and the risk from a confrontation with the United States large, the Soviet Union would probably have pressured Hussein not to attack.

The former Yugoslavia, a shotgun marriage of cultures, ethnic groups and religions, was held together to a considerable degree

[19]Farber and Gowa (1995) question whether it is democratic institutions or common interests that are the chief deterrents to militancy. Their thesis would imply that it is more important for the Asian countries to form economic unions, so that the costs of belligerency become very high, than for them to introduce democratic institutions.

by the threat of Soviet invasion should it waiver from its brand of communism, or fall into disarray. The Soviet Union's disintegration removed the threat of its invasion, and gave a green light to a dictator or general in any of the republics with the hubris to make a grab for land and power. Unfortunately, candidates with these qualifications were not in short supply. Thus, in Europe, in Asia, in Africa, and perhaps in still other parts of the world, the probabilities of small wars starting has increased since 1991. Since small wars often become big wars this development is an unfortunate consequence of the Soviet Union's demise. Some institution for preventing local wars must be found now that the bipolar nuclear stand-off can no longer achieve this end.

The most promising possibility for preserving peace in Europe is the gradual expansion of the European Union. It is easy to judge the Union as an economic success, and a political failure. Its biggest expenditure item is in an area where government has no business being, protection and support for agriculture. In the area of defense and foreign policy, where only governments can act, the European Union spends and does little.

But in one important respect the European Union has been a tremendous political success. It has prevented its members from going to war with one another. The probability that Germany and France would go to war again seems as low as the probability that California would declare war on Nevada. Today, Turkey, the Czech Republic, Poland, Slovakia, Slovenia, Hungary, the Baltics, and still more former communist countries are likely entrants into the Union. One can envisage its gradual expansion eastward, first absorbing these lands, and then moving on into the former Soviet Union until it eventually reaches the Pacific Ocean and the borders of China. If it continues to require entrants to be democratic countries, which guarantee basic civil rights and liberties to all of their citizens, then democracy will extend itself across the entire Euro-Asian landmass, and so too will the peace that democracy brings with it.[20]

What Eastasia lacks as a means for preserving peace is an institution like the European Union. Until it has such an institution, the possibility of a war breaking out in Eastasia cannot be dismissed. The most likely way in which such an institution might come into existence would be for increasing economic cooperation and integration eventually to lead to political integration, i.e., the same scenario that Europe followed. The process of economic integration seems well underway. But political integration will, I fear, have to wait until democratic institutions take deeper root in the individual Asian countries, and then the countries that are democratic reach out and join hands with their neighbors.

References

Adelman, Irma. "Stylized and Simulated Long-run Economic Development." *Journal of Evolutionary Economics* 5 (September 1995): 189–208.

Ameringer, Charles D. *Democracy in Costa Rica.* New York: Praeger, 1982.

Ames, Barry. *Political Survival.* Berkeley: University of California Press, 1987.

Bernholz, Peter. *The International Game of Power.* Berlin: Mouton, 1985.

Caplin, Andrew S. and Nalebuff, Barry J. "On 64%-Majority Rule." *Econometrica* 56 (July 1988): 787–814.

Carstairs, Andrew M. *A Short History of Electoral System in Western Europe.* London: Allen and Unwin, 1980.

[20]For a precocious discussion of this possibility, see Bernholz (1985).

Caves, Richard E. "Mergers, Takeovers and Economic Efficiency: Foresight vs. Hindsight." *International Journal of Industrial Organization* 7 (March 1989): 151–74.

Diamond, Larry, Linz, Juan J. and Lipset, Seymour M. Editors. *Politics in Developing Countries.* Boulder, Colo.: L. Rienner, 1990.

Eyck, Erick. *A History of the Weimar Republic*, Vol. 1. Cambridge, Mass.: Harvard University Press, 1962.

______. *A History of the Weimar Republic*, Vol. 2. Cambridge, Mass.: Harvard University Press, 1963.

Farber, Henry and Gowa, Joanne. "Common Interests or Common Polities? Reinterpreting the Democratic Peace." NBER Working Paper No. 5005, Cambridge , Mass., 1995.

Frieden, Jeffery A. *Debt, Development and Democracy: Modern Political Economy and Latin America, 1965-1985.* Princeton, New Jersey: Princeton University Press, 1991.

Frideman, Milton. *Capitalism and Freedom.* Chicago: University of Chicago Press, 1962.

Hermans, Ferdinand A. *Democracy or Anarchy.* Notre Dame: University of Notre Dame Press, 1941.

______. *Europe between Democracy and Anarchy.* Notre Dame: University of Notre Dame Press, 1951.

Jensen, Michael C. and Ruback, Richard S. "The Market for Corporate Control: the Scientific Evidence." *Journal of Financial Economics* 11 (April 1983): 5–50.

Kline, Harvey F. "Columbia: The Struggle between Traditional 'Stability' and New Visions." In *Latin American Politics and Development*, 3rd ed., edited by Wiarda, Howard J. and Kline, Harvey F., Boulder, Colo.: Westview Press, 1990: 231–57.

Lamounier, Bolivar. "Brazil: Inequality against Democracy." In *Politics in Developing Countries*, edited by Diamond, Larry,

Linz, Juan J. and Lipset, Seymour M., Boulder, Colo.: L. Rienner, 1990: 87–134.

Lepsius, M. Rainer. "From Fragmented Party Democracy to Government by Emergency Decree and National Socialist Takeover: Germany." In *The Breakdown of Democratic Regimes*, edited by Linz, Juan J. and Stepan, A., Baltimore: Johns Hopkins University Press, Part 2, 1978: 34–79.

Levy, Daniel C. "Mexico: Sustained Civilian Rule without Democracy." In *Politics in Developing Countries*, edited by Diamond, Larry, Linz, Juan J. and Lipset, Seymour M., Boulder, Colo.: L. Rienner, 1990: 135–73.

Lijphart, Arend. "The Political Consequences of Electoral Laws, 1945-1985." *American Political Science Review* 84 (June, 1990): 481–96.

Lindbeck, Assar. "Hazardous Welfare-State Dynamics." *American Economic Review Papers and Proceedings* 85 (May 1995): 9–15.

Manning, Maurice. "Ireland." In *Referendums: A Comparative Study of Practice and Theory*, edited by Butler, David and Ranney, Austin, Washington, D. C.: American Enterprise Institute, 1978: 193–210.

McDonald, Ronald H. "Uruguay: Democratic Regeneration and Realignment." In *Latin American Politics and Development*, 3rd ed., edited by Wiarda, Howard J. and Kline, Harvey F., Boulder, Colo.: Westview Press, 1990: 321–34.

Moulin, Herve. "The Proportional Veto Principle." *Review of Economic Studies* 48 (July 1981a): 407–16.

———. "Prudence versus Sophistication in Voting Strategy." *Journal of Economic Theory* 24 (June 1981b): 398–412.

Mueller, Dennis C. "The Effects of Conglomerate Mergers: A Survey of the Empirical Evidence." *Journal of Banking and Finance* 1 (December 1977): 315–47. Reprinted in *Financial Analysis and Planning: Theory and Application, a Book of Readings.*

edited by Lee. Cheng few, Reading, Mass.: Addison-Wesley, 1983, 450–82. Also reprinted in *Mergers and Acquisition*, edited by Marchildon, Gregory P., London: Edward Elgar, 1991.

______. "Voting by Veto." *Journal of Public Economics* 10 (August 1978): 57–75. Reprinted in Laffont, Jean Jacques. *Aggregation and the Revelation of Preferences.* Amsterdam: North-Holland Publishing Co., 1979. Also reprinted in *The Theory of Public Choice II*, edited by Buchanan, James M. and Tollison, Robert D., Ann Arbor: University of Michigan Press, 1984.

______. "Voting by Veto and Majority Rule." in *Public Finance and the Quest for Efficiency*, edited by Hanusch, Horst, Detroit: Wayne State University Press, 1984: 69–86.

______. *The Corporation: Growth, Diversification, and Mergers.* Chur: Harwood Academic Publishers, 1987.

______. "Antimerger Policy in the United States: History and Lessons." *Empirica* 23 (1996a): 229–53.

______. *Constitutional Democracy.* Oxford: Oxford University Press, 1996b.

Odagiri, Hiroyuki. *The Theory of Growth in a Corporate Economy: Management Preference, Research and Development, and Economic Growth.* Cambridge: Cambridge University Press, 1981.

______. "Antineoclassical Management Motivation in a Neoclassical Economy: A Model of Economic Growth and Japan's Experience." *Kyklos* 35 (1982): 223–43.

______ and Yamawaki, Hideki. "The Persistence of Profits: An International Comparison." In *The Dynamics of Company Profits: An International Comparison*, edited by Mueller, Dennis C., Cambridge: Cambridge University Press 1990: 169–85.

Porter, Michael. *The Competitive Advantage of Nations.* New York: Free Press, 1990.

Rae, Douglas W. *The Political Consequences of Electoral Laws.* Rev. ed., New Haven: Yale University Press, 1971.

Roett, Riordan and Sacks, Richard S. "Authoritarian Paraguay: The Personalist Tradition." In *Latin American Politics and Development*, 3rd ed., edited by Wiarda, Howard J. and Kline, Harvey F., Boulder, Colo.: Westview Press, 1990: 335–58.

Seligson, Mitchell A. "Cost Rica." In *Latin American Politics and Development*, 3rd ed., edited by Wiarda, Howard J. and Kline, Harvey F., Boulder, Colo.: Westview Press, 1990: 455–66.

Sigmund, Paul E. "Chile." In *Latin American Politics and Development*, 3rd ed., edited by Wiarda, Howard J. and Kline, Harvey F., Boulder, Colo.: Westview Press, 1990: 201–30.

Snow, Peter G. and Wynia, Gary W. "Argentina: Politics in a Conflict Society." In *Latin American Politics and Development*, 3rd ed., edited by Wiarda, Howard J. and Kline, Harvey F., Boulder, Colo.: Westview Press, 1990: 129–66.

"The Hole in Your Future." *The Economist* (1995): 88.

Valenzuela, Arturo. "Chile: Origins, Consolidation, and Breakdown of a Democratic Regime." In *Politics in Developing Countries*, edited by Diamond, Larry, Linz, Juan J. and Lipset, Seymour M., Boulder, Colo.: L. Rienner, 1990: 39–86.

Wiarda, Howard J. and Kline, Harvey F. Editors. *Latin American Politics and Development*, 3rd ed., Boulder, Colo.: Westview Press, 1990.

PART II

CONSTITUTIONAL PROCESSES

Constitutional Political Economy, 10, 119–148 (1999)

Fundamental Issues in Constitutional Reform: With Special Reference to Latin America and the United States

DENNIS C. MUELLER mueller@econ.bwl.univie.ac.at
Department of Economics, University of Vienna, BWZ - Bruenner Str. 72, A-1210 Vienna, Austria.

Abstract. This article describes the kinds of democratic institutions that citizens might include in a constitution that they themselves wrote to advance their common interests. It argues that no single set of institutions dominates all others, but rather that there are advantages and disadvantages to different institutions and, most importantly, that different parts of the constitution can either reinforce or contradict one another. Frequent reference is made to the experience of Latin American countries in the interest of making the arguments more concrete. Many of the same issues are also relevant for the United States, however.

JEL classification: D70, D72, H11.

Those who do not learn from history live to repeat it.

George Santayana

1. Introduction

An ideal constitution contains properties sufficiently desirable so that it *should* be followed, and incentives so that it *is* followed. Support for such a constitution can be expected to grow as citizens observe the positive consequences that flow from it. This has occurred in the United States, and helps explain the widespread support and respect Americans give to the Constitution. The first and most important step toward good, democratic government is, therefore, to choose a constitutional design that elicits the widest possible support, a constitution which ideally advances the interests of *all* citizens.

The design of such a constitution is no mean feat. Democratic politics almost inevitably produces winners and losers, and the state's powers to tax and spend provide groups great incentives to control the state and use its powers to advance their interests over those of other citizens. A constant struggle between different groups to control the state results, a struggle that can produce political instability, and thereby the democratic state's demise. Latin American constitutions have been patterned after that of the United States and often contain the same separation of powers, federalist structures and protections of civil liberties. In practice, however, central governments have dominated provincial and local governments, the judiciary has generally been dominated by the executive, and fundamental civil liberties—like freedom of the press and freedom from arbitrary arrest—have often been grossly violated. Latin American governments have often done that which they should not do, and too often have failed, miserably, in those activities that constitute the raison d'être of the state.

The challenge when writing a constitution is, therefore, to design institutions that allow the state to do those things that can benefit all citizens, and at the same time to prevent it from being used as an instrument through which some groups advantage themselves at the expense of others. With this goal in mind I describe democratic institutions that citizens might include in a constitution that they themselves wrote to advance their common interests.[1] This paper argues that no single set of institutions dominates all others, but rather that there are advantages and disadvantages to different institutions and, most importantly, that different parts of the constitution can either reinforce or contradict one another. The challenge in writing a constitution is to select a *set* of institutions that complement and reinforce one another.

Much of what needs to be done to advance the interests of individual citizens, they can do for themselves. The state's role here is merely to guarantee the citizen's freedom to make private choices. The criteria for defining such freedoms and the institutions for guaranteeing them are discussed in Part 2. A second important role for the state is to bring about the sorts of *collective actions* that can advance the interests of all citizens. The institutions of government for achieving this goal are the subject of Part 3. Part 4 closes the paper with a brief sketch of the three main sets of institutional options that a country faces. Although most arguments in the article could apply to any country, frequent reference is made to the experience and problems facing Latin American countries in the interest of making the arguments more concrete. We shall also argue that many of the same issues are relevant for the United States.

2. Constitutional Rights

We think of the constitution as a contract among the citizens creating the state. The conceptual starting point is a world without government, therefore. In entering into this contract, the individual gives up certain freedoms and takes on certain obligations. The individual thus runs the risk that the constraints on freedom and obligations imposed by the community may actually *reduce* his welfare, thus vitiating the sole purpose of government. To reduce this risk, the individual can place certain provisions in the constitutional contract that protect his freedom to act. In their most general form, these protections of freedom fall under the heading of *rights*.

2.1. Rights

Most actions, like scratching one's ear, affect only the actor. Thus, implicitly and perhaps better explicitly, the constitution should *allow* all individual actions *unless* they are specifically prohibited. Some actions, as driving 100 km/hr through the center of a city, adversely affect other individuals and the constitution must define the legislative voting rule to constrain or ban such actions. In choosing a voting rule, the likely losses to persons prevented from acting must be weighed against the gains to those harmed by this action.

The higher the majority required to pass an issue, the more protection an individual has against legislation that adversely prevents her from acting. If the actor's gain equals the loss imposed on others, the optimal voting rule is the simple majority rule.[2] As the loss imposed on an individual who is prevented from acting grows relative to the gains to the rest of the community from this prohibition, the optimal required majority to prevent the action grows.[3] An example requiring a high qualified majority might be a bill to arrest and detain indefinitely members of a particular ethnic, religious or political group, even though they were accused of no specific crime. At a time when the targeted group is a potential source of violent actions against other members of society, such a measure might reduce the anxiety of a vast majority of citizens. But the costs imposed on innocent members of the targeted group obviously could be enormous. At a constitutional convention, individuals who are uncertain about whether they or their descendants might someday be members of a targeted group would want to protect themselves against the possibility of such legislation passing. Requiring a high qualified majority to pass such legislation would provide protection. The greatest protection would be provided by the unanimity rule, for it would allow a threatened minority to veto all such legislation.

Since the unanimity rule would be used only for decisions in which minorities stand to suffer great losses, these minorities can be expected in most instances to exercise the veto that the unanimity rule gives them and vote against such proposals.[4] The transaction costs of collective decision making can be reduced, if issues of this type are not voted upon using the unanimity rule, but rather are dealt with by defining unconditional rights.

This logic implies the following criteria when defining rights: First, rights should protect specific actions or perhaps nonactions (the right to remain silent). Second, rights should be defined only where it is thought that some future subset of the community will attempt to block a particular action. Third, rights should be defined to protect only those actions where the gain to the actor is expected to be very large relative to any costs imposed upon second parties.

Although these criteria are fairly specific, it must be stressed that they *do not* define a *unique* set of rights for all countries. An action that one community deems worthy of protection may not be deemed so by another. For example, in a country with many religious minorities citizens may fear that a future legislative majority will try to prohibit some minority's religious practice. If the citizens perceive that the loss to the majority discomforted by this practice is likely to be small relative to the minority's loss from the prohibition, they will choose to protect the minority's freedom to practice its religion by defining a right to that effect in the constitution. In a community in which everyone is a member of the same religion, however, legislative action against the religion may seem inconceivable, and no constitutional rights protecting religion may be introduced. *All* definitions of constitutional rights are thus to some extent *relative* to the particular preferences and culture of each community.

2.2. *Protection of Market Exchange*

The constitution has two important roles to play in facilitating the gains from market exchange: First, it establishes the basic institutional structure that underlies a market system. Second, it places constraints on the state's ability to intervene and harm the market process.

The institutional structure underlying the market system could be a set of rights like the following:

1. Each citizen has the right to own and dispose of any and all property which has been obtained by legal means.
2. Each citizen has the right to enter into contracts to buy or sell goods in his possession, or to sell his services, or to buy the services of others. This freedom applies to transactions between citizens of the country, and between any citizen and a citizen of a foreign country.
3. Each citizen has the right to demand any price he chooses for the goods in his possession or for his services.
4. Each citizen has the right to start or terminate a business at a time of his choosing.

In certain situations state interference with the market may improve the allocation of resources. The constitution must therefore allow for state interference with the market, when it is in the broad public interest. This objective can be accomplished by stipulating in the constitution that *any* abridgment of the above enumerated rights requires the approval of a substantial majority, say 3/4ths, of the legislature. Such a provision would constrain the state's ability to distort the market process for the benefit of a few and at the cost of the many.

2.3. Economic Rights

Although the allocation of goods and services through market exchange can increase everyone's welfare, market systems do not guarantee that everyone has a minimally acceptable income. Such minimum guarantees can only be provided by the state. A minimum guaranteed income, financed out of a general tax, has the characteristics of a constitutional right described above. The minority receiving the subsidies obtains a huge benefit, and the larger population suffers a small loss. A person who put herself in the shoes of a middle class taxpayer paying for such subsidies and in those of the poor person receiving them, might well vote for the subsidies. Certain basic redistribution programs to the very poor might thus be written into the constitution as a form of "economic right" or entitlement.

Treating basic redistribution as a right and placing it into the constitution would take the most divisive issue a democracy faces "off the political agenda." It is no coincidence that democracy has frequently given way to dictatorship in times of economic uncertainty or at the onset of an economic contraction. The Bolshevik Revolution in Russia during World War I, the Nazi takeovers in Germany and Italy after World War I and, on a much smaller scale, Huey Long's rise to power in Louisiana all fit this pattern. The displacement of democracy in Latin America (e.g., Argentina in 1930, Costa Rica in 1948, Chile in 1973, and Uruguay in 1933 and 1973) has also often occurred, when the positive sum politics of a growing economy has been replaced by the zero and negative sum politics of how to distribute a shrinking pie. It is also no coincidence that Latin America's most successful democracies—Uruguay and Costa Rica—have had its most egalitarian distributions of income, and thus have been spared the intense distributional conflicts that have befallen countries with highly unequal distributions of income, like Peru.[5]

With economic entitlements in the constitution, other forms of *compulsory state-provided* redistribution, like unemployment compensation and old age benefits, could be eliminated with, of course, people free to contribute to private insurance programs.

If everyone with an income below a basic subsistence level is entitled to a subsidy, then other institutions can be designed to advance the interests of all citizens. To discourage interest group efforts to redistribute income involuntarily from the rest of the community to themselves, tax and expenditure bills should require high legislative majorities. Government activities that benefit the entire community—like defense and police protection—can secure the support of 2/3rds or 3/4ths of the legislature. Interest groups seeking subsidies and tax breaks will, on the other hand, find it more difficult to put together large redistributive coalitions.

In addition to a minimum income should each citizen not also be entitled to an education, health care, etc.? Arguments favoring entitlements can be extended in several directions. Where to draw the line? When answering this question, one must keep in mind the basic criteria that warrant defining a constitutional right. The welfare increase of the subsidy recipient should be very large relative to the welfare loss of the taxpayer. In a rich country the fraction of the population requiring subsidies of these types is small as is the burden placed on the average taxpayer. A relatively long list of entitlements might be chosen. In a poor country, each new entitlement increases the burden on the relatively small fraction of middle and high income taxpayers substantially. A short list of entitlements is more likely to be optimal. As is true of all constitutionally defined rights no single set of economic entitlements will fit all countries. The optimal set for a particular country depends on its income level, and the degree of empathy its citizens feel for one another.

2.4. *The Judiciary*

2.4.1. *The Selection of Judges*

The constitution, a kind of contract among the citizens, is like all contracts vulnerable to breach. Its drafters must take into account the potential opportunistic behavior of all parties covered by it, and the potential for conflict among these parties. An institution for arbitration is required. This task logically falls to the judiciary.

In private contracting the impartiality of an arbitrator can be secured by *all* parties agreeing to the arbitrator's identity, before the contract is signed. To secure an impartial judiciary ideally *all* citizens would concur in the selection of judges. Since this solution is impractical, the most obvious alternative is for the citizens' representatives to select judges. To ensure impartiality the optimal voting rule in the selection of judges by the legislature would be the unanimity rule. When less than unanimous agreement suffices to pass legislation, a dissenting minority can be tyrannized to a degree by the majority. If the same majority has the authority to choose those who judge the merits of judicial appeals by the minority, the probability of the minority's tyrannization increases. Requiring minority concurrence in the selection of judges is a safeguard against its inevitable defeat in both the legislature and the courts.

The higher the majority required to appoint a judge, however, the greater the likelihood that the legislature is unable to agree on any person, and that judgeships remain vacant to the community's loss. This danger warrants an institutional safeguard to avoid it. One possibility is to invest some person or group with the authority to nominate judges, and stipulate that nominees assume their posts after say, six months, *unless* the legislature substitutes by the required supramajority another person for the nominee. This procedure would ensure that judgeships do not remain vacant should the legislature not fill a judgeship, but allows the people's representatives to substitute a person they deem to be better suited than the one nominated, when they can agree on a substitute.

Should the nominators under this procedure be in the legislative, or the executive or the judicial branches? One of the complaints lodged against England in the Declaration of Independence concerned the impartiality of judges in the colonies who were appointed by the king. Early state constitutions often authorized the governor to appoint judges and were accused of having produced a "spoils system" by reformers in the Jacksonian era. The nomination of federal judges, including those to the Supreme Court, by a popularly elected President coupled with the requirement of Senate approval by a simple majority has had the predictable result that the selection of "judges in America is a political process with a political result."[6] The selection of judges is also the prerogative of the executive branch with the consequence that the judiciary in most Latin American countries is weak and lacking in independence.[7] The political nature of judicial appointments has been a controversial issue in Ecuador in recent years. To ensure the impartiality of the judiciary, the nomination or appointment of judges cannot be entrusted to either a simple majority of the legislature subject to partisan influences, or a popularly elected chief executive.

The third possible location of a nominator is in the judiciary itself. In a judicial hierarchy cases are tried in lower courts, appealed to intermediate levels, with a superior court of last appeal at the top. The career of a typical judge is to be appointed from private practice to a lower court, and perhaps from there to judgeships at higher levels. Those best positioned to observe which trial lawyers have the potential to be good judges are judges in the lower courts, i.e. those hearing cases prepared by the trial lawyers. Similarly, the talents of lower court judges can be best appraised by those in the higher levels who review lower court decisions on appeal. These considerations suggest that the best place to locate the nominators of judges is in the judiciary itself.[8] Vacancies at a particular level could be filled by nominees of the judges at that level at that time, *unless* the legislature votes by the constitutionally required supramajority to substitute some other person.[9] (In Costa Rica, where the judiciary has far more independence and authority than in most Latin American countries, the Supreme Court appoints members to the lower courts (Booth 1989: 400).)

Such a system might appear to present the danger that the judiciary becomes a self-selecting and self-perpetuating institution, possibly populated by individuals who were incompetent or corrupt. Two observations are warranted in this regard. First, there are incentives to encourage competency. The work at any level of the judicial hierarchy is lighter and more enjoyable for a given judge if his colleagues are industrious and intelligent rather than slothful and dull. Thus, judges at each level have a selfish interest in seeing the most competent candidates join them, as well as a social responsibility to nominate persons who will best serve the interests of the community. An individual ambitious to move to higher courts will carry out his judicial responsibilities to the best of his ability so as to impress his superiors.

The second line of defense is the legislature's authority to substitute its own nominees for those of the judiciary. The legislature could reform an incompetent or corrupt judiciary by substituting its preferred candidates for the judiciary's nominations. If the judiciary came in need of reform, the citizens through their elected representatives could replace the existing cadre of judges.

2.4.2. The Control of the Judiciary

The constitutional convention confronts a classic principal-agent problem. It must design institutions—executive, legislature, judiciary—so that their future members have incentives to act not in their own narrow self-interest, but in that of the citizenry at large. The most important check on the legislative branch is, of course, the necessity of its members getting reelected. The chief executive must also win the votes of either the legislature or the populace at large. An additional check is provided by granting the judiciary constitutional authority to overturn actions by the executive and legislative branches, when they violate the constitution. In this respect judges serve as direct agents of the citizens charged with protecting their interests as defined in the constitution from possible infringements by the legislative and executive branches.

But judges are also agents with interests and ideologies that may run counter to those of the citizens. What incentives can force them to act on the citizens' behalf? What institutional device checks the avaricious appetites of judges?

These are among the most difficult questions a constitutional democracy must face. It puzzled the Founders of the United States and has troubled thoughtful observers ever since. Abraham Lincoln posed the question most poignantly, "If the policy of the government, upon the vital questions affecting the whole people, is to be irrevocably fixed by the decisions of the Supreme Court the moment they are made, as in ordinary cases between parties in personal actions, the people will have ceased to be their own masters, having to that extent resigned their government into the hands of that eminent tribunal" (Corwin 1906: 40).

The solution the Founders of the U.S. republic decided upon was (1) judges are nominated by the President, but approved by the Senate, (2) appointments last for life, subject to good behavior, and (3) neither branch can reduce a judge's salary. The first solution has failed to keep the nomination and approval process from becoming politicized, but the second two have arguably freed judges to act without regard to any political obligations accumulated on their way to office.

Although lifetime appointments and financial security allow members of the judiciary to act in the citizenry's behalf, these provisions do not ensure that the judiciary always acts in the interests of the citizens. Impeachment procedures can remove corrupt or incapacitated judges, but are unlikely to induce judges to make the "right" decisions from the point of view of the citizenry. The opportunity to substitute someone nominated for a judgeship by the members of the judiciary at that level, if the substitute can secure a substantial fraction of the legislature, is one way the citizens through their representatives can keep a check on the judiciary. But if the citizens are "to remain their own masters" ultimately they must be prepared to remove their agents if the need arises. The ultimate check on the judiciary would be the possibility to reconvene a constitutional convention and appoint a new court.

3. The Organization of Government

The role of the state is to provide those goods and services that individuals cannot efficiently provide themselves, or which the market does not provide efficiently. To supply these goods and services optimally, the preferences of all citizens must be recorded, these preferences must be aggregated to reach a "collective decision," and then this decision must be implemented. This process is discussed in the next five sections. We first discuss the two main options for conveying information about voter preferences into the political process—two-party and multiparty representative systems.

3.1. The Legislative Branch

The constitution framers face a choice between two fundamentally different modes of representation—multiparty (proportional) representation (PR), and two-party representative government. Although many variants on each and several combinations of both exist, I consider only the polar cases to reveal their quite different underlying logics. Indeed, because their logics are so different, I argue against combining the two, for a combination is apt to contain the worst features of each system.

3.1.1. Multiparty Legislatures

The ideal assembly for aggregating citizens' preferences would include all citizens. Such an assembly is infeasible and so in the best feasible assembly *all* citizens' preferences are *represented.* A representative assembly can duplicate the outcomes from an assembly of all citizens, if different groups of citizens have similar preferences regarding public policies. In this case, an assembly in which each group is represented in proportion to its size mirrors the preferences of all citizens.

3.1.1.1. At Large List Systems

In the national assembly the preferences of all citizens should be represented in proportion to their numbers across the nation. When *parties* are the instruments of representation, preferences can be represented proportionally, when each party offers a single list of candidates to all voters. Citizens vote for their most preferred parties, and parties take seats in the legislature in proportion to their votes across the nation.

3.1.1.2. At Large List Systems with an Option to Express Preferences for Persons

An objection often raised against straight party list systems is that voters cannot express their preferences among the different *individual candidates*. Various modifications of PR-list systems allow voters to choose from among the candidates in each list, while ensuring that the final allocation of seats is roughly proportional to the votes for each party.[10]

3.1.1.3. The Issue of Stability

The major objection against PR is that it leads to parliamentary instability, and thus to weak and ineffective government. Parliamentary instability under PR can take two forms. First, there is the possibility of *cycling*—the structure of preferences across the parties may be such that no proposal for, say, the education budget can defeat all other proposals. The parliament gets "hung up" in an endless cycle. Second, under PR it may be difficult to form a cabinet, as already mentioned. This form of instability is another manifestation of cycling with proposals now being the composition of the cabinet instead of the composition of the education budget.

Although both forms of instability can arise under PR, neither need be reason to avoid this form of electoral system, if its other characteristics make it superior to two-party systems. Cycling on *issues* can be eliminated by the appropriate choice of voting rule. *Cabinet* instability can be avoided most simply by not requiring that the parliament choose the cabinet. The logic underlying PR fits most comfortably with a government structure in which the legislative and executive branches are *separated*. Even when such a separation does not occur, however, cabinet instability need not produce the Italian pattern of continually falling governments and new elections. Norway avoids this syndrome, for example, by simply not having any provision for calling new elections in its constitution. If a majority government cannot form, a minority government must carry on. So long as the parliament employs voting procedures that avoid endless cycles, the essential budget measures pass, and the country survives until the next election.

3.1.1.4. Discussion

The attraction of PR is its inherent fairness. Under a party list system with 200 or more seats in the legislature and *no minimum cut-offs* for taking seats, all but a handful of voters is represented by a party that they vote for, and each party's position on public issues is reasonably close to those its supporters favor. These features of PR stand in stark contrast to those of the so-called two-party systems in the UK, USA, and Canada. These systems share the feature that each delegate to the legislature is elected from a different district under a first-past-the-post rule. The consequence is that some 40 percent of the voters in the United States are "represented" in the House of Representatives by someone for whom they did not vote. This is 40 times the proportion of "wasted votes" that one expects from a PR-system without cut-offs. The 40 percent or so voter turnouts in Congressional elections in non-Presidential election years further imply that in the two years leading up to a Presidential election only about 15 percent of U.S. citizens are represented in the House of Representatives by someone for whom they voted. Add to this the fact that the position a representative takes on national issues can be far away from the positions favored by many of the voters in her district—even many who voted for her—and one sees why first-past-the-post systems score much higher than PR-systems when it comes to various measures of alienation like voter turnouts and violent civil disobedience (Powell 1982). The opportunity to vote and work for parties that share one's views on public issues ties voters in PR-systems more closely to both their favored parties and to the democratic process.

3.1.2. *Two-Party Legislatures*

The claimed advantage of two-party government is that it produces more *responsible* and *effective* government. In part this claim rests on the assumption that PR-systems are prone to the instabilities just discussed. Although these instabilities are not necessary features of PR as already explained, the institutional arrangements that ensure that these instabilities do not arise often make the democratic process more deliberate and consensual. It does not seem legitimate to call a more deliberate and consensual governmental process less responsible. However, if one defines effective government as the ability to make quick and bold collective choices, and to introduce radical reforms, then the kinds of PR-systems outlined here can be called less effective, for they are likely to be less capable of implementing bold new programs.

The "Anglo-Saxon two-party systems" of the United Kingdom, United States, Canada, Australia, and until recently New Zealand have two features in common: (1) they employ single-member-district representation (SMDR) with all but Australia using the plurality rule, and (2) they all, more or less, have tended to produce systems in which two parties play dominant roles. Despite these common features, it must be stressed that the U.S.-*presidential* system is quite different from the parliamentary systems in the other four countries. Indeed, the U.S. system with its separation of the legislative and executive branches, and checks and balances is even less capable of implementing bold new programs than most European PR-systems, as the terms "gridlock" and "deadlock," now frequent in American political discourse, so tellingly reveal. If what one seeks from a two-party system is *effective* government, then the U.S. version—SMDR in the legislative branch plus a separately elected chief executive with veto powers—is definitely not the way to go. Since SMDR is so obviously inferior to PR as a way of conveying information about voter preferences into the legislature,[11] the U.S. system comes close to combining the worst features of the PR- and two-party alternatives.[12]

Consider instead a parliamentary system in which there are literally only two parties competing for votes. Party *A* offers one platform, party *B* another. Each citizen votes for the party which he believes offers the best platform. Under fairly reasonable assumptions about the parties and voters,[13] one can show that the competition for votes between the two parties results in the selection of the platform that is optimal in the sense that it positively weights the welfare of the individual voters. Competition for votes in a two-party system can achieve the same sort of invisible hand theorem result as competition for profits achieves in private goods markets.

Once one takes into account the effects of rational ignorance on the part of voters, rent-seeking by interest groups, and the like, there is reason to doubt whether the outcomes from two-party competition are quite as wonderful as the elegant theorems that establish the results described in the previous paragraph might lead one to believe. Nevertheless, the outcomes should fulfill much of the claims of those who advocate two-party systems. Voters can choose between two sets of party leaders one of which will govern the country after the election, and between two sets of policy proposals. Although neither party is likely to offer a program as close to a voter's preferred program as is available under PR, under a two-party system the voter knows that his party will be able to implement the set of policies it has proposed. Under a PR-system a voter cannot make this assumption.

With only two parties competing for votes, one must win a majority of the seats and, if the parliamentary voting rule is the simple majority rule, it is able to implement its program. If radical measures are called for, and one party can convince a majority of voters that its radical proposals would improve the country's situation significantly, it will be able to implement its measures after the election. *Effective* government in this sense can occur under a two-party system. It is much less likely under PR.

Under the rules used to elect members of the parliament in the Anglo-Saxon systems, one representative is elected from each geographically defined district. In the UK and Canada, she is the candidate receiving the most votes in the district. When several parties compete for votes across the country under this electoral rule, two parties emerge as dominant at the national level *only if these same two parties are dominant across most if not all of the individual districts of the nation.* If there are several parties with significantly different levels of popularity in different areas of the country, no single party let alone a pair of parties may emerge as dominant. India uses SMDR, and yet the distribution of seats across parties in its parliament looks more like that of a European PR-system than like that of the UK, a result due to the significant religious and ethnic differences across India. The distribution of seats across parties in France also looks much like that of other continental European PR-systems, despite France's having had SMDR for much of this century.[14]

In addition to not guaranteeing only two dominant parties, SMDR gives the largest parties significantly larger fractions of the seats in parliament than their fractions of the popular vote.[15] The Labour Party won a landslide victory in the 1997 election in terms of the number of seats in parliament despite having won roughly only 44 percent of the popular vote—a percentage that is about what the *losing* presidential candidate obtains in a landslide election in the United States.[16] With SMDR a majority of the voters might even prefer a second party to the one that wins a majority of the seats, with the winning party's victory entirely due to voter disagreement over which of the other two major parties is most preferred.

To avoid these disadvantages SMDR should not be used to obtain a two-party system. Instead, all parties should compete for votes across the entire country as under a PR-list system. If one party wins a majority of the votes, then seats in the parliament are allocated as under a PR-list system. This party then has a majority of the seats and can implement its program just as it could, if there were only two parties. If no party obtains more than 50 percent of the votes, a second election is held between the largest two parties. These two parties are then assigned seats in the legislature in proportion to their votes in the second election. This procedure would ensure that some party always occupies a majority of the seats, and that a majority of voters either preferred this party to the second largest party, or preferred it to all other parties. At large elections, coupled with a run-off if no party wins an absolute majority on the first ballot, would both ensure the existence of a majority party and legitimate its election.

3.2. The Parliamentary Voting Rule

The choice of voting rule for the legislature under a two-party system is simple—the simple majority rule. Under the logic of a two-party system parties compete by offering packages of proposals along with the claim that they are the best party to govern the country. For the system to produce the effective government sought, the winning party must be able to deliver on its promises. It can do this, if the parliament employs the simple majority rule, since the winning party is assured a majority of the seats under the electoral procedures described above. The issue of which parliamentary voting rule to use in a multiparty-system is a good deal more difficult.

3.2.1. A Qualified Majority Rule with the Simple Majority as a Special Case

The justification for the state rests on the existence of market failures that are most efficiently resolved by government action. All citizens can be made better off through collective action, and the collective decision could be made using the unanimity rule. The standard objection to the unanimity rule is that it raises decisionmaking costs. As the required majority to pass an issue falls, however, the likelihood rises that the government undertakes actions that harm some citizens. The optimal majority for a parliamentary voting rule balances the increase in decisionmaking costs, which accompany higher required majorities, against the expected increase in costs borne by those who lose under a lower required majority.[17]

With lower required majorities, the likelihood of cycling increases, and with cycling the time required to reach the *final*, winning proposal. If the legislature concentrates on issues that potentially benefit all citizens, however, the probability of a voting cycle falls as the required majority increases reaching zero at a qualified majority of 64 percent.[18] Thus, if the parliament is largely concerned with issues likely to improve the welfare of all citizens, decisionmaking costs actually *rise* as the required majority falls below 64 percent. The optimal majority would be greater than this figure.

The concern is often raised that representative bodies sometimes pass measures in the heat of the moment that are later thought to have been ill-conceived. To avoid this danger, parliamentary rules often require that a measure be read before the parliament more than once before it can take effect, and stipulate intervals between each reading. One justification for a second legislative chamber is to delay a bill's passage, thus allowing its advantages and disadvantages to be more thoroughly understood.[19]

If these arguments have merit, then decisionmaking costs, i.e., the time spent debating and reformulating an issue to achieve a particular majority, are not costs at all, or at least are not costs until one reaches very high qualified majorities. Stated alternatively, the same objective as requiring a bicameral legislature, or second and third readings of bills, can be accomplished simply by requiring a large majority of a single chamber to pass any bill. These considerations favor requiring a majority of at least 2/3rds of the legislature to pass a bill.

Other justifications for a second chamber of parliament have been put forward, but we shall not discuss them here (see, Mueller 1996: Ch. 13). To represent individual preferences adequately on national issues one needs only one legislative chamber with groups having different preferences represented in proportion to their size. The competition for votes among the existing parties and the entry of new parties can be relied upon to ensure that those proposals that can potentially improve the welfare of all citizens get made.

A two-thirds or higher majority rule increases the possibility that no collective decision is reached. Sixty percent favors a five percent increase in education expenditures, the remaining 40 percent favors a three percent reduction. Neither proposal can obtain the 2/3rds needed to pass. The legislature is deadlocked. As the majority required to pass a bill increases, the importance of the *status quo* increases, for the *status quo* wins when no new proposal secures the required qualified majority. The most obvious choice for the *status quo* is the decision made last year. If a 2/3rds majority cannot be secured for a new education budget, then last year's budget is reinstated. If a 2/3rds majority cannot be secured for a new bridge, then no bridge gets built. In this regard, a PR-system coupled with a high qualified majority rule would be inherently conservative, conservative not in the sense of necessarily biased toward the positions of those on the right of the ideological spectrum, but conservative in the literal meaning of slow to change. Here we see why a PR-system may produce less effective government than a two-party system, when one defines effective government as the ability to make significant changes in policy.

I now describe, therefore, a voting rule that avoids cycles, eliminates all agenda setting problems and yet possesses the same normative properties as the simple majority rule.

3.2.2. Voting by Veto

Under voting by veto each member of the legislature proposes one outcome for the collective decision, for example the size and composition of the defense budget. If the legislature has n members, then their n proposals plus the *status quo* form a set of $n + 1$ proposals. The *status quo* could be to do nothing, to do what was done last year, or whatever. Unlike with high qualified majority rules, the *status quo* is an unlikely winner under voting by veto, and its content is of little importance. Once a proposal set is formed a random process selects an order in which the n members eliminate proposals from the set. After all n members have cast their vetoes, one proposal is left. It is the winning proposal.[20]

Voting by veto has a number of attractive properties. (1) Although its normative properties resemble the simple majority rule's,[21] unlike the simple majority rule it *always* determines a winning proposal. Cycling cannot occur. (2) When a stable majority coalition forms in a PR-system, parties not in the coalition are powerless. Their supporters, although fairly represented in the legislature, have no impact on the outcomes. Under voting by veto *all* parties have a chance to influence the outcome. Even a small party's proposal might win, if it stands relatively high in all members' proposal rankings. (3) The procedure encourages more responsible behavior by extremist parties. Rather than simply making wild proposals and having them eliminated, an extremist party can try and get its proposal selected by including in it features that are attractive to the other parties. Voting by veto establishes a competition among the parties to propose the *relatively most popular proposal.* (4) The procedure encourages more responsible behavior on the part of voters. In a normal PR-system, a voter can cast a "protest vote" for a party on the far left or right without running any danger that the party for which he votes will have any influence on public policy, since such extremist parties do not enter the coalitions that form governments. Under voting by veto, however, the citizen has more incentive to reflect on his party choice, since all parties can affect public policy.[22]

3.3. The Executive Branch

Two fundamentally different views exist regarding the function of the executive in a republican form of government.[23] One sees it as agent of the legislature, administrators who carry out its policies. The other sees the executive as a balance to the legislature, a separate location of legitimate authority that can check the legislature.

3.3.1. *The Chief Executive as Agent of the Legislature*

In a two-party system voters expect the winning party to carry out the mandate they have given it. To secure this end, the winning party's legislation should be implemented. Effective government requires a direct link between the bills passed by the legislature and their execution. By combining the executive and legislative branches, a two-party parliamentary system tries to forge this link. The party's leadership takes charge of each ministry, and conveys party policy into them.[24]

In a multiparty system each voter is represented by a party that takes a position close to that favored by the voter. The parliamentary voting rule selects the best outcome given this mode of representation. Additional input into *what* should be done is not required, under the logic of this mode of representation. The role of the executive branch should be, as under a two-party system, to see that what was voted to be done gets done. The chief executive must monitor bureaus in the executive branch to ensure that they carry out their tasks efficiently, and do not place their own objectives over those of the legislature. Under this interpretation, the chief executive is an agent of the legislature and logically is chosen by it.

The president is elected by the legislature in several countries today, and a proposal to have the House of Representatives elect the U.S. President was almost adopted at the Philadelphia convention (Sundquist 1986: 25). Given the public-good nature of the president's administrative role, if a supramajority (2/3, 3/4) of the legislature is required to pass public-goods issues, then the same majority should be required to elect the president. Such a rule would require the agreement of two or more parties in most instances, and thus favors the election of nonpartisan candidates, or at least individuals known to be fair and even-handed.

3.3.2. The Executive Branch as a Check on the Legislative Branch

The distinguishing feature of the U.S. Constitution is often viewed as the separation of the powers of government into three branches. But a more accurate characterization is that each branch jointly exercises the powers of government. Together they *share* these powers.[25] The President and both Houses of Congress are now popularly elected. Each can claim with some legitimacy to represent "the will of the people."

Once one conceives of the office of president as a separate location of legitimate authority and responsibility, several constitutional options arise for defining that authority. First, the president can be granted *sole authority* to act in some areas. The president can be designated the "commander and chief" with authority to commit the armed services to military action should the country be attacked. In a parliamentary system, the president can be given the authority to choose the "prime minister," to dissolve the parliament and call new elections, to dissolve the parliament and rule by decree, and so on. Most broadly and dangerously, the president can be allowed to suspend the constitution itself, and essentially assume dictatorial powers in times of national crisis.

The president can be given the authority to *initiate* action in certain areas subject to the approval of the legislature. Budget proposals might originate in the executive, but require the approval of the legislature, with the latter free to amend the proposals. The higher the required majority for passing such amendments, the greater the authority of the president. The U.S. Constitution grants the President the authority to initiate international treaties subject to the approval of the Senate.

A third option is to give the president the power to *check* legislative actions. In its mildest form, the constitution can allow a presidential veto to be overridden by the same majority of the legislature as is required on the first vote. The higher the majority required to override a presidential veto, the greater the president's power vis-à-vis the legislature.

The practice of dividing governmental authority between the executive and legislative branches evolved between the 14th and 16th centuries. The monarch was the representative of *all* of the people in Tudor England, and a Member of Parliament represented purely local or corporate interests.[26] Although by the end of the 18th century Europeans were well on their way to replacing this system with one in which governmental authority was vested in a single, parliamentary body, it was the Tudorial system of divided authority that the Founding Fathers enshrined in the U.S. Constitution. Its checks and balances reflect deep-seated fears of the potential excesses of an elected legislature,[27] and of a powerful chief executive who might assume the arbitrary authority of a king. This system has admirably prevented the legislative branch from acting rashly, while granting the President ample warmaking powers and authority for unilateral action in foreign affairs.[28]

Although the President has considerable latitude to commit the nation to war, he can implement his domestic program only with the concurrence of both Houses of Congress. Bills that become law are a compromise between the broad national interests represented by the President and the narrow geographic interests represented in Congress. There is no theoretical reason to presume that these compromises are the best outcomes a political system could produce. The U.S. system of checks and balances has produced frequent stalemates preventing either branch from implementing a coherent program.

Where an ambiguous division of authority in the United States of America produces deadlocks and frustration, in other countries the outcomes have been much worse. Max Weber wanted a strong presidency patterned after that of the United States defined in the Weimar Constitution, in the hopes of bringing political stability to post-war Germany. The Weimar Republic's collapse was arguably due to the ambiguous division of authority in its Constitution among the President, the Chancellor, and the Parliament.[29]

Latin American constitutions have also been patterned after that of the United States with strong presidencies. They typically have not included electoral rules that ensure a majority in the parliament for the president's party, however. "The combination of presidentialism and a fractionalized multi-party system seems especially inimical to stable democracy ... Chile is the only case in the world of a multi-party presidential democracy that endured for twenty-five years or more ... [Presidentialism] is inconducive to democratic stability because it easily creates difficulties in the relationship between the president and the congress."[30] Neither can deliver the programs promised during elections. The ineffectiveness of presidential government in Latin America "has been a precipitating factor in several democratic breakdowns" (e.g., Columbia in 1949, Brazil in 1964, Peru in 1968, and Chile in 1973).[31] The histories of both the Weimar Republic and Latin American presidential systems vividly illustrate the costs of not adopting a logically consistent constitutional structure.

3.3.3. Discussion

The logic supporting a multiparty system is the same as that supporting democracy itself. "The voice of the people" is to be heard, and since the citizenry cannot express their preferences directly, an assembly is formed in which all people are proportionally represented. The decisions of this assembly should reflect the preferences of all citizens. A voting rule is needed that gives all representatives a voice in the outcome. The unanimity rule is the obvious choice. A qualified majority rule compromises the goal of having all citizens influence the outcome. This compromise is smaller, the higher the majority required to pass legislation. Other rules, like voting by veto, can ensure that *all* representatives not just a half or 2/3rds of them, influence the outcomes.

Democracy has done best in Latin American countries like Costa Rica and Uruguay with "political culture[s that foster] a general striving toward compromise and consensus."[32] A voting rule cannot create a political culture, but it can foster compromise and consensus. Both a high qualified majority rule and voting by veto have this property.

If the voting rule leads to outcomes that reflect citizen preferences, then these outcomes should be implemented. Placing a second chamber or a president with veto powers between a multiparty legislature and the execution of its decisions thwarts its actions, and can induce the kind of "militant, uncompromising, confrontational" style of government that has frequently led to the breakdown of democracy in Latin America.[33]

The form of multiparty government described here differs from typical PR-systems in that the cabinet is not a part of the parliament. The cabinet-form of PR has two serious disadvantages relative to a PR-system in which the executive is separate from the legislature. First, cycling over the composition of the cabinet can lead to short-lived governments as in Italy since World War II, and the 4th Republic of France. Second, a cabinet-form of PR complicates the voter's choice and thereby distorts the information about voter preferences obtained through elections. A voter who prefers the program of Party *C* may not vote for Party *C*, because he thinks it has a small probability of joining the coalition that forms the cabinet, and thus of influencing public policies. Instead, of elections in cabinet-forms of PR conveying unambiguous information about the policy preferences of voters, these elections provide mixed signals of voters' policy preferences and their estimates of the probabilities that different parties will join the government. To avoid these disadvantages and to achieve multiparty PR's full potential, the legislative and executive branches should be separated.

The opposite is true in a two-party system. Here the voter chooses the government, i.e., the cabinet, directly. The voter knows that the winning party will form the government and can implement its program. The voter need not engage in any complicated strategic choices. He votes for the party whose program and administrative competence he prefers. Under a two-party system the majority party implements its program almost without opposition. A form of "tyranny of the majority" exists, since it faces only two real checks on its actions: (1) constitutional restrictions on the issues that can come before the parliament, and (2) the threat of defeat in the next election.

Presidentialism attempts to combine the advantage of broad diverse representation of a multiparty system with the decisiveness inherent in a strong executive. In Latin America presidentialism has produced governmental "immobilism," which in turn has frequently led to the truly strong executive authority of a dictator.

The choice of electoral system is made difficult by the fact that no one system is probably best for all countries, and the best system for a country at one point in time may not be best at some later date. For example, Russia and other post-Communist countries may have been better off adopting two-party forms of government. When Communism collapsed, many interrelated, fundamental structural reforms were needed. Had these countries chosen two-party systems, their governments would have been in a position to implement these reforms. But the post-Communist countries have followed their western European neighbors and introduced PR-systems with presidents having various degrees of authority. The result has typically been inconsistent actions by the parliaments, and clashes over policy and authority between presidents and parliaments.

Although the capacity of two-party systems to undertake bold reforms in times of crisis can be a great advantage, it also poses great dangers. If "the wrong party" wins the election, it may boldly lead the country into disaster, and the wrong party leader might even lead the country into dictatorship. In choosing to implement a two-party system these two possibilities must be carefully considered.

In contrast to the potential for bold initiatives that exists in a two-party system, with PR and a high qualified majority voting rule in the legislature bold initiatives would be possible only when they commanded broad support. One expects that a PR-system with a high qualified majority rule would engage in modest, incrementalist reforms. Such has been the case in Columbia's consensual, consociational style of government.[34]

3.4. Federalism

3.4.1. Preference Revelation in a Federalist System

A federalist structure can better match demands for local public goods and services and their supply. A strong federalist structure can also contribute to political stability by reducing interregional redistribution and rent-seeking. A strong federalism requires four elements: (1) elective representative bodies at each level of government, (2) administrative agencies at each level that are responsible to these representative bodies, (3) explicit authority for expenditures, and (4) explicit tax authority.

It is *crucial* that the constitution assign explicit authority for *both* expenditures and taxes to the different levels. The regional and local governments in the so-called federalist states of Germany and Austria do not have separate tax and expenditure authority. Consequently, their citizens exert little control over local governments, and public goods and services show little regional variation. The opposite is true in Switzerland, the only European country in which local governments have control over both their expenditures and sources of revenue.

3.4.2. The Problem of Overcentralization

Alexis de Tocqueville (1835: 165–71) thought that the United States had preserved the political liberty of a small country, despite its size, because of its federalist structure. The Founding Fathers placed language in the Constitution to constrain the federal government to specific activities. But broad interpretations by the Supreme Court have allowed a centralization of governmental activity at the federal level.[35] Many of the first Latin American constitutions were patterned after the U.S. constitution and contained strong federalist elements (e.g., Brazil's). They too have not prevented a tremendous centralization of governmental activity. The lesson to be learned from these experiences is that special effort must be made to safeguard a federalist system's integrity. We briefly discuss five constitutional provisions to secure this goal.[36]

3.4.2.1. A Constitutionally Defined Division of Authority

The constitution of the nation-state can delimit explicitly the issues that the national legislature can and cannot consider. Defense budgets are a legitimate national issue, urban police budgets are not. In addition, the constitution could define the conditions necessary to place an issue on the national legislature's agenda. Any issue that concerns citizens in *only* one lower political unit should not be decided at the national level. If only a few units are affected, they can negotiate a solution to the issue. Action at the national level is optimal only to save interjurisdictional bargaining costs, when an issue affects several lower governmental units. The constitution can provide for these cases by stipulating that only issues substantially impacting more than x regional jurisdictions can be included on the national agenda, where x might be half of the regional jurisdictions.[37]

3.4.2.2. The Choice of Voting Rule

No overcentralization problem would exist if the national legislature used the unanimity rule. The higher the majority in the national legislature required to pass an issue, the less likely overcentralization is.

3.4.2.3. The Method of Representation

Local issues are more likely to gravitate upward, if representatives are elected on a geographic basis than if they are elected at large at the national level. Under geographic representation, each district's representative to the national legislature becomes a lobbyist for projects that only benefit her district. In contrast, competition for votes across the nation forces candidates to focus on national issues.

3.4.2.4. A Second House of Parliament

Another way to protect a federalist structure is to represent regional governments directly in a second chamber. Each province could send a delegation with membership proportional to party representation in the provincial legislatures. The constitution could require either that all legislation pass in both chambers, or, more narrowly, that any legislation affecting the several provinces differentially pass both houses.

Both the Swiss Council of States and the *Bundesrat* (Germany's second house) function in this manner. In Germany, however, both the federal and regional (Länder) governments share overlapping authority in most governmental areas and the post-war period has seen a gradual shifting of power to the central government.[38] A second chamber representing regional interests might also result in the defeat of legislation that would benefit citizens across the nation. The control of representatives in Congress by state governors has sometimes had this effect in Brazil (Lopes 1996: 205). Thus, preserving federalism via a second chamber does not seem optimal.

3.4.2.5. Referenda

Swiss citizens can demand a referendum to approve legislation passed by the federal parliament. This option is one reason why the Swiss state remains smaller and more decentralized than in its European neighbors. Optional referenda are a check against all central government legislation that might harm a substantial number of citizens including that which benefits some regions, and harms others.

3.5. The Control of Government

Federalism can both facilitate the revelation of citizen preferences for public services and control the waste and efficiency of government. In this section, we describe several additional controls on government starting with those over the legislature.

3.5.1. Control over the Legislative Branch

There are three main checks on the legislature. First, the constitution can restrict the issues that can come before the legislature. If the constitution assigns elementary education to municipal governments, then the federal legislature cannot get involved in this activity.

The most effective check on the legislature is simply defeat in the next election. This check is the main constraint on government in a two-party system, but even in a multiparty system, a loss of seats is a threat to each party. The more fearful the constitutional convention is of the legislature's actions, the shorter the interval between elections should be.[39]

The third check on the legislature is the parliamentary voting rule. The higher the majority required in the legislature, the more likely it is that the legislature confines itself to actions that benefit all citizens.

3.5.2. Control over the Executive Branch

Presidentialism in Latin America has given ample evidence of the potential harm that can arise from the abuse of executive authority, and has led to a variety of institutional mechanisms for controlling the executive.[40]

3.5.2.1. Deny the President the Possibility of Being Reelected

Although democracy in the United States has never been threatened by a President's refusing to give up office, the Constitution was amended to limit a President to two terms of office following Franklin Roosevelt's unprecedented four electoral victories. Almost every Latin American country has also tried this method of controlling the president.[41] This option has three serious disadvantages: First, it makes the president a "lame duck" in perhaps his only term of office, and thereby eliminates an important incentive for him to perform his duties well—the desire to be reelected. Second, it removes the incentive even for his own party to work with him.[42] Third, it denies the country the services of a truly talented person, when such a person succeeds in becoming president. The supply of talented leadership in Latin America has not been so large that a country can toss away a truly great leader after six years or so. Accordingly, several Latin American countries have amended their constitutions in recent years—at the president's request and during his term in office—to allow him to succeed himself. Such actions, although understandable, discredit the constitution and the constitutional amendment process. Rather than turning a president out of office regardless of his performance, the constitution should include incentives and other constraints to induce him to do a good job in office, and to strive to remain in office.

3.5.2.2. A Plural Executive

Uruguay tried twice, 1919 and 1952, to contain the power of the presidency by dividing it into several offices. "This was a very interesting experiment. Unfortunately, the experiment failed ... In reaction to the plural executive, the 1967 constitution created a very strong presidency ... The Uruguayan experience with the plural executive demonstrates how strong is the desire to limit the power of the president and yet how powerful is the desire to have a strong president" (Kantor 1992: 103–04).

3.5.2.3. A Parliamentary System

In a parliamentary system, the chief executive is a member of the parliament and can be removed by it. Consequently, control over the executive is much less of a problem in a parliamentary system than in a government with a strong, separate executive. Several Latin American countries have tried replacing presidentialism with a parliamentary form of government. All have failed because of the difficulty of forming stable cabinets with many parties (Kantor 1992).

3.5.2.4. Appointment and Impeachment of Cabinet Ministers

The U.S. Constitution and many Latin American constitutions require that the legislature approve certain presidential appointments, and/or allow the legislature to remove a member of the executive branch from office. "In Latin America this has not been a real check upon the presidents because of the general weakness of the legislatures" (Kantor 1992: 105). In the United States, on the other hand, Congress has increasingly succeeded in blocking or delaying Presidential nominees for both executive and judicial branch positions. The result has been large numbers of vacant judgeships, ambassadorships, and high ranking positions in the executive branch with the concomitant inefficiency of government.

Impeachment is a crude and divisive way to try to affect politics. In Chile "the constitutional crisis that led to the [Pinochet] dictatorship came, in part, because President Allende several times broke the spirit of the constitution . . . by not removing impeached ministers . . . Similar clauses appeared in many of the constitutions adopted through the years. In all cases, however, the dominance of the presidency kept these constitutional rules from being really important limitations upon the power of the president" (Kantor 1992: 105). The divisiveness and impotence of Ecuador's politics has been enhanced by the legislature's repeated impeachment of cabinet members in an effort to exert control over the executive branch.

3.5.2.5. The Sharing of Executive Power

"The Costa Rican constitution of 1949 made a determined effort to weaken the power of the president by strengthening the legislature and the judiciary, and by requiring that executive power be exercised by a president and his ministers acting together . . . the Costa Rican president remains a strong executive with few limits upon his actions, except for the Supreme Court's power to declare his acts unconstitutional and the legislature's power to refuse him funds." In Costa Rica as in many Latin American republics, the "president . . . must have a cabinet minister counter-sign all presidential decrees and regulations, but as long as the president appoints and removes his ministers as he sees fit, this is no limitation on his power" (Kantor 1992: 106–07).

Although the president remains strong in Costa Rica, the importance of "the Supreme Court's power to declare his acts unconstitutional and the legislature's power to refuse him funds" (Kantor 1992: 106) should not be underestimated. No constitution is likely to control presidential power effectively, if it does not contain these two provisions. Costa Rica is one of Latin America's few successful democracies, and one of the few with a relatively strong and independent judiciary. Its success as a democracy is due in no small part to the checks placed on presidential power by its constitution, and the incentives it provides for consensual government.[43]

3.5.2.6. Impeachment of the President

Impeachment is the ultimate control over presidential power. In Latin America "impeachment [has not been] an easy method for removing a president from office . . . [and] generally . . . has failed to control presidents."[44]

The same might be said for the United States. During its first 175 years, only one U.S. President was brought to trial for impeachment, and the impeachment motion failed by a single vote. In the last generation one President has been threatened by impeachment, and another has been tried for it. These threatened attacks of the Legislative Branch on the Executive are symptomatic of the continual deterioration of the relationship between these two branches that has marked American politics since the Vietnam War. More such attacks can be expected. Whether the U.S. Congress's power to impeach the President proves to be a more effective means for controlling him than has been the case in Latin America is difficult to predict. What is easy to predict is that it will further advance the deadlocks and paralysis that have become characteristics of the United States's presidentialist system.

3.5.2.7. The Creation of Independent Agencies

"The independent agency has proved to be a real check upon the power of the president where constitutional government is the rule. It hampers the president in that he is not able to force the agency to follow his policy."[45]

Although independent agencies can serve as an effective check on the president, they can also be a remedy that is worse than the disease, by replacing the arbitrary abuse of power of an elected official accountable to the citizens with the arbitrary abuse of power of unelected officials accountable to no one. Indeed, Latin American presidents have often *created* independent agencies "as a means of enhancing their power and accomplishing their agendas" by circumventing congress (Mainwaring 1992: 115).

Nevertheless, independent agencies can play a limited role in avoiding some of the more egregious excesses of democratic politics. To justify the assignment of a governmental activity to an agency that is independent of democratic control, three criteria must be met: (1) The danger that the legislature or the president makes decisions regarding the activity that are harmful to the general welfare is significantly greater than for an independent agency. (2) The goals of the agency are few and well-defined. (3) It is easy to determine whether the agency has met its goals.

Two obvious choices for such independent agencies are the central bank and an authority for monitoring elections. The dangers that can arise when a president or parliament seeking reelection controls the money supply are well-known to all Latin Americans. The temptation to tamper with the election process is equally obvious and has also often been observed. The cause of liberal democracy in Costa Rica and Venezuela has been advanced by "the creation of powerful, independent agencies to administer the electoral process." The agency established in Costa Rica's 1949 constitution, the TSE, "has all but eradicated the incidence of fraud in Costa Rican elections. Costa Rica's reputation for fairness and honesty in elections is one of the highest in the world."[46]

3.5.3. A "Watchdog" Agency

A third possible activity for an independent agency is to monitor the actions of the rest of government to prevent inefficiency, corruption, and abuse of power. The General Accounting Office in the United States has uncovered numerous instances of government waste and has thereby helped to reduce it. Chile's Contraloria monitors the legality of actions of the executive branch.

3.5.4. A Free Press

Watchdog agencies accomplish much of their mission simply by publicizing governmental misdeeds. Their efforts are greatly facilitated by the existence of a press eager to expose governmental malfeasance. No constitutional right is more essential for the maintenance of a strong democracy than the right to free speech which preserves freedom of the press.

3.5.5. The Problem of Dictatorship

Latin America has had more than its share of dictators. Any new constitutional convention should reflect upon institutions that reduce the likelihood of future dictators. Subsection 2.5 listed several institutions that Latin America has tried—most unsuccessfully–to limits presidential power and avoid dictatorship. We now consider how the institutions proposed here can avoid dictatorship.

Our multiparty alternative would give the legislature authority to elect the president, and severely limits his policymaking powers. His chief responsibility would be to monitor the bureaus that implement policies enacted in the legislature to ensure that they carry out their duties honestly and efficiently. Thus, in the form of multiparty government proposed here, the president would act as agent of the legislature, and would himself play a "watchdog" role.

Some members of a multiparty legislature might possess the charismatic personalities that often are drawn toward dictatorship. Denied direct control over any of the country's bureaucracies, and in particular of the military, members of the legislature would find it difficult to convert their popularity into a platform for launching a dictatorship, however.

In a multiparty system, each party competes against all other parties for support. The potential that any one party or party leader offers a set of policies so popular as to invite an unauthorized seizure of power is unlikely.

The danger of dictatorship is perhaps greater with a two-party system. With only two dominant parties, one could come to be led by a demagogue who was tempted to try to become dictator. The most important check against this happening in a two-party system is the electorate, which must threaten any party that is led by such a person with defeat. A second effective check is in the hands of a potential dictator's own party. Its members must remove him from the party's leadership, if they perceive that he poses a danger to the party or the country. The British Conservative Party's removal of Margaret Thatcher indicates that such internal checks can be effective even against a person as powerful and charismatic as Mrs. Thatcher.

4. Conclusions

4.1. Common Features of All Constitutions

If the state is to advance the interests of all citizens, its political institutions must both *prevent* the state from doing harm, and *allow* it to do good. To achieve the first objective, the constitution must contain a clearly defined set of individual rights. These must protect not only the citizen's political freedom, but also his economic liberty. To prevent the state from encroaching upon the citizen's freedom, a strong and independent judiciary must be established and preserved.

A second important protection against abuse of state power is a federalist structure. A strong federalist structure not only prevents the state from harming its citizens, it facilitates the provision of those public services that improve their welfare.

4.2. Three Options

4.2.1. The Multiparty Option

There are two, fundamentally different options for revealing citizens' preferences on national issues. In the multiparty option, citizens across the country vote on a single set of parties or candidates. Parties are awarded seats in proportion to the number of votes that they obtain across the nation.

The logic underlying a PR-multiparty system rests on the fair representation and aggregation of all voters' preferences in the legislature. If electoral and voting rules achieve this objective, then the policies chosen by the legislature should be implemented as decided. The executive should be separated from the legislature, chosen by it, and its main assignment should be to *execute* the policies of legislature. The president becomes the *agent* of the legislature.

4.2.2. *The Two-Party Option*

Under a two-party system parties compete in an at-large election as under a PR-system, but to ensure that one party has a majority of the seats in the legislature a second, run-off election is held, if no party obtains a majority of the votes on the first ballot. The only difference between the electoral rules underlying these two systems, would be the requirement of a run-off between the two leading parties under the two-party system.

A two-party system would provide more scope for the government to act in ways which either benefit or harm the citizens. The importance of clearly defined rights, an independent judiciary, and a strong federalist system are all enhanced if the two-party option is chosen.

4.2.3. *Presidentialism*

The third option for an electoral system is to try to combine the first two—a multiparty legislature so that all citizens are fairly represented, and a popularly elected president who represents a plurality or perhaps majority of the citizens. In the ideal presidential system the legislature and the president *share* authority and the most attractive properties of multiparty and majoritarian democracy are achieved. In practice presidentialism has lead to *immobilism* and *ineffective government*, however. Immobilism can be avoided by weakening the power of the president, in particular by denying him a veto over legislative action. The weaker the president's authority is, the more a presidentialist system would resemble the PR-system described above with the president an agent of the legislature.

Ineffective government can be avoided by strengthening the powers of the president, e.g., by granting him veto powers, the authority to rule by decree, the authority to suspend parts of the constitution. Argentina's constitutions have granted its presidents such powers and have resulted in "hyperpresidentialism." "Presidentialism and especially hyperpresidentialism produce an executive branch that has enormous formal powers but that frequently lacks the consensus required to implement policy. This means immensely strong hyperpresidents—in the formal sense—are often remarkably weak in their capacity to have their policies carried out successfully. The weakness of hyperpresidents does not, however, imply strength in other democratic bodies. The case of Argentina shows that formal omnipotence in the executive branch is achieved at the expense of other democratic bodies, which are often seen as irrelevant. A formally strong, but in fact weak, hyperpresidentialism means a weak democracy *tout court*."[47] And, in Latin America, weak democracy soon gives way to no democracy.

"Some thirty-three Third World countries . . . have adopted presidentialist constitutions. Almost universally these polities have endured disruptive catastrophes, usually in the form of one or more *coups d'état* whereby conspiratorial groups of military officers seize power, suspend the constitution, displace elected officials, impose martial law, and promote authoritarian rule" (Riggs 1992: 218–19). For this reason, most students of electoral systems now agree with Dieter Nohlen (1996: 49) "that the combination of presidentialism and proportional representation is the worst of all possible scenarios." Either of the first two electoral options sketched here would be far better than the third, presidentialist option.

For much of its over 200 year history, the United States's presidentialist system succeeded in avoiding the impasses and instabilities that have characterized its southern neighbors, despite the close similarities in their political structures. But the logic of presidentialism applies equally to the United States as to any other country that adopts this system. During the last third of the 20th century, deadlocks between Congress and the President have become common. One President has been induced to resign by the threat of impeachment, a second has been brought to trial. It can only be a matter of time before Congress successfully exercises its ultimate power over a President, and removes him from office. The United States has as much to learn from Latin America's experience with presidentialism as Latin America can learn from the United States.

Acknowledgments

This article has been adapted from a background paper written for the Assembly that met during the first four months of 1998 to write a new constitution for Ecuador. The preparation of the original document was funded by the World Bank. The views expressed in this paper are mine alone, and do not necessarily reflect the position or policies of the World Bank.

Notes

1. This same approach is taken in my recent book, *Constitutional Democracy*, 1996 (hereafter referred to as *CD*).
2. See, Rae (1969), Mueller (1989: Ch. 6).
3. See Mueller (1991) or *CD*: 14.
4. Most instances but not all. Free speech is an issue that has the characteristics for which unanimity is likely to be the optimal voting rule. The publishers of pornography might be willing to vote for a ban on certain forms of pornography, however, if offered a high enough bribe by the rest of the community.
5. Gillespie and González (1989: 210); Booth (1989: 388); and McClintock (1989: 335).
6. Corsi (1984: 153, see also 117–32); and Murphy and Pritchett (1979: 122–61).
7. This can be said of Argentina (Waisman 1989: 96); Brazil (Lamounier 1989: 129, 137); Venezuela (Levine 1989: 273), and Columbia (Hartlyn 1989: 323).
8. Several U.S. states vest judicial nominations in a commission of lawyers selected by the State Bar Association. This system, often called merit selection, is in the spirit of the text's proposal. In practice, however, it has not generally succeeded in removing partisan politics from the judicial selection process (Watson and Downing 1969; Dubois 1980: 4–20; Marshall 1977).
9. Article II of the U.S. Constitution provides that the President nominate candidates for the Supreme Court. However, it further stipulates that "Congress may by Law vest the Appointment of such inferior Officers as they think proper, in the President alone, in the Courts of Law, or in the Heads of Departments." Should judges beneath the Supreme Court be deemed to be "inferior Officers," then the U.S. Constitution would allow a procedure like that described in the text at all judicial levels other than that of the Supreme Court.
10. For further discussion see, Lijphart and Grofman (1984); *CD*: Chs. 8, 10; Reynolds, Reilly and Grofman (1998).
11. This fact is becoming increasingly apparent even in the United States, where the combination of single-member-district representation and the plurality rule have been dominant at all levels of government since the founding. The goal of "fair" and "equal" representation for blacks put forward by Congress in the 1965 Voting Rights Act has proven devilishly difficult to achieve while adhering to single-member-district representation. Some success in meeting the goal was achieved through creative redrawing of district boundaries to produce black majorities, but the courts have recently turned hostile to this approach.

12. Those, who prefer slow deliberative forms of government—like the Founding Fathers of the United States—to *effective* forms capable of making bold new departures from existing policies, will of course regard gridlock as an attractive feature of the U.S. system. For these individuals the U.S. system of government can be seen as combining an attractive feature of PR-government with an unattractive and avoidable feature of existing two-party systems.
13. See Mueller (1989: Ch. 11; *CD*: Ch. 9).
14. France has not employed the plurality rule, but rather a double ballot majority system. This system would yield two dominant parties in France, if the same two parties were dominant across the different regions of the country. See, Macridis (1978: 93–174), Carstairs (1980: 178–86).
15. Lijphart (1984, 1990); *CD*: Ch. 10.
16. Because of the presence of third party candidate Ross Perot, the percentages for the winning candidate, Bill Clinton, in the last two presidential elections have looked much like those for UK parties.
17. Buchanan and Tullock (1962: 63–91).
18. Caplin and Nalebuff (1988).
19. *The Federalist*, No. 63 (1937: 409–10).
20. See, Mueller (1978, 1984); Moulin (1981a, b); *CD*: 161–64.
21. Mueller (1984).
22. Other attractive voting procedures are discussed in (*CD*: Ch. 11).
23. Gwyn (1986) lists *five* different theses justifying a separation of powers of which these are two. The other three are compatible with one or both of the two theses discussed in the text. One also encompasses a separate judiciary, which we discussed above.
24. In practice, since ministers frequently rotate they often have limited knowledge of the functions and operations of the ministry which they nominally supervise. A principal/agent problem exists between the minister and the ministry's more permanent and knowledgeable staff. The minister's goal is to carry out the program of the governing party, which may involve changes in the ministry that disadvantage its staff. The staff's goal is obviously to resist any such changes.
25. Neustadt (1960); Huntington (1968: 109–21).
26. Huntington (1968: Ch. 2).
27. This same fear originally led to the Senate's not being popularly elected.
28. See Schlesinger (1989).
29. See Eyck (1962: Ch. 3), Lepsius (1978: 47–50), Carstairs (1980: 165–66), and *CD*: 5.
30. Mainwaring (1992: 113–14).
31. Diamond and Linz (1989: 26). See also Sigmund (1990: 208–10), Valenzuela (1990: 66), Lamounier (1990: 129), and *CD*: Chs. 2, 18.
32. The quote is from Booth (1989: 403) and refers to Costa Rica. On Uruguay see Gillespie and González (1989: 227), and on Latin America in general, Diamond and Linz (1989: 14–15).
33. Diamond and Linz (1989: 14–15).
34. Hartlyn (1989: 329).
35. See Friedrich (1968: 17–24), Niskanen (1992), and Weingast (1992).
36. For a more detailed discussion see *CD*: 6.
37. By regional governments I mean states in the United States, provinces in Canada, and Länder in Germany.
38. Goldman (1973: 528–36); Smith (1989: 266–77); Wilson (1990: 282–83).
39. The fear of democracy in the United States at the end of the eighteenth century is also apparent in state constitutions that sometimes required that governors be elected biannually if not annually. James Madison, often cited as a champion of checks and balances, regarded frequent popular elections as "no doubt the primary constraint on the government" (Gwyn 1986: 71).
40. The following list is taken from Kantor (1992).

41. Harry Kantor (1992) writing in 1977 noted only two Latin American constitutions, Paraguay's and the Dominican Republic's, that allowed a President to be reelected.
42. Valenzuela (1989: 186).
43. Ameringer (1982), Booth (1989), and Seligson (1990).
44. Kantor (1992: 107).
45. Independent agencies were particularly popular in Ecuador during the 1950s, when they accounted for between 34 and 44 percent of the national budget (Kantor 1992: 108).
46. Peeler (1985: 113), as cited in Booth (1989: 395–98).
47. Nino (1996: 169).

References

Ameringer, C. D. (1982) *Democracy in Costa Rica*. New York: Praeger.

Booth, J. A. (1989) "Costa Rica: The Roots of Democratic Stability." In: Diamond, L., Linz, J. J., and Lipset, S. M. (eds.) *Democracy in Developing Countries: Latin America*, pp. 387–422. Boulder: Lynne Rienner.

Buchanan, J. M., and Tullock, G. (1962) *The Calculus of Consent*. Ann Arbor: The University of Michigan Press.

Caplin, A., and Nalebuff, B. (1988) "On 64%-Majority Rule." *Econometrica* 56: 787–814.

Carstairs, A. M. (1980) *A Short History of Electoral Systems in Western Europe*. London: Allen & Unwin.

Corsi, J. L. (1984) *Judicial Politics*. Englewood Cliffs, N.J.: Prentice-Hall.

Corwin, E. S. [1981 (1906)] "The Supreme Court and Unconstitutional Acts of Congress." *Michigan Law Review* 4: 616–30; reprinted in Loss, R. (ed.) *Corwin on the Constitution*, Vol. II, pp. 27–40. Ithaca, N.Y.: Cornell University Press.

de Tocqueville, A. [1945 (1835)] *Democracy in America*, Vol. 1. New York: Vintage Books.

Diamond, L., and Linz, J. J. (1989) "Introduction: Politics, Society, and Democracy in Latin America." In: Diamond, L., Linz, J. J., and Lipset, S. M. (eds.) *Democracy in Developing Countries: Latin America*, pp. 1–58. Boulder: Lynne Rienner.

Diamond, L., Linz, J. J., and Lipset, S. M. (eds.). (1989) *Democracy in Developing Countries: Latin America*. Boulder: Lynne Rienner.

Dubois, P. L. (1980) *From Ballot to Bench*. Austin: University of Texas Press.

Eyck, E. (1962) *A History of the Weimar Republic*, Vol. 1. Cambridge: Harvard University Press.

Eyck, E. (1963) *A History of the Weimar Republic*, Vol. 2. Cambridge: Harvard University Press.

Friedrich, C. J. (1968) *Trends of Federation in Theory and Practice*. New York: Prager.

Gillespie, C. G., and González, L. E. (1989) "Uruguay: The Survival of Old and Autonomous Institutions." In: Diamond, L., Linz, J. J., and Lipset, S. M. (eds.) *Democracy in Developing Countries: Latin America*, pp. 207–45. Boulder: Lynne Rienner.

Goldman, G. (1973) "The German Political System." In: Beer, S. H., et al. (eds.) *Patterns of Government*, 3rd ed., pp. 473–589. New York: Random House.

Gwyn, W. B. (1986) "The Separation of Powers and Modern Forms of Democratic Government." In: Goldwin, R. A., and Kaufman, A. (eds.) *Separation of Powers—Does it still Work?*, pp. 65–89. Washington, D.C.: American Enterprise Institute.

Hartlyn, J. (1989) "Columbia: The Politics of Violence and Accomodation." In Diamond, L., Linz, J. J., and Lipset, S. M. (eds.) *Democracy in Developing Countries: Latin America*, pp. 291–334. Boulder: Lynne Rienner.

Huntington, S. P. (1968) *Political Order in Changing Societies*. New Haven: Yale University Press.

Kantor, H. (1992) "Efforts Made by Latin American Countries to Limit the Power of the President." In: Lijphart, A. (ed.) *Parliamentary versus Presidential Government*, pp. 101–10. Oxford: Oxford University Press.

Lamounier, B. (1989) "Brazil: Inequality Against Democracy." In: Diamond, L., Linz, J. J., and Lipset, S. M. (eds.) *Democracy in Developing Countries: Latin America*, pp. 111–57. Boulder: Lynne Rienner.

Lamounier, B. (1989) "Brazil: Inequality Against Democracy." In: Diamond, L., Linz, J. J., and Lipset, S. M. (eds.) *Politics in Developing Countries*, pp. 87–134. Boulder, Colo.: L. Rienner.

Lepsius, M. R. (1978) "From Fragmented Party Democracy to Government by Emergency Decree and National Socialist Takeover: Germany." In: Linz, J. L., and Stephan, A. (eds.) *The Breakdown of Democratic Regimes*, part II, pp. 34–79. Baltimore: Johns Hopkins University Press.

Levine, D. H. (1989) "Venezuela: The Nature, Sources, and Future Prospects of Democracy." In: Diamond, L., Linz, J. J., and Lipset, S. M. (eds.) *Democracy in Developing Countries: Latin America*, pp. 247–89. Boulder: Lynne Rienner.

Lijphart, A. (1984) *Democracies*. New Haven: Yale University Press.

Lijphart, A. (1980) "The Political Consequences of Electoral Laws, 1945–85." *American Political Science Review* 84: 481–96.

Lijphart, A., and Grofman, B. (eds.). (1984) *Choosing an Electoral System: Issues and Alternatives*. New York: Praeger.

Lijphart, A., and Waisman, C. H. (eds.). (1996) *Institutional Design in New Democracies: Eastern Europe and Latin America*. Boulder: Westview Press.

Lopes, J. B. (1996) "Obstacles to Economic Reform in Brazil." In: Lijphart, A., and Waisman, C. H. (eds.) *Institutional Design in New Democracies: Eastern Europe and Latin America*, pp. 195–218. Boulder: Westview Press.

Macridis, R. C. (1978) "Politics of France." In: Macridis, R. C. (ed.) *Modern Political Systems: Europe*, 4th ed., pp. 93–174. Englewood Cliffs, N.J.: Prentice Hall.

Mainwaring, S. (1992) "Presidentialism in Latin America." In: Lijphart, A. (ed.) *Parliamentary versus Presidential Government*, pp. 111–17. Oxford: Oxford University Press.

Marshall, T. (1979) "Mr. Justice Marshall Comments on the Missouri Plan." Remarks by Justice Marshall before American College of Trial Lawyers, Coronado, California, March 14, 1977. In: Murphy, W., and Pritchett, C. H. (eds.) *Courts, Judges, and Politics*, 3rd ed., pp. 155–59. New York: Random House.

McClintock, C. (1989) "Peru: Regimes, Authoritarian and Democratic." In: Diamond, L., Linz, J. J., and Lipset, S. M. (eds.) *Democracy in Developing Countries: Latin America*, pp. 335–85. Boulder: Lynne Rienner.

Moulin, H. (1981a) "The Proportional Veto Principle." *Review of Economic Studies* 48: 407–16.

Moulin, H. (1981b) "Prudence versus Sophistication in Voting Strategy." *Journal of Economic Theory* 24: 398–412.

Mueller, D. C. (1978) "Voting by Veto." *Journal of Public Economics* 10: 57–75.

Mueller, D. C. (1984) "Voting by Veto and Majority Rule." In: Hanusch, H. (ed.) *Public Finance and the Quest for Efficiency*, pp. 69–86. Detroit: Wayne State University Press.

Mueller, D. C. (1989) *Public Choice II*. Cambridge: Cambridge University Press.

Mueller, D. C. (1991) "Constitutional Rights." *Journal of Law, Economics, and Organization* 7: 313–33.

Mueller, D. C. (1996) *Constitutional Democracy*. New York and Oxford: Oxford University Press.

Murphy, W. E., and Pritchett, C. H. (eds.). (1979) *Courts, Judges, and Politics*, 3rd ed. New York: Random House.

Neustadt, R. E. (1960) *Presidential Power: The Politics of Leadership*. New York: Wiley.

Nino, C. S. (1996) "Hyperpresidentialism and Constitutional Reform in Argentina." In: Lijphart, A., and Waisman, C. H. (eds.) *Institutional Design in New Democracies: Eastern Europe and Latin America*, pp. 161–74. Boulder: Westview Press.

Niskanen, W. A. (1992) "The Case for a New Fiscal Constitution." *Journal of Economic Perspectives* 6: 13–24.

Nohlen, D. (1996) "Electoral Systems and Electoral Reform in Latin America." In: Lijphart, A., and Waisman, C. H. (eds.) *Institutional Design in New Democracies: Eastern Europe and Latin America*, pp. 43–57. Boulder: Westview Press.

Peeler, J. A. (1985) *Latin American Democracies: Columbia, Costa Rica, Venezuela*. Chapel Hill: University of North Carolina Press.

Rae, D. W. (1969) "Decision-Rules and Individual Values in Constitutional Choice." *American Political Science Review* 63: 40–56.

Reynolds, A., Reilly, B., and Grofman, B. (1998) "The World of Electoral Systems." In: Rush, M. (ed.) *Voting Rights and Redistricting in the United States: An Encyclopedic Guide*. New York: Greenwood.

Riggs, F. W. (1992) "Presidentialism: A Problematic Regime Type." In: Lijphart A. (ed.) *Parliamentary versus Presidential Government*, pp. 217–22. Oxford: Oxford University Press.

Schlesinger, A. M. Jr. (1989) *The Imperial Presidency*. Boston: Houghton Mifflin.

Seligson, M. A. (1990) "Costa Rica." In: Wiarda, H. J., and Kline, H. F. (eds.) *Latin American Politics and Development*, 3rd ed., pp. 455–66. Boulder: Westview Press.

Sigmund, P. W. (1990) "Chile." In: Wiarda, H. J., and Kline, H. F. (eds.) *Latin American Politics and Development*, 3rd ed., pp. 201–30. Boulder: Westview Press.

Smith, G. (1989) *Politics in Western Europe*, 5th ed. New York: Holmes & Meier.

Sundquist, J. L. (1986) *Constitutional Reform and Effective Government.* Washington, D.C.: Brookings Institution.

The Federalist (1937) Indianapolis: Modern Library No. 63: 409–10.

Valenzuela, A. (1989) "Chile: Origins, Consolidation, and Breakdown of a Democratic Regime." In: Diamond, L., Linz, J. J., and Lipset, S. M. (eds.) *Democracy in Developing Countries: Latin America*, pp. 159–206. Boulder: Lynne Rienner.

Valenzuela, A. (1990) "Chile: Origins, Consolidation, and Breakdown of a Democratic Regime." In: Diamond, L., Linz, J. J., and Lipset, S. M. (eds.) *Politics in Developing Countries*, pp. 39–86. Boulder, Colo.: L. Rienner.

Waisman, C. H. (1989) "Argentina: Autarkic Industrialization and Illegitimacy." In: Diamond, L., Linz, J. J., and Lipset, S. M. (eds.) *Democracy in Developing Countries: Latin America*, pp. 59–109. Boulder: Lynne Rienner.

Watson, R. A., and Downing, R. C. (1969) *The Politics of the Bench and the Bar.* New York: John Wiley & Sons.

Weingast, B. R. (1992) "Federalism and the Political Commitment to Sustain Markets." Mimeo. Stanford, CA: Hoover Institute.

Wilson, F. L. (1990) *European Politics Today.* Englewood Cliffs, N.J.: Prentice-Hall.

Constitutional Political Economy, 9, 171–186 (1998)

Constitutional Constraints on Governments in a Global Economy

DENNIS C. MUELLER mueller@econ.bwl.univie.ac.at
Department of Economics, University of Vienna, BWZ - Bruenner Str. 72, A-1210 Vienna

Abstract. The continuing integration of Europe, the increasing mobility of its citizens and enterprises, and the globalization of the world economy place increasing pressure on Europe's redistributive regulations, taxes, and subsidies. The most attractive response for many European governments is to reduce the options of its citizens through tax and regulation harmonization, thereby avoiding the politically costly steps of taking away the subsidies and privileges to which the politically most powerful groups are accustomed. The danger Europe faces by responding to the pressure from globalization by tax harmonization, however, is that it preserves the resulting inefficiencies, and becomes increasingly unattractive for businesses to locate, people to work, and eventually for people to live.

This paper examines the cases for a redistributive state and an allocative (efficiency) state from the perspective of constitutional political economy. A constitutional democracy is described in which the state engages in those sorts of redistribution that all people favor, and provides only those goods, services and regulations that make all citizens better off.

JEL classification: H11, H20, D70.

1. Introduction

The tax and expenditure patterns in Europe, (e.g., in Austria, France, and Germany), and the rhetoric that surrounds debate about reform, often reflects a 19th century or at best 1930s conception of market economies. The struggle is between capital and labor over the distribution of the national pie. There is much talk of solidarity, whereby solidarity among members of factor groups is meant—workers, farmers, teachers, shopkeepers, and so on. This solidarity often takes the form of cartel activity with its usual adverse effects on allocative efficiency and consumer welfare. Current debates about economic reform in Europe raise, directly or indirectly, questions of possible trade-offs between redistributive goals and allocative efficiency, and more fundamentally questions concerning optimal constitutional structures.

In this paper I examine the cases for a redistributive state and an allocative (efficiency) state from the perspective of constitutional political economy. A constitutional democracy is assumed in which citizens first, *unanimously* select their political institutions, and then make their allocative and redistributive choices using these institutions. Section 2 discusses the kinds of institutions for redistribution citizens might place in a constitution, or agree to using the political institutions defined in the constitution. Section 3 discusses the kinds of institutions that are best suited for achieving allocative efficiency.

An important consideration in choosing optimal political institutions is the degree of mobility of goods, capital, labor, consumers and citizens. Section 4 describes the nature of the constitutional choices in an immobile world, in Section 5 the impact of mobility on these choices is examined. Mobility will be seen to place important constraints upon both the tax and expenditure options facing a community, and upon its choice of political institutions. In Sections 6 and 7 the implications of this analysis are drawn for allocative efficiency and redistribution choices in the European Union. I shall argue that a fundamental rethinking and redesign of European democratic and fiscal institutions is needed to cope with the consequences of the increasingly mobile and globalized European and world economies.

2. Redistribution in a Constitutional Democracy

It has become customary within the public choice literature since the publication of Buchanan and Tullock's (1962) classic book to imagine the constitution that defines the democratic institutions of the polity as being unanimously agreed to by all of the citizens at the time of the polity's inception. Although a poor description of how many constitutions are actually written, the assumption of unanimity at the constitutional stage has at least two important conceptual advantages. (1) It provides a normative underpinning to the constitution in that the assumption of unanimity combined with that of individual rationality implies that the institutions of the constitution must be expected to advance the interests of *all* citizens. The basic institutions of the polity are not designed to allow one group of individuals to exploit another. (2) The unanimity assumption has the further advantage of solving "the infinite regress problem" of what voting rule we use to choose a voting rule. All democratic institutions, including the voting rule to be used to make subsequent collective choices, are chosen unanimously.[1]

But if people have different and conflicting interests, how can we be sure that they unanimously agree on a set of institutions that advances their collective interests? Buchanan and Tullock's (1962:3–10) answer to this question is to assume that individuals at the constitutional stage are sufficiently uncertain about their future positions and preferences in the post-constitutional stage that they can unanimously agree upon a set of institutions to fulfill these preferences. This assumption about uncertainty over future position can be used to achieve unanimous agreement over redistribution at the constitutional stage.

2.1. Redistribution as Insurance

Abba Lerner (1944:23–40) was, I believe, the first to defend redistribution by assuming uncertainty over future position. Assume that there are two individuals i and j, with incomes, Y_i and Y_j. If their utilities depend solely on their incomes, and they have diminishing marginal utilities with respect to income, then the distribution of income that maximizes the expected utility of someone who is uncertain about whether she will be i or j must equate the marginal utilities of income for these two individuals.[2] If we assume that the utility functions of i and j are identical, then the distribution of income between the two individuals must be equal.

A decade later John Harsanyi (1953, 1955) presented a similar analysis. Individuals were assumed to make certain choices, like conceivably over the distribution of income, using their *ethical* preferences. The use of these preferences required that one assume that one had an equal probability of having the normal preferences and being in the same position as every other individual in the society. Although Harsanyi did not restrict individual utility functions to depending only on income, if one imposed such a restriction, his reasoning would take one to the same place as Lerner reached.

Nearly two decades later John Rawls (1971) presented a much more elaborate normative argument built on the assumption of uncertainty over future positions to justify a distributional principle that was likely to yield substantial if not egalitarian redistribution. Each of these is an essentially normative argument for redistribution devoid of any political analysis of how the favored degree of redistribution would come about. A related, but more politically oriented analysis was offered by Buchanan and Tullock.

They assumed uncertainty of future position at the constitutional stage of the collective decision process as a result of the *long-run* nature of the choices made at this stage. Although much of the analysis in *The Calculus of Consent* can be viewed as normative, the assumption of uncertainty due to the time dimension of constitutional choices is not totally unrealistic. If then we assume that the redistributional choices of a community are made at the constitutional stage, and are incorporated into the constitution, then the community's redistributional policies will have an insurance-like character, and will have some of the normative properties claimed by Harsanyi and Rawls.[3]

Lerner, Harsanyi, Rawls, and Buchanan and Tullock all describe conditions under which individuals could *unanimously* agree on insurance-like redistribution programs. There are several characteristics of such redistribution to note. First, the importance of uncertainty over future position in the explanation for this type of redistribution suggests that the programs that bring it about will either be literally part of the constitution or quasi-constitutional programs which enjoy widespread political support and change only slowly. Second, redistribution will go from the well-off to the less well-off, or from the recently unchanged or better-off to the recently worse-off. Third, the insurance-nature of the programs implies that they are actuarially sound. Money is transferred from one group of people in the program to another group within the program, and thus there is no scope for running deficits.

2.2. *Redistribution as Altruism*

A second explanation for redistribution that does not depend on the existence of uncertainty over future position sees redistribution motivated out of altruism. The person from whom the redistribution occurs is not and was not uncertain about being the recipient, but transfers money because she gets utility from the transfer. This form of redistribution can be modeled by either assuming that the recipient's *income* is in the giver's utility function, or assuming that the recipient's *utility* is in the giver's utility function and the recipient's utility is a function of his income level (Hochman and Rodgers 1969). Of course, individuals can in general achieve the utility gains from altruistic giving by giving money directly to the individuals whom they want to see made better off, or by contributing through a charity. More than just altruism is needed to rationalize governmental redistribution as the optimal way to achieve the gains from altruistic redistribution. The usual argument made here is the familiar free-rider problem with public goods. The giver does not want to see just one poor person better off, but all poor people. He is willing to contribute if all other similarly situated individuals contribute the same amount, but she is not willing to contribute by herself (Thurow 1971).

There are several implications that follow from this Pareto-optimal rationale for redistribution. First, although the recipients are of course made better off from the redistribution, this outcome is somewhat incidental to the reason for the government's undertaking it. As a governmental program it is driven by the need to make the givers better off and avoid the free-rider problem. Logically, the collective choice as to how much to transfer and to whom should be made exclusively by the givers. If as a practical matter the recipients are allowed to vote on the amount of redistribution, their vote should not be decisive. A redistribution proposal should be capable of winning unanimous support.

Second, redistribution should be exclusively to the lowest level or levels of the income distribution. A donor gets greater utility from giving a mark to j than to k, if $Y_j < Y_k$ (von Furstenberg and Mueller 1971). No funds should be transferred to k until $Y_j = Y_k$.[4] If k is the person with the highest initial income to receive funds, then *all* people with initial incomes below his have had their incomes raised to equal his, *no one* with an income higher than k's income receives a transfer, and *all persons* with incomes higher than k's contribute to the transfers going to those in the bottom income group(s).

3. The Allocatively Efficient State

The standard *normative economic* argument for government sees government as the provider of public goods, corrector of externalities, and facilitator of cooperation in prisoners' dilemmas.[5] The normative case for government sees it as providing those goods and services that can make all citizens better off, and the market for some reason does not provide in sufficient quantities. Since all individuals can be made better off from the provision of the public good or service, once again as with the two types of redistribution discussed above, the unanimity rule is the obvious choice for a collective decision rule to decide which of these goods to provide, in what quantities, and how to pay for them (Wicksell 1896).

Following the now classic discussion of Buchanan and Tullock (1962:63–91) it has been customary to argue that the constitution framers would not be likely to demand full unanimity for the voting rule to be used to make collective decisions in the post-constitutional stage owing to the potentially large decisionmaking costs this rule entails. Some, unspecified majority of less than unanimity must be optimal. Recent work by Andrew Caplin and Barry Nalebuff (1988) has sharpened the predictions as to what this majority is likely to be, however. They show that when the preferences of voters for publicly provided goods are like those one would expect to observe for pure Samuelsonian public goods, and the distribution of voters is single peaked in whatever number of dimensions that exist in public goods space, then the probability of a voting cycle falls as the required majority to pass an issue rises, reaching zero at a required majority of roughly 64 percent. Since voting cycles can be expected to contribute heavily to raising decisionmaking costs, these costs can be expected to fall as one increases the required majority above the simple majority. The optimal majority, *when voting is restricted to pure public good and similar allocative efficiency issues*, is likely to be substantially above a simple majority although below unanimity.

Optimal taxation in a voluntarily redistributive state follows the principles of taxation traditionally labeled as the "ability-to-pay approach" to taxation. Income and wealth are the obvious targets of taxation within the voluntarily redistributive state, with money going from rich to poor, from better off to worse off. In contrast optimal taxation in an allocatively efficient state should follow the principles of taxation traditionally labeled as the "benefit approach" to taxation.[6] For some public goods, benefits may correlate well with individual income or wealth, but for many it will not. Those who drive should be charged for the highways. Automobile owners may on average have higher incomes than the rest of the population, but some wealthy individuals may not own cars. Under the benefit approach it would be only those who drive on the highways who would pay for them. User taxes are the natural sources of revenue to finance highways, bridges, parks, and many other public goods for which these sorts of taxes are feasible.

Many public goods have a geographic dimension. An urban police force protects only those inside the city. The city's parks are frequented mostly by the city's residents. The beneficiaries of these sorts of public goods can be identified geographically. Applying the benefit approach to finance these sorts of public goods leads logically to a federalist structure of government, with local and regional governments responsible for both the determination of the quantities of public goods supplied and the taxes to pay for them. For those public goods for which the benefits are proportional to income and wealth, taxes on property are an attractive source of tax revenue, since property values correlate with income and wealth, are easily assessed, and unambiguously identify the beneficiaries of locally supplied public goods.

4. Redistribution and Allocative Efficiency in an Immobile World

The preceding two sections outline the kinds of redistribution, public goods and services, and forms of taxation one might expect to find in a polity in which the citizens themselves first draft the constitution, and then democratically make collective choices within it. If all citizens participate in the constitution-drafting process, and all agree on the outcome of that process, then this constitution can be expected to advance the interests of all citizens. Any redistribution that occurs through the constitution or the institutions it defines will benefit all citizens in at least an ex-ante sense, if not ex post. Publicly provided goods and services and the taxes that finance them will also be selected so as to advance the interests of all or nearly all citizens.

The ideal voting rule for achieving these ends at both the constitutional stage and for all post-constitutional decisions is the unanimity rule, or some "near" unanimity rule. No nation-state employs the unanimity rule for making its day-to- day collective choices. Almost all use the simple majority rule.

If all citizens can benefit from the provision of a particular public good, then so too can half of all citizens. Thus, any redistribution and public goods and services that we would find in a community that would use the unanimity rule, we should find provided under the simple majority rule. Under the simple majority rule, however, a proposal can win if it benefits only half of the community. Thus, to the list of proposals that benefit all members of the community are added proposals that benefit only a majority of the community. These can take the form of targeted public and private goods and services that only some members of the community consume (e.g., free university educations, publicly subsidized housing), of public goods and services that all members of the community consume but are financed with taxes that leave only a majority as net benefitters and, most simply of all, as zero-sum redistributions from a minority to the majority, which very often is a coalition of minorities.

The costs of voting, rational ignorance and the like make some groups more influential in the political process than others (Downs 1957: Chs. 11–13; Olson 1965). The more inelastic the supply of a particular factor group is, the greater the sensitivity of its income to shifts in the demand for its services. Thus, we can expect farmers, doctors, lawyers and the like to exert more effort and resources to protecting the demand for their services than say unskilled laborers who supply their services on local spot markets. Today's citizen has more political influence than tomorrow's. Thus, we expect retirement programs to be biased in favor of the current generation of retirees, governmental regulations over rental properties to benefit current occupants over future entrants into the market, and so on. Under the simple majority rule many governmental programs benefit some politically influential groups at the expense of others.

Public choice makes two quite different predictions with respect to the outcomes under majority rule. A now vast literature predicts the absence of an equilibrium.[7] Each winning package of issues is vulnerable to defeat by a newly proposed package. Each winning coalition can be defeated by a new coalition that adds one new group to replace another. If this prediction accurately characterized real world politics, we would expect to see considerable instability in the identities of the beneficiaries of government programs. This year the dairy farmers win huge subsidies, next year they lose them and renters enjoy a freeze on their rents. Such instability is not observed, however. Although the identities of the winners and the relative sizes of their winnings changes somewhat over time under majority rule, the relative strengths of the different interest groups appears to be such as to produce considerable stability in observed outcomes. Once price supports for milk and controls on rents are installed, they remain in place for decades. Real world outcomes under majority rule suggest the existence of the kind of stable majority coalition that has come to be called *the tyranny of the majority*. The biggest item in the European Union's budget is today, as it has always been, its redistributive agricultural program.

In an immobile world, the scope for involuntary redistribution is limited only by the elasticities of the targets' supply and demand schedules. The capitalist avoids a tax on capital only by ceasing to invest it, the successful opera singer avoids a highly progressive income tax only by ceasing to sing, the smoker avoids the tax on cigarettes only by giving up smoking. The higher the taxes imposed on a particular group, the more it suffers and the greater the incentive it has to organize, to join with other groups, and to try and overturn the tax. Thus, we expect the permanent targets of involuntary redistributive taxes[8] to be those who find it most difficult to organize—like consumers, and those standing lowest in the public's esteem and sympathy—capitalists, apartment building owners, upper income groups, gamblers, drinkers, and smokers. In an immobile world *voice* is the only option individuals have to express their unhappiness, and we expect redistributive taxes to fall most heavily upon the politically weak and unorganized.[9]

5. Redistribution and Allocative Efficiency in a Mobile World

In a mobile world individuals can use the *exit* option to express their unhappiness. The capitalist invests outside of the community, the opera singer takes up residence and records outside of the country, the smoker fills up the trunk of her car when traveling in countries where cigarettes are lightly taxed, or buys them from the smuggler who sells them around the corner from where she lives. Just as diners are unlikely to frequent a restaurant that continually overcharges them, if they have other options, a citizen who is overtaxed for the goods and services she receives seeks to avoid these taxes. In an increasingly mobile world, the scope for avoiding redistributive taxes expands, a majority's ability to impose such taxes upon minorities contracts.

Thus, as consumers and factor owners become increasingly mobile we can expect the scope for involuntary redistribution to decline. As smokers move to communities in which smoking is not taxed, and opera singers take up residence in communities in which the benefits they receive from governmentally provided goods and services are equal to the taxes they pay, communities are forced to rely on benefit taxation and to limit activities to those public goods and services that benefit all members of the community.[10] In the limit, mobility acts like a silent unanimity rule and produces the same outcomes as we would expect under this voting rule in an immobile world.

It should be noted that this result does *not* imply that there will be *no* redistribution in a mobile world, but rather that there will be no *involuntary* redistribution. A governmentally run unemployment compensation program can remain attractive to all workers so long as they perceive that they stand a chance of being unemployed. All may well choose to continue to contribute to it. What changes in a mobile world is the ability of workers to get *capital* owners, or opera singers, or smokers to cover the costs of their unemployment insurance, or to make other direct transfers to themselves.

Nor will redistribution based on altruism disappear. If the better-off members of the community get utility from redistribution programs that help the needier members of their community, then they will not try and exit the community to avoid the taxes that pay for this redistribution, for by doing so they remove themselves from both the benefits and the costs of the program. If the wealthier members of the community get benefits from police and fire protection, we can expect them to be willing to pay for these benefits. It would certainly be irrational for them to move to communities that do not provide police and fire protection just to avoid the taxes that finance these public services. It would be similarly irrational to move away from redistribution programs that provide them benefits in excess of the taxes they pay. In a mobile world, the redistributional programs that disappear are the ones that only benefit the recipients.

Thus, in a mobile world we can expect to see more revenue raised through user taxes, and greater emphasis on taxing that which remains immobile like property. More generally, there will be a greater concern to ensure that the benefits the citizen obtains from the government exceed the taxes she pays to it.

6. Allocative Efficiency in the European Union

The rhetoric with which European fiscal institutions are discussed is filled with references to social justice and social solidarity, and the discussions of reform reflect an almost exclusive concern with distributional issues. The view of the economic world underlying these discussions seems to be one in which capital, labor, and citizens are immobile, and the key question is how the fiscal burdens of the state *ought* to be shared. The traditional answers to this question—tax capital, the wealthy, those who are working, and the sinners who smoke, drink alcohol, gamble, etc.—are coming under continued stress as these targets of taxation are more and more able to avoid being taxed. Capital moves to countries where it is taxed only for the benefits government provides, workers move into the black market, or into the generous benefits provided to the unemployed, the retired, and so on. Federalist fiscal structures do not exist in most European countries, and where they do, as in Germany and Austria, they fail to achieve their potential, because the lower levels of government do not have the authority to raise their own taxes. Heavy reliance is placed on taxing that which is mobile, like capital, that which is immobile—property—goes lightly taxed or is even subsidized. That most countries seem to have difficulty matching expenditures to revenues is unsurprising.

The obvious solution to this problem is to shift to benefit taxes. This was the proposal that Knut Wicksell (1896) made just over one hundred years ago. He called his proposal "A New Principle of *Just* Taxation" (emphasis added). Wicksell's use of the word *just* is interesting in this regard. Wicksell thought that the only form of taxation that could be called "just" was one in which citizens received benefits for their tax payments that are at least as great as their costs. This notion of justice agrees with our common sense notions of justice in every realm of activity outside of government. When we eat in a restaurant we expect to pay the same price for the same quality and quantity of food as the person at the next table. We demand "equal pay for equal work" regardless of sex, religion, race, etc. Why should we not expect equal treatment from the government, in the sense that all citizens are taxed for goods that they wish to receive and in proportion to those benefits? As noted above, and in the following section, this principle does not imply that there *should* or *will* be no redistribution. It merely limits and defines the scope of such redistribution.

7. Redistribution in the European Union

We discussed two forms of *voluntary* redistribution that can in principle achieve unanimous support. One requires uncertainty over future positions on the part of all citizens, and seems best handled as a sort of constitutional right to certain insurance like protection from the state (Mueller 1996: Ch. 16). Given the importance of uncertainty over future position, this form of redistribution raises an intriguing question in the context of the European Union. At what level of aggregation would a European assume that she might trade places with another European? Would a Venetian assume because of true uncertainty or as an ethical act that she or her grandchildren might trade places with a German or a Swede? Would she limit her uncertainty horizon to Italy, to Northern Italy? These are impossible questions to answer in the abstract. The proper way to answer them is, of course, to ask the citizens.

If this form of redistribution is to replace existing involuntary redistributional structures, then the proper modus for answering these questions would be a constitutional convention in which citizens were present or properly represented.

Up to the present time the "constitution" of the European Union has been written in the form of treaties drafted by representatives of existing member-states. Paragraph 10 of the Social Charter states that:

> Every worker of the European Community shall have a right to adequate social protection and shall, whatever his status and whatever the size of the undertaking in which he is employed, enjoy an adequate level of social security benefits. Persons who have been unable to enter or re-enter the labour market and have no means of subsistence must be able to receive sufficient resources and social assistance in keeping with their particular situation.[11]

In keeping with the spirit of "worker solidarity" that underlies so many discussions of distributional questions in Europe, the focal point of social protection in the Social Charter is the European *worker* not the European *citizen*.[12] As with all "constitutional" developments in the European Union, citizen (and worker) participation in the drafting of this part of the Social Charter was minimal, to say the most. Since the Charter contains no specific language as to how the nobel intentions contained in the paragraph are to be achieved, it remains an empty statement of sentiments of the representatives of member-countries who drafted the Maastricht Treaty.

A more direct way to represent citizen preferences with respect to this sort of distributional issue would be through the European Parliament. One could convene the European Parliament as a constitutional convention and charge it with drafting a constitution that included insurance-like provisions that would cover all of Europe. To ensure that the parliament did not simply introduce yet another involuntary redistribution program, it should be required to employ some rather large qualified majority to implement any proposal. A further check would be to require that the proposal be ratified by a referendum in all member-countries. Yet a third option would be to have Europeans elect delegates to a special constitutional convention to deliberate this and perhaps other constitutional issues facing Europe (Mueller 1996: Ch. 21; 1997).

It is of course possible that such a procedure would produce no European-wide insurance scheme, or one which many Europeans would consider inadequate. If so, then the citizens of individual member-countries, or perhaps still more decentralized levels of government could introduce their own forms of social insurance to supplement that provided at the European level. If such programs were approved by the citizens of a given country, and were included in the constitution of that country, access to the program as well as obligations to pay into the program could and logically would be restricted to citizens of the country in question. If the citizens of Italy agree to implement a social insurance system, because they can or do imagine that they might be in the position of other Italians, then the program should be restricted to those persons whom Italians think of as Italians.

The second form of voluntary redistribution that we discussed takes the form of altruism. No uncertainty over future positions exists, one group votes to redistribute some of their income to another because they get satisfaction from doing so. Such redistribution might obviously arise at any level of government. The nature of the gains to the contributors and the voluntary nature of the redistribution imply that the contributors should be free to define the size of the redistribution and the identities of the recipients in any way that they choose.

8. The Alternative of Tax Harmonization

The increasing mobility that comes with rising personal incomes, economic integration, and globalization constrain a community's ability to engage in certain forms of involuntary redistribution. I have suggested that the response of governments to this development should be to shift from their heavy reliance on forms of involuntary redistributive taxes to benefit taxes from which citizens cannot or do not wish to run away. An alternative approach would be to attempt to reduce factor owner and consumer mobility and thereby defend the present forms of taxes. Such an approach usually comes under the heading of *tax harmonization*.

Consider first the case of commodity taxation. Country *A* has a lower VAT rate or lower excise tax on tobacco than *B*, and this leads consumers from *B* to do some of their shopping in *A*. Such cross-border shopping can have three effects leading to demands for tax harmonization: (1) It leads to wasteful increases in "transaction costs" as consumers waste time and money to travel across borders in the search of lower prices. (2) It redistributes tax revenue from the high to the low tax country. (3) It "may cause inefficiently low tax rates as countries engage in commodity tax competition" (Genser and Haufler 1996:61f.). When we think about the *private* sectors of countries engaging in competition, we usually think that the end result is *greater* efficiency. Why should we expect competition between governments to produce inefficiency, while competition between private sector agents produces efficiency?

Let us consider first the private sector analogue. Wages and property values are much higher in *B* than in *A*. Some individuals in *B* when contemplating whether to vacation in their own country or in *A* choose to go to *A* as the hotel and restaurant prices are lower there due to the lower wages and property values. One can object to this outcome on the grounds that the tourists from *B* needlessly incur wasteful transaction costs when traveling to *A*, that the outcome redistributes tourism revenues from *B* to *A*, and that it will encourage inefficiently low wages in both *B* and *A*. The latter argument would run as follows. To win tourists from *B* businesses in *A* know that they have to charge lower prices than in *B*. To do so, they cut back on their purchases of food and clothing for their children, move into tiny and overcrowded apartments, and so on. These tactics cause those in the tourist industry in *B* to cut prices and therefore wages. The families of people in the tourist industry in *B* now begin to suffer. The tourist industry in *A* makes further price cuts, and a "race to the bottom" in prices, wages and living standards ensues. The only way to avoid this catastrophe is to harmonize hotel, restaurant, and other prices in the two countries, and thereby discourage the wasteful journeys by *B*'s tourists into *A*.

When so stated the argument against intercountry competition takes on a rather obvious protectionist guise. A main purpose of creating the EU and of its competition policy, however, has been to destroy such protectionism and achieve the benefits to consumers from competition. But these benefits *require* that goods and services and *consumers* be mobile. If competition between businesses in *B* and *A* is good, why is competition between their governments bad?

The arguments that it is assumed that in the absence of tax competition the optimal levels of government expenditures are chosen and public goods and services are efficiently provided. Each country is restricted to raising revenue by means of a commodity tax, and thus the loss in tax revenue from tax competition harms the citizens in each country.[13] But surely one must allow for the possibility that competition between the governments of the two countries may result in some increases in the efficiency of the provision of governmental goods and services.[14] If it can, then we must weigh both the costs and the benefits of international tax harmonization proposals (Fuest 1997).

If we assume that the government is providing only those goods and services that its citizens want, and doing so efficiently, then the problem of taxation becomes that of charging the beneficiaries of government for its services. The first thing to note in this regard is that general taxes on commodities like the VAT, and excise taxes as on tobacco are not obviously the best proxies for the benefits citizens receive from government. What public service does the government supply a smoker for the tax she pays on each pack of cigarettes, that the government does not also supply to a nonsmoker?

The attraction of a broad-based commodity tax like the VAT over an excise tax on, say, shoes is that the tax elasticity is much lower for the broad-based tax, and thus also the deadweight losses from taxation. Revenue elasticity considerations also undoubtedly explain the great popularity among finance ministers of tobacco, alcohol, gambling, etc. as objects of taxation. The increasing mobility of consumers and differences in tax rates across countries makes the revenue from general commodity taxes and even some excise taxes more elastic. This elasticity can be reduced, of course, by eliminating differences in tax rates across countries. But this approach also eliminates any positive effects on governmental efficiency that tax competition can bring about. An alternative to allowing governments to form tax cartels is for them to shift to less elastic sources of tax revenue. Property taxes are an obvious choice. If country *B* imposes much higher taxes on property than *A* and uses this revenue to provide public services that all residents of *B* can consume, then residents of *B* enjoy better roads, parks, schools, etc. than those in *A* consume. A resident of *B* can avoid the higher taxes in *B* only by giving up the better government services. No "race to the bottom" will ensue, *if governments supply the goods and services that all of their citizens want*.[15]

Particularly troublesome normative issues are raised by the "sin taxes" on tobacco, alcohol, and the like, if we assume, as in this paper, that collective choices are made by rational individuals to advance their collective interests. The strongest *normative* argument that one can make for these taxes is the "merit good" argument put forward by Richard Musgrave (1957, 1959). But as several writers have pointed out, this argument rests on the questionable assumption that voters can decide the "right amount" of these goods which should be consumed, but consumers cannot. Such an argument is incompatible with the use of the unanimity rule for making collective choices, as then the set of voters and consumers is identical, and the argument would have to assume that individuals as voters make *wiser* choices than they do as consumers, an assumption that runs against much of the literature of public choice dealing with voter rationality.[16]

The merit good argument is compatible with the use of the simple majority rule for making collective choices, *if* one adopts an elitist posture *and* one assumes that the *majority* can decide the quantities of these items that should be consumed better than the individual consumers themselves. Such an elitist view of government is at direct odds with the postulate of *normative individualism* that underlies this paper. Even if we were to accept the proposition that *some elite* knows better what a group of citizens should consume, than these citizens themselves, there is no reason to assume that the majority coalition in a country constitutes that elite (Mueller, forthcoming).

Under the elitist interpretation of merit wants, the ostensible reason for high excise taxes on tobacco, etc. is to deter their consumption. But if this is the justification for the taxes, and not simply that they are a good source of revenue, then there is much less reason to be concerned about cross-border shopping with respect to these goods. Having to drive to another country to buy cigarettes is probably as effective as a deterrent for most people as having to pay a high tax at the shop on the corner. The consumption of people who cross borders to buy more lightly taxed tobacco and alcohol is probably not greatly different than it would be if they had to buy these products in their own country. What is affected are the taxes they pay, *and to whom they pay them.* And, I submit, it is the latter consideration that dominates concern about cross-border trade in these items, *not* the possible ill-effects on their citizens from the additional consumption of these products.[17]

Most objections to tax competition between governments on the grounds that it will lead to "social dumping" and "a race to the bottom" rest on an elitist view of government similar to that underlying the "merit want" argument. The "impartial observer" knows what the proper level of taxation for the country should be and how this money should be spent, and fears that any loss in tax revenue will harm these programs. Such fears are unfounded, *if governments provide the goods and services their citizens want, and use benefit taxes to finance them.* Citizens in the United States move *into* communities with high quality schools and good police forces, *not away* from them, and they are willing to pay the high property taxes that are needed to finance these high quality public services. They do move away from cities with high tax rates and *low* quality schools and other public services, however, like Washington, D.C.

The government programs that are most vulnerable to intergovernmental competition are the zero-sum transfers that occur under majority rule. If country *B* has higher taxes than country *A* because *B* provides generous tax subsidies to its farmers, subsidized housing and other attractive benefits to its governmental employees, subsidies to its nationalized firms to allow them to maintain large and well-paid work forces, etc., then those citizens of *B* who are not farmers, or government employees, etc. may be tempted to move to *A*. If *B* engages in considerable zero-sum transfers, and is inefficient in its provision of government services, it will not be able to switch from a system of redistributive taxes to one of benefit taxes as the benefits it now provides fall far short of the taxes that it charges. For such countries, tax competition is a paramount danger. Tax harmonization is the only way to preserve the status quo of high redistributive taxes on the politically weak, and subsidies to the politically powerful.

9. Conclusions

The continuing integration of the economies of European countries, the continually increasing mobility of its citizens and enterprises, and the continuing globalization of the world economy place increasing pressure on the system of redistributive regulations, taxes, and subsidies in Europe. The most attractive response for many European governments will be to reduce the options of its citizens by pressing for tax and regulation harmonization, and thereby avoid the politically costly steps of having to take away the subsidies and privileges to which the politically most powerful groups have become accustomed. In some cases harmonization measures can be an effective means for protecting involuntary redistributive taxes. Some Austrians can fairly easily cross into neighboring non-Union countries and buy lower taxed cigarettes, liquor, and gasoline. It is much more difficult for a Belgian. Uniform VAT and excise taxes across the EU would effectively eliminate a Belgian's ability to tax arbitrage.

In other areas, the scope for successful harmonization is more limited, however. Although uniform taxes on capital within Europe would stop the movement of capital from high tax countries like Germany into low tax countries like Ireland, they would not deter the flow of capital *outside* the EU, indeed they would stimulate it. Such a diversion in the long run seems highly likely, since capital is the most mobile of all factor inputs. Note that while low Irish taxes on capital can be said to have a negative externality on Germany, if they lead German firms to invest in Ireland instead of Germany, imposing higher tax rates on Ireland harms it in the long run by restricting its ability to attract capital not only from Germany, but from everywhere else in the world.

The danger Europe faces, if it responds to the pressure from increasing mobility and globalization by tax harmonization, is that it retains its system of high redistributive taxes and regulations, preserves the resulting inefficiencies, and becomes therefore an increasingly unattractive place for businesses to locate, people to work, and eventually for people to live.

The alternative model of the state which I have proposed for consideration is the allocatively efficient state. In this state government would engage in those sorts of redistribution that all people favored, and would provide those goods, services, and regulations that can make all citizens better off. Given a choice from behind the veil of ignorance between the present, highly inefficient redistributive state and the allocatively efficient state, all European citizens would choose the allocatively efficient state. If European citizens were to write a "constitution for Europe," they might also make such a choice, given the long-run nature of a constitution. But, of course, *European citizens* do not make constitutional choices, representatives of their elected governments do. These governments respond to the incentives inherent in the principles of majoritarian democracy extant in each country, and thus tend not to challenge the redistributive policies that this system generates. A system that benefits a majority in the short run blocks consideration of alternative systems that would provide greater benefits to all citizens in the long run.

Acknowledgments

I gratefully acknowledge the financial support of the Hochschuljubiläumsstiftung der Stadt Wien.

Notes

1. For further defense of the assumption of unanimity at the constitutional stage, Buchanan and Tullock (1962:3–10, 77–80); Mueller (1989:100–11, 410–11; 1996:65–67, 89–90, 221–22).
2. We must maximize $E(U) = .5U_i(Y_i) + .5U_j(Y_j)$. The demonstration rests on the important assumption that the sum of Y_i and Y_j is a constant.
3. Buchanan and Tullock (1962:Ch. 13) argue in favor of placing redistribution decisions in the constitution. See also Mueller (1996:Ch. 16).
4. This is also the case with respect to redistribution based on John Rawls's difference principle. See Mueller (1989:446–48), and again von Furstenberg and Mueller (1971).
5. See Hardin (1982, 1997), and Mueller (1989:Ch. 2).
6. For a now classic discussion of these two principles and the earlier debate over them, see Musgrave (1959:Chs. 4, 5).
7. For surveys, see Sen (1970), Mueller (1989:Ch. 5), Enelow (1997), and Pattanaik (1997).
8. I include here the *effective* taxes imposed on groups through price supports and ceilings as well as statutory taxes.
9. On the distinction between the exit and voice modes of expression, see Hirschman (1970).
10. For a demonstration of this result with respect to taxes on capital, see Oates and Schwab (1988, 1991).
11. Taken from Atkinson (1995:278). Atkinson discusses the desireablility of a "European social safety net" at some length in Ch. 14.
12. Atkinson (1995:219) reports that the word "worker" was substituted for "citizen" in the final draft of the Social Charter.
13. See again Genser and Haufler (1996), and for a survey Keen (1993).
14. See Cnossen (1990), and Edwards and Keen (1996).
15. A large literature has examined the potential of communities using property taxes to finance local government services and the efficiency gains from intergovernmental competition in the provision of these services starting with Charles Tiebout (1956). For a recent survey, see Inman and Rubinfeld (1997).
16. Geoffrey Brennan (1990) has made just this sort of argument, however. Brennan's argument is that voters employ their "expressive" preferences when they vote not their narrow, selfish ones, and that expressive preferences are likely to place more weight on what is good for the community. The smoker *knows* that smoking is a bad habit and thus votes for a high tax on cigarettes. Having done so she drives to the border to avoid paying the tax that she voted for. For further discussion and critique, see Head (1968, 1969, 1990), McLure (1968, 1990), Mueller (1990), and Musgrave (1990).

    A somewhat different argument would rely on intertemporal inconsistencies. The smoker wishes to give up smoking, but cannot do so by herself. She votes for taxes to help herself resist smoking. This argument seems more persuasive when applied to the constitutional stage, at which all citizens agree on provisions in the constitution contemplating being not only their future selves, but also their children, grandchildren, etc. With respect to taxes on cigarettes voted by a parliament, I suppose that *some* smokers support such taxes, but that the strongest support comes from nonsmokers and the strongest opposition from smokers.
17. A recent proposal by the Minister of Finance in Austria to raise the excise taxes on gasoline and cigarettes was *not* precipitated by new reports about the environmental and health effects of these products, but the projection of a larger than expected budget deficit for 1998. The proposal was quickly withdrawn, because of predictions by revenue experts that the higher taxes would only lead to greater "gastank tourism" and longer queues at the borders near duty free shops, and not to additional tax revenue.

References

Atkinson, A. B. (1995) *Incomes and the Welfare State*. Cambridge, Engl.: Cambridge University Press.
Brennan, G. (1990) "Irrational Action, Individual Sovereignty and Political Process: Why There is a Coherent 'Merit Goods' Argument." In: Brennan, G., and Walsh, C. (eds.) *Rationality, Individualism and Public Policy*,

97–118. Canberra: Centre for Research on Federal Financial Relations, The Australian National University.

Buchanan, J. M., and Tullock, G. (1962) *The Calculus of Consent. Logical Foundations of Constitutional Democracy*. Ann Arbor: University of Michigan Press.

Caplin, A., and Nalebuff B. (1988) "On 64%-Majority Rule." *Econometrica* 56: 787–814.

Cnossen, S. (1990) "The Case for Tax Diversity in the European Community." *European Economic Review* 34: 471–79.

Downs, A. (1957) *An Economic Theory of Democracy*. New York: Harper and Row.

Edwards, J., and Keen, M. (1996) "Tax Competition and Leviathan." *European Economic Review* 40: 113–34.

Enelow, J. (1997) "Cycling and Majority Rule." In: Mueller, D. C. (ed.) *Perspectives on Public Choice*, 149–62. Cambridge: Cambridge University Press.

Fuest, C. (1997) "The Political Economy of Tax Coordination." University of Munich, mimeo.

Genser, B., and Haufler A. (1996) "Tax Competition, Tax Coordination and Tax Harmonization: The Effects of EMU." *Empirica* 23(1): 59–89.

Hardin, R. (1982) *Collective Action*. Baltimore, Md.: Johns Hopkins University Press.

Hardin, R. (1997) "Economic Theories of the State." In: Mueller, D. C. (ed.) *Perspectives on Public Choice*, 21–34. Cambridge: Cambridge University Press.

Harsanyi, J. C. (1953) "Cardinal Utility in Welfare Economics and in the Theory of Risk-Taking." *Journal of Political Economy* 61: 434–35.

Harsanyi, J. C. (1955) "Cardinal Welfare, Individualistic Ethics, and Interpersonal Comparisons of Utility." *Journal of Political Economy* 63: 309–21; Reprinted in Arrow, K. J., and Scitovsky, T. (eds.) (1969) *Readings in Welfare Economics*, 46–60. Homewood, Ill.: R.D. Irwin.

Head J. G. (1968) "Welfare Methodology and the Multibranch Budget." *Public Finance* 23(4): 405–28.

Head J. G. (1969) "Merit Goods Revisited." *Finanzarchiv* 28(2): 214–25; reprinted in Head J. G. (1974) *Public Goods and Public Welfare*, 248–61. Durham, NC: Duke University Press.

Head J. G., (1990) "On Merit Wants: Reflections on the Evolution, Normative Status and Policy Relevance of a Controversial Public Finance Concept." In: Brennan G., and Walsh, C. (eds.) *Rationality, Individualism and Public Policy*, 211–44. Canberra: Centre for Research on Federal Financial Relations, The Australian National University.

Hirschman, A. O. (1970) *Exit, Voice, and Loyalty*. Cambridge, Mass.: Harvard University Press.

Hochman, H. M., and Rodgers J. D. (1969) "Pareto Optimal Redistribution." *American Economic Review* 59: 542–57.

Inman, R. P., and Rubinfeld D. L. (1997) "The Political Economy of Federalism." In: Mueller, D. C. (ed.) *Perspectives on Public Choice*, 73–105. Cambridge: Cambridge University Press.

Keen, M. (1993) "The Welfare Economics of Tax Co-ordination in the European Community: A Survey." *Fiscal Studies* 14(2): 15–36.

Lerner, A. P. (1944) *Economics of Control*. New York: Macmillan.

McLure, C. E. Jr. (1968) "Merit Wants: A Normatively Empty Box." *Finanzarchiv* 27(3): 474–83.

McLure, C. E. Jr. (1990) "Merit Wants." In: Brennan, G., and Cliff, W. (eds.) *Rationality, Individualism and Public Policy*, 178–85. Canberra: Centre for Research on Federal Financial Relations, The Australian National University.

Mueller, D. C. (1990) "Brennan's Coherent Merit Goods Argument." In: Brennan, G., and Walsh C. (eds.) *Rationality, Individualism and Public Policy*, 119–24. Canberra: Centre for Research on Federal Financial Relations, The Australian National University.

Mueller, D. C. (1989) *Public Choice II*. Cambridge: Cambridge University Press.

Mueller, D. C. (1996) *Constitutional Democracy*. Oxford: Oxford University Press.

Mueller, D. C. (1997) "Constitutional Public Choice." In: Mueller, D. C. (ed.) *Perspectives on Public Choice*, 124–46. Cambridge: Cambridge University Press.

Mueller, D. C. (1997) "Federalist Governments and Trumps." *Virginia Law Review*, forthcoming.

Musgrave, R. A. (1957) "A Multiple Theory of Budget Determination." *Finanzarchiv* 17(3): 333–43.

Musgrave, R. A. (1959) *The Theory of Public Finance*. New York: McGraw-Hill.

Musgrave, R. A. (1990) "Merit Goods." In: Brennan, G., and Walsh, C. (eds.) *Rationality, Individualism and Public Policy*, 207–10. Canberra: Centre for Research on Federal Financial Relations, The Australian National University.

Oates, W. E., and Schwab, R. M. (1988) "Economic Competition Among Jurisdictions: Efficiency Enhancing or Distortion Inducing?" *Journal of Public Economics* 35: 333–54.

Oates, W. E., and Schwab, R. M. (1991) "The Allocative and Distributive Implications of Local Fiscal Competition." In Kenyon, D., and Kincaid J. (eds.) *Competition Among States and Local Governments*, 127–45. Washington, D.C.: Urban Institute Press.

Olson, M. Jr. (1965) *The Logic of Collective Action: Public Goods and the Theory of Groups*. Cambridge, Mass.: Harvard University Press.

Pattanaik, P. K. (1997) "Some Paradoxes of Preference Aggregation." In: Mueller, D. C. (ed.) *Perspectives on Public Choice*, 201–25. Cambridge: Cambridge University Press.

Rawls, J. A. (1971) *A Theory of Justice*. Cambridge, Mass.: Belknap Press.

Sen A. K. (1970) *Collective Choice and Social Welfare*. San Francisco: Holden-Day.

Tiebout, C. M. (1956) "A Pure Theory of Local Expenditures." *Journal of Political Economy* 64: 416–24.

Thurow, L. C. (1971) "The Income Distribution as a Pure Public Good." *Quarterly Journal of Economics* 85: 327–36.

von Furstenberg G. M., and Mueller D. C. (1971) "The Pareto Optimal Approach to Income Redistribution: A Fiscal Application." *American Economic Review* 61: 628–37.

Wicksell, K. [1958 (1896)] "A New Principle of Just Taxation." In Musgrave, R. A., and Peacock, A. T. (eds.) *Classics in the Theory of Public Finance*, 72–118. London: Macmillan.

[7]

Interest groups, redistribution and the size of government

Dennis C. Mueller

One of the noticeable differences between the USA and Western Europe is the greater amount of and emphasis placed upon redistribution in Europe. Transfers are the single biggest item in most European countries' government budgets, even exceeding *all* of government consumption. It is largely the size of government transfers which explains why the government sector is so much larger in most European countries than in the USA.

Since the USA and all West European countries are democracies, an explanation for these dramatic differences must be found in the political process. Democratic politics in Europe simply results in greater amounts of governmentally driven redistribution. Why?

One possible answer is that Americans are more mean spirited than Europeans. Well-to-do Americans are more willing to see their neighbors living in poverty, more willing to allow their fellow workers to suffer when they become unemployed, more willing to see their parents slide into indigence when they enter old age. University students in Europe seem particularly quick to offer these sorts of explanations for why the public sector is so much larger in Europe than in the USA, but similar utterances are often also heard from European politicians as they defend the size of their welfare states. This explanation for the greater size of government in Europe presumes that European citizens - implicitly all European citizens - demand more redistribution from their governments.

Public choice scholars have offered a second explanation for differences in the size of government sectors across countries which is less benign. Government transfers do not come about to satisfy the will of *all* the people, but only of some of them - those who are members of well-organized and powerful interest groups. This explanation for the differences in the size of government between the USA and Europe would imply that interest groups are better organized and more powerful in the latter than in the former.

In this chapter I shall examine some of the implications of these two explanations for differences in the size of government sectors, and some of the empirical evidence that bears on these explanations. I begin with the essentially normative argument that governmental redistribution programs arise because of citizens' concern about their neighbors.

1. NORMATIVE ARGUMENTS FOR REDISTRIBUTION

A normative *raison d'être* for the state commonly invoked by public finance and public choice scholars is that the state exists to provide goods and services to its citizens that they cannot obtain in Pareto-optimal quantities without the state. Any state-provided good or service must, therefore, have the potential of making *all* citizens better off. By implication any state redistribution programs must have the potential of making all citizens better off. In this section we discuss three such normative arguments that have been put forward to justify state redistribution programs.

1.1 Redistribution as Altruism

Our normative criterion is that the state should undertake only those activities that benefit all citizens. Redistribution from one group, say the *R*s, to another called the *P*s is consistent with this normative criterion only if the *R*s also benefit from the redistribution. One way in which this might come about is that the *R*s get utility out of seeing the *P*s made better off, and are willing to have their own incomes reduced to bring this about. This sort of *Pareto-optimal redistribution* is quite plausible if the *R*s are richer than the *P*s, and have altruistic preference functions (Hochman and Rodgers, 1969).

Let U_R be the utility of an R, $U_R = U_R(Y_R, Y_P)$ where Y_R and Y_P are the incomes of an R and a P, and U_P be the utility of a P, $U_P = U_P(Y_P)$. An R experiences a utility gain from seeing P have a higher income, and can bring this about by transferring a sum, T, to P. R's optimization problem is then to maximize

$$U_R = U_R(Y_R - T, Y_P + T) \tag{8.1}$$

with respect to T, which yields as a first-order condition

$$\partial U_R / \partial Y_R = \partial U_R / \partial Y_P \tag{8.2}$$

The rich transfer money to the poor until the marginal utility that a rich person gets from keeping an extra dollar just equals the utility she gets from giving it to the poor.

One obvious question to ask is why the state must intervene to bring about these transfers. Why cannot the rich simply give money to the poor without the state? The usual answer given to this question is that a rich person does not want to see just one poor person made better off, but rather all poor persons. To accomplish this all rich persons must give to the poor, and a potential free-rider problem arises. State intervention is needed to solve this free-rider problem.

It is reasonable to assume that a rich person gets more utility from giving to someone whose income is one-tenth of the rich person's income than to someone with half of her income. Giving to the poorest person in the community provides a rich person with the highest utility. These considerations lead to the following two predictions with respect to state-induced redistribution for altruistic purposes: (1) both the rich and the poor benefit from and support such redistribution; and (2) transfers are first targeted to the lowest-income people in the community. When their incomes have been raised to that of the second-poorest group, transfers are made to both bottom-level groups and so on until a level of income below that of the rich is reached such that eq. 8.2 is satisfied.[1]

1.2 Redistribution as Social Insurance

All insurance programs involve redistribution of one form or another. Individuals voluntarily enter such programs to avoid certain risks. When they do, they (unanimously) agree to engage in *ex post* redistribution. All purchasers of fire insurance agree to a redistribution from those who do not have fires to those who do.

Although the market is capable of providing many sorts of insurance - like that against fires - optimally, in some cases there may be market failures of one sort or another that justify state provision of the insurance. For example, if it were possible while we were still ensconced in the womb to purchase insurance against our having future physical or mental handicaps that would cause us to be poor, we might all voluntarily sign the insurance contract. Such contracts are as yet infeasible, however, and by the time we are able to join such contracts our physical or mental handicaps are often already apparent, and those who need the insurance most cannot acquire it. Thus state-run involuntary programs of redistribution can be justified on market failure grounds.

Rawls (1971) argued that every adult *ought* to undertake the *Gedankenexperiment* of pretending he might be rich or poor, and that the proper amount of redistribution in a society would be that amount that was unanimously agreed to behind such a veil of ignorance. Thus we can again justify some forms of state-provided rich-to-poor redistribution as being consistent with the criterion that everyone is made better off by them. In addition to using income as a criterion for whether a person is badly off or not, we might also think of using other criteria. Blindness or other physical handicaps, mental deficiencies, sickness and unemployment are all obvious candidates. As with redistribution as altruism, redistribution as social insurance leads to the prediction that the recipients of state transfers are disadvantaged in some way.

2. REDISTRIBUTION IN PRACTICE

These normative arguments for state-sponsored redistribution are quite compelling. Unfortunately the patterns of redistribution observed in most countries do not correspond to those that these theories predict.

As a first example consider Table 8.1. It presents a summary of the major components of the EU's budget in 1985 and 1995. Almost 90 percent of the EU budget in 1985 went into redistribution programs, almost 80 percent in 1995. In both of these years and in every other year in the EU's history, the largest single item in its budget has been transfers to the agricultural sector. Neither normative theory of redistribution discussed in the previous section can account for this phenomenon. Farmers are not poor. Indeed, the average income of a farmer in the EU is slightly *above* that of the average taxpayer, and a disproportionate share of EU transfers go to the richest farmers (Koester and Tangermann, 1990). Nor can one defend state subsidies to farmers using a social insurance argument. No blue- or white-collar worker in Europe goes to bed each night wondering whether he will awake the next morning as a sugar beet farmer. If someone were to step behind Rawls's veil of ignorance and contemplate what a just distribution of income in a

Table 8.1 Distribution of European Union expenditures by budget category, 1985 and 1995 (percentages)

		1985	1995
Redistribution	Agriculture and fisheries	72.9	53.6
	Regional policy	5.9	13.6
	Social policy	5.7	11.9
Allocative efficiency	Research, energy, transport	2.6	5.6
	External policies	–	6.2
	Administrative costs	4.6	5.1
	Miscellaneous	4.4	4.5

Source: Goodman (1996), pp. 101, 105–6.

society should look like, it is difficult to imagine why she would single out farmers as the worst-off people in society. Farmers are not in any obvious way disadvantaged.

As a second example consider Table 8.2. It presents figures from the US federal budget for transfers in 1995. Over 90 percent of these transfers go into insurance-like programs, over 50 percent go to retirees. Once again it is not possible to rationalize such transfers using either of the two normative theories for redistribution presented above. Every retiree is not poor and every person working and paying social security taxes is not rich. A McDonald's worker in the year 2020 is unlikely to get any utility out of contributing to Bill Gates's retirement income. The theory of Pareto-optimal redistribution cannot be used to defend the kinds of redistribution that we observe in a typical pay-as-you-go pension system as in the USA, where wage income is taxed and the beneficiaries are identified by age and not by income. The same can be said of those programs that finance social security out of general tax revenue, where the payee is the average taxpayer. Insurance against the risk of growing old must be purchased during an individual's working life, and all of us have the opportunity to buy such forms of insurance. The only exceptions to this occur

Table 8.2 Federal transfer payments in the USA, 1995 (millions of dollars)

	Expenditures		As a percentage of all transfers	As a percentage of total budget
1. Insurance-like programs, total		630 316	90.4	38.7
a. Retirement	357 286		51.2	
b. Disability	49 430		7.9	
c. Unemployment	21 576		3.1	
d. Medicare	180 214		25.8	
e. Veterans' insurance programs	21 810		3.1	
2. Noninsurance transfers		67 271	9.6	4.1
a. Welfare and social services	47 120		6.8	
b. Other	17 981		2.6	
c. Veterans	1 412			
d. Housing	87		< 0.1	
e. Agriculture	90		< 0.1	
f. Labor training	581		0.1	
3. Total transfers net of interest payments		697 587	100.0	42.8
4. Total Federal Budget		1 628 419		100.0

Source: Survey of Current Business, October 1998, Tables 3.16 and 3.17.

when someone during her working life is too poor to purchase retirement annuities. This situation calls for rich-to-poor redistribution, however, not young-to-old. If a society undertakes the proper amount of redistribution to the poor, as justified, say, by Rawlsian-type arguments, there is no reason why the state has to intervene to provide old age insurance.[2] Indeed, if someone at the age of 20 was to engage in a Rawlsian experiment of imagining that she might live to be 80 or live to be 60, she would quite likely decide that it is the person who will die at 60 who is the most disadvantaged of the two. Were it feasible, she would favor taxing the person who will live to 80 during his working life and subsidizing the person who will die at 60 to compensate her for missing out on 20 years.[3] She would *never* favor taxing both persons throughout their working lives and then giving all of the money to the lucky one who lives to be 80, as to some extent happens with state-run pension schemes.

We conclude that it is not possible to rationalize the biggest item in the EU budget and the biggest component of government transfers in the USA using the two normative arguments for redistribution presented above. Farmers do quite handsomely in the USA also, of course, and the elderly are well taken care of in Europe. (In Austria they receive 15 percent of GDP.) Before turning to a *positive* account of why this is so, we shall pause to consider one additional quasi-normative justification.

3. REDISTRIBUTION AS A MERIT GOOD

In an ideal, individualistic society, the state would redistribute income and wealth from the rich to the poor to an optimal degree and each individual would decide how much to consume during each year of her working life, and how much to save and invest to protect against the possibility that she lives to a ripe old age. Each individual would choose her own lifetime consumption plan based on her own, personal rate of time-preference, expectations about her life expectancy, and so on. A heavy smoker might discount the likelihood that she lives to a ripe old age and consume more during her working lifetime than, say, a non-smoker who jogs every day.

State-provided old age insurance is sometimes justified in such a society by invoking the kind of merit good (wants) argument that Richard Musgrave (1959, pp. 13–14) first developed. Individuals are myopic and irrational and do not make the *optimal* choices about how much to save for their retirement. The state must make these decisions for them.

This justification of state-provided old age insurance is inherently élitist, and thus abandons the kind of *normative* individualism premise upon which the other two justifications for state-provided redistribution rest. Some political élite knows how much each citizen should save during her working life and consume in retirement, and it relieves the citizen of the responsibility of having to make these choices.

Such élitism is not only difficult to reconcile with the kind of normative individualism that underlies much normative theorizing in public choice;[4] its premises run counter to much *positive* analysis in public choice. Behind the state in a democracy stand the citizens, the same group of myopic creatures who fail to save the proper amounts for their retirement. A merit-want defense of state pension systems assumes that the individual *qua* saver and investor is myopic and irrational, but as citizen/voter is far-sighted and rational. The citizen/voter invests more time and energy to decide what the proper consumption pattern should be for society than she does for herself. Such an assumption clearly contradicts the proposition that voters are rationally ignorant, and would not seem to have much empirical justification.[5]

An alternative defense of state-provided old age insurance might be to argue that voters are not better informed or less myopic than the average person in a society, but that they somehow choose representatives that have these characteristics. This defense is also problematic, however, since most work in public choice suggests that elected politicians' time horizons do not extend much beyond the next election, and that voters' memories do not go further back than the last election.[6]

We conclude that it is not possible to obtain a justification for state-provided old age insurance that is consistent with the normative criterion that the state should adopt programs that advance the welfare of all citizens, and that these citizens are rational, utility maximizers.[7] The same arguments hold a fortiori for transfers to farmers and other groups. We turn now therefore to a positive analysis of state-provided redistribution.

4. INTEREST GROUPS AND GOVERNMENT TRANSFERS

If we cannot account for major redistribution programs as voluntary giving that could even come about under a unanimity rule, then we must explain them as involuntary taking that comes about because countries employ the simple majority rule. In Austria one out of every four citizens has retired. Many of the remaining three-fourths are ineligible to vote (for example children). Of those that are eligible to vote, pensioners have the highest turnout percentages of any age group. If pensioners are not already a majority of those who vote, they soon will be.

Pensioners are able to bring about involuntary taking under the simple majority rule merely because of their sheer numbers. Smaller interest groups must resort to other tactics. French farmers are fond of blocking all of the major highways until the government caves in, but most interest groups employ subtler tactics, like lobbying and contributing to the campaigns of individual candidates and parties. A large literature now exists examining this sort of political behavior.[8] It establishes unequivocally that *money buys votes.*

It does so in two senses. First, the campaign contributions of interest groups influence how Congressmen vote. A contribution from a farm group increases the probability that the recipient Congressman votes for the legislation favoring this group. A contribution from a labor union increases the probability that the recipient Congressman votes for a higher minimum wage. Congressmen's votes can be bought.[9]

The second way in which money buys votes is that when a Congressman turns around and spends the contributions from interest groups, they increase the probability of his being re-elected. Table 8.3 summarizes the main findings of 23 studies with respect to the efficacy of campaign spending. Seldom does the empirical literature produce such consistent findings. With one partial exception, campaign expenditures always increase the probability of a candidate's election in studies of elections outside the USA. Without exception, campaign expenditures increase the probability of a challenger's election in studies of elections inside the USA. The one piece of seemingly contradictory evidence comes from the fact that the coefficient on the incumbents' expenditures is statistically insignificant in some studies. This finding is readily accounted for, however, when one takes into account the investment-like nature of campaign expenditures.

Campaign spending is like the persuasive advertising of certain consumer products in that it builds up a stock of goodwill toward the candidate, which in turn translates into votes on election day (Mueller and Stratmann, 1994). The relationship between votes and campaign spending can be expected to look like that presented in Figure 8.1. At low levels of spending, campaign spending makes a candidate's name known to large numbers of voters, and has a large impact on the probability that they will vote for her. As the candidate and her platform become better known to voters through campaign spending, the increase in votes from additional expenditures declines. Eventually, the candidate is so well known that it is impossible to win any more votes through additional spending. The top of the curve has been reached.

In the USA many challengers for Congressional seats start off as nearly complete unknowns in their districts (states) and thus start near the origin in Figure 8.1. Even those who have some reputation in their districts are likely to be less well known than an incumbent running for re-election. Thus, even a challenger who is fairly successful at raising funds is not likely to reach the top

Table 8.3 Summary of the main results linking votes for candidates to their campaign expenditures

(a)

	Effect of expenditures by		
Election	Challenger	Incumbent	Study
US House			
1972	sig.	insig.	Glantz et al. (1976)
1972, 1974	sig.	sig. (1974, OLS)	Jacobson (1978)
1978	sig.	sig., wrong sign	Kau et al.[b] (1982)
1972-82	sig.	insig. (usually)	Jacobson (1985)
1972-90	sig.	insig.	Levitt[c] (1994)
1984	sig.	insig.	Coates (1998)
1980	sig.	insig.	Kau and Rubin[b] (1993)
	Dem.	*Rep.*	
1972	sig.	sig.	Welch (1974, 1981)
1980-86	sig.	sig.d	Snyder (1990)
US Senate			
1972, 1974	sig.	sig. (1972)	Jacobson (1978)
1972-82	sig.	insig. (usually)	Jacobson (1985)
1974-86	sig.	sig.	Abramowitz (1988)
	Dem.	*Rep.*	
1972	sig.	sig.	Welch (1974, 1981)
US Presidential			
1972	sig.	sig.	Nagler and Leighley (1992)

(b)

	Effect of expenditures by			
Election	Challenger	Incumbent	Candidate	Study
Provincial elections				
1966, 1970 Quebec			sig.	Palda[a] (1973, 1975)
1973 Manitoba			sig.	Palda[a] (1975)
California Assembly 1972, 1974	sig.	sig. (1974)		Glantz et al. (1976)
Parliamentary Seats, Scotland and Wales, 1974			mixed	Johnston (1978)
8 Provincial Elections in Canada, 1973–77			sig.	Chapman and Palda (1984)
Canadian Federal Election, 1979 (Ontario)			sig.	Palda and Palda (1985)

Notes:

a Palda (1973, 1975) uses votes for all candidates as dependent variable. Incumbency treated as a dummy variable (significant).

b Kau et al. (1982), and Kau and Rubin (1993) regress winner's margin on winner's and loser's expenditures. Given high success rate of incumbents, I have interpreted their results for winners as pertaining to incumbents.

c Sample restricted to contests in which both candidates faced each other more than once. Coefficient on challenger spending much smaller than in other studies.

d Snyder regresses Democrat's share of vote on Democrat's share of expenditures. Significance of Republican spending inferred from significance of Democrat's spending share.

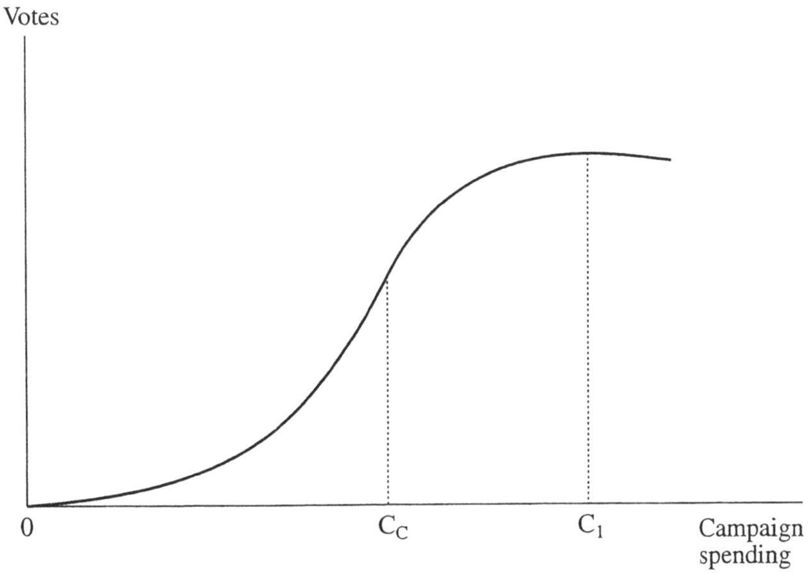

Figure 8.1 Relationship between votes and campaign spending

of the curve in Figure 8.1, but rather some point like C_C. The incumbent, on the other hand, starts the election with a large stock of 'brand recognition' from previous elections, appearances on television and in newspapers during her years in office, mailings to constituents, and so on. Given her high probability of being re-elected, interest groups seeking votes are more likely to give to the incumbent than her challenger. Thus an incumbent can generally outspend her challenger and is quite likely to wind up at the top of the curve in Figure 8.1. This reasoning explains why the estimated slopes of the vote/expenditure lines for challengers are always positive, while for incumbents they are often near zero. Rather than demonstrating that this implies that campaign spending does not help incumbents, it further illustrates its importance.

If members of interest groups are rational actors, they will not contribute to politicians' campaigns unless they expect to get something in return. Rational politicians will not seek donations to their campaigns and spend the donations that they receive unless they believe that they will help them get elected and re-elected. The empirical literature on campaign spending implies that both interest groups and politicians are rational actors. This literature can also explain why certain interest groups are so successful at using the political process to bring about involuntary transfers from the rest of the population to themselves.

5. WHY ARE INTEREST GROUPS IN EUROPE MORE EFFECTIVE THAN IN THE UNITED STATES?

Interest groups exist in Europe and in the USA. Farmers are treated handsomely by European governments; they also do very well in the USA. If interest groups account for a large fraction of the involuntary redistribution that governments undertake, and this redistribution accounts for a significant fraction of the difference in the size of the government sector in the USA and Europe, then it follows that interest groups must be more effective in bringing about involuntary redistribution in the latter than they are in the former. Why might this be so?

Consider an interest group in the USA with a fairly narrowly defined interest, say sugar beet farmers. They can count on the votes of Congressmen and Senators from districts and states where sugar beet farming is important, but these representatives make up a small fraction of the House and Senate. To get a piece of legislation passed that benefits sugar beet farmers and harms the rest of the population, the votes of at least 218 members of the House and 51 Senators are needed and, if the sugar beet farmers want to be sure that the bill is not vetoed, a sympathetic friend in the White House is needed. If this sympathy and these votes are to be won by contributing to the campaigns of the political actors, a great deal of money and organizational muscle is needed. Some interest groups - like the sugar beet farmers - may have what it takes; many will not.

Now consider the situation in a typical European parliamentary democracy. To get a piece of legislation through the parliament an interest group needs the support of the *government*, the party or more often a coalition of parties that effectively selects or supports the cabinet and is capable of passing legislation. The support of at most a few parties is needed. Campaign contributions in Europe go to parties, not to persons. It is most probably the case that an interest group needs to contribute more to a single party in Europe to win its support than an interest group in the USA must contribute to one member of Congress to win her support. It is most certainly the case that an interest group does not have to contribute 50 times as much money to win the votes of a party with 50 seats in the parliament as is needed to win the vote of one member of Congress. Advantage number one for interest groups in Europe is that there are *economies of scale* in winning votes through campaign contributions and other campaign activities.

When a member of the US Congress retires or is defeated in an election, an interest group's investments in that person are effectively wiped out. It must begin anew with one of the candidates from that district in the next election or try to buy the vote of some other member of Congress. Persons can die, retire or suffer defeats in elections; the parties that tend to form governments almost never do.[10] Even when a major party suffers what the newspapers call 'a defeat', it almost always wins enough votes to take seats in the parliament. It lives on to fight another day. Thus a second advantage that interest groups have in Europe is that it is easier for them to form *long-run* linkages to parties than it is for interest groups in America to form long-run relationships with members of Congress.

The proportional representation systems of Western Europe produce both a greater number of parties than exists in the USA, and a greater coverage of the ideological spectrum. Thus it is easy for a European interest group that is either on the right or the left of the ideological spectrum to find a party that comes close to its ideological position. The third advantage that interest groups have in Europe is, therefore, that they are *ideologically closer* to the parties to which they are linked and thus can form closer bonds. The greater importance of ideology in Europe than in the USA is symbolized in the names of parties. The names of the two dominant parties in the USA, Republican and Democratic, reveal nothing about their ideological stance. The names of European parties, on the other hand, often signal their ideological positions - the Conservative Party, the Liberal Party, the Social Democratic Party, the Socialist Party and, of course most vividly, the Communist Party, although this name is somewhat out of vogue now. Some party names in Europe signal direct links to economic interests - the Labour Party, the Farm Party.

For these three reasons we conclude that economic interest groups are more closely linked to political parties in Europe, and thus more effective politically in achieving their goals. Although we believe this to be true across all of Western Europe, it is particularly the case in countries like Austria and Sweden, which have adopted corporatist institutions that formally integrate economic interest groups into the political process, and in which membership in some economic interest group is generally obligatory. In these countries the Olsonian free-rider problem has essentially been solved for economic interest groups.

The two normative theories of redistribution discussed above predict that transfers go from the rich and advantaged to the poor and to those who are disadvantaged in some way. Since all members of society benefit from redistribution of this type, these normative theories can also be treated as positive theories in a democracy. *Some* transfers in every democratic country should be targeted to disadvantaged groups.

Many members of economic interest groups receive transfers or benefit financially in other ways from government programs although they are not disadvantaged. Where economic interest groups are strong, money will flow from the poor to the rich, from one segment of the middle class to another, and so on. The pattern of transfers will reflect the political advantages of different groups, not their economic disadvantages.

Table 8.4 reports the distribution of transfers by income quintile and the average level of transfers as a percentage of median income for 15 countries. Looking first at the last column, we see a great spread of values for the average level of transfers as a percentage of median income, ranging from 7.3 percent of median income in Switzerland to 35.5 percent in Sweden in 1987. Switzerland and the USA are the only two countries with transfer levels that are less than 10 percent of their median incomes. If all redistribution is from the rich to the poor and disadvantaged, then Switzerland and the USA look rather niggardly and mean-spirited in comparison to the 13 other rich countries in the table. If, on the other hand, redistribution largely takes the form of involuntary taking by interest groups rather than voluntary giving by all

Table 8.4 Distribution of transfers by quintile and average transfers as a percentage of median equivalent income

		Bottom	2	3	4	Top	Total	Average transfers as percentage of median equivalent income
Australia	1981	42.8	22.2	13.3	12.5	9.2	100.0	10.8
	1985	40.1	24.6	14.4	12.9	8.0	100.0	11.3
Belgium	1985	22.9	22.5	21.9	16.6	16.1	100.0	33.3
	1988	21.5	23.6	20.1	16.1	18.7	100.0	34.9
Switzerland	1982	38.5	19.2	15.6	13.3	13.3	100.0	7.3
Canada	1981	33.0	22.9	17.9	14.1	12.1	100.0	10.1
	1987	29.5	24.2	19.2	15.0	12.1	100.0	12.4
France	1979	19.7	21.2	18.8	17.7	22.6	100.0	22.2
	1984	17.5	21.8	18.4	17.7	24.7	100.0	25.0
Germany	1984	21.8	22.2	16.7	21.0	18.3	100.0	19.8
Ireland	1987	32.0	21.9	21.3	15.2	9.6	100.0	20.5
Italy	1986	15.6	16.4	19.7	20.7	27.6	100.0	21.4
Luxembourg	1985	17.3	18.3	19.5	22.5	22.4	100.0	23.7
Netherlands	1983	21.8	21.8	18.4	20.4	17.6	100.0	28.5
	1987	24.9	21.3	16.9	17.7	19.2	100.0	28.3
Norway	1979	34.0	20.9	16.4	13.6	15.1	100.0	13.5
Sweden	1981	18.0	23.9	19.8	19.5	18.7	100.0	35.0
	1987	15.2	25.8	21.7	19.9	17.4	100.0	35.5
UK	1979	30.6	20.0	17.4	17.0	15.0	100.0	18.5
	1986	26.7	25.9	19.4	16.1	11.9	100.0	24.3
USA	1979	29.7	21.1	17.4	14.7	17.1	100.0	8.9
	1986	29.2	21.2	17.1	17.5	15.1	100.0	9.4
Finland	1987	25.9	22.6	18.2	15.8	17.6	100.0	27.7

Source: Atkinson et al. (1995), Table 7.5, p. 107.

citizens, then economic interest groups would appear to be much more powerful in countries like Belgium and Sweden than they are in Switzerland and the USA.

Let us look now at the pattern of transfers across the five income categories. The first thing that stands out in Table 8.4 is that *every* income group from the bottom to the top receives a non negligible share of transfers. In only two countries is the share of transfers going to the richest 20 percent of the population less than 10 percent, and then just barely so. In only one country, Australia, does as much as 40 percent of all transfers go to the poorest 20 percent of the population. In France (1984), Italy and Sweden the poorest 20 percent of the population actually received the *smallest* share of the transfers; in France and Italy the largest percentage of all transfers went to the *richest* 20 percent of the population. These patterns clearly do not conform to what we would expect from the two normative theories of redistribution.

Nor do other theories of redistribution find much support in the table. The middle quintile, which presumably contains the median voter in terms of income, never receives the largest share of transfers. A Marxist prediction that the rich take from the poor also fails as a general proposition. Only the interest group hypothesis put forward here seems consistent with the numbers in Table 8.4. In majoritarian democracies economic interest groups at all levels of the income distribution succeed in obtaining transfers. Everyone wins at the redistribution game in a majoritarian democracy; some, however, win more than others.

Although the numbers in Table 8.4 suggest that interest groups are alive and well in all 15 countries, the patterns of transfers come closer to what the normative theories predict in the five countries with the lowest levels of transfers. In all five countries, the bottom quintile receives the highest fraction of transfers, with this fraction being roughly two-fifths in Australia and Switzerland. The bottom two-fifths of the income distribution in these two countries receives roughly 60 percent of all transfers. In Canada, Norway and the USA, over half of the transfers go to the bottom two quintiles. These numbers suggest that interest groups are somewhat less successful in playing the redistribution game in Australia, Canada, Norway, Switzerland and the USA, than they are in the other eight countries in the table.[11]

6. A PROPOSAL

If the playground pip-squeak asks the playground bully, after the bully has taken the pip-squeak's lunch money from him, 'What right do you have to do that?' and the bully replies, 'Because I'm bigger than you', he will have given an accurate positive explanation for the transfer. Few would regard it as an adequate normative justification, however. By the same token, a transfer of wealth from one group of citizens to another cannot be justified normatively with the argument that the recipients of the transfer were able to form a bigger coalition than the suppliers of the transfer. There are conditions under which the use of the simple majority rule can be justified normatively, but these conditions are *not* satisfied for issues involving pure redistribution.[12] The vast amounts of redistribution that occur in majoritarian democracies as a result of interest group politicking can be *explained* using standard public choice analysis; they cannot be defended by any normative analysis, however.

Suppose one wanted to change things. Suppose one wanted to eliminate, or at least reduce, the amount of redistribution as involuntary taking that takes place in a country, but not the redistribution as voluntary giving, what might one do?

Under the two normative theories of redistribution both the recipients and the payees are willing to vote for the transfers; under involuntary taking most of the recipients can be expected to vote for the transfers; while a large fraction of the payees vote against them. Many redistribution measures that involve only involuntary taking would presumably not succeed without the votes of the takers. With this in mind I make the following proposal for a constitutional amendment, or, where it will suffice, an act of parliament to reduce the amount of redistribution as involuntary taking.

Proposal Any legislation that involves a direct transfer of income or wealth from one group of citizens to another, or an indirect transfer as through a price ceiling, price floor or some similar device, must be put before the citizens in a national referendum. Only those citizens who will not directly benefit financially from the proposed legislation are allowed to vote in the referendum.

Since the normative theories of redistribution imply that the payees will unanimously support the redistribution, one might in addition require that the transfer legislation receive the support of a super-majority of those voting, as, say, two-thirds. I personally would be happy if the proposal were put into effect and only a mere majority were required to pass it. Even this threshold should be difficult to reach for many forms of redistribution as involuntary taking.[13]

Under the proposal, sugar beet farmers would not be allowed to vote on subsidies, quotas or price supports for sugar beets. Those currently receiving pensions would not be allowed to vote on legislation to extend or increase the payments under the current state pension system. Altruism among those not receiving pensions would undoubtedly result in the current generation of pension recipients still receiving most of, if not all, the payments that they expected. The reweighting of the votes of the young and those active in the labor market that the proposal would bring about would, on the other hand, increase the likelihood that a pay-as-you-go system might be replaced by an intelligently designed fully funded system, which would benefit all future generations of citizens.

One of the likely benefits of the proposal would be to bring involuntary redistribution out into the open. Dairy farmers would have to explain the benefits of higher milk prices for themselves and the rest of the community in trying to win support for them; consumer groups could explain their costs. With full information on the costs and benefits from such programs, citizens might well vote them down. If one believes that democracy is the best form of government, then having decisions made by a better-informed and active citizenry can only improve its outcomes.

Many will regard my proposal as radical and ultra-conservative. It has, however, a liberal pedigree. John Stuart Mill was one of the great thinkers of the nineteenth century. He was perhaps radical, but was no ultra-conservative. He was an early advocate of women's suffrage and favored proportional representation, because he believed that minorities deserved fair representation. Yet Mill felt that it was

> important that the assembly which votes the taxes, either general or local, should be elected exclusively by those who pay something toward the taxes imposed. Those who pay no taxes, disposing by their votes of other people's money, have every motive to be lavish and none to economize. As far as money matters are concerned, any power of voting possessed by them is a violation of the fundamental principle of free government – a severance of the power of control from the interest in its beneficial exercise. It amounts to allowing them to put their hands into other people's pockets for any purpose which they think fit to call a public one … (Mill, 1865, p. 133)

Most democratic countries did deny those with low incomes or without property the right to vote throughout much of the nineteenth century and in some cases into the twentieth.[14] The US Constitution originally denied US citizens living in the District of Columbia the right to vote for the President, Members of Congress or even representatives to the local government. The logic underlying this provision was a fear that those living in the District would be biased in their views as to the proper scope of and funding for government, since they directly or indirectly obtained their livelihood from it.

My proposal would not target the poor or any other group directly, but would instead prevent *all* interest groups from putting their hands into other people's pockets. As we have seen in Table 8.4, in many countries a disproportionate share of all transfers *does not* go to the very poor. My proposal would force the richest 20 percent of the Italian population to defend why they should receive 27.6 percent of all transfers, and would deny them the possibility of voting for the programs that bring these transfers about. By reducing the amount of redistribution as involuntary taking in a country, the proposal might actually lead to *more* redistribution to the poor, due to the reduction in taxes that accompanies this change and the increase in individual incomes that should result from reducing the deadweight losses that accompany high tax rates.

7. CONCLUSIONS

When the welfare state first came into existence at the end of the nineteenth and beginning of the twentieth centuries, its redistribution programs *were* targeted toward the poor, despite the fact that in many countries the poor had only a limited franchise (Ploug and Kvist, 1997, ch. 2). The theory of Pareto-optimal redistribution can be used to explain why this redistribution took place. Over the course of the twentieth century, the list of recipients of transfers grew along with the size of these transfers. By the end of the twentieth century, almost everyone in some countries was putting their hands in other people's pockets, and having their pockets picked at the same time. My proposal would to some extent put back the clock and limit redistribution to those who are truly deserving because they are poor or disadvantaged in some other way. The USA and Western European countries are much richer than they were 100 years ago; they can afford to be more generous to the poor. But the growth of incomes over the last century has not eliminated scarcity entirely. The high rates of taxation needed to feed huge transfer programs that do not target the poor result in significant deadweight losses that reduce everyone's income.[15] Pay-as-you-go pension systems reduce savings and slow economic growth, thus reducing everyone's income in the long run.[16] In the not-so-long run they threaten to eat up an ever-larger share of national income, and possibly drive out other more worthy social expenditure and transfer programs.

It is worth emphasizing that the gains some interest groups achieve at the expense of the rest of society not only lead to economic inefficiencies; often they also produce significant inequities. And it should also be repeated that benefits for interest groups often come in ways that do not involve direct government subsidies.

French truck drivers got their government to allow them to retire at 55 by blocking all of the major highways in France, thereby bringing auto and truck travel to a standstill. A few years ago, Austrian rail workers went two better. By merely threatening to strike and paralyze the country's rail system, they were able to induce the government to allow them to retire at the age of 53. These interest group victories obviously lower national income by taking people who are able to work out of the workforce prematurely. But they also introduce significant inequities into the state-run retirement system. Shoemakers cannot threaten to bring traffic to a halt; nor can they even make people go barefoot by going on strike. They are powerless compared to truck drivers and rail workers. Shoemakers must work until the mandatory retirement age. Their social security payments help finance the early retirements of those who are politically more powerful, like truck drivers in France and rail workers in Austria, and thus can be viewed as a form of transfer from people who retire at the 'mandatory' retirement age, to those who retire earlier. Neither the inefficiency caused by these early retirements nor their inequity can be discerned from any government statistics on incomes and transfers, however. Once they enter into retirement, the truck drivers and rail workers simply appear as any other retired person enjoying his 'well-deserved and earned' pension.

My proposal would not, of course, prevent Austrian rail workers from striking, if their request for a retirement age of 53 were turned down in a referendum. But it would change the confrontation to one directly involving the citizens who would be hurt by the strike and the rail workers. If a large majority of the citizens thought that the proposed retirement age was unfair, as opinion polls revealed they did, they might be willing to call the rail workers' bluff by rejecting the proposal. A large no vote in a referendum might even give the government the political courage to use whatever means it has at its disposal to end the strike.

Considerable concern has been expressed by political scientists and observers of politics about the dramatic decline in recent years in citizen support for the governments of their countries and for those who serve in these governments. Citizens in the leading democracies favor democracy over other forms of government as much as they ever have, but are disenchanted with those who get elected under the democratic rules operating in their countries.[17] One possible cause for this disenchantment might be that citizens have become unhappy about the scope of government activity in their country and the extent to which this activity serves special interests as opposed to the general interest. Each citizen may be aware that she has her hand in the pockets of other citizens, but that they at the same time have their hands in her pocket. Involuntary taking via the political process is a zero-sum game that all interest groups can play. If the payoffs sum to zero, what is the point in playing the game? Perhaps the growing alienation toward those in government that has been observed in several of the world's leading democracies in recent years has come about because citizens have begun to realize how much of government activity is of a zero-sum nature. In the long run most people's net gains are zero or even negative once the inefficiencies from zero-sum redistribution are factored in, and those who are net winners are not necessarily the most deserving players. Here it is interesting to note the dramatic surge in support for those in government that occurred in the USA after September 11th, 2001. Americans perceived that their government was acting in a way that benefited everyone, and their support for government soared. A reduction of the amount of zero-sum programs in a country might have a similar, although more modest, effect. My proposal would reduce the amount of zero-sum redistribution that goes on in a country, and place control over the redistribution that does take place directly in the hands of the citizens from whom any transfers will flow. Those who vote for redistribution programs must put their hands in their own pockets to pay for them, and all citizens will be able to vote directly against measures that would place other people's hands in their pockets. By reducing the scope for government actions that harm large fractions of the citizenry, the proposal should remove one source of citizen disenchantment. By giving citizens a direct voice in government decisions, the proposal should reduce another source, since each citizen will know that the government redistribution programs that are carried out were not decided by 'them', the politicians, but by 'us, the people'.

NOTES

1. For further discussion and a demonstration of this proposition, see von Furstenberg and Mueller (1971).
2. I do not mean to imply here that the amount of redistribution corresponds to that prescribed by Rawls's difference principle, but rather the amount that rational individuals would select, when uncertain of their future positions including their future incomes. See Mueller (1996, ch. 16).
3. A day may come, and perhaps quite soon, when life expectancies can be accurately predicted by DNA testing, and such forms of redistribution could take place.
4. See, for example, Buchanan and Tullock (1962).
5. The pros and cons of the merit-want justification for state intervention are put forward in a lively series of essays contained in Brennan and Walsh (1990).
6. See, for example, the literature on political business cycles as reviewed by Paldam (1997) and Mueller (2002, ch. 19).
7. For additional discussion and proposals in favor of old age pension systems that are consistent with a principle of *normative individualism*, see Peacock (1997) and Prewo (1997).
8. Most of this literature is concerned with the USA. For a review, see Mueller (2002, ch. 20).
9. See Silberman and Durden (1976), Chappell (1981), Kau et al. (1982), Kau and Rubin (1982, 1993), Peltzman (1984), Frendreis and Waterman (1985), Marks (1993), Stratmann (1991, 1995, 1996), and Kang and Greene (1999).
10. There are, of course, many small parties that enter politics to champion some ideological cause and then depart some time later because their followers have tired of the cause and/or they fail to make some minimum vote cut-off to obtain seats in the parliament. These parties are attached to ideological interest groups, but are not very attractive for the kinds of economic interest groups discussed here, since these parties do not have realistic chances of joining the government.
11. I hasten to add that interest groups can exert their political muscle to benefit their members in other ways than just by securing direct transfers, like minimum wages, agricultural price supports, tax breaks and so on. A full comparison of interest group strengths across countries would need to take these other dimensions of success into account.

12. See May (1952), Rae (1969) and Mueller (2002, ch. 6).
13. Swiss readers of this chapter and those familiar with Switzerland may be surprised by the discussion of the previous paragraph, which seems to imply that interest groups are not politically powerful in this country, given its corporatist institutions. The ability of Swiss citizens to call referenda and reverse government actions that benefit the few at the disadvantage of the many helps protect them against both the actions of their elected representatives and the interest groups that support them, and this helps to explain why Switzerland appears to fall into the weaker interest group category. My proposal is simply to make this happy Swiss institution mandatory for pure redistribution issues. On the important role the referendum plays in Swiss politics, see Kirchgässner et al. (1999).
14. See Ploug and Kvist (1997).
15. On this see Browning (1987).
16. See the various essays in Wise (1997) and Feldstein (1998).
17. See the various essays in Norris (1999).

REFERENCES

Abramowitz, Alan I. (1988), 'Explaining Senate Election Outcomes', *American Political Science Review*, **82**, June, 385–403.

Atkinson, Anthony B., Lee Rainwater and Timothy M. Smeeding (1995), *Income Distribution in OECD Countries*, Paris: OECD.

Brennan, Geoffrey and Cliff Walsh (1990), *Rationality, Individualism and Public Policy*, Canberra: ANUTECH.

Browning, Edgar K. (1987), 'On the Marginal Welfare Cost of Taxation', *American Economic Review*, **77**, March, 11–23.

Buchanan, James M. and Gordon Tullock (1962), *The Calculus of Consent*, Ann Arbor: University of Michigan Press.

Chapman, Randall G. and Kristian S. Palda (1984), 'Assessing the Influence of Campaign Expenditures on Voting Behavior within a Comprehensive Electoral Market Model', *Marketing Science*, **3**, 207–26.

Chappell, Henry W. Jr (1981), 'Campaign Contributions and Voting on the Cargo Preference Bill: A Comparison of Simultaneous Models', *Public Choice*, **36** (2), 301–12.

Coates, Dennis (1998), 'Additional Incumbent Spending Really Can Harm (at Least Some) Incumbents: An Analysis of Vote Share Maximization', *Public Choice*, **95**, April, 63–87.

Feldstein, Martin (ed.) (1998), *Privatizing Social Security*, Chicago: University of Chicago Press, 215–60.

Frendreis, John P. and Richard W. Waterman (1985), 'PAC Contributions and Legislative Behavior: Senate Voting on Trucking Deregulation', *Social Science Quarterly*, **66**, 401–12.

Furstenberg, George M. and Dennis C. Mueller (1971), 'The Pareto Optimal Approach to Income Redistribution: A Fiscal Application,' *American Economic Review*, **LXI**, September, 628–37.

Glantz, Stanton A., Alan I. Abramowitz and Michael P. Burkar (1976), 'Election Outcomes: Whose Money Matters?', *Journal of Politics*, **38**, November, 1033–8.

Goodman, S.F. (1996), *The European Union*, 3rd edn, London: Macmillan.

Hochman, Harold M. and James D. Rodgers (1969), 'Pareto Optimal Redistribution', *American Economic Review*, **59**, September, 542–57.

Jacobson, Gary C. (1978), 'The Effect of Campaign Spending in Congressional Elections,' *American Political Science Review*, **72**, June, 469-91.

Jacobson, Gary C. (1985), 'Money and Votes Reconsidered: Congressional Elections, 1972-1982,' *Public Choice*, **47** (1), 7-62.

Johnston, R.J. (1978), 'Campaign Spending and Votes: A Reconsideration,' *Public Choice*, **33**(3), pp. 83-92.

Kang, In-Bong and Kenneth Greene (1999), 'A Political Economic Analysis of Congressional Voting Patterns on NAFTA', *Public Choice*, **98**, March, 385-97.

Kau, James B. and Paul H. Rubin (1982), *Congressmen, Constituents, and Contributors*, Boston: Martinus Nijhoff.

Kau, James B. and Paul H. Rubin (1993), 'Ideology, Voting, and Shirking', *Public Choice*, **76**, June, 151-72.

Kau, James B., D. Keenan and Paul H. Rubin (1982), 'A General Equilibrium Model of Congressional Voting,' *Quarterly Journal of Economics*, **97**, May, 271-93.

Kirchgässner, Gebhard, Lars P. Feld and Marcel R. Savoiz (1999), *Die direkte Demokratie*, Basel: Helbing und Lichtenhahn/Vahlen.

Koester, Ulrich and Stefan Tangermann (1990), 'The European Community', in F.H. Sanderson (ed.), *Agricultural Protectionism in the Industrial World*, Washington, DC: Resources for the Future, pp. 64-111.

Levitt, Steven D. (1994), 'Using Repeat Challengers to Estimate the Effect of Campaign Spending on Election Outcomes in the U.S. House', *Journal of Political Economy*, **102**, August, 777-98.

Marks, Stephen V. (1993), 'Economic Interests and Voting on the Omnibus Trade Bill of 1987', *Public Choice*, **75**, January, 21-42.

May, Kenneth O. (1952), 'A Set of Independent, Necessary and Sufficient Conditions for Simple Majority Decision', *Econometrica*, **20**, October, 680-84.

Mill, John Stuart (1865) [1958], *Considerations on Representative Government*, Indianapolis: Bobbs-Merrill.

Mueller, Dennis C. (1996), *Constitutional Democracy*, New York: Oxford University Press.

Mueller, Dennis C. (2002), *Public Choice III*, Cambridge: Cambridge University Press.

Mueller, Dennis C. and Thomas Stratmann (1994), 'Informative and Persuasive Campaigning,' *Public Choice*, **81**, 55-77.

Musgrave, Richard A. (1959), *The Theory of Public Finance*, New York: McGraw-Hill.

Nagler, Jonathan and Jan Leighley (1992), 'Presidential Campaign Expenditures: Evidence on Allocations and Effects', *Public Choice*, **73**, April, 319-33.

Norris, Pippa (ed.) (1999), *Critical Citizens*, New York: Oxford University Press.

Palda, Filip and Kristian Palda (1985), 'Ceilings on Campaign Spending: Hypothesis and Partial Test with Canadian Data,' *Public Choice*, **45** (3), 313-31.

Palda, Kristian S. (1973), 'Does Advertising Influence Votes? An Analysis of the 1966 and 1970 Quebec Elections', *Canadian Journal of Political Science*, **6**, December, 638-55.

Palda, Kristian S. (1975), 'The Effect of Expenditure on Political Success', *Journal of Law and Economics*, **18**, December, 745-71.

Paldam, Martin (1997), 'Political Business Cycles', in D.C. Mueller (ed.), *Perspectives on Public Choice*, Cambridge: Cambridge University Press, pp. 342-70.

Peacock, Alan (1997), 'The Future Scope for Self-Reliance and Private Insurance', in H. Giersch (ed.), *Reforming the Welfare State*, Berlin: Springer, pp. 91-108.

Peltzman, Sam (1984), 'Constituent Interest and Congressional Voting,' *Journal of Law and Economics*, **27**, April, 181-210.
Ploug, Niels and Ion Kvist (1997), *Social Security in Europe: Development or Dismantlement?*, The Hague: Kluwer Law International.
Prewo, Wilfried (1997), 'From Welfare State to Social State: Individual Responsibility and Compassion', in H. Giersch (ed.), *Reforming the Welfare State*, Berlin: Springer, 295-309.
Rae, Douglas W. (1969), 'Decision-Rules and Individual Values in Constitutional Choice', *American Political Science Review*, **63**, March, 40-56.
Rawls, John A. (1971), *A Theory of Justice*, Cambridge, MA: Belknap Press.
Silberman, Jonathan I. and Garey C. Durden (1976), 'Determining Legislative Preferences on the Minimum Approach', *Journal of Political Economy*, **84**, April, 317-29.
Snyder, James M. Jr (1990), 'Campaign Contributions as Investments: The US House of Representatives 1980-86', *Journal of Political Economy*, **98**, 1195-227.
Stratmann, Thomas (1991), 'What Do Campaign Contributions Buy? Causal Effects of Money and Votes', *Southern Economic Journal*, **57**, January, 606-20.
Stratmann, Thomas (1995), 'Campaign Contributions and Congressional Voting: Does the Timing of Contributions Matter?', *Review of Economics and Statistics*, **77**, February, 127-36.
Stratmann, Thomas (1996), 'How Reelection Constituencies Matter: Evidence from Political Action Committees' Contributions and Congressional Voting', *Journal of Law and Economics*, **39**, October, 603-35.
Welch, William P. (1974), 'The Economics of Campaign Funds,' *Public Choice*, **20**, 83-97.
Welch, William P. (1981), 'Money and Votes: A Simultaneous Equation Model', *Public Choice*, **36** (2), 209-34.
Wise, David A. (ed.) (1997), *Frontiers in the Economics of Aging*, Chicago: University of Chicago Press, pp. 125-72.

Constitutional Political Economy, 12, 161–172, 2001.

Centralism, Federalism, and the Nature of Individual Preferences

DENNIS C. MUELLER*
dennismueller@econ.bwl.univie.ac.at
Department of Economics, University of Vienna, Brünnerstr. 72, 1210 Vienna, Austria

Abstract. Almost all of economic theorizing takes individual preferences as givens, and then proceeds to analyze individuals' choices within the constraints that they face. This paper takes into account the fact that preferences are to some extent endogenous, and that the state typically plays an important role in shaping individual preferences through its education and other policies. It analyzes the consequences of assuming both exogenous and endogenous preferences, and homogeneous and heterogeneous preferences for the choice between centralized and decentralized (federalist) government structures. Given the increasingly heterogeneous nature of individual preferences, more decentralized, federalist structures are deemed likely to be optimal. Ironically, at the same time an increasing tendency to proclaim and impose cross nationally a set of "universal values" can be discerned.

Keywords: federalism, endogenous, preferences, centralization

JEL classification: D71, H70

Introduction

Almost all of economic theorizing takes individual preferences as givens, and then proceeds to analyze individuals' choices within the constraints that they face. Some economists go so far as to dismiss all economic modeling, which does not assume exogenous preferences, as unscientific (Stigler and Becker 1977). If preferences are truly exogenous, and all individual choices are attempts by rational actors to maximize their utilities, it is difficult to understand why individuals in northern Germany overwhelming choose to be Protestants, while southern Germans opt to be Roman Catholics; why Italy is overwhelmingly Roman Catholic, while neighboring Greece is overwhelmingly Greek Orthodox. An important objective of religious instruction is presumably to *shape* individual preferences, so that the targets of instruction favor one particular religion over all others.

Much the same can be said about education in general. In addition to instruction in reading, writing and arithmetic, schools invariably attempt to inculcate *values*. In religious schools these values include the basic tenets of the religion. In state-financed schools these values typically encompass civic virtues, patriotism, and the like. Since education is an important activity of the state in virtually every country in the world, one must conclude that any theory of the state, which treats citizen preferences as exogenous, rests on a false premise. How damaging this inadequacy is will, of course, depend on the questions asked. If one's goal is to explain differences in highway expenditures across communities using the median voter model, then assuming exogenous preferences seems quite reasonable. If, on the other hand, one's goal is to analyze the consequences of different constitutional

* I would like to thank the two discussants of my paper at the workshop in Sweden, Olof Petersson and Torsten Persson, for their very helpful comments on the first draft of this paper.

definitions of the state, then one presumably wants to consider all of the functions of the state, including education, and one may wish to allow for the possibility that the state both shapes individual preferences and is shaped by them.

My goal in this paper is to contrast centralized and federalist state structures. At this basic level of analysis, it seems prudent to recognize that the state can play an important role in forming individual preferences. I shall, therefore, consider the consequences of assuming both that individual preferences are exogenous, and that they can be, at least partially, formed by the state.

If one wished to analyze the collective choices of Italians and Greeks with respect to, say, the determination of public holidays, it would be reasonable to assume that Italians have homogeneous, Roman Catholic preferences, and Greeks have homogeneous, Greek Orthodox preferences. If one wished to analyze the collective choices of Americans on religious questions, one would need to assume considerably more preference heterogeneity. In addition to allowing for the endogeneity of individual preferences, therefore, we shall allow for their possible heterogeneity. With this additional factor, we have eight possible combinations of state structures and preferences: centralized state, homogeneous and exogenous preferences; centralized state, homogeneous and endogenous preferences; and so on. Four of these eight seem implausible combinations, however. For example, if we assumed a centralized state with homogeneous and exogenous preferences, we would be assuming that all Greeks just happened to prefer Greek Orthodoxy to all other religions, all Syrians happened to prefer Islam to all other religions, and so on. This hap-and-stance seems so unlikely that we shall not consider it. We focus instead upon the four most likely combinations: a centralized state with homogeneous and endogenous individual preferences; a decentralized state with heterogeneous and exogenous preferences; a decentralized state with heterogeneous and endogenous preferences; and a centralized state with heterogeneous and exogenous preferences. The first four sections of the paper discuss the normative characteristics of each of these possibilities. In section 5 we briefly discuss the possibility of transitions from one form of state to another. Section 6 examines the impact of introducing certain kinds of externalities. In the final section we consider the implications of the analysis for the choice of constitutional structures with special reference to recent developments in the United States, the European Union and Sweden.

1. Centralized State with Homogeneous and Endogenous Individual Preferences

An extreme version of this case is the totalitarian state.[1] In its religious form, a religious elite controls the state and its schools. All children are taught the state religion, all adults are expected to obey its laws or commandments. There is no need for democratic institutions, since there is no need to consult individual citizens as to what state policies should be. The holy books of the state religion define what is right and wrong, and should there be any ambiguity as to what these books imply about specific state actions, the holy (almost without exception) men at the top of the religious elite, who speak for and sometimes with God, can clarify what is to be done.

In its secular form, the totalitarian state is controlled by a *party* and led by a party elite. Some secular *ism* is substituted for religion, and the state's holy books become the past writings of members of the party elite, or the works that inspired them. The state-controlled education system indoctrinates children and adults alike in the virtues of the party's principles, and attempts to instill in them loyalty to the state and the party. Democratic institutions are again not needed to determine state policies, since all citizens are expected to have the same preferences for that which the party recommends.

Under both religious and secular totalitarianism the state makes all of the important choices *for* citizens. To the extent that such systems have any normative justification at all, one must assume that all citizens have the same preferences and that these match the ideology of the state's religion or party. The ruling elite determines what is best for the citizens, and its education and propaganda programs attempt to shape individual preferences to conform to the ideology that underlies the state.

Democratic socialism resembles totalitarianism in so far as the state continues to make many of the important choices facing citizens for them. Citizens are assumed to be incapable of deciding how much to save for their retirement or for their children's education, thus the state saves for them, and provides the same levels of education and retirement benefits for all. Citizens are unable to choose the proper level of health insurance, and so the state chooses it for them, and provides the same, optimal level for all. Citizens are incapable of deciding what is healthy to eat, drink, read, smoke, etc. and so the state regulates, bans and taxes all sorts of products to induce citizens to consume the "proper bundles" of goods and services.

If we assume that the state acts for the benefit of the citizens under democratic socialism, then we must assume that citizens have homogeneous preferences for many of the goods and services that the state provides, since it tends to provide the same levels of social insurance, housing, etc. to all. This assumption becomes more plausible, when one notes that under democratic socialism the state makes great efforts to ensure that its citizens *have homogeneous* preferences. The state owns the television and radio stations, and broadcasts programs, which are "good" for the citizens, which educate them to and help preserve their cultural values, which make them good citizens. The same goals underlie the state's education policy. All citizens no matter where they live or what their incomes are receive the same education, an education whose content is determined by the state's education department, and which seeks to instill in citizens a common set of values.

Democratic socialism in the extreme form just described is quite compatible with economic models of the state, which see "the social planner" choosing the optimal actions of the state by maximizing a social welfare function whose arguments include the preferences of all citizens. Although in principle this function could allow for heterogeneous citizen preferences, since the social planner cannot know what these preferences are, in practice most people who work with social welfare functions assume a single utility function for all citizens. This "organic" view of the social-democratic state differs from that of the totalitarian state only in so far as the citizens in a social democracy are allowed to choose which among *two* or more competing party elites will maximize the social welfare function for them.[2]

A normative defense for this elitist form of centralized democratic system can be derived with the help of Condorcet's Jury Theorem, if we assume that the underlying preferences of all citizens for government policies are homogeneous, but citizens differ in their beliefs as to which of two competing elites will best carry out its assignment. That is, we assume, say, that citizens want honest politicians, who adopt economic policies which produce full employment, balance of payments equilibria, low inflation, etc. Two parties compete for the right to form the government and provide the policies that produce these outcomes. The citizens are uncertain as to which party will best fulfill these goals, but each citizen has a better than 50 percent chance of choosing the best party. The simple majority rule in this case acts as a sampling device which selects the best party—that is the best ruling elite—with a probability approaching one as the size of the electorate grows.[3]

If the only government policies of interest to citizens concerned things like unemployment, the assumption that underlying preferences were homogeneous might seem realistic enough to provide a defense for a competing elites theory of the state. But the underlying preferences of citizens with respect to issues like abortion seem both fundamentally different and opposed. No government can provide a single policy with respect to abortions that will be viewed as optimal by all citizens. We consider next, therefore, the state as a system of multiple governments.

2. Federalist State with Heterogeneous and Exogenous Individual Preferences

At the other pole from a centralized, elitist model of the state, in which a dictatorial or an elected elite makes for the citizen many of the decisions, which she could make for herself, stands an individualist model in which the individual as both consumer and citizen is assumed to have the capacity to decide what bundle of goods she wishes to consume. This model of the state rests upon a premise of *normative individualism*. All normative statements are based on the effects of specific actions on the welfare of individuals. The Pareto principle becomes the logical normative bench market.

Advocates of normative individualism favor free markets for the allocation of private goods, because the unconstrained choices of individuals in free markets are expected by the invisible hand theorem to produce Pareto-optimal allocations of private goods. The unanimity rule is the preferred "voice mechanism" for revealing individual preferences for public goods, because it ensures that no collective action is undertaken unless it constitutes a Pareto improvement for the community.

Exit can also be an effective mechanism for revealing individual preferences for public goods, when the goods are *local* public goods, that is to say that they have limited geographic spillovers, and are provided by competing governments in a federalist system. Under these conditions citizens reveal their preferences for public goods by choosing to live in the community that promises them the best bundle of public goods.[4]

The voting-with-the-feet model of government sees local polities as coming into existence, because political entrepreneurs spot opportunities to attract citizens and earn profits by providing bundles of local public goods for which there is an unsatisfied demand, just as capitalist entrepreneurs are motivated to provide products for which there exists an unfilled demand. Again in analogy with the model of market competition, the competition for mobile citizens in the voting-with-the-feet model eliminates entrepreneurial profits and results in a Pareto-optimal allocation of local public goods and citizens.[5]

The voting-with-the-feet model as originally developed rests on the assumption that citizen preferences for local public goods are exogenous and fixed. It allows for heterogeneous preferences in the wider community, while at the same time achieving Pareto-optimality in the allocation of local public goods within this wider community by allowing citizens to sort themselves into local communities of homogeneous preferences. Elementary and secondary education are classic examples of local public goods, and one thus assumes that one of the local public goods that will be supplied in different quantities and qualities in a federalist system of competing governments is education. If we continue to consider education as a government policy, which *changes* individual preferences, then we must allow for the possible endogeneity of individual preferences in a federalist system.

3. Federalist State with Heterogeneous and Endogenous Individual Preferences

In a "classical democracy" the citizens rule the state and it is their preferences, not those of a political elite, which are reflected in the state's policies (Schumpeter 1950:250–52). This same image of democracy dominates the public choice literature with the policies of the state reflecting the preferences of the median voter or a winning coalition of voters. In a federalist system with highly mobile citizens, each local polity is composed of citizens with identical preferences or preferences, which vary over a narrow range. In principle the unanimity or a very high qualified majority rule could be used to determine the polity's policies.

In an individualistic, federalist state the preferences of the citizens in each local community can be expected to determine the characteristics of its education system including its content. Communities composed of specific ethnic and religious groups can ensure that their values are emphasized in the curriculum. Communities dominated by citizens with advanced educational and scientific backgrounds can ensure that their local school curriculums emphasize science and contemporary issues and values.

In today's society education and preference formation do not stop on the day one leaves school. Today's citizen receives masses of information from an array of sources and this information can have a continuing impact on her attitudes and preferences. Thus, today's community filled with citizens with homogeneous tastes can tomorrow be split apart by a new issue upon which its citizens cannot agree. If the range of issues confronting citizens continues to expand and change, and individual preferences adapt accordingly, becoming ever more heterogeneous, the dynamics of the Tieboutian process imply a continual reconstitution and mitosis of communities. With an expanding issue set, the optimal number of communities grows and their optimal size shrinks.

Thus, in a federalist system in which preferences can be both heterogeneous and endogenous, no equilibrium distribution of citizens into communities may exist. As the issue set evolves, becoming ever larger and more complex, the incentives to move and form new communities are continually renewed. In the limit, the optimal-sized community contains a single individual, who provides herself exactly the bundle of goods that matches her preferences, and educates her children in accordance with those preferences.

4. Centralized State with Heterogeneous and Exogenous Individual Preferences

It has been known since at least the 1930s that hypothetically the state can accomplish everything that the market can. In an age of high-powered computers, gigantic data banks on individual buying habits, financial status and the like, this potential is far more realizable than ever before. A centralized state, which took individual preferences as givens, could in principle duplicate both the outcomes of the market and of a decentralized, federalist system. A retirement community with good hospitals and plenty of golf courses is constructed here; a community for young families with good elementary schools and plenty of daycare centers there. Armed with computers and data banks, the political elite is able to select a sufficiently diverse array of public goods and services to maximize the social welfare, however heterogeneous its arguments happen to be. In a democratic, centralized state, the citizens could again choose which among the competing elites it wished to have solve this maximization problem.

5. Transitions

These constellations of governmental structures are, of course, not necessarily stationary. One might give way to another and, one might try to test whether one structure is better than all others in some Darwinian sense by seeing whether there is a tendency over time for governmental structures to converge on this structure. Even confining our attention to these four constellations of governmental structures would, however, still give us 16 possible transitions from one to another to consider. Such an analysis would require an article in and of itself. Nevertheless, it is perhaps useful to take up briefly the issue of how and why one structure may give way to another.

Three of the governmental structures involve heterogeneous preferences. Under what sorts of circumstances might we expect a country to move from one of the structures in which the citizens have heterogeneous preferences to a centralized state with homogeneous, endogenous preferences. Here we do not need to theorize, because the centralized, totalitarian states of the past century have all followed a common pattern. The leaders of the elite who will eventually run the totalitarian state identify a common element in the preferences of most citizens. Propaganda is then used to enhance the saliency of this element until it dominates many other elements in the citizens' preferences. A form of homogeneous preferences is thereby created in so far as one part of each citizen's preferences, which is common to all citizens, becomes dominant.

In each case, the common element seems to be a fear of or prejudice against a particular group or groups, which is common across most of the country's population. In Germany it was against the Jews, Gypsies and other "non-Aryan" minorities; in Russia it was against the capitalists and imperialists; in Iran it was against the secularists and those espousing Western culture. To achieve such a massive transformation of preferences (beliefs) and institutional structure requires overcoming great inertia, of course. Not surprisingly, therefore, one finds in each case a major, cataclysmic event that catalyzed the population and allowed an ideological elite to succeed. In Germany it was defeat in World War I, a humiliating peace settlement, and the economic crisis of the 1920s and '30s; in Russia it was also defeat in World War I and ensuing economic crisis; in Iran it was the corruption and collapse of the Shah's regime.

In contrast, one expects the transition from a centralized state with homogeneous, endogenous preferences to a state with heterogeneous preferences to be much more gradual. As time elapses, the fraction of the population that remembers or was even alive when the cataclysmic event occurred declines. Hatred of "the enemies of the state" subsides, other elements in citizens' preference functions begin to become more important.[6] The leaders of the centralized state will, of course, wish to prevent this transition from happening through their control of the schools, newspapers, magazines, publishing houses, radio and television. The advent of satellite dishes for broadcasting television programs, video recorders, the Internet, etc. make this increasingly difficult even in a country as poor and as vast of China.

Thus, one expects that a centralized state with homogeneous, endogenous preferences will eventually become a centralized state with heterogeneous preferences, preferences whose formation is increasingly out of the control of the leaders of the state. In a centralized, democratic state this transition should eventually lead to pressures by the citizens to introduce federalist structures so that government policies can be more closely tailored to the preferences of those it serves. Thus, one expects a natural transition from a centralized state with homogeneous preferences, to a centralized state with heterogeneous preferences, to a federalist state with heterogeneous preferences.

6. The Problem of Externalities

The four constellations of governmental structures and citizen preferences sketched above are polar cases, which match no actual political systems perfectly. Nor does any one of them necessarily constitute an ideal type. The one which probably comes closest to an ideal type is the last one for it, in its democratic form, essentially describes an omniscient, benevolent and democratically-elected dictator model.

Even in an age of high-powered computers and gigantic data banks, however, it is questionable whether the state can gather sufficient data on individual preferences to allow it to maximize their collective welfare, *even if it wished to do so*. The public choice literature also gives ample arguments and evidence to suggest that political elites do not selflessly maximize social welfare, but rather factor into their calculations their own personal interests to a considerable extent.[7]

These considerations suggest that the optimal governmental structure may be a federalist system, first because federalist democratic institutions facilitate the gathering of information on individual preferences, and second because competition among federalist governments may constrain the self-serving behavior of government officials.

A federalist system can also be a potentially attractive way for solving many externality problems. Some citizens are annoyed by seeing or hearing people who have drunk too much alcohol, others appreciate the option of purchasing an alcoholic drink in a restaurant or for consumption at home. Banning or constraining the purchase of alcoholic beverages in some communities while allowing it in others is a potential way to accommodate the preferences of both types of citizens.

Such resolutions of externality problems are only effective, however, if the extent of the spillover from the externality is not too large. Indeed, a necessary condition for the optimality of a federalist system with preferences revealed by individuals' voting with their feet is that there not exist significant cross-community externalities.[8] Two, quite different types of externalities are relevant for the design of state structures—*physical* and *psychological* externalities.[9] We examine each in turn.

6.1. Physical Externalities

The optimal dimensions of communities in a federalist system are determined by the magnitudes of the geographic spillovers caused by the public goods that they provide, and the externalities that they control. The optimal size of a community that determines the emissions of smoke from a factory includes all citizens affected by the smoke. When discussing externalities in the context of federalist design, we generally think of externalities like smoke and sewage, which third parties literally consume. It is externalities such as these that I have in mind with the term *physical externality*.

The amount of sewage community *A* deems optimal to spew into a river may not seem optimal to the downstream community *B*. Two possibilities exist for obtaining optimality in this situation: (1) The two communities engage in Coasian-contracting and agree on the Pareto-optimal quantity of sewage for *A* to discharge into the river. (2) A central government to which both *A* and *B* belong determines the optimal level of sewage discharge for *A* and ensures that this level is realized by implementing the appropriate tax, subsidy or regulation policy. When large numbers of activities involve cross-community externalities, the transaction costs involved with Coasian solutions to these problems may become so large that resolution by the central government becomes optimal. Indeed, if *A* and *B* do not already belong to a larger state, it may be optimal to create one.

Thus, the existence of numerous physical externalities with broad spillovers may negate the advantages of a highly decentralized federalist state in favor of a centralized state in which welfare-function-optimizing bureaucrats determine the socially optimal levels of the different activities for each community.

While the existence of physical externalities may justify the substitution of a centralized state for a federalist one, it need not do so. Many physical externalities have quite limited spillovers, and therefore the overall optimality of the decentralized federalist state remains a possibility even though not an inevitability. The same cannot be said, however, for psychological externalities.

6.2. Psychological Externalities

Luv lives in Lund a long way from the rainforests of Brazil. Nevertheless, she experiences displeasure from the thought that the rainforests are being felled. She fears an increase in the risk of global warming. She fears that rare species of birds, insects and other plant-and-wildlife may become extinct and that as a result possible cures for cancer and other diseases may go undiscovered. She experiences mental anguish from the thought that some animal species will become extinct, even though she has never seen them and expects that she never will. Luv's first listed fears of global warming and cancer can be regarded as a form of *anticipated* physical externality. Her unhappiness over the potential extinction of unseen animal species is, however, an example of what I call *psychological* externalities.

Whereas a federalist structure can help mitigate externality problems when the effects of the externality are direct and physical, they are of no help when the externalities are psychological, for psychological externalities know no geographic bounds. Luv's anguish from contemplating the possible disappearance of a species is independent of the distance of the species from her.

Psychological externalities have become increasingly important in the politics of many democratic countries in recent years. Very often the externality issues are couched in terms of *rights*. One group is concerned about the treatment of animals who are transported and slaughtered for food, and demands their protection by appealing to the existence of animal rights. Another group is concerned about the welfare of asylum seekers, and claims for them certain rights. Rights are claimed for fetuses by those who oppose abortions. Rights are claimed for children or prisoners by those who oppose child labor or forced labor by prisoners. In the latter cases, the claims may be an attempt to disguise the protectionist goals of their proponents, and thus may be a simple manifestation of selfish rent seeking. But in many of these cases, no narrow selfish motivation is discernable. The issues involve pure psychological externalities engendered by the value preferences of those experiencing the externality.

Interpersonal conflicts over alcohol consumption can be eliminated or at least mitigated by banning alcohol consumption in some communities and allowing it in others. Such a solution to conflicts over abortions are infeasible, however, if opponents of abortion experience psychological pain at the thought that abortions occur, regardless of where they occur. The existence of psychological externalities makes the centralized state the optimal form of government for resolving these issues within a country. Obviously if such issues are salient within a country, one must reject the assumption of homogeneous preferences on all issues. These issues must be resolved through the imposition of one solution upon the entire community by the ruling elite. In a democracy, this elite will be chosen by a majority of the citizens, and thus the outcome will be a form of "tyranny of the majority," at least in the eyes of the losing minority. Psychological externalities of the type described here present a particularly difficult problem for the optimal design of political institutions at the beginning of the twenty-first century. We close this paper by discussing why this is so.

7. Constitutional Issues in Federalist Design

Although a polar case, the model of the centralized state with endogenous and homogeneous preferences sketched in section I does resemble in important respects the secular, totalitarian states of the Third Reich, the Soviet Union, and its Communist satellites. It also resembles theocracies as Iran has been in recent years. It its less extreme form, this model of the state can also be seen in the many social democracies, which gave rise to the welfare state. *Social solidarity* is stressed in the ideologies of the social democracies, and a uniform education system available to all is considered an integral part of both implementing and maintaining this solidarity. In countries like Sweden, preference homogeneity often appears to be not only an attribute of the society, but a virtue and goal of its government.

The ideology that underlies the social-democratic state stems directly out of the 19th and early 20th century class struggles between capital and labor. Labor was poorly educated and disorganized, and thus was thought to need the protection of the state against capital. The intellectual elites that led the workers' movement and helped establish the social-democratic welfare state knew what was in labor's interests, and succeeded in providing it. The helpless worker did not have to concern himself about unemployment, the education of his children, sickness or old age. The elites who ran the welfare state ensured that the worker-citizen was protected from "cradle to grave."

The socio-economic model that best fits the welfare-state model does not seem to describe very well the developed countries at the beginning of the 21st century. Most workers are educated, many highly so. Many are capitalists in the double sense that they carry considerable *human* capable around with them in their heads, and own shares in capitalist companies. The interests of these modern capitalist/workers are not always identical with those espoused by leaders of the worker movement.

The modern, educated capitalist/worker is often capable of deciding for himself how much to save for retirement, the level of health insurance, which for him is optimal, etc. In short, the model of the social-democratic state which presumes that all citizens have homogeneous preferences, that all citizens are incapable of caring for themselves, and thus that a political elite must decide what is best for them, no longer corresponds to reality. An alternative model of the state, which allows for the diversity of interests of citizens, and allows for their capacity to make decisions for themselves is called for. Federalist democratic structures would seem likely to be a potentially important component of such a model.

Strong federalist states have existed for some time, of course, in Canada, Switzerland and the United States. Federalism arose in these countries to accommodate preexisting cultural heterogeneities, and by-and-large have succeeded in doing so. Signs of stress are apparent in all three countries, however. In Canada the preferences of some within the French-speaking Province of Quebec are sufficiently out of skew with the rest of the country that they favor complete separation. In Switzerland, one segment of the population favors further integration into Europe through membership in the European Union, while another expresses hostility toward both integration with Europe and the assimilation of non-Swiss residents already present in the country.

In the United States federalism has allowed and fostered considerable diversity across communities. Today the heterogeneity of preferences across individuals and communities appears as large as at any time in the history of the country. Consistent with the discussion above, the increasing heterogeneity of preferences in the United States has produced centrifugal pressures favoring further political mitosis. Differences in views as to what the proper content of education should be have led many individuals to remove their children from public schools and considerable heterogeneity across states and school districts with Darwinian evolution banned in some school districts, taught in others. Further implementation of voucher systems to finance education seems inevitable, and with it will come a further reduction of the harmonization of preferences and values that publicly funded education has traditionally brought. Symbolically the ultimate form of mitosis in the provision of education has been increasing most rapidly in recent years—children educated by their parents at home.

At the same time that this process of decentralization and increasing diversity has been going on in the United States, psychological externalities have been increasing in both number and apparent saliency. Many Americans demand policies with respect to abortion, birth control, environmental protection, child labor and so on, that are uniform not only across all of the United States, but across all of the world.

A similar schizophrenia with respect to federalism can be seen within the European Union. Movements toward more decentralization if not outright separation are visible from Scotland to Belgium to the Basque region of Spain and the northern hills of Italy. At the same time, however, current and prospective members of the European Union are having to *harmonize* their tax and legal structures to conform with those of the Union. Common definitions of animal and human rights are being proclaimed. (When the highest court in Turkey ruled in fall, 1999 that the execution sentence against the Kurd leader Öcalan could be carried out, one EU official remarked that Turkey's entry into the EU might be jeopardized if they carried out the execution, since the death penalty was inconsistent with European Union values.)

Thus, in both North America and Europe two, almost contradictory developments are taking place simultaneously. A process of decentralization if not outright dissolution of political structures to allow for the expression of more cultural heterogeneity can be observed in some areas, while at the same time efforts are being made by central governments to impose forms of institutional and cultural homogeneity cross-nationally. Although citizens are often directly involved in the decentralization process, the process of defining and imposing a common set of "human values" internationally has been driven by central government leaders. What seems to be emerging is a federalist governmental structure in which local units of government possess considerable leeway, when it comes to maintaining and strengthening cultural diversity—a cultural diversity which presumably extends to the definition of certain values—while at the same time central governments proclaim the existence of common, cross-cultural values. If and how these two tendencies can be reconciled in a single, institutional structure remains to be seen.

Notes

1. For an analysis of totalitarianism from a public choice perspective see Bernholz (1991, 1993).
2. Buchanan's (1954) early critique of Arrow's social-welfare-function approach emphasized the organic view of the state, which underlies it.
3. See Mueller (1996a:157–59) for a discussion of the Condorcet Jury Theorem in the context of two-party democracy, and Young (1997) for a more general discussion.
4. The pioneering discussion of this model was of course that of Tiebout (1956). See also Oates (1972), Mueller (1989, Chap. 9), and Inman and Rubinfeld (1997).
5. Epple and Zelenitz (1981) show that mobility is not sufficient for eliminating entrepreneurial rents in the voting-with-the-feet model, it is also necessary that citizens have the right to vote on government tax and expenditure policies.
6. Ironically, the United States's embargo of Cuba has made it easy for Castro to remind Cubans of who their enemy is, and thereby no doubt has helped to perpetuate his regime.
7. See, McCormick and Tollison (1981), and Brennan and Buchanan (1980).
8. See again Oates (1972), Mueller (1989, Chap. 9), and Inman and Rubinfeld (1997).
9. I have discussed the concept of psychological externalities in a different context elsewhere (Mueller 1996b).

References

Bernholz, P. (1991) "The Constitution of Totalitarianism." *Journal of Institutional and Theoretical Economics* 147(3): 425–40.

Bernholz, P. (1993) "Necessary Conditions for Totalitarianism: Supreme Values, Power and Personal Interests." In: G. Radnitzky and H. Bouillon (eds.), *Government: Servant or Master?* pp. 267–312. Amersterdam and Atlanta: Rodopi.

Brennan, G., and Buchanan, J. M. (1980) *The Power to Tax: Analytical Foundations of a Fiscal Constitution*. Cambridge: Cambridge University Press.

Buchanan, J. M. (1954) "Social Choice, Democracy, and Free Markets." *Journal of Political Economy* 62: 114–23.

Epple, D., and Zelenitz, A. (1981) "The Implications of Competing among Jurisdiction: Does Tiebout Need Politics?" *Journal of Political Economy* 89(6): 1197–1217.

Inman, R. P., and Rubinfeld,D. L. (1997) "The Political Economy of Federalism." In: D. C. Mueller (ed.), *Perspectives on Public Choice*, pp. 73–105. Cambridge: Cambridge University Press.

McCormick, R. E, and Tollison, R. T. (1981) *Politicians, Legislation, and the Economy*. Boston: Martinus Nijhoff.

Mueller, D. C. (1989) *Public Choice II*. Cambridge: Cambridge University Press.

Mueller, D. C. (1996a) *Constitutional Democracy*. Oxford: Oxford University Press.

Mueller, D. C. (1996b) "Constitutional and Liberal Rights." *Analyse & Kritik* 18: 96–117.

Oates, W. E. (1972) *Fiscal Federalism*. London: Harcourt Brace.

Schumpeter, J. A. (1950) *Capitalism, Socialism, and Democracy*, 3rd ed. New York: Harper and Row.

Stigler, G. J., and Becker, G. S. (1977) "De Gustibus Non Est Disputandum." *American Economic Review* 67(2): 76–90.

Tiebout, Ch. M. (1956) "A Pure Theory of Local Expenditures." *Journal of Political Economy* 64: 416–24.

Young, H. P. (1997) "Group Choice and Individual Judgements." In: D. C. Mueller (ed.) *Opicit*, pp. 181–200.

[9]

Defining Citizenship

*Dennis C. Mueller**

This article employs the methodology of public choice, or constitutional political economy, to the question of how citizenship should be defined in a constitution. All members of a community or an assembly representative of all members writes a constitution. Each participant in the constitution-drafting process is uncertain of his or her future identity under the constitution and thus chooses a constitution that maximizes the expected utility of all future citizens. The article describes the optimal conditions within this framework for: (1) granting citizenship to those born and raised in the country; (2) granting citizenship to those immigrating into the country; and (3) withdrawing citizenship from those who emigrate from the country. The article also discusses why it might be desirable to require that people pass certain tests and take a loyalty oath to the constitution before being awarded the privilege of voting.

Introduction

Virtually all of public choice implicitly assumes that the set of individuals who form the polity are defined exogenously prior to the beginning of the analysis. The one major exception to this statement is the literature on clubs and voting with the feet, but even this literature assumes that the pool of potential members of each club or local polity is predefined. The set of individuals who make up the largest political unit is known; only their distribution across local polities is unknown. In this paper, I take up the question of how a polity, which is autonomous from all other polities, should define its citizenship. There is some overlap with the club literature, but several separate issues are raised.

I first became interested in this question when I wrote *Constitutional*

* University of Vienna.

Democracy.[1] My goal in writing that book was to apply public choice analysis to all of the basic issues that arise when a constitution is written. The question of citizenship is certainly one of them, and thus I felt that I had to address it. Somewhat to my surprise, I found that there is not only very little written on this topic in the public choice literature, but also that very little has been written, recently at least, by political scientists.[2] Thus, I had to begin with first principles. I do so again in this paper, but also attempt to push the analysis somewhat further than I did in the earlier work.

To begin, I adopt the familiar starting-point of constitutional political economy. Individuals behind a veil of ignorance must write a constitution in which they define conditions for citizenship so as to maximize their expected utility at the constitutional stage. I then go on to consider non-utilitarian options.[3]

I. Utilitarian Definitions

To make the analysis simple, let us assume that the people living on Utopia, an isolated island in the Blissful Ocean, decide to create a state. The potential set of citizens is thus easily identified: all individuals currently living on the island.

A. Optimal Citizenship with Homogeneous Preferences

Consider first the case in which every individual on the island has the same preference function and income. The purpose in forming a state is to provide a single, lumpy public good, G. Since all potential citizens have the same preference functions, they realize that the optimal provision of the public good will involve equal tax shares. In the absence of crowding, each citizen's share of the public good's cost falls as the size of the polity increases, and its optimal size is infinity. Utopia is a small island, however, and therefore the possibility of crowding must be taken into account. Let each citizen's utility, U, be written as a function of her private good consumption; X, the public good; and the size of the polity, n.

$$U = U(X,G,n) \qquad (1)$$

1 Dennis C. Mueller, Constitutional Democracy (1996).

2 *But see* Joseph H. Carens, Citizenship and Community: A Contextual Exploration of Justice as Evenhandedness (2000).

3 I use the term *utilitarianism* simply to imply utility-maximizing behavior by rational individuals and not in any deeper, philosophical sense.

Since all individuals pay the same fraction of the public good's costs, we can define the prices of the public and private good to make $X = G/n$. Using this expression to replace X in (1) and maximizing with respect to n yields:

$$\frac{\partial U}{\partial X}\frac{G}{n^2} = -\frac{\partial U}{\partial n} \qquad (2)$$

Utopians would maximize their expected utilities by limiting the size of the population on the island so that the marginal gain in terms of a reduced share of the public good's costs from adding another person to the island just equals the marginal costs in terms of increased crowding that this person causes.

If the n that satisfies (2) is less than the population of the island, then the task of individuals at the constitutional stage is simple. All current residents are made citizens. Moreover, it will be in the interests of the current residents to allow immigration up until the community reaches the optimal size. The situation is potentially more complicated when the optimal population size for Utopia is less than its current level.

One possibility here would be to make all current residents citizens and allow free emigration. If other islands like Utopia exist, upon which the population size is less than optimal, Utopians will have an incentive to migrate to them up until the point where the population of Utopia reaches its optimal level.

A second possibility is that no such attractive options for emigration exist. Utopians will then have no other alternative but to make everyone a citizen, prohibit immigration, and perhaps take additional steps to reduce the population of Utopia by discouraging births or encouraging emigration.

B. Optimal Citizenship with Heterogeneous Preferences

Consider now the consequences of citizens having different preferences. Let there be two groups, the Blues and the Greens. The sole public good that the new state will provide is a highway across the island, whose costs will be shared equally by members of both groups. It is technologically infeasible to prevent members of either group from using the highway once it has been built. Blues favor a high quality, four-lane highway, which will allow high-speed driving with minimal delays. Greens favor a low quality, two-lane highway, which will cause low-speed driving with many delays. Looking forward into the post-constitutional stage, both groups can see that if everyone on the island is made a citizen, the outcome of the political process will be a compromise in which some parts of the highway have four lanes and other parts only two. Both groups can expect higher utility gains if they are free to construct the highway as they prefer. It would not make sense for the Greens to construct a two-lane highway alongside a four-lane one. Knowing this, the Blues have an incentive to form the state by themselves, that is, to define citizenship for only Blues, and build a four-lane highway. This is obviously true if individuals at the constitutional stage know whether they will be Blues or Greens in the post-constitutional stage. But it is also possible that all Utopians unanimously agree to form a state in which only Blues have citizenship from behind the veil of ignorance. A sufficient condition for such unanimous agreement would be, for example, that the Blues be in the majority and the utility gain for each Blue from choosing the type of highway equals the loss to each Green.[4]

If the Blues are in the majority, they could achieve the same outcome by granting Greens citizenship and simultaneously selecting the simple majority rule as the voting rule to be used for making collective decisions in the post-constitutional stage. Here we have reached an important result. For the majority group, the definition of citizenship and the choice of voting rule are substitutes. A group with an absolute majority of the population can ensure that it dictates all outcomes in the post-constitutional stage *either* by excluding members of the other group(s) from citizenship *or* by choosing a voting rule requiring a majority below that which they have, as say a simple majority. Buchanan and Tullock[5] introduced the concept of *external costs of collective decisionmaking* and used it to define the optimal voting rule from the point of view of citizens at the constitutional stage. In our example, inclusion of the Greens in the collective decision process creates a negative externality for the Blues, an externality that they can eliminate either by excluding the Greens from the collective decisionmaking process entirely or by effectively excluding them through the choice of a voting rule.

The same two options do not exist for a minority group. If the Greens constitute 35% of the population, they cannot dictate outcomes in the post-constitutional stage by choosing a one-third majority rule at the constitutional

4 Let U_B and U_G be the utilities that a Blue and Green expect to experience, if only Blues have citizenship. Let V_B and V_G be the utilities that each expects to experience, if both Blues and Greens have citizenship. Then, from behind the veil of ignorance, sole citizenship for Blues will be unanimously preferred to citizenship for both groups if

$$pU_B + (1-p)U_G > pV_B + (1-p)V_G$$

where p is the probability of being a Blue. If $p > 1-p$, then this condition is satisfied when $U_B - V_B = V_G - U_G$.

5 James M. Buchanan & Gordon Tullock, The Calculus of Consent (1962).

stage, for the Blues would easily satisfy this requirement. The Greens' only option if they want their most-preferred outcomes to win would be to create a state in which only Greens have the right to decide for the combined community of Blues and Greens.[6]

Although limiting citizenship to only certain groups is a *possible* outcome from the constitutional process, when individuals have heterogeneous preferences, it is of course not an inevitable one. The possibility that both groups obtain citizenship and compromises emerge out of post-constitutional politics exists when individuals define citizenship from behind the veil of ignorance. The likelihood of this happening increases if we expand the number of post-constitutional collective choices and allow for more groups, so that every group has a chance of being part of the majority on some future issues. Although such assumptions increase the likelihood of inclusive definitions of citizenship, they do not guarantee it, when individuals choose definitions of citizenship that maximize their expected utility. With sufficient preference heterogeneity, the expected utility of an individual at the constitutional stage will be maximized — *even from behind the veil of ignorance* — by excluding some groups from affecting future collective choices. This can always be accomplished by excluding these groups from citizenship. When these groups constitute a minority of the population, they can be effectively excluded even when granted citizenship, by choosing the simple majority rule as the community's voting rule.

If one group of Utopians can create a state and exclude the other group from citizenship, it might, of course, be possible for this group to force the non-citizen residents to pay for all of the public good or even to become slaves of the dominant group. By appropriate choices of utility functions and group sizes, we could even show that both Blues and Greens would unanimously agree from behind the veil of ignorance that, say, the Greens would become slaves to the Blues in the post-constitutional stage. Such possibilities, however remote they might be in reality, have often caused some observers to reject utilitarian defenses of certain actions and institutions in favor of non-utilitarian options. We consider next one of these.[7]

---

6 Thus, the only way Whites could dictate outcomes in South Africa was by denying Blacks voting rights. Blacks, on the other hand, can dictate outcomes even when Whites are allowed to vote under the simple majority rule.

7 Among economists, Amartya Sen has been one of the most forceful opponents of "welfarism." Amartya K. Sen, *Rational Fools: A Critique of the Behavioral Foundations of Economic Theory*, 6 Phil. & Pub. Aff. 317 (1977); Amartya K. Sen, *Personal Utilities and Public Judgements: or What's Wrong with Welfare Economics?*, 89 Econ. J. 537 (1979).

II. A Just Definition of Citizenship

John Rawls'[8] contractarian alternative to utilitarianism is, perhaps, the most obvious place to begin to define criteria for citizenship that do not rely upon a utilitarian calculus. A *just* definition of citizenship is chosen instead of one that maximizes the expected utility of every person behind the veil of ignorance.

Rawls eliminates utilitarian calculations by denying individuals behind the veil of ignorance all information about both the preferences of future citizens and the probabilities of being any one of them. It would thus be a trivial extension of Rawls' reasoning to show that Utopians would choose to grant both Blues and Greens equal citizenship from behind a Rawlsian veil of ignorance.

Rawls defends his characterization of the veil of ignorance with the following arguments:

> Somehow we must nullify the effects of specific contingencies which put men at odds and tempt them to exploit social and natural circumstances to their own advantage. Now in order to do this I assume that the parties are situated behind a veil of ignorance. They do not know how the various alternatives will affect their own particular case and they are obliged to evaluate principles solely on the basis of general considerations.
>
> It is assumed, then, that the parties do not know certain kinds of particular facts. First of all, no one knows his place in society... . More than this, I assume that the parties do not know the particular circumstances of their own society. That is, they do not know its economic or political situation, or the level of civilization and culture it has been able to achieve.[9]

And a bit further on,

> Now the reasons for the veil of ignorance go beyond mere simplicity. We want to define the original position so that we get the desired solution. If knowledge of particulars is allowed, then the outcome is biased by arbitrary contingencies.[10]

8 John A. Rawls, A Theory of Justice (1971).

9 *Id.* at 136-37 (citation omitted).

10 *Id.* at 141.

Rawls spends considerable time discussing the implications of his theory for thc issue of intergenerational justice, but it would seem rather obvious that the theory should apply equally to *where* one is born as to *when* one is born. Knowledge of the country in which one lives would seem to be one of the "arbitrary contingencies" that Rawls seeks to remove from the original position with the veil of ignorance. If "parties do not know the particular circumstances of their own society..., its economic or political situation, or the level of civilization and culture it has been able to achieve," they cannot know whether they have been born onto a rich and democratic island, to which many will wish to migrate, or on a poor and desperate island, from which many will wish to flee. The kind of liberal society that Rawls seeks to create would certainly allow Utopians to migrate to other islands and people from other islands to move to Utopia. Thus, someone behind the veil of ignorance *ought* to assume that she might be born on Utopia or born anywhere else in the world. Accidents of birth — including location — are just that — accidents — and thus have no place in determining the set of just institutions that emerge from behind the veil of ignorance. A person born on Utopia has no more right to the riches of this island than does a person born on any less well-endowed island. The just definition of citizenship in Utopia would make it available not only to all persons living on Utopia, but to all persons currently living anywhere else and, of course, to all future persons regardless of where they are born.

Application of the Rawlsian logic thus would lead to a definition of citizenship that would not only grant it to all current residents of the island, but would imply liberal criteria for new residents. If Utopia happened to be a very rich island, migration from poorer places could be expected. Such migration would continue until the average level of utility on Utopia were reduced due to crowding to that of the poorest island/country in the world.[11] If all countries adopted the same, just definitions of citizenship and all of the people of the world were free to migrate, migration could be expected to continue until the average level of welfare in every country of the world is the same.

If a rich country like Switzerland were to adopt such a just definition of citizenship, literally millions of people from the poor countries of the world would flock to it. Congestion costs would eventually mount and the Swiss standard of living would sink toward that of the poor countries supplying it with population. The equilibrium obtained would

11 See discussion in Frank Flatters et al., *Public Goods, Efficiency, and Regional Fiscal Equalization*, 3 J. Pub. Econ. 99 (1974).

not be Pareto-optimal, since the migrants would be ignoring the *marginal* impacts of their movements, but this alone would not necessarily overturn the justness of a liberal definition of citizenship, since under Rawls' theory it is only the possibility of improving the welfare of the worst-off person in the world that carries weight. Since the poor can always be expected to be better off in a rich country, application of the difference principle would always imply free migration between poor and rich countries.

Such a liberal definition of citizenship would seem likely to result in a great destruction of wealth in the process of redistributing it. Regardless of whether such an outcome is desirable or not, it is obviously never going to come about. No rich country like the United States or Switzerland is going to open its doors to unlimited immigration. Applying Rawlsian criteria, this may only go to show how unjust these countries are. Alternatively, we might conclude that the logic of Rawls' theory of justice is too demanding and continue our search for other criteria. In doing so, we must recognize, however, that we are taking a long step back toward the utilitarian position, for we are in effect rejecting a very liberal definition of citizenship on the grounds that no veil of ignorance could ever be thick enough to induce the current occupants of Utopia to adopt a definition of citizenship that would ensure that they are all made much worse off in the post-constitutional stage.

Thus, on pragmatic grounds, we are driven back to some utilitarian approach to defining citizenship and to the question of how those individuals who are not among the initial group of citizens as defined by the constitution can attain citizenship. In exploring this question, we again adopt the assumption that individuals from behind the veil of ignorance choose definitions of citizenship that maximize their expected utility, but we now grant them knowledge of the island upon which they are born and its state of economic and political development.

III. Acquiring Citizenship

A. By Place of Birth

It seems so obvious that the first generation of Utopians will wish to have their children and grandchildren become citizens, that we need not spend considerable time defending this assumption. We shall, however, come back to consider the *kind* of citizenship each child can claim.

Our first candidate for a criterion for acquiring citizenship in Utopia is, thus, that one be born in Utopia to parents who are already citizens of Utopia.

This criterion raises two obvious questions, however: (1) What should be the status of persons born in Utopia, if their parents are not citizens? (2) What should be the status of persons born outside of Utopia, if their parents are citizens?

When answering these questions from behind the veil of ignorance, the constitution-framers will again wish to consider the two criteria mentioned above: the size of the population relative to the optimal size and the effect of easy citizenship on the heterogeneity of the population. If Utopia's population were far below its optimal level, extremely liberal criteria for citizenship would be a possible way of expanding the population. Granting citizenship to babies born to temporary visitors might then be optimal. Presumably, the extreme imbalance between land and people in the United States at the end of the eighteenth century explains why it chose such a liberal policy. Absent an extreme shortage of population, however, it is not obvious why any country would choose such a policy today, since temporary visitors are not likely to have the same preferences for government policies as long-time citizens.

Citizens' views about government and preferences for government policies are formed by the education they receive from their parents, their schools, and churches and the other institutions in their community. In short, citizens' preferences are a product, at least in part, of the culture in which they grow up. Automatically granting citizenship to persons who happen to be born in a country risks increasing the heterogeneity of the citizenry and the attendant costs in terms of altered collective choice outcomes and higher decisionmaking costs. The writers of the constitution of a country that is not short of population would not find it optimal to grant citizenship solely based on the location of birth.

B. By Pedigree

To ensure freedom of movement, the constitution must grant citizenship to persons born to citizens who are temporarily outside of the country. What, however, should be the status of children of citizens who have taken up *permanent* residence abroad? What, moreover, should be the status of their parents?

If the constitution-framers do not wish to discourage mobility, they will not require that citizens living abroad forfeit their citizenship after living, say, x years abroad, but will strip citizens of their citizenship only if they acquire citizenship in the new country of permanent residence. If the constitution-framers were to withdraw citizenship from anyone who has lived more than x years abroad, they would effectively be forcing all citizens living abroad to return within those x years.

The situation is somewhat different, however, for citizens who live abroad and acquire citizenship in their new country of residence. Their children will presumably also acquire citizenship in that country. Their children's preferences will be shaped by the culture in which they grow up and are likely to differ from those of the typical Utopian. Weighing from behind the veil of ignorance the cost and benefits of granting dual citizenship to such children living in another country who have citizenship in that country, those writing Utopia's constitution may well choose to deny Utopian citizenship to children of its citizens living abroad.

Indeed, the constitution-framers may wish to strip any citizen of Utopia of her citizenship once she acquires citizenship in a second country in which she permanently resides. Central to the modern conception of citizenship is the right to vote. Citizens of Utopia living abroad can be assumed to be allowed to vote in Utopia's elections, at least at the national level. A citizen living abroad who pays taxes to finance education, highway construction, etc., in Utopia is likely to have quite a different perspective on the optimal level of taxes and expenditures than a citizen living in Utopia. The citizen abroad experiences little, if any, benefits from such outlays, while bearing the full brunt of their costs. Including the votes of citizens residing outside of the country is likely to shift the chosen levels of taxes and expenditures downward from those that the resident Utopians would select and thereby lower the welfare of the latter. The expected utility of a citizen behind the veil of ignorance might well be maximized, therefore, by denying dual citizenship to persons living abroad. This would provide those abroad with the great benefit of not having to pay taxes in Utopia, but at the cost of not being able to vote in or retain a passport from Utopia.[12]

An alternative would, of course, be to exempt citizens abroad from paying taxes in Utopia, while allowing them to retain their citizenship. Tax exemption would eliminate their incentive to vote for very low government outlays. But what then would be their incentive to vote at all or to become informed about the issues if they do vote?

The specter of rationally ignorant voters deciding tax and expenditure policies has haunted normative justifications for democracy for over fifty

12 One might be concerned that a Utopian living abroad would lose her right to return to Utopia if she lost her citizenship after x years abroad. This cost could be removed by allowing x-citizens the right to re-attain citizenship quickly upon their return to Utopia.

years.[13] A citizen living abroad who neither consumes most of the public goods provided by the country nor pays for them has far less incentive to become informed about the issues in an election than does the citizen who resides in the country. The citizen abroad also is much less likely to obtain information about the issues in an election inadvertently by reading newspapers, watching television, talking with friends, etc. Thus, it is difficult to see how the inclusion of the votes of citizens abroad could improve the collective outcome for Utopia. These votes must be regarded as, at best, white noise. Recognizing this, one can well imagine that the constitution-framers would, after x years, strip citizens living abroad either of their citizenship[14] or, at a minimum, of their right to vote in Utopian elections.

The possible desirability of separating citizen voting rights from the other rights that accompany citizenship is an important implication of the analysis, for it raises the possibility of having different levels or degrees of citizenship, a point to which we shall return in the next section. But first, I take up a third possible criterion for citizenship.

C. By Length of Residence

Visitors to Utopia on business are concerned about the quality of police protection, public transportation, laws governing business transactions, the quality of the judiciary, and perhaps a few more governmentally-provided goods and services. They are not going to be concerned about the quality of public education and many other publicly-provided goods, however. Even if it were feasible to do so, it would not be in the interests of Utopians to grant visitors to Utopia temporary citizenship and rights to vote.

The same can be said, however, with respect to those immigrating from abroad and taking up residence in Utopia. These persons will, presumably, be consumers of the full spectrum of publicly-provided goods and services and will pay the same taxes as any Utopian citizen in a similar situation. Thus, a foreigner who is a permanent resident of Utopia might well desire the right to vote and the other rights that accompany citizenship, but it will typically not be to the advantage of the citizens of Utopia to grant foreign-born residents these rights — or at least not until they have resided in Utopia

---

13 *See* Joseph A. Schumpeter, Capitalism and Democracy 260-64 (3d ed. 1950); Anthony Downs, An Economic Theory of Democracy at chs. 11-14 (1957).

14 A possible opposite bias to the one just discussed is introduced when citizens abroad pay no taxes. They may now favor much larger outlays for foreign service, international organizations, development aid, etc., than resident, tax-paying citizens desire.

for a considerable length of time. The foreign-born resident who benefits Utopia's citizens through the taxes that he pays could harm Utopians by voting, if his preferences are significantly different from those of Utopians. By not granting immigrants citizenship, Utopia's citizens enjoy the benefits from the taxes paid by the immigrants, without incurring the possible costs of allowing them to vote. When Utopia's constitution is written, if its writers consider only the possibility of being descendants from the initial group of citizens and not from immigrants, they will not choose to grant immigrants citizenship.

There are three considerations that might change this calculus and lead to the initial constitution providing for immigrants to acquire citizenship after, say, y years of residence. First, there may be costs to Utopia's citizens from having long-time residents not possess full citizenship. Immigrant groups may become alienated, and this alienation may lead to frictions that impose costs on Utopia's citizens as well as on the immigrants.

Second, and related to the first point, Utopia's citizens may bear psychological costs from seeing their immigrant friends and neighbors devoid of citizenship. The utility functions of Utopians may have, or with time may come to have, the welfare of immigrants as an argument. Utopians may experience utility gains, therefore, from seeing immigrants made better off through the attainment of citizenship.

Third, the costs of granting immigrants the right to vote that arise due to heterogeneity of preferences should decline with time as immigrants absorb the culture of Utopia and their preferences become more like those of Utopia's citizens. All of these considerations suggest that the Utopians who write the constitution may find it optimal to include a provision that allows immigrants to obtain citizenship after some y years of residence.

IV. Citizenship Tests

A. For Immigrants

If one drops a sponge into a bucket of water, it begins to absorb the water immediately and continues to do so until it becomes saturated. All sponges absorb water at about the same rate. All persons who are "dropped" into a country do not "absorb" its culture at the same rate, however. The speed of absorption will depend on whether the newcomer must learn a new language as part of absorbing the culture; the effort that she expends to learn the language and/or to absorb the culture; etc. Similar considerations apply to the newcomer's children. Thus, a policy of allowing immigrants to apply for citizenship after y years of residence, on the grounds that they should be granted citizenship only after they have absorbed a sufficient amount of Utopia's culture so that their participation in the political process does not produce significant negative externalities for existing Utopian citizens, is likely to result in some persons receiving citizenship before they have fully adopted Utopia's culture, whereas other persons have to wait too long for their citizenship. An alternative to granting citizenship on the basis of years of residence, therefore, would be to require that immigrants pass a test before they can attain citizenship, a test to determine how much of Utopia's culture has been absorbed.

What would be the content of such a test? The language of Utopia is one obvious component, since language opens the door to the learning of all other aspects of a country's culture. Knowledge of the country's political institutions is another, since one cannot participate effectively in a political process unless one knows something about how it functions; knowledge of Utopia's history, its religion perhaps, if its people all practice a single religion, and so on. Obviously, the more criteria one includes in the test, the more difficult it will be to satisfy these criteria, and the harder it will be to acquire citizenship. It is equally obvious, however, that the easier Utopia makes it for immigrants to acquire citizenship, the greater the costs that its citizens will bear, because of the differences between their preferences for public goods and services and those of the immigrants. Different countries can be expected to resolve this tradeoff differently.

B. For Non-Immigrants

Once one recognizes that someone else's vote can cause a negative externality for a citizen, if the other person's preferences differ from those of the citizen, it becomes obvious that this is true, regardless of whether the other person was born outside of Utopia to parents who were not citizens or was born within Utopia to citizens. A person who favors the overthrow of Utopia's democracy poses a threat to its citizens that is more or less independent of her origin of birth and parentage. Should, then, persons who meet the normal criteria for citizenship in terms of place of birth and parentage *also* have to pass a test before they are allowed to vote? Should they have to pass the same test as immigrants seeking citizenship?

It is difficult to see how the answer to the first question can be anything other than a qualified yes. Costs are costs. If a country chooses to exclude persons from citizenship if they lack an understanding of the country's language, history, and culture, it should logically apply the same standard to persons who would otherwise qualify for citizenship, for the failure of the latter to meet the requirements demanded by the test imposes the same costs on the rest of the community as would that of an immigrant. The qualification to this statement comes from the possibility that the education levels and cultural homogeneity of a country may be such that it would expect a very high percentage of those born and raised in it to be able to pass the required test. Transaction costs could thus be saved by not requiring those who would automatically obtain their citizenship by birth to take such a test. In countries where education levels are not uniformly high and cultural heterogeneity is significant, the participation of everyone in the political process is likely to impose significant costs on others. Those who weigh these costs from behind the veil of ignorance might well, therefore, choose to restrict citizenship to those who can demonstrate knowledge of the country's political system, history, and culture, *independent* of their origin of birth.

V. Loyalty Oaths

In most countries, individuals convicted of serious crimes are not allowed to vote. Why? The social benefit from removing a bank robber from society for a period of time is clear, but what does society gain from denying him the opportunity to vote? Perhaps he has children and is interested in the quality of their education. Why should he not be allowed to express his preferences on this issue? Why should he not be allowed to express his preferences on national defense, foreign aid, and the treatment of the poor? He certainly has a strong interest in the quality of prisons and the treatment of prisoners. Communities do not forbid hospital patients from voting on issues related to medical care funding, nor students from voting on issues related to education spending, so why treat prisoners differently?

If there is a justification for denying prisoners the privilege of voting, it is presumably because their past actions have revealed them to be in a real and meaningful sense "enemies of the people." Their views as to what is good for society and themselves are sufficiently different from those of the average citizen, so that significant costs would be imposed on society from recording the preferences of prisoners with respect to public policies.[15]

But are convicted felons serving time the only enemies of the people? Is the neo-Nazi or anarchist who advocates the overthrow of the democratic

15 Given the minute probability that a prisoner's vote affects the outcome of an election, it is doubtful that many persons place sufficient value on the privilege of voting to be deterred from commiting crimes for fear of losing this privilege.

state not just as much an enemy? Indeed, are they not greater enemies? In addition to demanding that people know something about thc political institutions and history of a country before they are allowed to become full citizens, the writers of Utopia's constitution might wish to demand that they take some sort of oath of loyalty to its political institutions. At a minimum, such a requirement would help to ensure that those who are allowed to vote know something about these political institutions. In addition, it might just deter some of those who are opposed to these institutions from trying to undermine them.

VI. Discussion

In his celebrated description of life in anarchy, Thomas Hobbes[16] vividly illustrated the problems that arise when individual interests are in conflict. Hobbes' solution to these problems was to grant all individuals citizenship in a newly created polity, in which they became subservient to a monarch. In such a polity, conflicts of interests and heterogeneous preferences would not matter, since the implicit "voting rule" would only weigh the preferences of a single person.

John Stuart Mill,[17] although a great champion of democracy and ardent advocate of proportional representation because of its greater inherent fairness than two-party government, was opposed to extending the franchise to those lacking in education and property, for fear that it would lead to "mediocrity."

Most advocates of two-party democracy place its greater stability high on their list of its advantages. To the extent that two-party systems are more stable, it is because they tend to limit the choices of voters to two, rather centrally positioned candidates or parties. Individuals with preferences that are far askew from those of the median voter have the right to vote, but are not offered parties or candidates who espouse their views on the major issues. Even in so-called proportional representation systems like those of Germany and Austria, groups with heterodox preferences are often denied representation in the legislatures by setting high minimum cutoffs for the percentage of votes that a party must win before it can claim seats. In Germany and Austria, these cutoffs are set at 5% of the vote.

The third and most commonly used way to deny groups with preferences that deviate dramatically from those of the "mainstream" is, of course, to employ the simple majority rule to decide issues in the legislature. Knut

16 Thomas Hobbes, Leviathan (1651).

17 John Stuart Mill, On Liberty at ch. 8 (1859).

Wicksell,[18] writing at a time when most of the poor were not enfranchised, considered one of the important advantages of the unanimity rule to be that it increases the political power of the poor.

Thus, in practice, societies have recognized the costs of enfranchising individuals whose knowledge or preferences deviate dramatically from those of the bulk of the community and have implicitly, if not explicitly, tried to ensure that the enfranchisement of such groups does not place undue costs on the rest of the community, by choosing either electoral rules or a voting rule that effectively disenfranchises those with deviant preferences. In this paper, I have instead focused on the more fundamental question of whom to enfranchise.

It is clear from history that those who have created democracies have been aware of the costs of enfranchising people with preferences and interests that differ from their own. Thus, for many years the indigenous populations of Australia, South Africa, and the Americas were barred from voting by the European populations that migrated to these continents. In none of these cases were the political institutions that were put into place designed by people who had stepped behind the veil of ignorance and imagined that they had equal probabilities of being members of each group. Had they done so, it is unlikely that they would have created the kinds of institutions that they did. But it is also unlikely, given the vast cultural differences that separated the different populations, that constitutional conventions that fairly represented all communities would have been capable of drafting democratic constitutions that made citizens of all members of both communities. The European invaders and indigenous populations were effectively in a state of anarchy at the time that the Europeans first created democratic institutions for themselves, and they remained so for some time afterward.

We live in an increasingly mobile world. It is also a world in which democratic values are given increasing weight. More and more people can be expected to choose to live for long periods, if not permanently, in countries in which they initially do not possess citizenship. These migrants can be expected to seek citizenship in their newfound homes. Granting them citizenship can present costs and benefits for the existing population of citizens. One way to increase the cost-benefit ratio is to establish criteria and tests for citizenship. There are good reasons for also requiring that those who are born within a country and would ordinarily acquire citizenship automatically satisfy these same requirements for citizenship.

---

18 Knut Wicksell, A New Principle of Just Taxation (1896), *reprinted in* Classics in the Theory of Public Finance 72 (Richard A. Musgrave & Alan T. Peacock eds., 1967).

Public Choice **90:** 255–280, 1997.

Federalism and the European Union: A constitutional perspective*

DENNIS C. MUELLER
Department of Economics, University of Vienna, BWZ-Brünner Str. 72, A-1210 Vienna, Austria

Abstract. Constitutional questions have resurfaced in the last few years with regard to the European Union. The Maastricht Treaty is a kind of constitutional reform. The rejection of this treaty by Denmark in its first referendum, and the subsequent debate of the treaty that has taken place, raise questions about both the nature of the European Union, and the process by which its rules (constitution) get revised and approved. Similar questions surround the entry of Austria and the three, additional Scandinavian countries into the Union. Perhaps, no event called the European Union's constitution, or lack thereof, into question more that way in which a new President of the Commission was chosen during the summer of 1994. This paper will reexamine the European Union's structure and procedures from a constitutional perspective. Drawing upon the author's recently completed book, *Constitutional Democracy*, the paper will review the purpose for the Union's existence, the implications of this purpose for the structure of the Union (federalism versus confederation), the rules for making collective decisions in the Union, citizenship, and in particular, the procedures by which the European Union's "Constitution" is written and revised. The constitutional perspective adopted is taken from public choice. The political institutions of the European Union are examined relative to those rational, self-interested individuals would choose to advance their interests.

1. Introduction

Denmark's first rejection of the Maastricht Treaty and the ensuing questions raised about the treaty in other countries have again brought to the fore the issue of whether a true European federalism can (should) be created. This is essentially a constitutional question, and the Maastricht Treaty, like its predecessors signed in Rome and Paris, is a form of constitution for Europe, although a rather unusual one written in a rather unusual manner. These features may help to explain the indecisive response to the treaty by citizens and governments across Europe.

Understandably, the post-Denmark debate within Europe focussed on the Maastricht Treaty's provisions and their likely impact on different countries

* The financial support for this research of the Ludwig Boltzmann Institut is gratefully acknowledged.

and groups in Europe. But the treaty implicitly raises, and answers, more basic issues about the desirability of a "United States of Europe", the structure it should have, and the process by which it should come into existence. These are old questions in Europe having been debated on and off since the Community's founding after World War II. They have assumed renewed importance, since the first vote of the Danes. This article's thesis is that the process by which European integration has moved forward has in effect dictated the form that integration takes, and that European citizens have not been allowed to decide whether or not they want a true federalist structure for the European Union.

The most basic question to be asked, of course, is whether such a European government should exist in the first place. This question is taken up in the next section. We then turn to the issue of the structure of government, and in particular whether a federalist structure as in North America and Switzerland, or a confederation, as has existed up until now in the European community, is more appropriate (Section 3). The answer to this question has important implications for the choice of representational structure (Section 4), and voting rules used (Section 5). It also impacts the criteria for citizenship (Section 6), and the process by which a European government should be created (Sections 7 and 8). Should Europe adopt a fully federalist structure, a key question for it would be how to maintain that structure given the pressures toward centralization that seem to exist in all federalist nations. This issue is addressed in Section 9. In Section 10 the admission of additional members is discussed. After taking up each of these issues in a general way, we return in the closing section to the Maastricht Treaty, and the constitutional questions it raises.

2. The purpose and role of government

We shall assume that the purpose of government is to advance the interests of the citizens. A citizen's interests include those things that advance her welfare narrowly defined, e.g., the pleasure she gets from owning a car, the pleasure she gets from driving her car on a road built and maintained by the government, etc. But they can also be construed to include preferences for outcomes that do not impact directly and narrowly on the citizen. The happiness she gets from, and thus interest in, food relief for starving citizens in another country, or more meanly the pleasure from knowing that a religious minority has been prevented from practicing its religion.

Many of these interests can be advanced without having to resort to governmental institutions. This is obvious for the pleasures one gets from consuming private goods, but it may even be true for the joint consumption of "public goods". All farmers in a valley may benefit from damming a stream to prevent flooding and aid in irrigation. Such a dam would be a public good for the community of farmers. But it might well be provided without the need for a government or government intervention, if the number of farmers is small. They might simply agree to build the dam with each voluntarily contributing time, effort and money to achieve the goal (Coase, 1960). Citizens across the world can enjoy the satisfaction from knowing that they have helped to relieve the pain from a disaster in a particular part of it by contributing to voluntary relief organizations like the Red Cross.

The farmers building the dam and the Red Cross may be thought of as voluntarily formed "clubs", ad hoc in the one case, permanent in the other, for providing particular public goods. They can accomplish this task efficiently so long as numbers are small, and free-riding is not significant. But if the valley and stream (river) are large with hundreds of thousands of inhabitants with different occupations, and differing benefits (some perhaps even negative) from the dam, the costs of finding out what each would be willing to contribute to build the dam, and of actually raising the money and building it may be large. Government, a form of "involuntary club" to which all members of the community belong and contribute, may be the lowest cost institution for determining what public goods and other collective actions should be undertaken and how to pay for them (Dahlman, 1979; Mueller, 1989: Ch. 2). Democratic government is an institution for revealing this information by voting.

Thus, each member of a community has an interest in seeing that institutions of government are created to provide public goods and other public policies that potentially can benefit all members of the community. Of course, each action of government will not make every member of the community better off. But we take it as axiomatic that the combined actions of government ought to make all citizens better off, and that the kinds of decisions that are peculiarly within government's domain of activity are those that could potentially make every citizen better off. Moreover, even these actions are undertaken by government only when other voluntary organizations, like private clubs and charities, cannot carry them out efficiently because of the high decisionmaking costs that accompany free-riding and other forms of opportunistic behavior in large communities.

We have here what is obviously a *normative* description of what government ought to do, not a positive description of what real governments actually do. Countless actions that governments undertake do not fulfill the requirement that they even *potentially* might increase the welfare of all members of the community. A tariff on shoes protects the wages and dividends of those who supply labor and capital to shoe manufacturers to the loss of all shoe buyers.

258

A small dam financed by the central government benefits a handful of farmers to the loss of all taxpayers.

That actual governments undertake actions that make some citizens better off at the expense of others can be easily understood once one recognizes that the individual interests that government advances are often quite narrowly focussed, and the democratic institutions that register those interests, like the simple majority rule, give those in government strong incentives to advance the interests of only *some* members of the community. But actual governments, of course, already exist. No community would agree to create a government just so that one part of the community could be made better off at the expense of the rest. Most purchasers of shoes would presumably oppose the creation of a government, if the only planned activity of that government was to impose a tariff on shoes.[1]

These arguments imply that, if no European-wide political institutions existed today, and the citizens of Europe were to contemplate creating a European-wide government, they would rationally do so only if they all expected to benefit from it. The citizens of France would not help found a European government, if all that this government would do is tax the French and subsidize the Germans. Thus, to determine whether or not a European government should exist, we must inquire whether there are European-wide public goods and other sorts of public policies which *would* benefit all Europeans, but would *not* be provided in the absence of such a government, because of the high decisionmaking costs from doing so. Both conditions are necessary. If there are no pan-European public goods, e.g., all environmental problems have no cross-national spillovers, no European government is needed. Even if individual environmental problems involve more than one country, a European-wide government is not required to solve them if the decisionmaking costs of solving these problems by say bilateral or multilateral negotiations among the affected countries are lower than the implicit costs of resolving them within the governmental structure of a European-wide government.

The European unification agenda has, of course, contained several items that would potentially meet the definition of a public good, e.g., a common currency.[2] I shall not pause here to discuss whether this or other items on the agenda would or would not in fact potentially benefit all Europeans. The point to be made is that such pan-European public goods must exist, *and* a European government must be the lowest cost way of obtaining them to justify its creation. Whether a European-wide government is the lowest cost method for Europeans to consume European-wide public goods jointly cannot be determined, however, without knowing more about the structure that should underlie this government. We turn to that question now.

3. A federation or a confederation of Europe?

We can conceptualize three distinct governmental structures:[3]

(1) *Unitary government.* A single level of government exists in which all citizens participate directly or are represented directly by a person or party which they elected. All collective decisions affecting the citizen are made by this level of government.

(2) *Federalist government.* Two or more levels of government exist, each of which has primary if not sole responsibility for particular collective decisions. An individual is a citizen of the federal state and of each of the lower levels of government in which she resides. She participates directly or elects representatives to the legislative assemblies for each level.

(3) *A confederation of governments.* Separate autonomous governments are represented in an assembly to make collective decisions. Individuals are citizens in the constituent governmental units, but are represented only indirectly through their elected governments in the confederation's assembly.

The city states of ancient Greece or Renaissance Italy are examples of unitary states. Switzerland and the United States are prototype federalisms. NATO is a typical confederation of governments.

Which of these three governmental structures is best for making the collective decisions a community faces depends on its size, location and degree of heterogeneity. A community living on a small island may be able to make all of its collective decisions with a single governmental unit. A community living on a big island, like Australia, may find it optimal to subdivide its decision process in the form of a federalist structure. The invasion of any part of Australia by a foreign army puts all Australians at risk, thus all Australians have a common interest in defense against foreign invasion. But Australians who live in Melbourne are not affected by burglaries and fires in Perth. Optimal levels of fire and police protection and the taxes to finance them are better decided at a local level of government in a country the size of Australia. Federalism is the obvious form of government to employ.[4]

Under an ideal federalism the citizens at a given level of government consume the same government good or service, e.g., defense at the national level, police protection at the local level. Citizens may have different views as to the optimal quantity and characteristics of a public good provided at a particular level, but these views are not determined by the geographic location of the citizens. Hawks on defense are just as likely to be found in Sidney as in Perth. The task of democratic procedures is to aggregate these differing views and determine the optimal policy for the entire community.

It can happen, however, that the views on a particular government action are to a large extent defined by the location of their holders. For example, one's hawkishness on defense may depend in part on one's distance from the

260

likely point of an initial attack. When this is the case, and when the views of all citizens in a given area are already represented in a government, their views on more macro collective action can be adequately represented by the governments to which they already belong. If the views of Americans about common defense policies with Europeans were fundamentally the same, and the same was true for members of each European country, then the NATO confederation can be claimed to be an optimal governmental structure. The issue facing Europe is whether the common issues that it faces, and the attitudes of its citizens to these issues, are such as to make a federation or a confederation the optimal governmental structure.

Consider the following two environmental issues. The thinning of the ozone layer, let us assume, affects all Europeans equally. Some Europeans spend more time outdoors than others, some are genetically more vulnerable to skin cancer, some are more risk averse. But these characteristics vary uniformly across all of Europe. A Frenchman is no more likely to feel strongly about protecting the ozone layer than a Dane. For this type of issue, the optimal representational structure would weigh the preferences of each Dane for environmental protection identically to those of each Frenchman. If all collective choice issues that extend beyond national borders in Europe were of this type, then the optimal governmental structure for Europe would be a federalism. Environmental issues like the thinning of the ozone layer and global warming would be decided at the highest level of government in a European parliament in which Europeans were represented on the basis of their preferences with respect to these pan-European issues, not their place of residence. Given the importance of cultural and language differences, regional governments corresponding to the present nation states would most certainly exist with public issues like education assigned to them. Still other lower levels of government to handle police and fire protection and other local issues might also be present.

Now consider a second type of transnational environmental issue. A river's source is in country *A*, its mouth is in *C*, and in between it flows through *B*. The preferences of the citizens of each country for clean water, economic development, etc., are similar. Local communities and businesses along the banks of the river all contaminate it to an equal degree. The citizens of *A* suffer the least from the river's pollution, however, since the river starts off unpolluted and obtains only a modest level of pollution while flowing through its borders. Citizens of *C* suffer the most from the river's degradation, since it contains not only the pollutants its residents put into it, but also those remaining from *B* and *A*. The antipollution policies advocated for protecting the river advocated by citizens in *A* can be expected to be somewhat similar and quite different from those advocated by citizens from *B* or *C*. For this kind of collective decision all citizens of *A* may be adequately represented by a delegate from their government, as is true for *B* and *C*. If the only transnational issues to be decided in Europe were of this type, a confederation would suffice.

Thus, the question of whether a federalist or a confederalist structure of government is appropriate for Europe can be seen to depend on the nature of collective decisions Europeans have to make. If they are pan-European in the sense that they potentially affect all Europeans equally, a federalist structure is most appropriate. If they are transnational but not pan-European, i.e., they affect the citizens of more than one country, but not necessarily all Europeans, and certainly not all Europeans in the same way and to the same degree, then a confederation is more appropriate. We shall not venture an opinion on whether collective issues in Europe are more of one form or the other. We turn instead to the issues of optimal representation in each case.

4. The representation of citizen preferences

Many types of representation systems exist, but they can be broadly grouped into two categories – two-party and multiparty systems. The rationale behind the two is quite different. The objective under a two-party system is to "choose a government", i.e., to choose that party or party leader who a majority of citizens believe will best run the government until the next election (Bagehot, 1872; Mueller, 1996: Chs. 9, 10). The logic underlying a multiparty form of government is to have all the different views and preferences toward government action represented in the parliament, which in turn will decide government policy based on these preferences. A case can be made for each form of government. I shall not make that case here.[5] With the exceptions of the United Kingdom and sometimes France, all European countries have opted for some form of multimember-district representation which generally produces multiparty systems. I shall assume, therefore, that a European parliament would have its membership chosen by a proportional representation (PR) formula.

Within the PR systems one can again distinguish two broad categories: those which require that a citizen vote for a party, and those which allow her to designate her choice of person within the party. If the former were employed, its logical structure would have all parties listed on the ballots each voter marks regardless of the voter's country of residence. The voter would select the party she most preferred to have represent her views in the European parliament and seats in the parliament would be allocated in proportion to the number of votes each party received.

262

Most countries use a variant on the above system in which the electorate is divided into geographic districts within which the procedure is followed to elect a subset of the total number of seats in the parliament. This procedure is also used to elect representatives to the European Parliament in Strasbourg. The disadvantage of this variant is that it prevents those in a district who favor a minority party from being proportionally represented. If there are ten parties running, and there are ten seats, say, to be filled from a district, the major parties will fill a majority of them and the smallest parties will fill none.

The goal of having representatives from different countries taking seats in the parliament can and would be achieved under a party list system that treated all of Europe as a single electoral district, if each party chose members from the several countries to occupy positions on its list. Alternatively, a single-transferable-vote (STV) system could be used in which the voters designated not only the party they preferred, but their ranking of candidates within the party. If European citizens favored candidates of their own nationality, they could indicate that by ranking them higher. An STV system could lead to both proportional representation of parties and of nationalities of representatives. But it would also allow voters to disregard such provincialism if they chose, and simply vote for the persons from their favored parties whom they most preferred, regardless of their nationality.[6]

In a purely confederate form of government, all citizens within a country are presumed to have the same or at least very similar preferences with respect to the issues to be decided by the confederation. Thus, one delegation from the country, indeed one person, could adequately represent all of the citizens' views. Having a single parliament in which all citizens are represented, but the representatives are selected by country, as occurs in the European Parliament, is, therefore, a kind of halfway house between a fully proportional parliament in which Europeans are represented qua-preferences and regardless of where they reside, and a fully confederate assembly in which Europeans are represented exclusively according to where they reside.

5. The voting rule

If the role of government is to provide those goods that can potentially benefit all citizens, then the obvious choice for the voting rule is the unanimity rule. The main objections to its use are that it can take too long to find a formulation of a proposal that benefits all even when all participants vote sincerely, and that it encourages the strategic misrepresentation of preferences by individuals who "hold out" for a greater share of the gains from collective action (Black, 1958: 146–147; Buchanan and Tullock, 1962: Ch. 6; Barry, 1965: 242–250;

Samuelson, 1969). For these reasons the optimal voting rule is generally thought to be some qualified majority less that unanimity.

Under any qualified majority rule less than full unanimity, some individuals can be made worse off by a collective action. Under a federalist governmental structure, these individuals can be expected to be spread throughout the entire community. For example, assume a federalist structure existed in Europe with a European Parliament with the authority to take certain actions on behalf of all citizens. Defense would be an obvious policy to assign to the highest governmental level. A Pacifist Party might come into existence, but it would probably win only a small fraction of seats in the European Parliament. Under any reasonable choice for a qualified majority voting rule, the Pacifist Party would not have enough votes to prevent the European Parliament from passing defense appropriations and authorizing other defense related actions. Supporters of the Pacifist Party would be net losers on defense issues.

Thus, under a federalist system where each party represents citizens from across all of Europe, the winners and the losers on any issue would tend to be spread throughout the community. In contrast, if a qualified majority voting rule were used in a confederate assembly, the losers on any vote would be the representatives from specific countries. If the kinds of issues voted on in a confederation are those that favor its creation, i.e., issues with benefits and costs which vary by country, then the losers on any vote in a confederation under a qualified majority rule would be the citizens – in principle all of the citizens – of one or more specific countries. Both gains and losses would be geographically concentrated.

Any individual or group which is a net loser over the set of *all* collective actions of the community has a strong incentive to exit the community, of course. For an individual, exit is often very costly, however. It is also costly for a group, if it is widely dispersed across the community. In a confederation, on the other hand, the losers are geographically concentrated. Moreover, they are already organized into a political unit. Exit is easy. Accordingly, the threat of exiting is more effective, and the assembly of confederate delegates must take more care to ensure that every member, i.e., each constituent country, is a net gainer from its actions. In practice, this can be expected to result in greater constraints upon the kinds of issues that can come to a vote in a confederate assembly, and a higher required majority to pass proposals with unanimity being the likely choice for important issues.[7]

6. Citizenship

The constituents in a federalist state are the citizens of that state. The constituents in a confederation are the autonomous states conjoined. These differences have important implications for the criteria by which citizenship is established.

If a federalist structure is optimal, the nature of the issues decided at each level of government is such that a person living anywhere within a given governmental jurisdiction can be presumed to have *potentially* the same preferences for government action as the person at any other location. Pacifists and hawks are equally likely to be found anywhere. Logically, individuals should have the same rights and obligations as citizens of a particular governmental unit regardless of where they reside within that jurisdiction. If Europe were constituted as a federalist state with defense assigned to the highest level of government, and its federal parliament decided to introduce the draft, all citizens of Europe regardless of where they resided, should be equally obligated to serve in the military. In addition to considerations of fairness, this form of equality would be necessary to discourage individuals from migrating from one part of Europe to another to avoid military service. Both the taxes and benefits from collective action should be uniform across a given governmental jurisdiction for equity and efficiency reasons.

This logic also suggests that a single set of criteria should exist to define citizenship in a particular governmental jurisdiction. If a Federation of Europe existed, the same minimum residency requirement should apply before an immigrant is eligible for European citizenship regardless of whether the immigrant lives in England or Italy. Were this not the case, migrants seeking citizenship in Europe might tend to concentrate on the countries with the most lax citizenship qualifications.

There is no reason, however, to require identical qualifications for citizenship in any lower level of government across the different governmental units. In a federalist Europe, the present nations would most certainly exist as rather powerful "regional" governments. If citizenship in a Federation of Europe required a minimum of five years residence, say, there is no reason why Italy could not require two years or ten years residency before an immigrant could apply for citizenship and participate in Italian politics. Each regional government (i.e., current nation state) would be free to define the criteria for citizenship in its polity as it so chose. The same could, in principle, hold for smaller regional governments and cities and towns.

In a confederation, definitions of citizenship are logically the prerogative of each autonomous state. If the confederate structure is optimal, then the costs and benefits from collective action at the cross-national level must be presumed to be unequal. The assembly of national delegates to the confederate assembly might choose to require equal contributions on a particular occasion, say for a military action, but it need not do so. Given the asymmetry of benefits and costs of collective action that makes the confederation the optimal structure, it most certainly would not choose equal contributions on all occasions. Since the benefits and costs of participation in the European confederation are presumed to differ across states, there is no reason to assume that a common set of criteria for citizenship should exist across states. Each state could define its own set of rights and obligations according to its perception of its needs.

7. The European Union as a constitutional democracy

A constitution can be thought of as the set of rules that define a community's political institutions. By this definition all communities, even dictatorships, have a constitution.

In many cases history delineates the boundaries of the community and writes the provisions in its constitution. Great Britain is a collection of disparate peoples formed into a political community by a history of wars both amongst themselves and against common enemies. Its constitution, like the political community it defines, has evolved through a series of steps large and small over the course of centuries.

In contrast the United States, originally, was a far less diverse collection of people forged into a political community by the necessity of fighting a war against Great Britain. Having been suddenly apprised of their political identity, they were forced to choose consciously the political institutions that would govern them. The United States is the archetype of a constitutional government created by design and with purpose.

Europe, like Great Britain, is a collection of disparate peoples, whose history is characterized more by the wars fought among them than by their cooperative efforts to achieve common ends. But World War II, like the Revolutionary War in North America, made many Europeans like Jean Monnet (1978) suddenly aware that they too had common interests that were far more important than their differences, namely the interest in preventing future wars in Europe. Thus, the Europeans began the process of consciously crafting a constitution for Europe. But they did not choose to do so like their North American predecessors two centuries ago, in one fell swoop at a single convention. Rather they have chosen to proceed by small steps much more reminiscent of the evolutionary process by which Great Britain's constitution has been formed. This choice has important consequences to which we shall return. But first let us consider the various options, which Europe might have chosen and still could choose, if it wished to draft a constitution in a single step.

266

8. Founding a European government

Before one could call a constitutional convention one would have to decide what sort of union of European states one wished to create, a federation or a confederation. If one wished to create the latter, the obvious procedure for selecting delegates would be for each potential member state to send a delegation.[8] Although in principle the constitutional assembly could employ any voting rule it pleased, *de facto* a convention to create a confederation must employ the unanimity rule with each state effectively receiving one vote. Should any state not approve the agreement creating the confederation, it is free to remain apart from it. It is an autonomous state to begin with and can remain so, if it does not expect to be a net winner from joining the confederation. A confederation of *n* states can be formed only if all *n* think they will benefit from its creation.

Where a confederacy's constitution is necessarily an agreement, a contract, among its member states, a unified or federalist state's constitution is *ideally* a contract among its individual citizens. The purpose of the state is to advance the interests of all citizens, and it is most likely to achieve this goal if all citizens participate in its creation. Some method for representing the views of all citizens at the constitutional convention is required. Consider the following four options.

(1) Members of an existing government. By far the most common method by which nation states draft new constitutions is for a part of an existing government to draft the rules by which the future governments will function. If the existing government is a parliamentary democracy, its current parliament, or a subcommittee thereof, might write the constitution. Dictators often appoint commissions to draft new constitutions. The new constitutions in several post-communist European countries have been written in this way.

(2) Representatives from existing states. When a suprastate is to be formed out of several existing states, each state may send delegations to the convention in much the same way as they would if a confederation was to be formed. These delegations might be from either the parliaments of the individual states or from their executive branches. This format is essentially the same as that for creating a confederation.

(3) A specially elected assembly. Delegates from across the community could be elected for the sole purpose of drafting the constitution. Costa Rica's first constitution was drafted in this manner in 1812 (Seligson, 1990: 460), as was its present constitution, drafted in 1948 (Ameringer, 1982: 37). The Philadelphia convention of 1787 was made up of specially chosen delegates, albeit delegates chosen as under (2) by the several states that were to be conjoined.

(4) A randomly chosen cross-section of the citizens, selected in much the same way as one would select a jury.

Each of these alternatives differs with respect to the competencies of the delegates to carry out their task, and the incentives they have to do so in a way which is optimal for the future citizenry. Members of an existing parliament will, of course, have considerable expertise regarding the processes of government. But they may also think of themselves as representatives of particular interests and not of the interests of all future citizens. Members of the Labor Party may press worker interests to the exclusion of all others, members of the Green Party environmental interests. So long as *all* interests are adequately represented this partisanship may not be harmful, although it could stand in the way of achieving the kinds of compromises that are inevitably needed to reach agreement on constitutional questions.

A more serious form of partisanship arises with respect to the delegates own personal stakes in the outcomes of the constitutional process. In deciding what structure of government will be best for the future, a member of an existing parliament, or a prospective member of a future parliament, may find it difficult to abstract from the consequences of the various alternatives for her own political future and that of her party. Members of large parties will favor first-past-the-post systems and large minimum cut-offs for party representation under a PR system. Small parties will favor elections from large, multi-member districts and low cut-offs. If the current chief executive has a hand in the constitution writing process, she will favor provisions that produce a strong executive office. What best serves the citizens' interests gets adopted only by chance.

This point is well illustrated by European experience in constitution writing at the nation state level. For example, Italy's current constitution was drafted shortly after World War II by members of the parties that existed prior to Mussolini's takeover. They drafted a constitution designed to protect incumbent parties not to advance citizens' interests. It has achieved the former goal admirably, with the major parties (except for the Communists) playing dominant roles in the myriad governments that have come and gone since the end of World War II. How well the Italian constitution has served Italy's citizens is a more debatable issue (Spotts and Wieser, 1986). Several attempts have been made to improve the situation by reforming the constitution, but these too have been blocked by the parties in parliament fearful of the consequences of reform for their future.[9] Resentment against the major parties has reached new highs in recent years and some changes in the constitution now seem likely.

Olaf Ruin (1988: 329–331) has made the following observations concerning the revision of Sweden's constitution in 1974 by the Swedish Parliament. "...

268

the agreement ... hammered out [did not] rest on any version of the right constitutional framework for an advanced welfare society of the Swedish type. Rather, the agreement was characterized by calculations from different quarters of what maximally favored or disfavored their own political party. The Swedish version of constitutional politics appeared as the interest politics of political parties *par excellence*."

The same type of partisanship appears under the second method of selecting delegates to a convention, except in this case the partisan interests have a significant geographic flavor. If a federalist state is to be created out of autonomous smaller states, having each of these represented can help to ensure that the central level of government does not engulf the smaller levels, since the latter will wish to preserve as much authority as possible. On the other hand, if voters are represented at a constitutional convention only through existing, geographically defined governments, the latter's interests in preserving their autonomy may well stand in the way of creating the kind of central government that will best serve all citizen interests.

Although the United States' Constitution was not written by members of an existing Parliament, nor were many delegates likely to have expected to serve in the national assembly in the future, they were selected by state, and many saw themselves as representatives of the states that sent them and of their various economic interests.[10] Thus, the Philadelphia convention was a cross between a convention to create a confederation and one to create a federation. The results of this confusion of purposes are most blatantly apparent in the compromise that resulted in the overrepresentation of the small states in the Senate.[11] The ambiguity as to the United State's governmental structure created by the constitutional process also contributed in no small way to the belief of the Southern states in 1860 that they retained the right to secede from the Union. Canada's recent tribulations in trying to write a federal constitution through assemblies of representatives of each provincial government is a further illustration. Not surprisingly, given this mode of representation, one of the proposals surfacing in Canada during this process has been to convert its upper house into the kind of anachronistic, gerrymandered institution that the U.S. Senate is. The British Government's threat in the summer of 1994 to veto the entry of new members into the EU, because of the implication of their entry on the power of Great Britain to block initiatives in Brussels, is yet another illustration of geographically based representatives viewing an essentially constitutional choice, that affects the whole community (i.e., Europe), only in terms of its impact on the narrow, geographic interests directly represented.[12]

These considerations underline the importance of selecting delegates to a constitutional convention to write a *federalist* constitution, who are representatives of all citizens regardless of location of residence, and are chosen for the sole purpose of writing this constitution. If they are elected as under the third of the four procedures enumerated above, the delegates should be chosen from common lists of candidates that are presented to all voters. Ideally, the delegates should be chosen on the basis of their expected skills in writing a constitution that takes into account and advances the interests of future generations of citizens. To further ensure the impartiality of the delegates to the constitutional convention, provisions might be adopted to bar them from serving in any capacity in the federal government designed by the convention for a fixed number of years after the convention. More generally, impartiality could be fostered by having the entire constitution not go into effect for several years after the convention.[13]

The goal of impartiality might best be achieved by having the delegates to the constitutional convention selected, like members of a jury, by a random draw from the entire population. To my knowledge no constitution has ever been written by such an assembly, and if one were to be constituted it would obviously be somewhat lacking in expertise. But the latter objection can and has been levied against the use of the jury system, and yet it is believed by many in the Anglo-Saxon countries that use it to function well. A constitutional convention, like a jury, could call upon the advice of experts to assist it in its work.

John Rawls (1971) placed considerable stress on the role of impartiality in the selection of the provisions of the social contract to the subsequent willingness of individuals to comply with the terms of that contract. James Buchanan and Gordon Tullock (1962) placed similar emphasis on impartiality in the choice of a constitution (see also Buchanan, 1975). Citizens are more likely to identify with a constitution's provisions and attempt to comply with them, if they believe their interests were fairly represented at the convention that created it. Either of the latter two methods for selecting delegates is likely to be superior to the first two by this criterion.

The issue of compliance is also relevant for the choice of a voting rule to be used at the convention. While only a unanimous agreement among the participant states at a convention will lead to the founding of a confederacy, unanimity among the delegates is not necessary for a unitary or federal government to come into existence. The difficulty in exiting from a community may force some individuals to remain in a polity, even if they oppose the rules adopted at its creation. But such opposition bodes ill for the future success and stability of the polity. Thus, the heavy emphasis on unanimity at the constitutional stage to foster future compliance with the constitutional contract in most contractarian writings (Buchanan and Tullock, 1962; Rawls, 1971; Buchanan, 1975).

270

9. Maintaining a federalist structure

The optimality of federalist governmental structure stems from the geographic characteristics of the kinds of goods government should provide. Some of these public goods, like defense, are ideally provided to large numbers of people across great expanses of land. Others, like fire protection, can be optimally supplied to small communities. The ideal federalism consists of several levels of government, each responsible for those public goods whose geographic impact most closely corresponds to it. In the European context this idea has been referred to as the "subsidiarity principle" in recent discussions.

There appears to be a tendency in all federalist systems for responsibility for government services to shift upward in the federalist hierarchy (Aranson, 1992a). The highest level of government serves as a kind of magnet drawing ever more government activities away from the regional and local governments that are under it. This process of centralization is perceived to result in a federal government which is too large and unresponsive to the local and regionally defined needs of the citizens. A challenge facing those who would design a federalist system is to construct effective safeguards against the overcentralization of government activities that seems inevitably to transpire. Five possible safeguards are as follows:[14]

(1) Perhaps the simplest and most effective safeguard against overcentralization is to avoid having lower level *geographic* interests represented at each level of government. Every representative, who seeks reelection, has an incentive to bring before the parliament in which she sits issues of concern to those who elected her. If the Green Party of Belgium elects a delegate to a European parliament, it is the environmental issues of most concern to Belgians that she will press upon the parliament. Some of these may concern mainly or exclusively Belgians, and could better be resolved by the Belgian Parliament than by a European one. But this is of no concern to the delegate, who seeks only to please her constituents in every way that she can so as to retain their favor and thereby her seat. An important step toward preserving the integrity of a federalist system is to have the delegates to the legislative bodies at each level elected from common lists available to all voters across the areas covered by the respective governmental units.

(2) When a federalist structure is formed as a constitutional democracy, the framers may attempt to forestall the future concentration of government activity at the higher levels by explicitly assigning in the constitution specific governmental functions to each level of government. The U.S. Constitution did this for the federal level of government, and the federal government by and large stayed within its proscribed set of activities *until* the 1930s. The activist New Deal government sought the permission of the Supreme Court to expand the scope of federal government *greatly*, and was given it.[15] Although

the device of assigning each governmental unit specific functions ultimately (after 150 years) failed in the United States, it is not obvious that this must inevitably be so.

(3) The constitution framers could not anticipate all types of collective decisions that a federalist state will have to make in the future, and assign each to a level of government. Therefore, they will need to devise a general principle for assigning new issues. One possibility, which would seek to preserve the federalist structure, would be a provision in the constitution that prohibited any issue from coming before the parliament that did not promise substantial benefits for the citizens in at least 50 percent, say, of the constituent states. Thus, in a federalism composed of 15 states, a proposal to construct a dam would have to have anticipated benefits for the citizens in at least 8 of the 15 states. Such a provision would prevent purely local issues (a small dam) from being funded at higher levels of government than necessary.

(4) To protect federalist institutions, constitutional provisions must not only be written, they must also be enforced. Given the likely importance of this issue in Europe, the best way to ensure effective enforcement might well be to create a special federalist court charged with the responsibility for preserving European federalism and settling jurisdictional disputes among the member states. If a proposal came before the parliament of a federalist Europe that materially affected the citizens of only one or two states, any member of parliament could challenge the bill under the aforementioned provision. The constitutional court would then decide whether it was appropriate to consider the proposal in the parliament before a vote was taken.

(5) Yet another device for preserving federalism's strength is the referendum (Schneider, 1992; Frey, 1993). Of all federalist states, Switzerland has been without doubt the most successful at maintaining its decentralized federalist structure, and it has done so in large part by a liberal use of the referendum. Rather than challenging a proposal of merely local or regional interest in court, when it comes before the national parliament, the Swiss can petition for a referendum on it. If it would benefit only those in a small area of Switzerland, it is likely to be defeated in a national referendum. Those seeking funding for public goods of limited scope must do so at the level of government that corresponds most closely to the beneficiaries of the action, i.e., to those who are most likely to support it. The example of Switzerland illustrates that federalism need not give way to a giant, oversized government. The principle of subsidiarity can be withheld, if institutions for doing so are set into place.

272

10. The admittance of additional member states

Expanding an existing confederate or federalist state does not raise any fundamentally new issues. All parties should anticipate being made better off by such a move. A unanimous agreement among the delegates from the existing members of the confederation is obviously needed, and correspondingly the citizens of a federalist state should unanimously approve the entry of a new subunit into their system. Once again full unanimity cannot practically be required, but a large supramajority of either the representative assembly of the federalist state, or of its citizens directly in a referendum could be. Similarly, the new entrant needs to poll its citizens regarding the desirability of the move.

Indirectly, the expansion of a federalist state raises another potentialy important issue, however. The choice between a federalist and a confederalist structure should rest on the nature of the collective decisions to be made. The federalist structure is to be preferred if the benefits and costs from the collective decisions are likely to be spread uniformly across the polity. The confederalist structure is more appropriate when the costs and benefits are spread unevenly, and the asymmetries tend to be related to existing state boundaries. The benefits and costs of a collective action, say regulations to curb air pollution, are more likely to be uniform across a polity, the smaller its size. Thus, as a federalist state grows by adding new territory of once autonomous other states, the number of collective decisions it makes *at its highest level of government*, which satisfy the uniformity-of-benefits-and-costs condition that favors a federalist structure, can be expected to decline. If it retains its federalist structure as it expands, it will eventually find it optimal to add new sublevels which better match the distribution of benefits and costs of the collective decisions that need to be made. As it expands, the collective decisions a federation makes may begin to resemble more and more the kinds of decisions that favor a confederate governmental structure.

It is perhaps because of this that enthusiasm for an integrated, federalist-type structure for the EC has been strongest among the original six members. The United Kingdom and Greece, which are situated more on the periphery of the community, along with Denmark, have exhibited the most lukewarm attitude to further integration and appear more to favor the confederate over the federalist structure (Holland, 1992: 149–150).

11. Implications for the Maastricht Treaty and further European integration

11.1. *The European Community's confederate past*

Jean Monnet's original vision for Europe was for it to become a "federation of the West" (Holland, 1992: 5–6). The steps by which it has progressed toward this goal have been a series of treaties and more informal agreements among representatives of the several governments. Thus, the decisionmaking process by which integration has advanced has taken the confederate form. Not surprisingly, therefore, it has moved forward only when consensus has been reached. Not surprisingly, consensus has often come at the cost of compromise between alternative views of what the community should be, and in particular alternative views regarding federalism and confederation. Given that the process of integration has been governed by a confederate structure, it is not surprising that the end product resembles much more closely the confederation model than it does the federalist one. The bulk of political power lies with the Council of Ministers in Brussels, not with the European Parliament in Strasbourg. Jean Monnet's vision of a European federalism remains unfulfilled.

There are several, perhaps unintended, consequences of the Community's continued reliance on a confederate decisionmaking structure. Not only is a confederate structure better suited to resolving issues in which the gains and losses differ across countries, it tends to focus the Community's attention on such policies. No better example exists than European Farm Policy.

Subsidies to farmers have been for a generation and remain the Community's biggest budget item. But the "gains" and costs of this policy differ greatly across the member countries. If a true federalist structure existed with parties elected to a European Parliament using a European-wide party list system, a Farm Party might come into existence and win some, but undoubtedly not many, seats. It might be able to find enough support among the other parties for some general protection and subsidies for farmers. But it is inconceivable that it could induce a broadly representative parliament to institute the kind and scale of protection for farmers that now exists.

Farmers' demands for assistance within each country are more concentrated and specific than they are across Europe. In one country it is the dairy interests which are most powerful, in another wheat growers, in a third soybean farmers. These specific interests can put relatively more pressure on the governments of their respective countries than they would be able to muster under proportional representation in a European parliament. Moreover, the effectiveness of protests which disrupt traffic and the lives of ordinary citizens is much greater under the present confederate structure than it would be under a federalist system. The protests of French farmers affect mostly other Frenchmen and can put great pressure on the French Government to give in to the farmers' demands. But demonstrations by French farmers would put far less pressure upon a European parliament to act. No single party, other than a Farm Party if one existed, would feel the necessity to take up the French farmers' cause. Each party would gather its support from across all Europe, not just from France, and would feel less pressure to give into the French farmers to spare the rest of the French the inconveniencies caused by the protests. The unwillingness to give in to the demands of protesters would be strengthened by the losses imposed on other Europeans from giving in to the French farmers. Of course, simultaneous protests by all European farmers would put considerable pressure on a European parliament, but protests on such a scale are far more unlikely to occur because of the differences in farm interests that exist across Europe, and because of the sheer transaction costs of organizing effective protests on that scale.

Not only does the confederate structure of collective decisionmaking in the community tend to focus its attention on issues with disparate benefits and costs across the members, but it blocks taking up the kinds of pan-European issues that would be a federalist Europe's *raison d'être*. If one pan-European issue exists, it is most certainly defense. All Europeans benefit from a peaceful and secure Europe and do so, presumably to an equal degree. Yet the community has failed to come up with an effective security force and policy under its confederate organizational structure (Nugent, 1991: 39–40; Holland, 1992: Ch. 5). Again the problem undoubtedly stems from each government's ministers viewing European defense policy from the perspective of its own *marginal* benefits and costs from participation.[16]

With the exception of the United Kingdom, and from time to time France, all European countries have adopted some form of multimember district representation. Incongruously, the system of representation that is used to decide European community policy resembles much more closely that employed in the United States and the United Kingdom than that used throughout Continental Europe and Scandinavia. Just as a citizen from the south side of Chicago is represented in the lower House of Congress by the person who got the most votes in her district, regardless of whether she voted for that person or shares his ideology, a German citizen is represented in Brussels by the party or coalition which got the most votes in the last German parliamentary elections, regardless of whether she voted for that party or shares its ideology. All German citizens can be adequately represented in this manner on only those issues that affect all Germans in the same way. The European Community continues to function largely as a confederation of independent states with its political agenda constrained to those kinds of issues that a confederation can resolve.

Are there other issues of a pan-European nature like defense or some environmental problems that are best suited to a federalist decisionmaking structure that are not being dealt with optimally, or perhaps not at all, due to Europe's political organization as a confederation? This was the key question Europeans needed to answer when the idea of a European political community was first broached. It remains the single most important question to be answered before further changes in Europe's political structure take place. It is a question for all Europeans to ponder and answer.

11.2. *The European Community's federalist future?*

The European Community's "constitution" is based on three treaties: two signed in Rome, one in Paris. Thus, from its inception it has been a confederalist structure (Nugent, 1991: 42). Its institutions have been created through negotiations between the representatives of the member governments, and these institutions have lodged authority in an assembly of representatives from these same governments. The basic elements of the Maastricht Treaty, the most ambitious step toward European political and economic integration to date, were conceived in Brussels and, not surprisingly, retain most political authority in Brussels. So long as the institutions of European government are designed by the ministers of its constituent governments, it will always retain a largely confederate structure.

This is the lesson, as noted above, to be learned from the experience individual countries have had when writing their constitutions. If the constitution is written by members of the parties who expect to hold seats in future parliaments, then the constitution will be designed to favor their interests. Nowhere is this lesson more apparent than in Great Britain's actions with respect to representation in the European Parliament. All members of the EU elect members to the European Parliament in Strasbourg using some variant of a PR formula except for Great Britain, which uses the same form of single-member-per-district representation as it uses in its domestic elections. Single-member-per-district-representation overrepresents the larger parties in the Parliament relative to a strictly proportional system (Rae, 1971; Lijphart, 1986, 1990). The usual defense made for this type of system is that it is more likely to award a majority of seats to the largest party and thus produce strong and effective government. When applied throughout the polity, this argument has merit. But the use of single-member-per-district representation by the UK, while all other EU countries use PR formulas, is not going to result in a single party having a majority of seats in the Strasbourg parliament. It does, generally, result in the largest parties in the British Parliament being overrepresented in Strasbourg (Jacobs and Corbett, 1990: 16–17), and this of course explains why the British Parliament opts for this mode of representation. (An exception to this general tendency occurred in the 1994 elections to the European Parliament, however, when British voters revealed their displeasure with the Conservative Government's handling of domestic issues by sending a disproportionately *small* number of Conservatives to Strasbourg. Perhaps, no single event better illustrates the inadequacies of the present rules for electing a European Parliament, then that voters in one country should use an election to the European Parliament to express their preferences *not on panEuropean* policies, but on policies of purely domestic concern.)

European political unification has gone the furthest, perhaps, in creating a common set of rights for Europeans (Magiera, 1991; Holland, 1992: Ch. 6). If there is such a thing as a European citizen, with common civil and political rights and obligations, which are identical regardless of where he resides in Europe, then there must exist a European citizen with interests in government which he shares in common with other Europeans regardless of where each lives. If the institutions of government are to advance the common interests of all European citizens, then they should have a hand in their creation and ratification.

To date the European citizen's role in the creation of the EU's political institutions has been indirect and reactive. His most direct participation has come through the occasional *national* referenda that have been held regarding entry into the EU or approval of the Maastricht Treaty. But such participation has always been after the fact. Does the Briton want to join the EU as it exists in 1973? Does the Dane want to adopt the treaty of Maastricht? A more participatory role for European citizens would have them involved in the drafting of the treaties, as say through a constitutional convention.

If a government of Europe is to advance the interests of all Europeans, then the constitution which creates this government should reflect the interests and ideas of all Europeans. The surest way to accomplish this goal is to hold a constitutional convention with delegates selected from across Europe. The delegates should not be members of existing national governments or parliaments for they will have difficulty divorcing their own political futures and interests under the constitution from those of the citizens on whose behalf they must act. Rather a special convention with delegates chosen solely for the purpose of drafting the constitution is required. If the delegates were elected, the best procedure would have them elected from across all of Europe, as ideally would be the case for a European parliament. Although most Europeans might be expected to vote for delegates from their own country, a widely respected European statesman might well win votes from many countries. Most importantly, the delegates to the convention should not think of themselves as representing the interests of any specific group or country, but rather of all Europeans. To help accomplish this goal one might bar individuals, who hold elective office in any country from running as candidates to be delegates to the European Constitutional convention.[17] The ideal candidates would be, like the octogenarian Benjamin Franklin at the Philadelphia convention, senior statesmen and stateswomen capable of looking beyond their own personal interests in the outcome of the convention, or even that of their country of birth, to the interests of all Europeans.

Given that the areas that would form a European federalism are currently autonomous states, no federalist constitution drafted by a convention, however constituted, could take effect if a majority of the citizens of any country opposed. Thus, the delegates to a constitutional convention would have to consider its impact on each country and be confident that it benefited all, but again this can be accomplished without having delegates selected to *represent* each country. As a further check on the convention, a European wide referendum to ratify it would be appropriate, so that citizens would be forced to weigh the likely benefits and costs of the constitution on themselves, and express their opinion on them.

The United States' Constitution was written by delegates from the individual states who kept in mind the interests of their constituents. Thus, it suffers from some of the same maladies upon which I have laid stress. Yet, this constitution is generally given credit for this country's maintaining its democratic institutions for more than two centuries, and is widely respected by its own citizens. There are several reasons for this. First, although the citizens played little role in the selection of delegates to the convention in Philadelphia, and were kept in the dark regarding its deliberations, they were informed of its content and treated to an active debate on its merits by the Federalists and the Antifederalists during the interval between the convention and the Constitution's ratification by the individual states. Second, the participants in the convention included men like Washington, Madison and Franklin, whose intellect and character added lustre to the outcome. Most Americans today probably identify with the Constitution not because they took part in its creation, but because they cannot imagine that they would have done any better than the men who did, if they had.

In contrast, the Maastricht Treaty was neither widely debated nor understood by Europeans before the first Danish vote. Whatever the talents of the people who drafted it are, they were not selected by Europeans for this task, and are not widely regarded as statesmen and intellectual leaders. Although the actual content of the Treaty has much merit, there is nothing in the process by which it was drafted or the personages who drafted it to make Europeans identify with it as *their constitution*, and the same is largely true of the Treaties

278

of Rome and Paris that preceded it. To bring about such an identification, a different process would be required.

The participants at the constitutional convention in Philadelphia recognized that they were at an important juncture in world history, and that they were engaging in an experiment with possibly profound consequences for future generations both in the United States and elsewhere. The events in Europe commencing in 1989 make the present another historic juncture in world history. Democratic experiments are taking place today, as they did in North America 200 years ago, that might define the character of European life for centuries to come. Even if it wanted to, the European Union could not stand by and ignore what happens to its east, since events like those in Bosnia will inevitably impinge upon it. But given its location and its resources, it is obviously in a position to be able to do much more. But before it can it must decide what it is, and what its interests are. Is it mainly a cartel for regulating agricultural prices, steel production, airline landing rights and the like? Is it mainly a customs union for encouraging free trade within its borders? Is it mainly a confederation of nation states capable of making only those collective decisions that are perceived to benefit all countries by the governments which hold majorities in each? Or is it a full-fledged democratic community, composed of individuals with common interests, and governed through political institutions that allow its citizens to express and advance these common interests?

Notes

1. There are some special cases, like infant industries, in which all members of a community might benefit from a tariff, but these are far rarer than the number of tariffs one observes. Nor can one argue persuasively that all members of the community might benefit from a set of many tariffs that protected most/all wage earners and capital suppliers. A central tenet of economics since its inception has been that the entire community is better off with no tariffs than with many. The initial "public good" the European Community consumed was, of course, the benefits from free trade within the "common market" created by the Treaty of Rome.
2. For a discussion of monetary union and other issues of European integration from a constitutional perspective, see Kirchgässner (1994).
3. For a distinction between federation and confederation in the European context similar to that made here, see Forsyth (1981).
4. Oates (1972) and Tullock (1969) provide classic discussions of the allocation issue, Inman and Rubinfeld (1996) and Tullock (1991) provide more recent discussions.
5. See my discussion in (1996, Chs. 8–10), however.
6. The voting system used in Luxembourg also allows voters to express their preferences for the *persons*, whom they want to see represent them as well as the parties.
7. Several alternatives to simple qualified majority rules have been developed, which have superior properties, but we shall not take the space to discuss them here. See descriptions in Mueller (1989: Ch. 8; 1996, Ch. 11).

8. States may send delegations of several individuals, and voting at the convention could be by delegate or by state. The convention could also agree to adopt a qualified majority rule to pass on each proposal for inclusion in the constitutional contract. But the final vote approving the constitution must *de facto* be a unanimous vote of the *delegations*, although not necessarily of the delegates. Even if balloting on this final vote were by delegate using a qualified majority rule, if a majority of one state's delegation opposed the constitution it could simply withdraw leaving the remaining delegations to form a confederation without it.
9. See Hine's (1988: 218–223) discussion of the fate of the Bozzi Commission's proposals for reform.
10. For further discussion of the roles of self- and constituent interests of the delegates at the convention in Philadelphia, see McDonald (1958), Roche (1961), Jillson (1988), and McGuire (1988).
11. For further examples of jockeying by party representatives at constitutional conventions see Merkl (1963: 90–103) on the Federal Republic of Germany's Constitution and Bonime-Blanc (1987: 77) on Spain's.
12. Worse still the British delegation in Brussels appeared not even to be weighing the impact of entry and the choice of voting rule on the welfare of *all* British citizens, but rather to be most concerned with placating the anti-Europe faction of the Conservative Party.
13. For further discussion of these options, see Mueller (1996, Ch. 21).
14. Several authors have wrestled with this and other questions of institutional structure and protections in the EU, for example, Bernholz (1993), Frey (1993), and Schneider (1992).
15. See Ackerman (1991), Aranson (1992a, b), and Niskanen (1992).
16. Burgess (1989: 95) stresses that politics at the European level continues to be dominated by the member states, despite the progress toward federalism that has been made.
17. Gordon Tullock suggested this to me.

References

Ackerman, B.A. (1991). *We the people.* Cambridge: Belknap Press.

Ameringer, C.D. (1982). *Democracy in Costa Rica.* New York: Praeger.

Aranson, P.H. (1992a). Federalism at founding. Mimeo. Emory University.

Aranson, P.H. (1992b). Federalism: Doctrine against balance. Mimeo. Emory University.

Bagehot, W. (1872/1961). *The English Constitution*, 2nd ed. Garden City: Doubleday, 1961 (reprint of 1872, ed.).

Barry, B. (1965). *Political argument.* London: Routledge and Kegal Paul.

Bernholz, P. (1993). Constitutional aspects of the European integration. In S. Borner and H. Grubel (Eds.), *The European Community after 1992.* London: Macmillan.

Black, D. (1958). *The theory of committees and elections.* Cambridge: Cambridge University Press.

Bonime-Blanc, A. (1987). *Spain's transition to democracy.* Boulder: Westview Press.

Buchanan, J.M. (1975). *The limits of liberty: Between anarchy and Leviathan.* Chicago: University of Chicago Press.

Buchanan, J.M. and Tullock, G. (1962). *The calculus of consent.* Ann Arbor: The University of Michigan Press.

Burgess, M. (1989). *Federalism and European Union.* London: Routledge.

Coase, R.H. (1960). The problem of social cost. *Journal of Law and Economics* 3 (October): 1–44.

Dahlman, C.J. (1979). The problem of externality. *Journal of Law and Economics* 22 (April): 141–162.

Forsyth, M. (1981). *Unions of states: The theory and practice of confederation.* Leichester: Leichester University Press.
Frey, B. (1993). The role of direct referenda in institutional reform. Paper presented at a conference at Universita degli Studi 'La Sapienza', Rome.
Hine, D. (1988). Italy (1948): Condemned by its constitution? In V. Bogdanor, *The people and the party system*, 206–228. Cambridge: Cambridge University Press.
Holland, M. (1992). *European Community integration.* New York: St. Martin's Press.
Inman, R.P. and Rubinfeld, D.L. (1996). The political economy of federalism. In D.C. Mueller (Ed.), *Perspectives on public choice.* Cambridge: Cambridge University Press.
Jacobs, F. and Corbett, P. (1990). *The European Parliament.* Boulder: Westview Press.
Jillson, C.C. (1988). *Constitution making: Conflict and consensus in the Federal Constitution of 1787.* New York: Agathon Press.
Kirchgässner, G. (1994). Constitutional economics and its relevance for the evolution of rules. *Kyklos* 47: 321–339.
Lijphart, A. (1986). Degrees of proportionality of proportional representation formulas. In B. Grofman and A. Lijphart (Eds.), *Electoral laws and their political consequences*, New York: Agathon Press.
Lijphart, A. (1990). The political consequences of electoral laws, 1945–85. *American Political Science Review* 84 (June): 481–496.
Magiera, S. (1991). A citizen's European personal, political and cultural rights. In L. Hurwitz and C. Lequesne (Eds.), *The state of the European Community*, 153–164. Essex: Longman.
McDonald, F. (1958). *We the people.* Chicago: University of Chicago Press.
McGuire, R.A. (1988). Constitution making: A rational choice model of the federal convention of 1787. *American Journal of Political Science* 32 (May): 483–522.
Merkl, P.H. (1963). *The origin of the West German Republic.* New York: Oxford University Press.
Monnet, J. (1978). *Memoirs.* Trans. R. Mayne. New York: Doubleday.
Mueller, D.C. (1989). *Public choice II.* Cambridge: Cambridge University Press.
Mueller, D.C. (1996). *Constitutional democracy.* Oxford: Oxford University Press.
Niskanen, W.A. (1992). The case for a new fiscal constitution. *The Journal of Economic Perspectives.* 6 (Spring): 13–24.
Niskanen, W.A. (1992). Autocratic, democratic and optimal government. Mimeo. Cato Institute.
Nugent, N. (1991). *The government and politics of the European Community.* Durham: Duke University Press.
Oates, W.E. (1972). *Fiscal federalism.* London: Harcourt Brace.
Rae, D.W. (1971). *The political consequences of electoral laws*, revised edition. New Haven: Yale University Press.
Rawls, J.A. (1971). *A theory of justice.* Cambridge: The Belknap Press of Harvard University Press.
Roche, J.P. (1961). The Founding Fathers: A reform caucus in action. *American Political Science Review* 5: 799–816.
Ruin, O. (1988). The New Constitution (1974) and the tradition of consensual politics. In V. Bogdanor (Ed.), *The people and the party system*, 309–327. Cambridge: Cambridge University Press.
Samuelson, P.A. (1969). Pure theory of public expenditures and taxation. In J. Margolis and H. Guitton (Eds.), *Public Economics*, 98–123. New York: St. Martin's Press.
Schneider, F. (1992). The federal and fiscal structures of representatives and direct democracies as models for a European Federal Union. Mimeo. Linz.
Seligson, M.A. (1990). Costa Rica. In H.J. Wiarda and H.F. Kline (Eds.), *Latin American politics and development*, 3rd ed., 455–466. Boulder: West View Press.
Spotts, F. and Weiser, T. (1986). *Italy: A difficult democracy.* Cambridge: Cambridge University Press.
Tullock, G. (1969). Federalism: Problems of scale. *Public Choice* 6 (Spring): 19–30.
Tullock, G. (1991). *The new federalism.* Mimeo. Tucson, AZ.

[11]

Constitutional issues regarding European Union expansion

Dennis C. Mueller[1]

Introduction

The original intent of Jean Monnet and the other founders of the European Union was to join Germany, France and enough other European countries sufficiently closely economically to make certain that they would never go to war against one another again. Thus, the motivation behind the founding of the European Union was to provide a form of public good for all of Europe. In describing the European Union's *raison d'être* today, we would expand the list of collective goods that can be provided more efficiently at the European level, and would explicitly include the gains to all Europeans from free trade. The European Union's *raison d'être* is to help Europeans achieve the possible gains from a more efficient allocation of goods and services.

To achieve the collective benefits from providing public goods to all Europeans, one must determine the types and amounts of public goods Europeans want, and then supply them. There are essentially two types of institutional structures for accomplishing these tasks: a federalist or a confederalist structure. Which structure is best suited to these tasks depends upon the characteristics of the distribution across Europe of citizen preferences for public goods, and thus, of course, also on the characteristics of the public goods themselves. The European Union's institutional structure has both federalist and confederalist attributes. This mixture creates certain problems in optimally providing public goods within the EU, and in deciding whether or not to admit new members and upon what terms. These issues are the subjects of this contribution.

States as clubs: federalism

Optimal club size

Imagine people distributed in varying densities across a given land mass living in anarchy. They produce that which they need to survive, supplemented by that which they can obtain through exchange. Certain goods exist – roads, fire protection – that no single person or family can supply optimally. Thus, incentives exist for groups of individuals to agree to provide these goods collectively. In the tradition of contractarianism and the new constitutional political economy we can imagine various groups of individuals reaching separate agreements to provide different public goods. Let us call each union of a group of people to provide one or more public goods a 'club'.

The characteristics of a public good – joint supply and non-exclusion from benefits – often give a *geographic* dimension to any club formed to provide a particular good or service. The fire station benefits only those within a certain radius that covers the distance that its trucks can reach in a reasonable amount of time; the dam protects only those who live lower down along the river. This property of public goods leads us to expect that many clubs are formed to provide public goods with a geographic dimension to them.[2] The natural self-interest of individuals should thus lead them to create and join many clubs of different geographic dimensions to provide the many possible public goods that could make them better off.[3]

The essence of a club is that it is a *voluntary* association of individuals to achieve some mutually beneficial goal. As such, the formation of clubs to provide public goods is much in the spirit of Knut Wicksell's (1896) 'voluntary exchange' approach to government, and of Frey and Eichenberger's FOCJs (1996). Consistent with these approaches, one might simply define *a* state as a club formed to provide one or more public goods. Given the many sorts of public goods that individuals might wish to consume and the different geographic dimensions of their benefits, one might well expect that a given individual would be a citizen of several club/states, some of which would provide public services to individuals in a small geographic area, others to larger numbers of individuals spread across much larger areas. Although there is nothing that we have said so far that would imply that a series of voluntarily joined clubs would take on the hierarchical structure of a federalist state, these clubs would resemble the optimal federalist state, as described in the economics literature on federalism, in that governmental *functions* would be associated with different levels of government in accordance with the geographic spillovers from the various public goods, and the relationship between the benefits from membership in a club and the size of the club.

The public good benefits from club membership may be of two, fundamentally different types: (1) benefits that grow without bound as club size expands, or (2) benefits that eventually decline with club size, and may even turn negative on the margin beyond some size. Under the first heading we can place the benefits from free trade to members of a customs union, or the net benefits to a club member from providing a public good when there is no crowding. In the latter case, if the benefits to a member do not fall as the club size increases, his *net* benefits from membership increase as the club size grows and the fixed costs of providing the public good are spread over more and more dues/tax payers.[4]

For many public goods, like transportation, environmental and recreation systems, adding consumers leads to congestion costs beyond some club size. When crowding occurs, an optimal club size exists at which the benefits to existing members from spreading the costs of providing the public good over one more member just equal the additional congestion costs that this new member brings with her.[5]

The costs of heterogeneity under federalism

Although all citizens can in principle benefit from the provision of a pure public good, all do not necessarily have the same preferences for it. Institutions must be established to aggregate the diverse preferences of the citizens in a given polity to determine the optimal quantities and characteristics of the public goods offered by that polity. In all European countries except for Great Britain these institutions take the form of a proportional representation electoral system to elect members of parliament, and a simple majority rule within the parliament to aggregate the preferences represented there. This method of aggregating preferences imposes certain costs on some or even all citizens, when citizen preferences differ from one another.

To see what is involved, assume that a polity provides a single public good, say roads, and its citizens must decide the amount, x, to be spent on roads. The population can be divided into five groups, each of which favours a different expenditure. Let x_1 be the expenditure favoured by group 1, x_2 the expenditure favoured by group 2, and so on. Assume that $x_1 < x_2 < x_3 < x_4 < x_5$. An election is held and the parties representing groups 2 and 3 together win enough seats to form the government and decide the amount of x for the community. It is reasonable to assume that the expenditure on roads that this coalition chooses, x^* falls between x_2 and x_3, i.e., $x_2 \leq x^* \leq x_3$. Under this assumption, x^* must differ from the most preferred quantity of x of one of these two groups, and most likely differs from the quantities most preferred by both groups. Thus, the need to form a coalition to be able to decide the quantity of the public good imposes costs on each group in comparison to what it would experience, if it could decide the quantity of the public good alone.[6]

Similar losses obviously also exist for members of the other three groups, and these losses are likely to be even greater than those experienced by the groups whose representatives were able to form the government. Thus, the necessity of all members of a community having to consume the same quantity of any public good it provides imposes some loss of utility on virtually all members, as opposed to what would occur if all members had the same tastes. Two consequences follow: first, we can now identify a second possible cost to the existing members of a community from expanding its membership. Even when no crowding takes place, the existing members may be made worse off from the admittance of new members, if the new members have different preferences from old members, and the increased heterogeneity of the community shifts the chosen quantities of public goods supplied away from those favoured by the old members. Second, gains may exist for all individuals from free migration across communities, if this migration can result in communities with more homogeneous preferences for public goods.[7] A possible advantage of having a federalist governmental structure with numerous communities within the federation providing similar bundles of public goods is that it would allow citizens the opportunity to improve the levels of utility that they obtain from publicly provided goods and services by re-sorting themselves into communities of more homogeneous preferences.

Summary

Rational, self-interested individuals can be expected to form and join clubs and communities, which provide public goods. The characteristics of public goods are likely to make the formation of multiple clubs and polities optimal, so as to better match the beneficiaries of publicly provided goods to those who decide upon their characteristics and pay for them. When a club or a community provides a pure public good to its members, *all* members must consume the same public good. If members differ over the quantity or quality characteristics of the good that should be supplied, then these characteristics will deviate from those considered optimal by some, perhaps all, members. A second possible advantage of a federalist governmental structure is that it facilitates migration to achieve better matches between the preferences of citizens for public goods, and the characteristics of the public goods provided.

Confederations as clubs

My *American Heritage Dictionary* defines a 'confederation' as a group of states united for a common purpose. One might well also define a 'club' as a group of individuals united for a common purpose. A confederation is thus a kind of club of nations,[8] and we expect it to share the following two properties of clubs: (1) membership is voluntary, and (2) members voluntarily join because they expect to be made better off. The 'common purpose' that brings them together involves their obtaining mutual benefits. The benefits from membership in the club or confederation are a form of a public good to club members.

When the members of a club are autonomous states, the issue arises of whether it is the interests of the citizens of these states that are being advanced by the confederation, or the interests of the members of the governments that represent these citizens. The simplest case to consider, and the one which is most compatible with the confederate form of government being the optimal way to advance the interests of the *individual citizens* within it, is to assume that every person within a given state has identical preferences for the public goods that the confederation provides, and that the representatives of the governments of each member state faithfully represent the preferences of their citizens.

Under these assumptions, a club of states has all of the properties of a club of individuals. Namely, optimal club size is infinite in the absence of crowding or preference heterogeneity across club members, while optimal club size is likely to be finite when either of these two phenomena are present.

When every person within a given state has identical preferences for the public goods provided by the confederation, an obvious and simple way to represent these preferences is to have each constituent state government send representatives to an assembly, and for these state delegations to have seats or voting rights in this assembly proportionate to their populations. Such a system of representation would produce an assembly of representatives that would resemble that which one would expect to arise under a system of proportional representation in which the citizens of the confederation directly elected representatives to the assembly.

The situation can be quite different, however, if the preferences of the citizens within each state are heterogeneous. Assume, for example, that the population of each state can be divided into five groups as in the previous section, with the five groups in each of the states having the same five most preferred quantities of the public good x, $x_1 < x_2 < x_3 < x_4 < x_5$. Assume further that there are ten states in the confederation. In five of these, parties representing the groups favouring x_1 and x_2 form governments with narrow majorities, in the other five states parties favouring x_3 and x_4 form governments with substantial majorities. If the populations of the five states favouring x_1 and x_2 give them a slight majority in the confederation's assembly, and this assembly uses the simple majority rule, then the quantity of the public good chosen using the confederate form of representation will lie between x_1 and x_2, where a quantity between x_3 and x_4 would have been chosen using the simply majority rule under a system of proportional representation in which the citizens elected their representatives directly.

With heterogeneous preferences within states, the outcomes from a confederate form of representation can differ from those under proportional representation when citizens elect representatives directly, even if the unanimity rule is used in the confederate assembly. In the above example, individuals who favour the quantity x_5 are not represented in any of the ten governments, and thus their preferences would presumably receive no weight in any compromise over x that representatives of the ten governments were able to reach under the unanimity rule.

The benefits and costs of membership in a newly formed confederation

Much of the public choice literature that deals with constitutions, and essentially all of the recent constitutional political economy literature, assumes that constitutions are written by the citizens of a country and are *unanimously* agreed to by these citizens.[9] Although these assumptions are highly unrealistic as *descriptions* of the way actual constitutions of nation states are written, they do accurately describe how confederations come into being. Since the potential members of a new confederation are themselves nation states, it is possible for each of them to remain in the current 'state of anarchy' should they not find the conditions for joining the confederation to their advantage. Unanimity is not merely a hypothetical ideal when it comes to the formation of a confederation, it is a practical necessity. Although all countries that meet to discuss forming a confederation may not choose to join it, the agreement among those which do join must be unanimous. The contract all joiners sign must be seen as a Pareto move *by all signatories*.[10] Both the contractarian perspective on the initial constitution and the assumption of unanimous agreement among all signatories is fully justified when the polity created by the constitution is a confederation of previously autonomous states.

Let us assume now that ten nations meet to consider forming a confederation to provide some set of public goods to its members. The ten countries are identical in size and preferences for the public goods, and thus there are no obvious, natural coalition partners. Let us further assume that the properties of the public goods and the potential members' preferences are such that the optimal size of the confederation, is seven. Obviously, an effort may be made to form a confederation of seven, and leave three countries out. But which three? If all potential members are identical no obvious way may exist to determine which countries are in the lucky seven, and which are the unlucky three. The deliberations may well result in all ten countries entering the confederation, with the benefits from membership falling below their maximum potential value.

The benefits and costs of adding members to an existing confederation

In joining a confederation, a nation risks losing some of its autonomy. The confederation may reach decisions that make the citizens of one of the member states worse off. This possibility can, of course, be avoided by requiring that all collective decisions of the confederation be made using the unanimity rule. The decision-making costs accompanying the unanimity rule may preclude its use for *all* collective decisions of the confederation, but one assumes that it will be retained for some decisions that are particularly likely to pose large potential losses for the individual members. One such collective decision would be whether or not to admit a new member. We shall assume, therefore, that the admission of new members to an existing confederation requires the unanimous approval of current members. If an existing confederation cannot *compel* other countries to enter by, say, threatening military action, then the unanimous agreement required to found any confederation will also be needed to expand it.

Let us now assume again that the optimal size of a confederation is seven nations, but that a confederation of this size already exists. Three countries, identical to the seven already in the confederation, wish to join. The situation is now quite different from that described in the previous section. The membership of the optimal coalition of seven is obvious: the existing confederation's members. The *status quo* constitutes a Schelling point for a coalition that creates one confederation of optimal size, and one of suboptimal size. If the three potential entrants are to succeed in joining the other seven countries in a confederation of ten, they are going to have to bribe the seven to let them in. The bribes must be large enough to leave the original seven members no worse off than before the confederation expands. If it is in the interest of the three potential entrants to offer such bribes, then the total benefits from a confederation of ten must exceed those arising from two clubs of sizes seven and three. The rational self-interest of both sets of countries produces the Pareto-optimal outcome, as in the previous example; only the distribution of benefits among the confederation's members differs.[11]

Implications for European Union expansion

The existing European confederation of fifteen nations is undoubtedly too small to supply some public goods optimally, and too large for others. The optimal membership of a confederation to address some environmental problems, like global warming, is perhaps all nations of the world. The existing confederation, however, is too large to address some more localised environmental problems, like pollution in the Rhine and Danube rivers.

If we assume for the moment that the optimal institutional structure for the European Union is a confederation, then the preferences with respect to EU policies of all citizens within each of its fifteen nations should be identical, with all preference heterogeneities existing *across* the fifteen members. One example of a public good that might fit this characterisation to some degree would be environmental protection, on the assumption that environmental protection is a luxury good. The richer countries in the existing confederation can then be expected to favour high environmental standards, its poorer members lower ones. European Union policies, regarding automobile and truck emissions, for example, should then be a compromise between the different policies favoured by each member country. On these assumptions we can also expect significant differences between the policies adopted by the existing members and those that the potential entrants would want to see enacted. Those heading the list of entrants into the European Union – Cyprus, the Czech Republic, Hungary, Poland and Slovenia – are much poorer on average than the existing confederation's members. Current EU environmental standards regarding automobile and truck emissions, and the like, are undoubtedly more stringent than those that this list of entrants would like to see enforced. Thus, although expansion of the European Union is likely to provide existing Union members benefits in areas where the Union is still too small, it is also likely to impose costs on the existing members in other areas due to the increased size and heterogeneity of the confederation.

If on balance the existing members of the European Union will benefit from expansion, then expansion will be a Pareto move for them, and there is no need for the entering countries to compensate or bribe the existing members. Given the heterogeneity of the existing membership, it is possible that expansion will harm some members and benefit others. If the net effect on the current fifteen members is positive, then there will again be no need for the new entrants to compensate existing members as a group to make their entry a Pareto move. Compensation can be from existing members who gain from expansion to those who lose.

If, of course, the net effect on the current fifteen members of the European Union from expansion were negative, then the entrants would need to compensate the existing members to make entry a Pareto move. Such compensation would be from relatively poor countries to relatively rich ones, and thus would run counter to normal notions of equity. However, if the entrance of additional countries into the Union is to obtain unanimous support, such compensation would have to take place, and the entering countries would still be better off following entry than they were before, despite having to compensate the existing members.

The biggest differences in preferences are probably between the richest current EU members – like Luxembourg and Germany – and the new entrants. Thus, to the extent that the costs of admitting Cyprus and the former Communist countries are due to the heterogeneity between existing and new members, it will be the richest current EU members who will lose the most from entry. If the existing members experience net gains from an enlargement, but these gains are unevenly distributed, it seems likely that the poorer current members would need to compensate the richer ones. Despite the obvious ethical and political difficulties with this solution, it could be necessary in order to obtain unanimous support for admitting countries that differ significantly from current members.

It is a logical possibility that the potential entrants would be made worse off by joining the European Union, but that the existing members would be made better off, and thus that the EU would have to bribe candidate countries to induce them to enter. Such bribes were given to Portugal, Spain and Greece at the time of their entry. Although this is a logical possibility, the need for compensation from existing to new members to avoid the latter being made worse off seems unlikely. *If* the rationale behind the European Union is to create political institutions to better supply European-wide public goods, then the benefits from membership must be much greater for the potential new members than for the existing ones. No transfers from existing to new members are likely to be needed to compensate the new members for the losses they experience from membership.

Representation and citizenship in the European Union

The European Union has evolved during the last fifty years through the conclusion of several treaties among the governments of European countries. Its evolution resembles that which one would expect for a *confederation* of autonomous states, and it seems most accurate to characterise the European Union as a confederation rather than as a federation. Consistent with this interpretation, we observe that the locus of political power in the European Union has been the Council of Ministers located in Brussels. Each member country is represented on the Council, with some collective decisions being made using the unanimity rule, and some made using a qualified majority rule, with larger countries receiving more votes than smaller ones. As discussed above, such a system of representation can accurately transmit information on *individual* citizen preferences only if all citizens within a country have the same preferences regarding European Union policies.[12] Since each country's representatives in the Council of Ministers are chosen by the country's elected government, representation in the Council reflects the preferences of the dominant parties and coalitions of the member countries. Only when all citizens in a given country have identical preferences with respect to EU policies will the preferences of all citizens and the ruling majority be concurrent.

If people with identical preferences on European Union policies reside in different member countries, then the mode of representation in the Council of Ministers does not adequately represent the preferences of different groups of European citizens. Those who favour a strong foreign policy for the European Union will go unrepresented in the Council, if the elected government in the country in which they have citizenship does not favour a strong foreign policy for the European Union. When individual preferences for EU policies differ within countries, but can be similar across countries, the optimal way to represent these preferences is to elect parties or persons to a European Parliament in proportion to their support across all of Europe. This is, of course, *not* the mode of representation in the European Parliament today, where representatives are selected from within the individual member countries. Because all countries except the United Kingdom employ some sort of proportional representation formula, the differences in preferences among EU citizens for EU policies are likely to be better reflected in the European Parliament than they are in the Council of Ministers. Given the relative strengths of the Council and the Parliament in determining EU policies, one should not expect these policies to correspond very closely to those that would best reflect the preferences of all Europeans, *if* the preferences of Europeans toward these policies are not homogeneous within each country.

Let us assume for the moment that the European Union has chosen the correct mode of representation given the kinds of public goods it provides, and thus that all citizens residing in a given member country have identical preferences on EU policies, but their preferences are likely to differ from those of citizens in other member countries.[13]

The existence of cross-national heterogeneities of preferences implies that all Europeans suffer from some of the costs of having to compromise on the characteristics of the public goods provided, as described above. It follows that these costs are likely to increase following the entry of new members that differ as widely from the existing members as, say, Germany and Poland differ. It further follows that the entry of these countries into the European Union, and the ones that will follow, must certainly impose some costs in terms of shifting the packages of public goods bundles offered away from those favoured by current members, under the assumption that the European Union's current mode of representation has been chosen correctly. It is still possible that there are other benefits for current members from European Union expansion that outweigh these costs. These additional benefits must be greater than the costs engendered by the preference heterogeneities, however, to allow the new entrants to join the European Union without having to compensate the existing members.

The existence of preference heterogeneities between residents of the new entrants and existing European Union members has an additional important implication. If the citizens of one country have preferences for public goods provided by the European Union that are relatively homogeneous as compared with the preferences for these public goods of citizens in other countries, it is also quite likely that their preferences for the public goods provided by their own country are more homogeneous than would be true of a cross-section of individuals from different European countries. Thus, membership in the European Union will entail additional costs due to individual preference heterogeneities, *if* the citizens of one member country have the right to take up citizenship and vote in another. This issue is explored further in the following section.

Why should there be a European Union? What form should it take?

Allocative efficiency or redistribution?

As Knut Wicksell (1896) first emphasised, since all citizens can benefit from a more efficient allocation of resources, the appropriate voting rule to employ when making collective decisions to improve allocative efficiency is the unanimity rule.

Until fairly recently, the unanimity rule was used exclusively in the Council of Ministers to make collective decisions. Since the European Council, which contains all heads of state of EU members, must approve any expansion of membership, the enlargement process still effectively requires the unanimous agreement of all existing members' governments.

If the purpose behind the European Union is to make collective decisions that benefit all member countries, and there are collective goods that the European Union provides that do make all members better off, then existing member countries should welcome new members, and European countries outside of the Union should be eager to join. There should be no need to *bribe* countries outside of the Union to join. Yet such bribes were extended to Spain, Portugal, Greece and Ireland when they joined. Why?

The most obvious explanation, of course, is that Spain, Portugal, Greece and Ireland were when they joined much poorer than the existing member countries. This fact in itself, however, offers neither a *positive* nor a *normative* explanation for the creation of transfer programmes to these entrants *if* the purpose of the Union is to provide community-wide public goods. If there are gains to being a member of a large confederation, then a single new entrant can expect to gain much more from its entry than the set of existing members. Add to this the well-documented 'catch-up' phenomenon, and one now expects new members following their entry to thrive relative to the incumbent countries, as to a considerable degree they have.

The presumption that the European Union's *raison d'être* is to help Europeans achieve the possible gains from a more efficient *allocation* of goods and services does not receive much support when one examines the distribution of the Union's budget between the provision of traditionally defined public goods and redistribution activities. Table 3.1 breaks the EU budgets in 1985 and 1995 down into various large categories. Outlays that were purely or largely redistributional made up almost 85 per cent of the EU budget in 1985 and almost 80 per cent in 1995. Activities that could be fairly clearly identified as having salient public good

Table 3.1 Distribution of European Union expenditures by budget category, 1985 and 1995 (in percentages)

	1985	*1995*
Redistribution		
• agriculture and fisheries	72.9	53.6
• regional policy	5.9	13.6
• social policy	5.7	11.9
Allocative efficiency		
• research, energy, transport	2.6	5.0
• external policies		6.2
• administrative costs	4.6	5.1
• miscellaneous	4.4	4.5

Source: Goodman (1996: 101, 105–6).

properties accounted for only 2.6 per cent of the EU budget in 1985. Even if we categorise the EU's aid to non-EU countries (External Policies) as a 'Pareto-optimal redistribution', and thus a form of allocative efficiency activity, outlays to improve allocative efficiency accounted for only 11.2 per cent of the EU budget in 1995.

Because the Council of Ministers has hitherto made the vast majority of its collective decisions using the unanimity rule, one must infer that the transfers to agriculture, poor regions, etc. have also been a form of Pareto-optimal redistribution.[14] If we make the further assumption that a confederate governmental structure is the optimal way to reveal the preferences of Europeans for EU policies, then all citizens in a given country have homogeneous preferences for EU policies, and the unanimity achieved in Brussels implies that *all Europeans* favour large subsidies to European farmers. Every European taxpayer has been willing to fund these large redistributive programmes, because she gets positive utility from seeing her fellow Europeans working on farms, or living in rural areas, have higher incomes – indeed, in the case of European farmers, even higher than the average European taxpayer.[15] If one assumes that past EU redistribution policies can be explained in this way, then one must wonder whether the average European taxpayer will get as much utility out of seeing the farmers of Poland and Hungary better off, as one must assume that she has got out of seeing French and German farmers better off?

This question becomes even more salient if one pursues the logic of Pareto-optimal redistribution to its conclusion. This explanation for government transfers sees the wealthier taxpayer as having the poorer transfer recipient's welfare in the taxpayer's utility function. Following this logic, the taxpayer gets more utility out of transfers to a person with one fourth of her income than she does to someone earning one half of her income (von Furstenberg and Mueller 1971). Since most potential entrants have much lower average incomes than even the poorest current members of the EU, the logic of Pareto-optimal redistribution would require that virtually all programmes transferring income to the poor or to poorer regions in current EU countries be abandoned in favour of similar – indeed more generous – programmes targeting individuals and regions in the new entrants.

Confederation or federation?

An alternative way to explain the size of redistribution programs in the European Union is to assume that the conditions that warrant a confederate governmental structure *are not met*. Each country's representatives in Brussels reflect only the preferences of the voters that support that country's government. Farm interests have not had to convince *all* Europeans that they deserve large subsidies, only a majority in each country. Indeed, they most likely have not even had to do that, but rather have had to join forces with other groups representing narrow interests in each country to form majority coalitions.

If in fact preferences toward EU policies like agricultural subsidies are not homogeneous within each country, a federalist structure for representing these preferences should result in a better match between the policies enacted at the

EU level, and those desired by its citizens. It is inconceivable that agricultural interests could exert as much influence in the European Parliament as they do in the Council of Ministers or the European Council, if the Parliament were elected under a PR formula at the European level – even assuming that the Parliament uses the simple majority rule. With redistribution a much smaller fraction of the EU budget than it now is, the potential budgetary costs to existing EU countries from admitting additional members would be greatly reduced, and the question of entry would be reduced to that of the potential for mutually beneficial outcomes, as discussed above. Thus, the mismatch between the existing structure for revealing the preferences of European citizens for EU-level goods and that which would be optimal results in both a serious distortion of existing policies and a serious hindrance to the admission of new member countries.

Citizenship and mobility

The issue of whether the European Union is or should be organised as a federation or a confederation also arises with respect to the rights of citizens within the EU, and in particular to their rights to employment and citizenship in other member countries. As discussed above, mobility across lower levels of government within a federation can increase the welfare of all citizens, if it results in more homogeneous preferences for the public goods provided at the local level, and there are no offsetting externalities from migration. Thus, a policy of granting the citizens of each EU country equal rights to employment, and eventually to citizenship in the other EU countries can be defended, if the conditions exist that make a federalist structure optimal for Europe.

If we assume, on the other hand, that the optimal structure for the European Union is that of a confederation, and thus that Europeans' preferences are homogeneous within countries but heterogeneous across them, then it is highly unlikely that the optimal EU policy is to provide its citizens broad rights across all Union countries. If the reason why a Dane has different preferences regarding EU policies from those of an Italian is because he is Danish, i.e., has grown up in Denmark and has absorbed the Danish culture, and not simply because he currently resides in Denmark, then there are likely to be costs imposed on the Dane by an Italian's moving to Denmark and participating in the political process there. Free migration is likely to increase preference heterogeneity in each member country and thereby worsen the collective decisions made in each country. Conversely, if migration does not have these negative consequences – if two people living side by side in Denmark are as likely to have similar preferences with respect to the public goods provided in Denmark, when one is Danish and the other Italian, as when both are Danish – then a confederation is *not* the ideal form of government for Europe (Mueller 1996: Chapter 21; 1997b).

This issue becomes particularly important with respect to the question of the entry of new members, because the countries in the queue to enter the EU are definitely homogeneous with respect to one important determinant of 'tastes' and heterogeneous with respect to existing members – namely income. If citizens in new member countries have immediate and equal claims to jobs in existing member countries as their own citizens do, then the substantial differences in wages that exist between the new entrants and the existing members could in itself become a major cause of migration. When deciding whether to migrate to a new community, the potential migrant compares the utility level he can enjoy in her new community to the utility she experiences in her present community. If newcomers can secure the same living standards as those already present in the community, migration will continue until the average utility levels in both communities are equal.

So long as migration causes no negative externalities, however, there is no reason to be concerned about it. Indeed, in the absence of negative externalities, migration leads to a rise in the utilities of the migrants without any fall in utilities to members of the recipient countries, and thus results in Pareto improvements. There are, however, reasons to expect that people living in countries experiencing inward migration will be harmed by it. We have discussed two sorts of negative externalities from migration already. First, migration can lead to population growth and reductions in welfare from crowding and congestion. Second, if the arrivees are allowed to participate in the political process, and their preferences for collective goods differ from those of the indigenous population, the outcomes from the political process may be altered to the disadvantage of the indigenous population. A third fear often expressed concerning migration from poorer countries is that the migrants compete for jobs with the indigenous population, and bring about higher unemployment and/or lower wages.

The most obvious ways to avoid the second and third sources of welfare loss are to deny new arrivees the right to vote and an equal right to employment. Such measures would directly contradict what have until now been basic tenets of European integration policy, namely that all European Union citizens have equal rights to employment and, in time, to citizenship in other EU countries. But such restrictions are fully consistent with a *confederate* form of government, where individuals are seen as similar within countries, but different across them, and primary citizenship is defined at the level of the member country, not at the level of the confederacy. Equal rights to jobs and citizenship are difficult to defend, even within a federalist system, however, if migration has negative consequences for the indigenous population.

The standard approach to any negative externality problem is to levy a Pigouvian tax on the source of the externality.[16] In the present case, this would entail taxing immigrants in some way so as to discourage their migration. Subsidies are substitutes for taxes, of course, and so one could in principle achieve the same end by subsidising immigrants to induce them to remain in their homelands. An alternative to the Pareto-optimal redistribution explanation for the European Union's programme of interregional transfers might be that these transfers are in the narrower interests of citizens in wealthier areas, because they prevent the reductions in the welfare of these citizens that would otherwise occur, if people from the poorer areas were to migrate in great numbers to the richer areas. The same arguments could be used to explain the large subsides offered to Greece, Spain, Portugal and Ireland upon their entry.

Such interregional transfers from existing Union members to poorer new entrants are an extremely inefficient form of subsidy, however, if the goal is to discourage migration. The optimal tax or subsidy to achieve this objective would target potential migrants. The difficulty in administering such a tax is to identify who the potential migrants are. A tax levied on actual migrants solves this identification problem by waiting until the potential migrants identify themselves. Offering subsidies to would-be migrants before they identify themselves is obviously far less likely to hit the correct targets exactly and are thus far more expensive.

Actual EU transfer policies fall even further from their mark, however. Transfers from the richer countries to regions and industries in new entrants will at best slow migration. Suppose, for example, that the average income in an existing Union member is 100, and in a new entrant is only 50. Income is growing at a 3 per cent rate in the new entrant and at a 2 per cent rate in the existing member. Transfers from the existing Union member to the new entrant raise the growth rate of the new entrant to 5 per cent, while leaving the growth of the existing member unchanged. With a 3 per cent growth rate it will take the new entrant over seventy years before its income reaches that of an existing Union member; at a 5 per cent growth rate the new entrant catches the existing member in around twenty-four years. Although people in the new entrant have less of an incentive to migrate if their country grows at 5 per cent than if it grows at 3 per cent, they still have some incentive for more than twenty years. Transfers from wealthier to poorer EU member countries to stimulate the poorer countries' growth are likely to be a far less effective way to discourage migration than imposing negative incentives directly on the migrants themselves.

Conclusions

We conclude that there is little reason why existing Union countries should offer subsidies of any kind to the countries in the queue to join it, and more generally for any other form of inter-country transfers to discourage cross-national migration. If cross-national migration has adverse effects on the countries receiving migrants, then these countries should, of course, be allowed to take actions to discourage this migration. Such actions would undoubtedly run counter to existing EU policies that provide citizens of EU countries broad rights across all EU countries. Although granting citizens of EU countries maximum freedom of movement within the European Union would obviously seem to be welfare enhancing in the absence of negative externalities from migration, in the presence of such externalities, broad rights to encourage mobility may not be optimal. The occasion of the possible entry of several countries which are much poorer than the average EU member presents an opportunity for, and indeed to some extent requires, a rethinking of the extent to which it is in the interest of all EU citizens that each one of them possess broad citizen rights across the several countries.

The issue of how citizenship in the European Union should be defined and what rights should go with it is related to the more fundamental issue of whether the European Union should be organised as a confederation or as a federation of states. The current structure of the European Union is essentially that of a confederation of autonomous states. The locus of political power in the Union has been the Council of Ministers and increasingly on major issues like enlargement the European Council where the heads of state meet. In both bodies EU citizens are only indirectly represented through their national governments. As noted above, such a structure of decision-making and modes of representation can be optimal, *if* all citizens within a country have the same preferences regarding European Union policies, and citizen preferences towards these policies differ across countries.

Common citizenship rights for all Europeans makes eminent sense, on the other hand, if the distribution of preferences for public goods provided at the level of the European Union is such as to make the optimal governmental structure that of a federation. Indeed, if citizen preferences for public goods at all levels of government can reasonably be assumed to be randomly distributed among Europeans at birth, then the migration of Europeans may actually have *positive* externalities by sorting individuals into communities of more homogeneous tastes, and common citizenship rights to encourage mobility can be strongly defended.

The European Union is often described, favourably, as a unique and original combination of federalist and confederalist principles. An elephant with wings might also be described as a unique and original combination, but whether one judged it favourably or not would probably depend upon how well it could fly.

Up to now, the European Union has been able to fly reasonably well despite the inadequacies and logical inconsistencies in its constitutional structure. These structural deficiencies are likely to prove more harmful to the European Union's ability to make collective decisions and to provide collective goods to its citizens as it grows in size. The occasion of the entry of several new members provides an ideal opportunity to reconsider what this structure should be.

Notes

1 The research on this contribution has received financial support from the Hochschuljubiläumsstiftung der Stadt Wien.

2 Exceptions exist, of course. One category would be that of 'cultural clubs', like religions. It may be possible to join a religious club and receive the benefits from membership regardless of where one lives. See Mueller (1996: Chapter 20).

3 Schmidt-Trenz and Schmidtchen (in Chapter 4 of this volume) emphasise the likelihood of different-sized protective states being optimal for different laws.

4 If B is the benefit to each member of a customs union from free trade, and n is the number of members of the union, then it is reasonable to assume that B initially grows rapidly as membership expands, but eventually its growth, although still positive, tapers off as the bulk of the gains from free trade have been realised. This relationship can be captured by positing an exponential relationship between B and n.

$$B = \alpha + \beta \ln n \quad (3.1)$$

A similar relationship between B and n arises for a pure public good, when there is no crowding. If α is the utility a club member experiences from consuming the pure public good, and β is the public good's total costs, then the benefits an individual obtains from club membership, net of his share of the public goods costs, are

$$B = \alpha - \beta/n^2 \quad (3.2)$$

Both Equations (3.1) and (3.2) imply an optimal club size of infinity.

5 Congestion costs can be introduced into Equation (3.2) by adding a term as given in Equation (3.3).

$$B = \alpha - \beta/n - \gamma n^2 \qquad (3.3)$$

Equation (3.3) implies an optimal size for club membership, $n^* = (\beta/2\gamma)^{1/3}$.

6 Let the members of group i have identical preferences for spending on roads, $U_i = K_i - b_i(x_i - x^*)^2$, where x_i is the amount each member of this group wishes to see spent on roads, and b_i is an intensity weight specific to group i. If $x_i = x^*$, a member of the group experiences a utility level K_i. The loss L to a member from having to consume x^* rather than x_i, increases linearly with its intensity weight, and exponentially with the distance between $x_i - x^*$, $L = -b_i(x_i - x^*)^2$.

7 See Tiebout (1956), Mueller (1989: Chapter 9), and Inman and Rubinfeld (1997). The latter two references also discuss the kinds of externalities from migration that negate the potential benefits from 'voting with the feet'.

8 Indeed the European Community was often referred to in its early years as the Club of Rome.

9 This is of course the approach pioneered by Buchanan and Tullock (1962).

10 It is, of course, possible that countries that choose not to or are not allowed to join are adversely affected by the formation of a confederation. Hence, the emphasis in the text.

11 Two confederations with six and four or five members each might dominate a single confederation of ten. Here too, however, it is the three outsiders that will have to offer the bribes.

12 See also Mueller (1996: Chapter 21; 1997b).

13 The fact that the Council of Ministers has felt it necessary to adopt a qualified majority rule for some collective decisions strongly suggests that cross-national heterogeneities of preferences exist. If the preferences of citizens were homogeneous across countries, then the Council could simply use the unanimity rule. Even the threat of 'hold-up' under the unanimity rule would be weak in this case, since the representatives of each country would know that the other countries had the same preferences as they did, and would call the bluff of any country that tried to hold out for more favourable treatment.

14 Although the Council of Ministers has made its collective decisions using the unanimity rule, this of course does not imply that Europeans have unanimously endorsed these policies. Since the country delegates to the Council represent the governments of their countries, they do not represent the citizens who oppose their governments' policies.

15 See Koester and Tangermann (1990).

16 A Pigouvian tax equals the marginal cost imposed on the rest of the community by the activity causing the externality.

References

Buchanan, J.M. and G. Tullock (1962) *The Calculus of Consent*, Ann Arbor: University of Michigan Press.

Frey, B. and R. Eichenberger (1996) 'FOCJ: competitive governments for Europe', *International Review of Law and Economies* 16: 315–27.

Furstenberg, G.M. von, and D.C. Mueller (1971) 'The Pareto optimal approach to income redistribution: a fiscal application', *American Economic Review* 61: 628–37.

Goodman, S.F. (1996) *The European Union*, London: Macmillan (3rd edition).

Inman, R.P. and D.L. Rubinfeld (1997) 'The political economy of federalism', in D.C. Mueller (ed.) *Perspectives on Public Choice*, Cambridge: Cambridge University Press, 73–105.

Koester, U. and S. Tangermann (1990) 'The European Community', in F.H. Sanderson (ed.) *Agricultural Protectionism in the Industrial World*, Washington, D.C.: Resources for the Future, 64–111.

Mueller, D.C. (1989) *Public Choice II*, Cambridge: Cambridge University Press.
Mueller, D.C. (1996) *Constitutional Democracy*, New York and Oxford: Oxford University Press.
Mueller, D.C. (ed.) (1997a) *Perspectives on Public Choice*, Cambridge: Cambridge University Press.
Mueller, D.C. (1997b) 'Federalism and the European Union: a constitutional perspective', *Public Choice* 90: 255–80.
Tiebout, C.M. (1956) 'A pure theory of local expenditures', *Journal of Political Economy* 64: 416–24.
Wicksell, K. (1896) *Ein neues Prinzip der gerechten Besteuerung: Finanztheoretische Untersuchungen*, Jena; translated as 'A new principle of just taxation', 1958; reprinted in R.A. Musgrave and A.T. Peacock (eds) (1967) *Classics in the Theory of Public Finance*, London: Macmillan, 72–118.

PART III

TAX AND SUBSIDY RESPONSES

Public subsidies for private firms in a federalist democracy

Dennis C. Mueller

A normative theory of democracy sees the government as created by the citizens to advance their collective interests (Buchanan and Tullock, 1962, Chapter 1; Mueller, 1996). Given the now almost-universal recognition of the role private markets play in advancing individual interests, any democratic constitution written today would certainly establish institutions that encourage and protect market competition.

The movement of firms from one location to another, and their occasional disappearance through bankruptcy, are normal occurrences in a market economy. In general, such firm movements and disappearances can be expected to improve the long-run efficiency of the economy by locating capital where it is most productive and eliminating inefficient producers. Governments that seek to promote economic efficiency should welcome capital mobility and tolerate, if not celebrate, the disappearance of weak competitors.

Occasionally, however, the impending departure or demise of a company induces public concern, calls for public assistance, and then some form of subsidy or other government action to keep the firm from moving or dying. Such government interventions advance the interests of *all* citizens only in the presence of some sort of "market failure" that makes the survival of the company a form of "public good." Alternatively, such subsidies and other forms of protection may be examples of "rent-seeking" interventions that harm one group to benefit another. Subsidies, for example, might well be harmful, not only to the citizens who pay taxes to fund them, but also to competitors of the subsidized companies, and thus to the competitive process itself. Considerations such as these have led the European Union (EU) to adopt a policy of opposing subsidies by member countries to their domestic firms, which in turn has led to clashes between the EU Commission and individual national governments, as in 1994 over France's subsidies to its troubled national airline, Air France, and again in 1996 over Saxony's subsidies to Volkswagen. Since the EU itself engages in various forms of subsidies and other sorts of protection for individual firms as a part of its industrial and agricultural policy programs, clashes such as these raise questions over both when subsidies should be allowed and what level of government should provide them.

In this chapter we explore conditions under which subsidies can produce a Pareto-optimal allocation of resources in the context of a federalist governmental structure (section II), and in cases where subsidies to private firms are justified whether they should be made by the central government or a lower level government. This latter question is part of the general "assignment problem," with which Albert Breton and Anthony Scott (1978) were concerned in their pioneering study of federalism. In section III we examine whether communities may enter into a form of destructive competition for businesses that leads to Pareto-inferior outcomes. We then consider the impact of public subsidies on the competitive process (section IV), and the proper policy to apply to public subsidies to protect consumer welfare (section V). The public choice of the origin and effects of public subsidies is discussed in section VI. In section VII we contrast the implications of our analysis with current EU policies. Conclusions are drawn in section VIII. We begin by briefly examining the issue of the optimal taxation of capital in a federalist system.

I The optimal taxation of capital under federalism

Let us assume that the citizens of a nation have sorted themselves into communities with identical tastes to consume optimal bundles of local public goods (Tiebout, 1956; McGuire, 1974). Each member of a particular community has the identical utility function, $U(x, s, g, H)$, where x is a private good imported into the community, s are services supplied by other members of the community, g is local governmental services, and H is the stock of housing owned by an individual citizen. For simplicity, we begin by assuming that H is a function of past investments, and does not depreciate. Thus, the representative individual must choose x, s, and g so as to maximize U, subject to the budget constraint, $y = P_x x + P_s s + T$, where T is her local tax payments. With n members of the community, $T = P_g g/n$. From the first order conditions it is easy to derive the usual optimality relationships for private and public goods

$$\frac{\partial U/\partial x}{\partial U/\partial s} = \frac{P_x}{P_s}, \quad n\frac{\partial U/\partial g}{\partial U/\partial x} = \frac{P_g}{P_x} \tag{1}$$

Ideally, T would be raised as a lump-sum tax on all citizens. Taxing either x or s would result in the usual deadweight losses, as would a tax on y if the individual could trade off leisure for income. With H fixed, it becomes an alternative to a head tax as an ideal basis for taxation.

Suppose that the only source of outside income for the community is a single firm that employs m members of the community. It has a capital stock K, and the owners of this capital reside outside of the community. Assume further that the parameters of a community member's utility function are such that $y/3 = P_x x = P_s s = T$. Each employee of the firm spends a third of her income on local private services and a third on local public services. Thus, every three employees of the firm directly support one service worker in the private sector and one in the public sector. Each of these divides his income of y in the same way as an employee of the firm, however, so that taking into account multiplier effects, the community has n members, $n = 3m$, divided equally across the three sources of employment.

The existence of the firm in the community provides another possible source of tax revenue. Indeed, if K is totally sunk, i.e., does not depreciate, then the community can effectively export its taxes by taxing K up to the value of K itself. This potential is reduced, however, to the extent that the capital of the firm depreciates.

Let δ be the depreciation rate on K, and r_c the gross of depreciation return on capital in the community. If other communities do not tax capital, then the suppliers of capital will demand $r_o - \delta$ as a net return in this community, where r_o is the gross return on capital in other communities. If the community's tax rate on capital is t_k, then r_c must satisfy the following relationship:

$$r_c - \delta - t_k = r_o - \delta \qquad (2)$$

under the assumption that δ is the same in all communities. The unexpected introduction of a tax on K by the community will therefore cause the owners of the firm to reduce the capital employed in it until r_c rises enough to satisfy equation (2). If the elasticity of capital with respect to return were one, a new tax on capital of 10 percent would result in a 10 percent reduction in the firm's capital stock, and with a fixed coefficient production function an eventual 10 percent fall in employment. Since, given the multiplier effect, each employee of the firm supports two other members of the community, a 10 percent tax on the capital of the firm will reduce employment and income in the community by 10 percent.

A community that set a given percentage tax on the value of capital employed in the firm could look forward to a steady state in which the firm continued to operate in the community, but at a lower level of activity, assuming that the return on capital invested in the community rose fast enough as capital was reduced to fully offset the effect of the tax on the net returns on capital. If the return on K in the community was constant and equaled r_o, the community could not raise *any* revenue by taxing K, as *all* of the capital would earn a lower return than elsewhere and would be withdrawn.

Now consider what happens if a community tries to raise a fixed amount of revenue, say mT, through a tax of t_k on capital. Two possibilities exist. If the present value of the tax (mT/r_o) exceeds the value of the firm's capital, K, the firm exits immediately. If $mT/r_o < K$, the firm will choose to stay in the community, but to reduce the value of its capital stock. To raise a constant amount of revenue, the community must continually *raise* t_k, as the firm's owners adjust the capital stock downward. At some point the present value of the firm's taxes exceeds the value of its capital, and it exits the community.

Even when the firm does not exit, there are costs to its reducing its capital stock, *unless* other firms move into the community to replace it. The loss in income caused by the contraction of the firm must either be shared by all of the community through some employment insurance program, or fall entirely on the subset directly affected. If these persons leave the community, then they lose the consumption benefits associated with their fixed housing stocks, and/or suffer a capital loss as the price of these assets falls due to the reduction in demand for them. The Tiebout literature argues that individuals group themselves into local communities with homogeneous tastes. Someone leaving the community because of the contraction of the firm might therefore be forced to enter a community with different tastes for local public goods than his own, and thus will experience a utility loss from the move. Nevertheless, if the depreciation rate on the firm's capital is low, some of the community's members may benefit enough from taxing the firm's capital rather than themselves to bring about this policy.

We conclude that the attractiveness of taxing externally owned capital declines with its mobility. If local public goods are not inputs into a local firm's production process, then its capital goes untaxed if it is perfectly mobile (Gordon, 1986). If local public goods are inputs into local production, then the local community adopts benefit tax formulas such that the marginal local tax paid by capital just equals the marginal benefits it receives from local public goods and services (Oates and Schwab, 1988, 1991). With capital perfectly mobile, capital will not be able to exploit local communities, nor will local communities be able to exploit capital.

II The private firm as a public good

In the previous section we have seen that a community will wish to raise all of its revenue by taxing externally held capital when it is completely immobile, and none of its revenue from such a tax when this capital is completely mobile. Since, by definition, complete or perfect mobility is the upper bound of mobility, it would seem that a zero tax on capital must be the lower bound for this tax. How then can one explain *negative* taxes on externally owned capital; how can one rationalize subsidies?

We have also seen in the previous section that some, perhaps all, members of a local community may be hurt by a withdrawal of capital from it. Any unexpected event that causes the firm to incur losses, not just a tax increase, may induce the firm's owners to withdraw some or all of their capital from the community. Two polar cases are of interest: a one-time loss of L, and an annual flow of losses f.

If the unexpected, one-time loss of L is less than the value of the firm's capital stock K, the firm's owners will simply absorb the loss and continue operating as before, since once the loss is covered the firm's capital is again worth K. If $L > K$, however, it is in the owners' interest to walk away from the firm, declare bankruptcy, and cap their losses at K. In the extreme case that no new external source of employment comes to fill the departing firm's place, the loss of L causes those employed by the firm to exit and eventually destroys the community, taking with it all of its fixed capital, nH, and any additional benefits associated with membership in this particular community. Even ignoring the latter, members of the community are obviously better off preserving the firm and with it the community, if $nH > L$.

When the loss is a constant flow, f, the same logic applies as when the community tries to raise a fixed amount of tax revenue over time. If the present value of the loss exceeds K, the firm exits immediately; if not, it continually reduces its assets until $f/r_o > K$, and then it exits.

Some unexpected shocks, for example, a permanent downward shift in demand, are better treated as shifting the demand for the firm's capital, resulting in, say, a constant percentage reduction in the return on its capital, λ. The firm then reduces its output and capital stock until

$$r_c - \delta - \lambda = r_o - \delta \tag{3}$$

holds. This action reduces employment and income in the community and, if it results in the emigration of α fraction of the community, wipes out privately held assets with a value of αnH. If the community's discount rate is i, it will gain by imposing an annual tax on itself of λK and subsidizing the firm to offset this loss, if $\alpha nH > \lambda K/i$.

The attractiveness to a community of taxing externally owned capital depends on the capital's mobility. The attractiveness of *subsidizing* externally owned capital depends on the mobility of both capital and the members of community. If the departure of one firm would be immediately offset by the arrival of another, the community would not tax itself to retain a particular company. If residents possessed no fixed assets or other benefits specific to this particular community, they would not tax themselves to remain there. But if *members of the community are immobile* – because they own immobile assets, because they have personal attachments to other members of the community, because they cannot obtain as attractive a bundle of local public goods for the same taxes elsewhere – then taxes on community residents to subsidize externally held capital may be optimal.

III Tax and subsidy competition across communities

It is sometimes argued that when communities compete for businesses by offering tax breaks, a "race to the bottom" occurs in which the communities themselves are harmed through the erosion of their tax bases and the consequent reduction in their local public goods supply.[1] Such a race to the bottom could presumably lead to negative taxes, and thus this critique applies to local subsidies for firms as well. As noted in section I, however, with perfect capital mobility local communities will level zero taxes on capital or, if they provide capital public goods benefits, will merely charge for these benefits. No community would rationally make itself worse off through a tax to subsidize a particular firm, if another firm would enter the community without such a subsidy. For the race-to-the-bottom argument to have merit with respect to taxes and subsidies for firms, capital must not be available to communities in infinitely elastic supply.

To see what is involved, let us consider an example where there is a perfectly inelastic supply of capital. Assume first that there are N communities, each containing one firm with capital stock K, and employing m workers. The technology is such that neither a larger nor a smaller firm is viable. Each community has a population of $n = 3m$, as in the earlier example, and each resident of community c owns fixed, nondepreciating housing capital of H_c, $c = 1,N$. The values of housing capital are assumed

[1] Although the fear of a "race to the bottom" is often expressed, there is scant empirical evidence to support such fears (Levinson, 1996). Wilson (1996) also questions the logical foundations for such fears.

to be identical within a community, but possibly different across them. We assume that the initial equilibrium arose at a time when both individuals and capital were perfectly mobile, so that firms are untaxed, and all local public goods are financed through benefit taxes on their residents. Capital is perfectly inelastic to the nation, but perfectly mobile within it.

Now assume that an external shock destroys one firm, say that of community *d*. No new capital can flow in from outside of the nation to replace community *d*'s firm, but firms can move from other communities into *d*. If community *d* must disband, its residents lose capital with a value of nH_d. It is prepared to offer up to this amount to attract a firm with capital *K* from another community. Any other community *c* will offer nH_c to retain its firm, however, so that a bidding war ensues with the community with the lowest value capital stock, nH_l, being the ultimate loser. Every other community must match the loser's bid to keep its firm, so that the shortage of capital results in a massive transfer of $(N-1)nH_l$ from residents of the $(N-1)$ communities to the owners of the $(N-1)$ surviving companies. Nevertheless, each winning community is better off from bidding by the difference in value between its housing stock and that of the losing bidder. The bidding process is efficient in that the limited available capital is allocated to the communities that have the most to gain from it.

A more realistic assumption would be that capital is in relatively inelastic supply in the short run, but in elastic supply in the long run. The unexpected and sudden departure of a major source of employment in an isolated rural community might lead it to offer generous subsidies to firms willing to enter the community. But in the long run the general mobility of capital should eliminate these subsidies, and bring about the zero-tax-and-subsidies outcomes predicted with perfect capital mobility.

Thus, there is no reason to expect competition for capital across communities to result in a misallocation of resources. Communities will not bid for capital that is in infinitely elastic supply; bidding for inelastically supplied capital will allocate it to the communities having the most to gain from it.

IV Protecting competition or competitors

A *Subsidies and competition policy*

A second and independent objection against local subsidies for private firms is that they harm other *firms* rather than other communities. That public subsidies to private firms might harm competitors by allowing the subsidized firms to underprice unsubsidized firms is obvious. But it is equally obvious that consumers benefit from the lower prices brought about by the subsidies. If consumers are better off, and taxpayers are better off (or they would not have taxed themselves to pay for the subsidies), why worry about other firms?

One reason to worry about other firms is that their survival may be necessary to maintain the health of the competitive process. Whether this is so at all, or if so under what conditions, has been much debated throughout the more than 100-year history of the U.S. antitrust laws (Neale and Goyder, 1980, pp. 439–44). Most American economists today would probably agree with Robert Bork (1978, Chapters 2, 3) that the antitrust laws *should be* used exclusively to protect and improve consumer welfare. Sections 85 and 86 of the Treaty of Rome recall the language of the U.S. Sherman Antitrust Act, and so one can argue that this is also the major goal of the European Union's competition policy. Other language in the EU's treaties calls this interpretation into question, however. For now, I shall assume that the exclusive goal of competition policy is to improve consumer welfare, and judge the competitive effects of subsidies by this criterion. The goals and consequences of EU competition policies are taken up in section VII.

We have seen that the only rational reason a community would have for subsidizing a firm would be to preserve valuable community capital dependent on this firm. Suppose, however, that these subsidies allow the firm to survive by underpricing other firms in its industry. If other firms must cut their prices to survive, they too may have to obtain subsidies from their communities. They shall succeed in obtaining these subsidies only if the value of community capital protected exceeds the value of subsidies paid. The situation is no different from the one discussed in the race-to-the-bottom example except that the consumers of the product are better off at the local taxpayers' expense, as well as at that of the capital owners.

Suppose, on the other hand, capital were sufficiently mobile so that the communities of the subsidized firm's competitors did *not* respond by subsidizing their firms. They let them go out of business and allowed other, more profitable firms to enter in their place. Our original subsidized firm becomes a monopoly, and then raises its price to earn monopoly rents. We now have an argument – indeed, the only legitimate argument – against public subsidies on consumer welfare grounds. Public subsidies for private firms can injure competition when they are part of a strategy to create a monopoly, which will eventually raise prices and impose welfare losses on consumers. The proper competition policy to apply to public subsidies for private firms is thus an antipredation, antimonopoly policy.

B *Antipredation policies and public subsidies*

A variety of proposals to deal with predatory practices have been put forward. We shall not review and analyze all of them, but rather confine ourselves to three proposals that seem particularly relevant and feasible for dealing with public subsidies.

1. Price less than short-run marginal cost: Areeda and Turner (1975) reason that any transaction at a price greater than marginal cost provides consumer benefits greater than the costs of producing them, and thus improves economic efficiency. They thus propose that any price equal to or greater than short-run marginal cost should be presumed to be nonpredatory.

A lump-sum subsidy to help a firm survive some presumably short-run difficulty would not affect its short-run marginal costs and thus would not figure in the application of the Areeda-Turner criterion to public subsidies. In the unlikely event that the subsidy were per unit of output, one would have to decide whether short-run marginal costs would be calculated net or gross of this subsidy. If firms were allowed to calculate short-run marginal costs after deducting any per-unit subsidies, then the Areeda-Turner criterion would in general allow firms to survive through public subsidies.

The Areeda-Turner criterion allows firms to set prices below long-run average total costs so long as they are above short-run marginal costs. It thus allows short-run transfers from the capital owners of a firm to the buyers of its product, if the firm could have charged a price that covered its full costs.[2] If firms are allowed to calculate short-run marginal costs net of any wage concessions by employees, then the Areeda-Turner rule would allow transfers from both capital owners and workers to consumers. If firms are allowed to calculate marginal costs net of per unit subsidies, then the rule would also allow transfers from the community of the subsidized firm to consumers. If the logic of the Areeda-Turner rule is accepted, that is, that the welfare of consumers in the short run is to dominate all other considerations, and transfers from capital and labor suppliers are construed as improving social welfare, then transfers from

[2] Such transfers may of course be in the long-run interests of the capital owners if they allow the firm to prey successfully on its rivals.

the firm's community should also be construed as doing so. All would seem to be on an equal footing.

2. Sustainable price: The Areeda-Turner rule abstracts entirely from the intertemporal aspects of predation. If a predator succeeds in driving its rivals out of business and then raises prices to monopoly levels, it is allowed to keep the rents it earns, so long as it did not set prices below short-run marginal costs in so doing.[3] Baumol's (1979) rule avoids this problem. It allows a dominant firm to set any price during the period of rivalry, but requires that this price be maintained in the period after rivals have been driven from the field. Baumol's rule forces the potential predator to choose a long-run sustainable price, that is, one equal to or greater than long-run average costs. Thus, if a company succeeds in driving its rivals out, it does so only if it has lower long-run average costs than they do. Moreover, consumers are allowed to benefit from the dominant firm's efficiency through the requirement that prices be kept low after the rivals depart.[4]

The Baumol rule requires no examination of company costs. Thus, its application would implicitly allow public subsidies. It would, however, raise the potential costs of these subsidies by requiring that the price, and thus perhaps the subsidy, be sustained in the long run. If this feature of the rule did not discourage the subsidies, however, application of the rule would not either.

3. Sustainable monopoly: Joskow and Klevorick (1979) treat predation as a question of sustainable monopoly. Because no firm can survive indefinitely at a price less than long-run average costs, they recognize that such prices must be inherently short-run in nature, and inevitably followed by either higher prices or reduced costs. Prices less than long-run average costs pose a potential threat to competition, however, only when a firm possesses sufficient market power to be able to raise its prices in the future – for example, when it is a dominant firm (market share at least 50 percent) in a market with high entry barriers.

If one suspected that a community was subsidizing its "local champion" with the intent of becoming a monopolist and charging monopoly prices, then one would calculate long-run average costs *before* deducting

[3] Areeda and Turner actually soften the criterion further by allowing a defense if price is at least equal to short-run average costs on the grounds that short-run marginal costs are difficult to measure. Since the cost data must be supplied by the firms, this either/or provision allows the firm to choose that cost criterion that is easier for it to meet.

[4] As a practical matter, a limit would have to be placed on the length of the post-departure period of constant prices.

local subsidies. If the firm's price were below unsubsidized long-run average costs, one would know either that price would later rise or that the community would have to go on indefinitely subsidizing the firm. If the firm is already dominant in an industry with high entry barriers, one might suspect the former motive and disallow the subsidies on the grounds that they are an attempt to create a monopoly. If the market structure conditions are not satisfied, the firm will not be able to raise prices in the future, and the subsidies pose no threat to consumer welfare. In this situation, the local community should be allowed to subsidize the firm as long as it chooses.

4. Discussion: Some observers believe that predation seldom, if ever, occurs.[5] To succeed, a predator must incur large immediate losses. The gain if he succeeds is the uncertain, discounted future profits. Under reasonable assumptions, the former typically exceed the latter. By this logic, predation that is harmful to consumers seems likely to be so rare that public subsidies to private firms as predation strategies could safely be ignored.

The predation-is-irrational logic figured heavily in the U.S. Supreme Court's decision *not* to hear the case brought by U.S. television manufacturers Zenith and National Union Electric against Matsushita and several other Japanese television manufacturers.[6] The court reasoned that it would not have been consistent with rational profit-maximizing decision making for the Japanese companies to charge such low prices and incur such large losses to obtain the possible future profits of monopoly. But what if the Japanese companies were not maximizing profits? What if they were rational growth maximizers àla Robin Marris (1964), and were willing to accept low returns on investment to achieve a substantial fraction of the U.S. television market?[7] While such an explanation refutes the logic of the court's decision, it does not lead to the conclusion that the outcome of the Japanese firms's actions harmed U.S. competition. If Japanese television manufacturers are willing to accept low returns on investment to supply U.S. consumers televisions at low prices, why should U.S. competition policy prevent them?

Similar arguments can be made with respect to public subsidies.

[5] See McGee (1958, 1980), Koller (1971), and Easterbrook (1981). For counterarguments and further debate, see Adams, Brock, and Obst (1996a,b), Elzinga and Mills (1996), and Rosenbaum (1996).

[6] For accounts of this case from both protagonists' sides, see Elzinga (1994) and Schwartzman (1994).

[7] Hiroyuki Odagiri (1981, 1992) has argued that Japanese managers are Marris growth maximizers.

Indeed, the public-choice literature implies an even higher probability that collective decisions by a community are "irrational." But, as argued at greater length in section VI.D, even if one doubts that a community's subsidy to one of its firms will provide net benefits to its citizens, this does not justify the actions of a higher level of government in preventing it from offering the subsidy. If there appears to be no danger that the subsidy will lead to a monopoly and subsequent consumers' surplus losses, there is no reason to prevent it.

The market conditions that are necessary for predation to succeed, as discussed by Joskow and Klevorick, are not the ones usually present for publicly subsidized firms. These companies are typically tottering on the brink of bankruptcy. If predation is occurring, it is more likely that the subsidized firms are its targets than that they are its perpetrators. We conclude that local public subsidies for private firms are unlikely to pose a threat to competition, and when they do, the appropriate policy response is not to prohibit them outright, but to challenge them under prevailing competition policy.

V European Union policy and local community taxes and subsidies

A *Taxes*

We noted in section I that local communities will find it attractive to tax externally held capital if it is immobile. When capital is mobile, however, a community's freedom to export its taxes is limited by the opportunities capital owners have to invest in other communities. Should some communities not tax capital at all, pressure is brought on the other communities not to tax capital.

Much discussion and some progress has been made in the European Union in the direction of "tax harmonization." The Ruding committee proposed, for example, a uniform 30 percent withholding tax on dividends across Union member countries, and a range of from 30 to 40 percent for taxes on corporate profits (European Community Commission, 1992). Although the latter is below some countries' corporate profits' tax rates – for example, that of Germany – it is considerably above that of others, for example, Ireland's 15 percent rate. The proposed withholding tax on dividends is also higher than those in several countries. The unanimity rule requirement for passing proposals in the EU Council prevented the adoption of a minimum 15 percent withholding tax on dividends in 1989 (Genser and Haufler, 1996, p. 74). But the pressure to raise or maintain taxes brought about by the EMU criteria, combined with the reluctance of Union member governments to cut expenditures, can be expected to produce additional efforts for the harmonization of taxes on capital within the European Union.

The implementation of the EMU will increase capital mobility within Europe, and make it even more difficult for individual countries to export their tax burdens by taxing externally held capital. If there were significant barriers to capital's movement out of the Union, "harmonized" taxes on capital within the Union could be defended if they substituted for more elastic sources of revenue, like the value-added tax or taxes on labor income. At the same time, however, such tax harmonization can be expected to reduce the pressure on individual national governments to match benefits from expenditures to the taxes that pay for them.[8]

B *Subsidies*

An unexpected drop in a company's profits falls first of all on the owners of its capital. Assuming that the firm is able to survive the loss, and no other measures are taken, the loss is borne entirely by capital. In this case, capital can be said to have subsidized the firm to help it stay in business. Current EU policies do not prohibit capital owners from subsidizing their companies in this way.

If the present value of the unexpected loss, L, exceeds the value of the capital invested in the firm, K, the firm's owners will walk away from it. If the firm's workers expect that no other firm will replace the company, and that they will have to leave the community, they will be willing to offer wage concessions with a present value of up to mH, the value of the fixed assets that they own, to keep the firm operating. If $mH + K > L$, it will be possible to keep the firm alive through some combination of reduction in wages and payments to capital owners, that is, through effective subsidies from capital and labor to the company. Other suppliers of factor inputs will accept lower prices to keep the firm alive, if they do not expect to replace its lost business, and if they possess assets that will be lost as a consequence.

Such "subsidies" to distressed companies are regarded as normal parts of the competitive process, and do not run afoul of EU strictures against subsidies, nor of any of its competition policies. But workers, capital owners, and other input suppliers will accept reductions in their incomes only if they own fixed assets that stand to be lost in the event of the firm's

[8] For further discussion of the pros and cons of tax harmonization, see Cnossen (1990), Keen (1993), Genser and Haufler (1996), and Haufler (1996).

demise. Public infrastructure is also one of the inputs to a firm's production. The "price" of this input is the firm's local taxes. Thus local tax reductions and subsidies are both reductions in the prices a firm pays for some of its inputs, as are cuts in dividends and wages. A collective decision to cut company taxes or provide subsidies forces either a reduction in expenditures or an increase in other taxes, and thus, ceteris paribus, lowers community welfare. The community will make such a move only if it fears a greater harm from the company's departure than from the other fiscal moves. As with other inputs' suppliers, a local community suffers from a firm's departure only if capital is not mobile, so that the firm will not be quickly replaced, *and* the community is not perfectly mobile, in the sense that it possesses assets that will be lost along with the departing firm.

There is nothing to distinguish between the four subsidy options in terms of their Paretian properties. Workers will not accept a reduction in wages unless they collectively think that they will be better off, nor will capital owners, nor will other inputs' suppliers, *nor* will the citizens of the local community. The main differences among the four ways of keeping the firm alive are in the distributions of their costs. These costs will fall on one of the factor owner groups or on a subset of the community, such as the employees of the company, or they will be spread over all members of the community. Equity considerations would seem to favor spreading the costs across the entire community. Thus, a justification for disallowing this alternative by forbidding subsidies must rest on efficiency considerations, and these must go beyond the company and the community in which it is located to consider, for example, the impact of the subsidies on competition in the firm's industry.

But, since there are possible efficiency gains from preserving the assets of the local community, improvements in efficiency cannot be guaranteed by an outright ban on local subsidies. The proper kind of policy to apply when considering the possible inefficiencies caused by local subsidies is, as discussed in the previous section, a competition policy against predation.

VI The public choice of public subsidies

A *Redistribution within the community*

We have until now assumed that the preferences and incomes of all members of a community are identical. Thus, all Pareto-improving collective decisions could be made using the unanimity rule. Most communities are not made up of individuals with identical tastes, of course, and none that I know of uses the unanimity rule. If the community makes decisions with the simple majority rule, a coalition of the firm's owners, employees, and those who have close economic connections to it might succeed in passing a tax-subsidy proposal over the rest of the community's objections, even when the losses of the firm were not large enough to threaten its existence. Indeed, if they can form a majority coalition, they can achieve such a transfer even when the firm is incurring no losses whatsoever. The subsidy would in part be a redistribution from one part of the community to the other.

All collective decisions made with the less-than-unanimous support of the community are likely to involve *some* redistribution, however. A park built in the southern part of the community, whose funding is opposed by residents in the north, redistributes income from north to south. Public schools redistribute from families without children to those with children, and across generations. We have seen that there can be circumstances under which a tax on a community to subsidize a major employer would benefit all, and thus would meet the definition of a pure public good, just as parks and schools can satisfy this definition. There is no obvious difference among these sorts of issues in this respect. There is no obvious reason, therefore, for allowing the central government to "trump" a community's collective choice in one case and not the other.[9] The only reason to allow the central government a veto over local government collective decisions is when they have significant negative external effects on other communities. As discussed previously, there is no reason to presume that subsidies to firms are likely to have this effect.

If one wants to eliminate redistribution within local communities, one should choose a voting rule different from simple majority rule. Although only the unanimity rule ensures that *no* redistribution takes place, higher qualified majorities reduce the amount of redistribution from that which occurs under the simple majority rule (Buchanan and Tullock, 1962, pp. 131–210; Mueller, 1989, pp. 58–63). Redistribution *within* local communities does not produce direct negative external effects on other communities, however. There is no reason to grant the central government authority to forbid such redistribution, therefore, regardless of the form it takes. The decision regarding the proper amount of intracommunity redistribution to allow, and how to achieve it, is essentially a constitutional question that is best resolved by the citizens

[9] The issue of who should be able to trump whom in a federalist system is discussed by Gillette (1997). See also Mueller (1997).

directly involved in the collective decision process, that is, by members of the local community.

B *Redistribution across communities*

Often when a community experiences an unexpected decline in the demand for its main employer's product, it chooses not to levy a tax upon itself to subsidize the local firm, but rather to appeal for a subsidy to the higher level polity of which it is a part. If there are other local communities also seeking subsidies, and the larger polity uses the simple majority rule to decide subsidy issues, then a coalition of local communities may succeed in inducing the larger polity to subsidize the local ones. If the winning coalition is of minimum size, a local community's share of the tax burden is roughly half the value of the assets saved. This situation resembles Gordon Tullock's (1959) famous overinvestment-logrolling example. Unlike the situation in Tullock's example, however, the tax-subsidy package *might* achieve a Pareto improvement. For example, a one-time lump-sum tax would produce a Pareto improvement if it were used to preserve some real assets, no matter how small the value of the assets. The one-time lump-sum nature of the tax would ensure that it introduced no distortions or inefficiencies into the larger community. Any real assets saved by the transfer would constitute a Pareto improvement. Even if the redistributional component of the tax-subsidy package were dominant, it would be Pareto-improving because of its one-time lump-sum nature.

Nondistortionary taxes are rare, however, and one-time subsidies have a way of turning into second- and third-time subsidies, and eventually into constant flows. The redistributional component of broad-based taxes to subsidize particular firms and industries on a continual basis can lead to an overinvestment in declining firms and industries, as predicted by Tullock's logrolling model. If a community benefiting from a firm's survival has to pay the full costs of these benefits, it lets the firm die. But if the larger jurisdiction picks up most of these costs, the community happily accepts the transfer. Inefficient firms and industries survive, and a nation's capital is trapped in the technologies of the past. Such inefficiencies would never arise if the potential beneficiaries from private subsidies bore the full burden of the taxes to pay for them.

Subsidies for private firms are not unique in bringing about inefficient logrolling, of course. Federal financing for urban transit redistributes from the rest of the nation to the largest cities. Farm subsidies redistribute from city to countryside. Subsidies to private firms are neither unique nor necessarily the most egregious forms of geographic redistribution that can occur under the simple majority rule. In addition to raising the required majority in the higher jurisdiction's Parliament, inefficient geographic redistribution could be reduced or eliminated by a procedural rule that prohibited bills of only local interest from coming before the central Parliament (Mueller, 1996, Chapter 6). Such a rule would force the subsidizing of private firms back onto the communities that are the prime potential beneficiaries of such subsidies.

C *Redistribution from consumers to producers*

Very often, companies in trouble (and some that are not in trouble) seek help from the state in the form of tariff protection, restraints on the entry of firms into their industries, price supports, exemptions from cartel prohibitions, and the like. Here the redistribution sought is from consumers to producers, and thus differs fundamentally from the other sorts of redistribution just described, in the sense that there are definite losers as well as winners as a result of the government action.

Competition policy has, or at least should have, as one of its primary objectives the advancement of consumer welfare.[10] Prohibitions against cartels are central elements in any effective competition. To allow a cartel in one industry to benefit its constituents for whatever reason contradicts the logic of competition policy, and violates the laws upon which it rests. Restrictions on entry, price supports, and even tariffs, to the extent that they are instigated at the behest of producers, fall into the same category. These policies, unlike public subsidies, are likely to result in consumers' paying higher prices for the products of the firms helped, not lower prices. The institution of a competition policy is a collective decision to place consumer interests above producer interests insofar as interference with the market process is concerned. Consistent with this revealed preference for consumer welfare, communities should refuse to suspend competition policy when asked to do so by individual firms or industries. One way to accomplish this would be to authorize the agency charged with enforcing competition policy to challenge actions by other parts of the government, be they federal or local, that violate this policy. A more powerful approach would make free trade and competition part of the federal constitution to deter if not prohibit both federal and local governments from interfering with the market in ways that lower social welfare, such as price floors and government-sponsored cartels (Mueller, 1996, Chapter 15).

[10] Robert Bork (1978) has forcefully argued that it should be the *sole* objective of competition policy.

D *Governmental inefficiency*

Many arguments have been put forward to explain why governmental institutions produce inefficient outcomes. Oates and Schwab (1988), for example, after demonstrating the optimality of local provision of public goods and taxation when capital is fully mobile, show that a Pareto-inferior outcome arises if local governments are run by budget-maximizing bureaucrats as first modeled by Niskanen (1971). Such an argument can be used to justify constraining local bureaucrats and governments vis-à-vis the market, say, by requiring larger than simple majorities for these *and other* collective decisions. It cannot be used, however, to justify locating authority for subsidizing private firms at the highest level of a federalist government. The relevant comparison in a federalist context is not the outcome when local governments are run by budget maximizers against the first-best outcome. The relevant comparison is the outcome when local budget-maximizing governments have authority to subsidize local firms against the outcome when a budget-maximizing central government has this authority. One expects governments at both levels to expand beyond the socially optimal size. In the case of local governments, however, citizens can resort to Tieboutian migration to avoid excessive taxes. This option is more limited at the highest level of government, since it requires citizens to migrate to another country, or in the case of the European Union to leave the Union. Thus, one expects that bureaucrats in the central government have if anything *more* discretion to pursue their interests than do bureaucrats in local governments, and consequently that greater inefficiencies will result when only central governments are allowed to subsidize private firms, as opposed to when these subsidies are restricted to the communities that pay for them.

A second concern about the efficiency of government actions stems from the belief that individuals act less rationally when they participate in the democratic process than when they make private decisions (Buchanan, 1954; Brennan and Buchanan, 1985). These arguments are equally valid against *all* collective decisions, however, and thus again cannot justify singling out public subsidies for private firms. Nor can they be used to defend placing the authority for making public subsidies with the highest level of government. An important justification for the claim that citizens make less rational choices when they vote is that they have poorer incentives to gather information about collective decisions than about their own private decisions. A citizen of Denmark is much more likely to be informed about the possible benefits and costs to her of the Danish government's subsidizing a Danish firm than about those of the European Union's subsidizing a Spanish firm. Arguments against government intervention that stress citizens' lack of information buttress the case for placing authority for subsidizing private firms with local governments.

VII Implications for EU policy

The competition policy of the EU has been designed to complement the "free trade" goals that first led to the Union's formation. Hay and Morris (1991, p. 617) have gone so far as to claim that "the promotion of effective competition is the *sole* focus of this policy" (emphasis added). Many provisions of the Treaty of Rome and subsequent refinements support this claim. Articles 85 and 86 of the treaty, for example, are sufficiently close to the language of the U.S. Sherman Act that one might reasonably assume that their intended beneficiaries are only consumers.

Other dimensions of EU competition policy and other EU policies raise some doubts, however. In its ninth Report on Competition Policy (1980, p. 9 ff.), the Commission explicitly set "fairness" as one of this policy's goals, and stated that this goal would be pursued by preserving equal chances for persons and companies engaged in business. Equal chances in turn would be promoted by preventing member states from aiding their domestic firms and thereby harming companies in other member states.[11] EU industrial and agricultural policies allow cross-national subsidies and interference with market processes to benefit certain firms and industries.[12] Thus, current EU policies with respect to subsides prohibit member states from engaging in the kinds of subsidies that are most likely to be efficiency enhancing, those where there is a large overlap between possible beneficiaries and possible losers. At the same time, EU policy allows the Commission to implement the kinds of cross-community tax/subsidy programs that are most likely to be driven by rent-seeking considerations. Ironically, given the reference to fairness in the ninth Report on Competition Policy, current EU policy allows capital owners, workers, and other factor input suppliers to subsidize a company in trouble, but does not allow the fairest sharing of this cost, namely, its distribution across the entire community that benefits from the subsidy.

A set of policies that was both fair and consistently sought to promote economic efficiency and consumer welfare would: (1) allow member

[11] See discussion in Schmidt and Binder (1996, pp. 92–4).

[12] For critical discussions of EU industrial policies from the perspective of optimal competition policy, see Möschel (1992), Hamm (1993), Streit (1993), and Oberender and Okruch (1994).

states and regional governments to subsidize their own firms out of their own tax revenues, (2) apply the Union's competition policies to these subsidies, (3) severely constrain or eliminate cross-national subsidies, and (4) severely constrain or eliminate all other Commission programs that interfere with market processes, where no obvious externalities or other market failures are present.

VIII Conclusions

The central goal of competition policy should be to protect consumers, not competitors. The only situation in which public subsidies for private firms are clearly inconsistent with this goal is when they are part of a predatory strategy to create a monopoly. As such, they should be subject to the laws and regulations that define competition policy. The typical firm seeking public subsidies is not on the verge of monopolizing an industry, however. The typical beneficiary of subsidies is on the brink of exit rather than in the process of driving rivals out of business. Public subsidies to such companies cannot harm competition.

In a world of perfect competition and perfect mobility, public subsidies would neither pose any threat to competition nor benefit the community providing them. Perfectly mobile capital owners would not accept a reduction in the value of their capital assets; perfectly mobile workers would not accept lower wages; and community members who could either costlessly exit, or could costlessly find a replacement for a departing firm, would not tax themselves to subsidize a firm in danger of leaving or closing. If the main employer in a community cannot survive competition in a world in which competition and mobility are not perfect, its workers and capital suppliers must bear the transaction costs of exiting to other firms. If their departure brings an end to the community, its residents must bear the transaction costs of departing to other communities. If one of these groups offers to accept a financial sacrifice to keep the firm alive, it implies that these transaction costs exceed the magnitude of the offer.

If the death of a firm results in the death of a community, it wipes out all tangible and intangible (friendships, for example) assets that the community's residents might own, and imposes the transaction costs of dislocation upon it. Citizens would not agree to tax-subsidy schemes to keep a major employer in their community going, if they did not think that they would be better off bearing the costs of the subsidies than bearing the costs of the firm's departure.

In each of these cases a group – bondholders, workers, or citizens of a community – accepts a reduction in its income to keep a firm alive, because it believes it is in its best interests to do so, given its current mobility and the prospects of the company.[13] In each case a redistribution occurs from a group making a sacrifice to all other groups that would be harmed by the firm's death, including its customers. Each voluntary decision by a group to sacrifice income to keep the firm alive may constitute a Pareto move. There is no reason consistent with the Pareto criterion to favor one group's sacrifice over any other's.

In the United States, in which state and local communities have independent taxation authority, numerous examples of interventions by local communities to save local firms can be cited. For example, TWA's probable demise was prevented by joint action by the city of St. Louis and the state of Missouri. Several cities and states have provided subsidies to professional sports teams to prevent their departures. Here the fixed assets at stake are probably a form of "intangible capital" consisting of community pride, the loyalty of fans, and the like. Similar forms of intangible capital are presumably associated with national efforts to save flagship airlines in Europe.

A particularly striking example of community effort to save a local firm occurred in the early 1950s, when people in and around the tiny city of Green Bay, Wisconsin, prevented the departure of their financially troubled football team by purchasing shares in the team, shares that promised zero financial return. These purchases were voluntary contributions to the provision of a public good. In this instance, the voluntary contributions sufficed to keep the team alive and in Green Bay; but the danger of free-riding makes this method of preserving community assets inferior to a local tax/subsidy package. Changes in National Football League policies have made a similar rescue effort impossible today, just as European Union policy opposes such solutions to local economic crises.

The integration of the East German and West German economies made much of East Germany's industrial sector economically nonviable. East Germans faced two options: abandon their homes and communities and migrate to the West to find jobs, or attract industry into their region. Given the low productivity levels and poor infrastructure in East Germany, this latter option could be pursued only with the help of subsidies for private firms. The subsidies to Volkswagen to locate a plant in

[13] Note that it may be in a community's interest to share some of the costs of keeping the firm alive even if it could impose all of them on capital. In the long run, capital is the most mobile of the three groups involved. By showing a willingness to bear some of the costs of keeping the firm alive, the community lowers the price of attracting new capital to the community in the future. The action may save the community by inducing another firm to enter, even if the subsidized firm eventually dies.

Saxony appear to be the kind of community-asset-preserving policy that can produce Pareto improvements.[14] They do not seem likely to lead to Volkswagen's monopolization of the automobile industry. They should not be of concern to the rest of the European Union.

In the typical subsidy case, one of two scenarios ensues: either the difficulty of the firm is temporary, it returns to profitability, and the subsidies cease; or alternatively, the difficulty of the firm is chronic and the subsidies must persist indefinitely. In this latter case, residence in the community is less attractive ceteris paribus than residence in other communities, since taxes are higher per unit of public benefits *not including the survival of the firm*. In the earlier example, we assumed that all citizens owned identical housing stocks, and that these did not depreciate. But real housing stocks differ in value and do depreciate. A scenario similar to that for the local firm can be predicted for the local community, if the former must be subsidized indefinitely. Citizens with small stocks of housing or long time horizons exit; immigration into the community does not offset emigration to other communities. The tax base erodes, and the firm and the community die anyway. But even in this case, one cannot claim that the initial decision to allow the subsidies is necessarily wrong. If assets are to some degree fixed, a gradual run down can be superior to wiping them out all at once. If the community votes for subsidies, it must be assumed that it believes at the time that they are the optimal policy.

References

Adams, Walter, Brock, James W., and Obst, Norman P., "Is Predation Rational? Is it Profitable?", *Review of Industrial Organization*, 11(6), December 1996a, pp. 753–58.

Adams, Walter, Brock, James W., and Obst, Norman P., "Is Predation Rational? Is it Profitable? – A Reply," *Review of Industrial Organization*, 11(6), December 1996b, pp. 767–70.

Areeda, Philip, and Turner, Donald F., "Predatory Pricing and Related Practices Under Section 2 of the Sherman Act," *Harvard Law Review*, 88, 1975, pp. 697–733.

Baumol, William J., "Quasi-Permanence of Price Reductions: A Policy for Prevention of Predatory Pricing," *Yale Law Journal*, 89, November 1979, pp. 1–26.

Bork, Robert H., *The Antitrust Paradox*, New York: Basic Books, 1978.

[14] In contrast, the "bail-out" of U.S. automaker Chrysler by the federal government resulted in a poor match between potential beneficiaries and taxpayers. Because the assistance offered Chrysler took the form of federal loan guarantees, however, and Chrysler recovered, U.S. taxpayers actually bore no costs from this rescue effort.

Brennan, Geoffrey, Buchanan, James M., *The Power to Tax*, Cambridge: Cambridge University Press, 1980.
Breton, Albert, and Scott, Anthony, *The Economic Constitution of Federal States*, Toronto: University of Toronto Press, 1978.
Buchanan, James M., "Individual Choice in Voting and the Market," *Journal of Political Economy*, 62, August 1954, pp. 334–43.
Buchanan, James M., and Tullock, Gordon, *The Calculus of Consent*, Ann Arbor: University of Michigan Press, 1962.
Cnossen, Sijbren, "The Case for Tax Diversity in the European Community," *European Economic Review*, 34, 1990, 471–79.
Cnossen, Sijbren, and Shoup, C. S., "Coordination of Value-Added Taxes," in S. Cnossen, ed., *Tax Coordination in the European Community*, Deventer: Kluwer, pp. 59–84.
Devereux, M., "The Ruding Committee Report: An Economic Assessment," *Fiscal Studies*, 13(2), 1992.
Easterbrook, Frank, "Predatory Strategies and Counter-strategies," *University of Chicago Law Review*, 48, Spring 1981, pp. 263–337.
Edwards, J., and Keen, Michael, "Tax Competition and Leviathan," *European Economic Review*, 40, January 1996, pp. 113–34.
Eichengreen, Barry, "European Monetary Unification," *Journal of Economic Literature*, 31, September 1993, pp. 1321–57.
Elzinga, Kenneth G., "Collusive Predation: *Matsushita v. Zenith* (1986)," in Kwoka, John E., Jr., and White, Lawrence J., *The Antitrust Revolution*, 2nd ed., New York: Harper Collins, 1993, pp. 238–59.
Elzinga, Kenneth G., and Mills, David E., "Is Predation Rational? An Answer to Adams, Brock and Obst," *Review of Industrial Organization*, 11(6), December 1996, pp. 759–64.
European Communities-Commission (Ruding Report), "Report of the Committee of Independent Experts on Company Taxation," Brussels, 1992.
Genser, Bernd, and Haufler, Andreas, "Tax Competition, Tax Coordination and Tax Harmonization: The Effects of the EMU," *Empirica*, 23(1), 1996, pp. 59–89.
Gillette, Clayton P., "The Exercise of Trumps by Decentralized Governments," *Virginia Law Review*, 83(7), October 1997, pp. 1347–1417.
Gordon, Roger, "Taxation of Investment and Savings in a World Economy," *American Economic Review*, 76, December 1986, pp. 1086–102.
Hamm, Walter, "Die europäische Wirtschaftsunion – eine Gefahr für die Marktwirtschaft?" *Ordo*, 44, 1993, pp. 3–14.
Haufler, Andreas, "Tax Coordination with Different Preferences for Public Goods: Conflict or Harmony of Interest?" *International Tax and Public Finance*, 3, January 1996, pp. 5–28.
Hay, Donald A., and Morris, Derek J., *Industrial Economics and Organization*, 2nd ed., Oxford: Oxford University Press, 1991.
Joskow, Paul L., and Klevorick, Alvin K., "A Framework for Analyzing Predatory Pricing Policy," *Yale Law Journal*, 89, December 1979, pp. 213–69.
Kanbur, Ravi, and Keen, Michael, "Jeux sans Frontières: Tax Competition and Tax Coordination when Countries Differ in Size," *American Economic Review*, 83, September 1993, pp. 877–92.
Keen, Michael, "The Welfare Economics of Tax Coordination in the European Community: A Survey," *Fiscal Studies*, 14(2), 1993, pp. 15–36.

Knieps, Günter, "Wettbewerbspolitik," Discussion Paper 19, Albert-Ludwigs-Universität Freiburg, February 1995.

Koller, Roland H., "The Myth of Predatory Pricing: An Empirical Study," *Antitrust Law and Economic Review*, 4, Summer 1971, pp. 105–23.

Levinson, A., "Environmental Regulations and Industry Location: International and Domestic Evidence," in J. N. Bhagwati and R. E. Hudec, eds., *Fair Trade and Harmonization*, vol. 1, Cambridge, MA: MIT Press, 1996.

Marris, Robin, *The Economic Theory of "Managerial Capitalism"*, New York: Free Press, 1964.

McGee, John S., "Predatory Price Cutting: The Standard Oil (N.J.) Case," *Journal of Law and Economics*, 1, October 1958, pp. 137–69.

McGee, John S., "Predatory Pricing Revisited," *Journal of Law and Economics*, 23, October 1980, pp. 289–330.

McGuire, Martin, "Group Segregation and Optimal Jurisdictions," *Journal of Political Economy*, 82, January/February 1974, pp. 112–32.

Mintz, J., and Tulkens, H., "Commodity Tax Competition Between Member States of a Federation: Equilibrium and Efficiency," *Journal of Public Economics*, 29, 1986, pp. 133–72.

Möschel, Wernhard, "EG-Industriepolitik nach Maastricht," *Ordo*, 43, 1992, pp. 415–21.

Mueller, Dennis C., *Public Choice II*, Cambridge: Cambridge University Press, 1989.

Mueller, Dennis C., *Constitutional Democracy*, Oxford: Oxford University Press, 1996.

Mueller, Dennis C., "Federalist Governments and Trumps," *Virginia Law Review*, 83(7), October 1997, pp. 1419–32.

Neale, A. D., and Goyder, A. G., *The Antitrust Laws of the U.S.A.*, 3rd ed., Cambridge: Cambridge University Press, 1980.

Niskanen, William A., Jr., *Bureaucracy and Representative Government*, Chicago: Aldine-Atherton, 1971.

Oates, Wallace E., and Schwab, Robert M., "Economic Competition among Jurisdictions: Efficiency Enhancing or Distortion Inducing?", *Journal of Public Economics*, 35, April 1988, pp. 333–54.

Oates, Wallace E., and Schwab, Robert M., "The Allocative and Distributive Implications of Local Fiscal Competition," in Daphne Kenyon and John Kincaid, eds., *Competition among State and Local Governments*, Washington: Urban Institute Press, pp. 127–45.

Oberender, Peter, and Okruch, Stefan, "Gegenwärtige Probleme und zukünftige Perspektiven der europäischen Wettbewerbspolitik," *Wirtschaft und Wettbewerb*, 44, 1994, pp. 507–20.

Odagiri, Hiroyuki, *The Theory of Growth in a Corporate Economy: An Inquiry into Management Preference, R&D and Economic Growth*, Cambridge: Cambridge University Press, 1981.

Odagiri, Hiroyuki, *Growth through Competition, Competition through Growth: Strategic Management and the Economy in Japan*, Oxford: Oxford University Press, 1992.

Rosenbaum, David I., "Comment to Adams, Brock and Obst: 'Is Predation Rational? Is it Profitable?'", *Review of Industrial Organization*, 11(6), December 1996, pp. 765–66.

Schmidt, Ingo, and Binder, Steffen, *Wettbewerbspolitik im Internationalen Vergleich*, Heidelberg: Recht und Wirtschaft, 1996.
Schwartzman, David, "*Matsushita v. Zenith*: An Economic Analysis," *Review of Industrial Organization*, 9, February 1994, pp. 1–23.
Streit, Manfred E., "European Industrial Policy: An Economic and Constitutional Challenge," *Staatswissenschaften und Staatspraxis*, 4, 1993, pp. 338–416.
Tiebout, Charles M., "A Pure Theory of Local Expenditures," *Journal of Political Economy*, 64, October 1956, pp. 416–24.
Tullock, Gordon, "Some Problems of Majority Voting," *Journal of Political Economy*, 67, December 1959, pp. 571–9, reprinted in Arrow, K. J., and Scitovsky, T., eds., *Readings in Welfare Economics*, Homewood, IL.: Richard D. Irwin, 1969, pp. 169–78.
Wilson, J. D., "Capital Mobility and Environmental Standards: Is There a Theoretical Basis for a Race to the Bottom?", in J. N. Bhagwati and R. E. Hudec, eds., *Fair Trade and Harmonization*, vol. 1, Cambridge, MA: MIT Press, 1996.

[13]

What ought to be taxed?

Considerable concern has been expressed in Europe in recent years about the potentially undesirable consequences of tax competition, and a large literature has sprung up analyzing this question.[1] As in much of the public finance literature, the analysis of this question has separated the tax and expenditures sides of the fisc. The Government is assumed to have initially set the optimal quantity of public expenditures and taxes, and then the potential adverse consequences on tax revenue of tax competition are explored. There are two things wrong with this approach from the perspective of normative public choice: it ignores the purpose for which the expenditures are intended, and any potential links between these expenditures and the tax instruments used to finance them. This chapter seeks to remedy this deficiency.

More generally, we take up the question of the proper targets of taxation in a democratic state. This question has a long history in economics. One approach, traditionally referred to as "the ability to pay" approach, sees the issue as one of the proper sharing of the burden of taxation. The tax and expenditure sides of the state's budget are separated, and the only question to be resolved is that of determining an equitable distribution of tax obligations. Implicitly this has been the perspective of much of the tax competition literature.

The second perspective on taxation, traditionally referred to as "the benefit" approach, links the expenditure and tax sides of the state's budget. Ideally under this approach the citizens decide both what to tax and at what level at the same time they decide the purpose for which the tax revenues will be used.[2] As we shall see, conceiving of taxation in this way casts the question of tax competition in an entirely different light. Rather than concentrating on harmonizing tax rates and thereby eliminating the pressure on states to be efficient when benefit taxes are used, the issue becomes one of the harmonized reporting of tax sources and, perhaps, of the coordinated collection of taxes.

We shall proceed as follows. The first two sections discuss the taxation of individuals by a state that seeks to advance the interests of all citizens. The third examines redistribution in a democratic state under the simple majority rule. The following four sections examine issues that arise in the taxation of business, allowing for the possibility of factor mobility. Next the question of the taxation of individuals is taken up, under the assumption that they are mobile. The special case of sin taxes is then discussed. A comparison of the predictions of this analysis with the actual patterns of taxation in Europe follows. Some conclusions are drawn in the final section.

The taxation of individuals

The normative theory of the state within the public choice tradition can be traced back to Knut Wicksell's classic essay on "A New Principle of Just Taxation" (1896).

This chapter has received financial support from the Hochschuljubiläumsstiftung of the City of Vienna.

Wicksell put forward the argument, equally as radical in our day as in his, that the state ought to provide only those goods that make all citizens better off. To determine what those goods are, each proposed governmental expenditure would be coupled to a tax which would cover it, and the expenditure/tax package would be voted upon using the unanimity rule. All citizens could determine whether their expected benefits from the expenditure would exceed their share of its costs, and thus any proposed expenditure/tax combination that secured unanimous support would achieve the desired goal of improving the welfare of all citizens.

A classic example of a government expenditure that can potentially provide net of tax benefits to all citizens is a pure public good. More than a half-century elapsed between the time that Wicksell outlined his criteria for the state provision of goods and Paul Samuelson (1954) derived the criterion for the Pareto-optimal allocation of public and private goods. If each individual i's utility is defined over a composite private good X, and a pure public good G, $U_i = U_i(X_i, G)$, then the Samuelsonian condition can be written as

$$\sum_{i=1}^{n} \frac{\partial U_i / \partial G}{\partial U_i / \partial X} = \frac{P_G}{P_X}. \qquad (13.1)$$

To satisfy this condition the Government must determine both a quantity for the pure public good and a distribution of the private good. If we take the distribution of pre-tax income as given, the Government must select a set of taxes that will satisfy (13.1). One such set was proposed by Wicksell's countryman Erik Lindahl (1919). Each individual i's tax price, t_i, is set equal to her marginal rate of substitution between the public and private goods,

$$t_i = \frac{\partial U_i / \partial G}{\partial U_i / \partial X}, \qquad (13.2)$$

with the sum of the t_i constrained to equal P_G / P_X.

Lindahl taxes can be viewed as capturing elements of both the benefit principle to taxation and the ability-to-pay principle. If all individuals have the same preferences toward the composite private good, and all have the same potential command over the private good, so that $\partial U_i / \partial X_i = \partial U_j / \partial X_j$, for all $j \neq i$, then (13.2) demands higher Lindahl taxes for those who experience higher marginal utilities from the public good. Conversely, if all is have identical utility functions, $U_i(X_i, G)$, but different incomes, then (13.2) requires lower Lindahl taxes for those with lower incomes.

A vast literature beginning with Lindahl has explored the possibility of eliciting the information from citizens that is required to satisfy (13.1).[3] Although no procedure has been designed that will reveal this information perfectly, in many cases taxes could be designed that might reasonably approximate the demands of eq. (13.1). The benefits from fire protection to an individual are proportional to the value of the property protected, the value of public highways is proportional to the amount of driving the individual does. Property taxes to finance fire protection and tolls or gasoline taxes to finance highways are reasonable means for approximating Lindahl taxes for individuals. With roughly similar incomes, the amount of property owned or the amount driven are good proxies for the benefits a person receives from fire protection and roads. With roughly similar preferences the rich can be expected to own more property than the poor and to make more use of public roads, and thus to pay higher fractions of their costs.

The value of a person's property is likely to be a good proxy for the benefits derived from many locally provided public goods (for example, police protection), and property taxes are thus an attractive choice of tax instrument for achieving Wicksell/Lindahl taxes. Other forms of user charges, like gasoline taxes and road tolls, can also be designed. For some public goods – like the financing of the judicial system – income may be a good proxy for the benefits an individual receives. Wealthy individuals make more use of the judicial system than the poor and in general have more to gain or lose financially from the outcome of a given judicial proceeding. Thus in these cases personal income taxes could constitute reasonable approximations to Lindahl taxes.

It is not the goal of this chapter to link up each category of public service that potentially has the property of a public good to a specific tax that would reasonably approximate a Lindahl tax. These examples hopefully suffice to show, however, that such linkages are not beyond the realm of possibility. Were such linkages forged, and voters were allowed to express their preferences toward various publicly provided services, the voters themselves would reveal the appropriateness of the particular tax/expenditure link made through their (dis)approval of the proposed tax/expenditure package.

Redistributive taxation under the unanimity rule

Eq. (13.1) in the previous section defines the condition for Pareto optimality in the allocation of a pure public good. Lindahl taxes are usually treated as possible means of attaining allocative efficiency in the provision of a public good, and Wicksell's voluntary exchange approach to government is also assumed to apply only to the allocative side of the Government's ledger. Redistribution decisions are generally thought to be quite different from allocative efficiency decisions and to require different taxes and different voting rules – like the simple majority rule – from those that might be used to make allocative efficiency decisions. Before discussing redistribution under the simple majority rule, let us briefly review the possible ways in which redistribution might come about in a community, even under the unanimity rule.

Positive theories

Pareto-optimal redistribution Under this theory a better-off group, R, gets utility from seeing a worse-off group, P, become better off.[4] This assumption can be modeled by assuming that the utility of R, U_R, is a function of the private good consumption of both an R and a P, $U_R(X_R, X_P)$. If T is the transfer from R to P, and Y_R and Y_P are R and P's incomes, then the budget constraints of R and P, $X_R = Y_R - T$ and $X_P = Y_P + T$, can be used to replace X_R and X_P in U_R, yielding

$$U_R = U_R(Y_R - T, Y_P + T). \tag{13.3}$$

Maximizing (13.3) with respect to T and setting the first derivative equal to zero gives us

$$\frac{\partial U_R}{\partial X_R} = \frac{\partial U_R}{\partial X_P}. \qquad (13.4)$$

An R transfers her income to a P up until the point where the marginal utility that she gets from her own personal consumption equals the marginal utility that she gets from another unit of consumption by P. The marginal utility that P gets from consumption figures only indirectly, if at all, in R's decision to redistribute her income to P.

As such the Pareto-optimal approach to income redistribution explains why a given person R might give to a given person P or, perhaps, why an R might give to a charity that gives to a group of Ps. It does not explain, however, why government intervention is needed to bring about this transfer. To rationalize government intervention under the Pareto-optimal approach to income redistribution one must assume that an R only gives to the Ps, *if all other similarly situated* R*s give*, and the Government intervenes to resolve the usual free-rider problem (Thurow, 1971; von Furstenberg and Mueller, 1971).

Income redistribution as insurance Fire insurance pools redistribute income from those who do not have fires to those who do, unemployment insurance redistributes from the employed to the unemployed. Risk averse individuals who are uncertain about whether they will be a victim of a fire or lose their job may raise their expected utilities by joining programs that insure against these risks. As with the altruistic behavior described in the Pareto-optimal approach, the question with this explanation for voluntary redistribution is not whether it could plausibly happen, but why the Government is needed to bring it about. Why cannot private insurance clubs achieve these ex ante Pareto gains?

The answer typically given invokes asymmetric information and moral hazard behavior. Individuals know whether they are industrious or not, and thus whether they are likely to lose their jobs or not. Employers and insurance companies cannot evaluate these probabilities. Thus highly industrious people would find it optimal to self-insure against unemployment, less industrious people would join insurance programs, and the familiar "lemons problem" leads to the insurance market's disappearance.[5] By forcing everyone to "buy" unemployment insurance, the Government solves the lemons problem and recreates a market for insurance.

Normative theories

Both of the preceding "positive" theories explain why a community might unanimously agree to implement a redistribution program. Each theory might also be given a normative interpretation. A rich person *ought* to obtain utility from altruistic behavior toward the poor; a rich person *ought* to assume that he might someday be poor. The latter prescription can lead to the conclusion that the income distribution *ought* to be egalitarian. To see this, assume again the existence of two individuals, R and P. The utility of each is solely a function of his own private goods consumption, $U_R = U_R(X_R)$, $U_P = U_P(X_P)$. T is again the transfer from R to P, and Y_R and Y_P are R and P's incomes with $Y_R > Y_P$. Each individual assumes that with probability π_R he will be R and with probability $(1 - \pi_R)$ he will be P. After substituting the budget constraints, $X_R = Y_R - T$ and $X_P = Y_P + T$, into U_R and U_P, each individual chooses T to maximize the same expected utility function,

$$E(U) = \pi_R U_R(Y_R - T) + (1 - \pi_R) U_P(Y_P + T). \quad (13.5)$$

The first order condition from this maximization yields

$$\frac{U'_R}{U'_P} = \frac{(1 - \pi_R)}{\pi_R}. \quad (13.6)$$

If one makes the further assumption that an ethical individual assumes that he has an equal probability of being R or P, and that they both have identical utility functions, then the right-hand side of (13.6) becomes one, and the optimal T equates the incomes of the two individuals. Uncertainty over future position produces an egalitarian distribution of income.[6]

Redistributive taxation under the simple majority rule

Under the simple majority rule redistribution can take place without any uncertainty on the part of those who are taxed, or without any altruism on their part. If the Ps are in the majority, they can take advantage of this fact under the simple majority rule. The simplest of all explanations for redistribution in a majority rule democracy is that a winning majority uses its political authority to transfer income to itself from the losing minority.

Taxes on business

Benefit taxes – financing highways

Businesses benefit directly from a variety of goods and services provided by the state. An obvious example of such a public good is highways. The annual costs of a system of highways can be divided into the amortization of their initial cost, A, and maintenance of the highways, M, which we can think of as including the cost of highway police, and so on. Maintenance costs can be expected to be proportional to traffic on the highways. Thus the maintenance costs that must be incurred because of the activities of a given firm are proportional to the amount of goods it ships. To begin, let us assume that the initial costs of constructing the highways have been entirely amortized, $A = 0$. Let m be the highway maintenance cost per unit of output shipped in industry X, c_i production costs per unit of output for a firm I in this industry. If the state levies a tax on firm I to cover the highway maintenance costs, which the firm forces the state to incur, then the unit costs of the firm are $c_i + m$. Assume that X is a differentiated product and each firm i faces a demand schedule, $p_i = a_i - bx_i$. A firm with a higher a_i can be thought of as having a higher-quality product, as consumers are willing to pay a higher price for this firm's product at any level of output. Under Cournot behavioral assumptions, a profit-maximizing company in this industry chooses an output $x_i = (a_i - c_i - m)/2b$, and earns a profit $\pi_i = (a_i - c_i - m)^2/4b$. Firms with higher-quality products as measured by a_i, or lower costs of production, c_i, have larger outputs and profits in the industry.

This method of financing the highways constitutes a form of benefit taxation. Each firm covers that proportion of highway maintenance costs that arises because of its use of the highways. Each firm chooses an output at which its marginal revenue just equals the cost of producing the last unit of output plus the social cost of shipping it to a customer. If all markets were perfectly competitive this method of financing highways would result in a Pareto-optimal allocation of resources. We have however assumed that each firm faces a negative sloped demand schedule and thus possesses some market power. This market power allows each firm to earn a profit, and these profits become an alternative source of tax revenue for the state.

The taxation of profits

If one wished to apply the ability-to-pay principle to firms, the obvious target of taxation would be profits. Suppose therefore that the state chooses to cover the maintenance costs of the highway by leveling a proportionate tax t on each firm's profits, instead of charging it a user fee proportional to its shipments over the highways. With $m = 0$, each firm I's output and profits become

$$x_i = (a_i - c_i)/2b,\ \pi_i = (a_i - c_i)^2/4b. \tag{13.7}$$

The state must choose a profit tax rate, t, that will cover the total maintenance costs incurred with $m = 0$.

$$m\sum_{i=1}^{n} \frac{(a_i - c_i - m)}{2b} = t\sum_{i=1}^{n} \frac{(a_i - c_i)^2}{4b} \tag{13.8}$$

which yields a value for t of

$$t = \frac{2m \sum_{i=1}^{n} (a_i - c_i - m)}{\sum_{i=1}^{n} (a_i - c_i)^2}. \tag{13.9}$$

A given firm i's taxes under the profit tax exceed its taxes when charged a fee proportional to use, depending on the direction of the following inequality

$$\frac{t(a_i - c_i)^2}{4b} \gtrless \frac{m(a_i - c_i - m)}{2b}. \tag{13.10}$$

This inequality is equivalent to

$$\frac{(a_i - c_i)^2}{\sum_{i=1}^{n} (a_i - c_i)^2} \gtrless \frac{(a_i - c_i - m)}{\sum_{i=1}^{n} (a_i - c_i - m)}. \tag{13.11}$$

A firm whose share of industry profits exceeds its share of industry output pays a greater share of the costs of highway maintenance. Under the assumptions made in this example, firms with higher-quality products and lower costs have both higher outputs and profits. Since output increases proportionally to $(a_i - c_i)$, while profits increase in proportion to $(a_i - c_i)^2$, substituting a proportional tax on profits for a highway user fee shifts the burden of paying for the highways on to the more efficient, higher-quality firms.

Applying the ability-to-pay approach to the taxation of firms can reduce the efficiency of the economy in two ways. First, it reduces the costs of shipping goods, and thus leads to greater outputs for firms that ship their goods over the highways. In a perfectly competitive industry, this would imply that the marginal social benefits from the last units produced were less than the marginal social costs of producing and delivering them. In industries where competition is imperfect, and some firms earn economic profits, taxing profits rather than applying user fees, subsidizes low-quality/inefficient firms at the expense of high-quality/efficient companies. Should there be additional fixed costs that need to be covered, the use of a profit tax rather than a user fee could result in an inefficient firm's survival under the profits tax, where it would have disappeared if it had to pay for the costs it imposes on society.

Sharing the fixed costs

The task of charging a user fee to cover the costs of public highways is relatively easy when all of these costs are maintenance related and proportional to use of the highways. Consider now the problem when $A > 0$ and these fixed amortization costs must be covered. Here we have a situation in which the optimal tax package is a two-part tariff with each highway user charged for the maintenance costs he induces, and the overhead amortization costs are covered through lump sum taxes. If we rule out lump sum taxes on feasibility grounds, the most obvious way to cover highway amortization costs that is consistent with the benefit approach would be to pro-rate them to use. Thus each firm would pay a user charge, u, for the highways that was proportional to its output. This user charge would equal the highway maintenance costs plus a share of A, $u = m + s$, where s is defined by

$$s\sum_{i=1}^{n} \frac{(a_i - c_i - u)}{2b} = A. \tag{13.12}$$

With $A > 0$, the user fee a firm pays to ship goods on the highways exceeds the marginal social costs of using the highways, $u > m$. If all industries were perfectly competitive this property would result in a welfare loss relative to the first-best method of covering A through lump sum taxes. But when competition is imperfect, as we have assumed, such a change in output might increase or decrease social welfare.[7] Covering A through a tax on economic profits, on the other hand, would leave output unchanged from the level that would be optimal under the perfect competition assumption. Such a method of covering social overhead costs might seem attractive, therefore. Use of the profits tax would continue to shift the burden of taxation from the relatively less efficient/low-quality producers to the relatively more efficient/high-quality producers, however.

Business taxation and tax competition

Consider now the case of two countries, *Ö* and *S*, which are situated next to one another. Both have highway systems with identical maintenance cost structures and identical initial costs that must be amortized. Producers to the north of the two countries ship goods across them to customers to the south. Transit routes through the two countries are identical in all respects. Producers choose shipping routes entirely on the basis of costs. We continue to assume that there are no crowding or other external costs to shipping.

Suppose that each country decides to charge a user fee to cover both the maintenance and amortization costs of their highways. Each uses eq. (13.12) to fix s, setting n equal to the number of domestic users, d, plus one-half of the total number of potential transit users. Call this s, s_n. Under the assumption that d is the same in both countries, both initially set the same u and divide the transit traffic equally. By cutting its user fee slightly, however, one of the two countries can capture all of the transit traffic and cover a greater fraction of its A out of the user fees levied. A competition between the two countries for transit traffic ensues with the much lamented "race to the bottom" in user fees.

There are two things to note about this outcome. First, bottom in the case where the countries attempt to cover the costs of the highway system through user fees, is $u = m$, not $u = 0$. Neither country has an incentive to subsidize transit by charging transit vehicles a price that does not cover the maintenance costs the transitor causes. Assuming that the Bertrand equilibrium is reached with each country setting $u = m$, each country must cover the highway amortization costs out of other sources of tax revenue. If we assume that the transitors are incorporated outside of *Ö* and *S*, then each of these two country's own citizens must bear the full amortization costs of their highway system. If we ignore the differences in tax burdens within each country, a country's citizens are no worse off financially setting $u = m + s_d$, where s_d is determined using eq. (13.12) under the assumption that the number of highway users is just the number of domestic users, d, than they are setting $u = m$. With $u = m$ at the Bertrand equilibrium, a country can expect to have half of the total potential transitors crossing its borders, with $u = m + s$, and s based on $n = d$, a country can expect no transitors. If there were any costs at all beyond highway maintenance fees to having foreign firms ship their goods across a country, the second solution would dominate the first, and each country would set its user fee at the higher level.

Of course, if both countries set the same user fees under the assumption that with these fees they would have no transitors, they would again share the perhaps now lower total number of transitors. The transitors would now be covering more than their proportional share of the highway amortization costs and implicitly subsidizing other activities in each country. One might expect in this case that user fees would begin to fall, and a downward spiral would again ensue, but one might not. Once each country's politicians understand the nature of the competitive game they realize that they are unlikely to be able to choose a positive s that is just less than that of the other country and capture all of the transit traffic. The three outcomes that might be expected to be sustained are $s = 0$, $s = s_d$ and $s = s_n$. Since the first is the least attractive of the three for each country, there is little reason to expect it to be the likely outcome.

Paying for the highways by taxing profits, or by some other method that corresponds to the ability-to-pay approach, obviously has no attraction for either country. Such taxes could be levied only on each country's own citizens. Transitors would cover none of the costs of the highway system. The advantages of benefit taxes to finance highway systems are enhanced once the highways are opened to transit traffic, even in the presence of potential intercountry tax competition.

Other forms of public goods

City fire departments protect business property from fire; city police protect business property from theft and vandalism; city sanitation departments dispose of the trash and sewage of businesses. Each of these services, and many others that governments provide, benefits businesses in obvious ways. Each of these services could easily be financed by some form of benefit taxation. The benefits from fire protection are proportionate to the value of the plant and equipment of a business. So too, to a large extent, are the benefits from police protection. Property taxes are the obvious source of revenue for these public services when they are financed under the benefit principle.

In other cases the benefits from government services, as with highway use, may be more closely related to output or value added. In all cases, however, businesses' benefits from government services are far more likely to be proportional to some measure of the scale of the business – replacement costs of capital stock, output, value added – than to profits or other measures of company financial success. Thus, taxes on property, sales and value added become logical choices for financing government activities when business is taxed under the benefit principle. As in the case of taxes to pay for highways, if a government service like fire protection is financed out of a proportional tax on profits, rather than say by a property tax, the share of the costs of the services borne by the relatively more efficient/high-quality producers rises. Applying the ability-to-pay approach to business taxation, rather than the benefit approach, effectively redistributes tax burdens to subsidize inefficient producers at the cost of more efficient ones.

Business taxation and tax competition with factor mobility

As with highways, the costs of most public services can be separated into a fixed component that does not vary with output and a variable component proportional to output. Considerable empirical research estimating a so-called "degree of publicness" parameter for urban public services implies, however, that in the long run the fixed costs for these services are zero and variable costs are constant.[8] A city with a population of 1 million spends roughly twice as much on police, fire protection, and so on, as a city of 500 000. Thus, for the kinds of public services that local communities supply, the task of choosing a benefit tax is fairly simple, as no formula for sharing the fixed costs of the service needs to be determined. Each business can be charged a share of the average costs of providing a service that is proportional to its benefits from the service.

When the long-run marginal costs of providing a public service are constant, and communities rely on benefit taxation to finance these services, no community needs to be concerned about tax competition and races to the bottom, *provided that it is as efficient as other communities at providing public services*. No business will move into a community that does not provide fire protection and the other public services, and it will willingly pay for these services if they are provided as efficiently as in other communities and thus charged for at the same levels. No community will charge businesses a price for these public services that is less than its costs of providing them, because to do so would raise their average tax burden and thus lower their welfare from living in this community. Any community that followed a strategy of taxing its citizens to subsidize the costs of providing public services to business would find that in the long run its citizens would move to other communities where businesses are not subsidized and thus the net of tax incomes of citizens are higher. In the long run communities must compete for both businesses and citizens, and if they discriminate against either one they can expect to see them leave.[9]

The taxation of individuals when they are mobile

Benefit taxes

When all communities employ benefit taxes and individuals are mobile, their movement from one community to another can increase the welfare of all individuals. This is the famous Tiebout (1956) proposition. Individuals who seek higher-quality schools for their children move to those communities that provide such schooling, and are willing to pay the higher taxes that are required. Some communities offer many high-quality public services and have high tax rates, others attract citizens who prefer minimal public services and low taxes. No race to the bottom results, unless we assume that all communities start the race with bundles of public goods and services that are of a higher quality than their citizens want. Even under this assumption, "bottom" will consist of public goods bundles that match the preferences of each community's citizens.

Tiebout's demonstration that the free mobility of individuals improves the allocation of publicly provided goods and services rests on a variety of assumptions that may not be reasonable in a real-world context (Mueller, 2003, Ch. 9; Inman and Rubinfeld, 1997). For example, crowding may result in some communities that attract citizens, while a community that loses population may find itself left with a stock of public goods that exceeds the desires of its remaining residents. But even in this situation the problem is not one of an excessive tax competition between the two communities, nor would tax harmonization improve matters. Indeed, one way to deal with this problem would be for the community that is gaining population to *raise* its taxes to keep new residents away.

Any community that is inefficient in its provision of public services and sets higher taxes than other communities which provide comparable levels of services, is likely to lose population, of course. Its Government will feel a pressure to improve the efficiency with which it supplies its public services and then to lower taxes (or raise quality). Requiring that the more efficient communities raise their taxes to harmonize them with those of the less efficient ones would only worsen the welfare of citizens in both communities. We conclude that allowing for citizen mobility in a world in which all communities employ benefit taxation to finance their bundles of goods and services will not result in a downward spiral in taxes that harms the citizens in each community and may actually benefit citizens in some by making their governments more responsive and efficient.

Redistributive taxation

All of the forms of redistribution that could conceivably come about, even if a community used the unanimity rule, provide each citizen benefits and could therefore be financed by a benefit tax of some sort. With Pareto-optimal redistribution, the rich benefit from seeing the poor better off. A tax on the incomes of the rich with the funds transferred to the poor is perhaps the most obvious way to bring about this redistribution, but other tax–transfer combinations are also possible. For example, if many local services like fire protection are financed through proportional property taxes an additional tax on high property values could be levied, converting the property tax into a progressive tax, with the additional funds raised transferred to the poor.

In any case, there would be no reason for the rich to try to avoid paying the tax by exiting the community if they obtain utility from seeing the poor members of their community better off. If the rich exited they would not pay this tax, but they would also not receive the benefits from seeing their poorer fellow citizens better off. It would be no more rational for a rich person to exit from a community to avoid a tax that was used to finance the kind of redistribution she favors than it would be to exit to avoid a tax that was used to provide the level of education she wanted for her children.

A similar argument holds with respect to government-run insurance schemes. If unemployment benefits are financed out of a pool that is created through a tax on the incomes of potential beneficiaries, no one has an incentive to exit the community to avoid the tax so long as they remain uncertain in their new community about the chances of being unemployed. If the argument that the market cannot supply unemployment insurance efficiently is valid, then no one would have an incentive to leave a community that provides unemployment insurance at its actuarial value and enter a community that does not provide unemployment insurance.

The same is true for anyone who supports redistribution because she accepts one of the normative arguments for it. If someone votes to tax themselves because they believe that one ought to behave altruistically toward the poor, or assumes that she has an equal chance of being herself or a poor person, after the tax that she voted for is implemented she is unlikely to decide to move to another community to avoid paying it.

Someone might move to avoid paying a tax which they did not vote for, of course. Redistribution from a losing minority to a winning majority, as occurs under the simple majority rule, does provide the losing minority with an incentive to move to a community which does not engage in this form of redistribution. Thus, citizen mobility might constrain a government's ability to redistribute the income of the community toward its supporters, and would then encourage it to try to prevent the targets of its involuntary redistributive programs from moving to other communities in which they were not so heavily taxed. Tax harmonization agreements, which equate tax rates across communities and thereby discourage migration, are likely to be attractive to any government that seeks to engage in involuntary redistribution.

Sin taxes

Social concern about drinking arose most prominently during the nineteenth and early twentieth centuries in Scandinavia, Northern Europe and North America. "Temperance movements" were led by women (wives) who sought to prevent their husbands from stopping at the local pub on the way home from work and squandering the family's resources. Thus, the original opposition to alcohol consumption was based on its financial impact on working-class families, and the proposed solution to the misery caused by alcohol consumption was to prohibit or significantly restrict its consumption.

Such policies could be rationalized using standard externality arguments. The consumption of alcohol by men imposed significant costs on the women and children who depended on their incomes. A similar rationale for constraining the consumption of alcohol cannot be sustained today in the developed countries of the world, however, first because families are less dependent today on one member's income, and second because alcohol consumption today, even in extreme cases, would constitute a far smaller proportion of most families' income than it did a century ago.

The rationale often stated today for restricting the consumption of alcohol through taxation, and analogously tobacco, rests on their likely adverse effects on health. These effects are borne by the consumer herself, however, and thus cannot justify state intervention to curb an externality.[10] Nor can taxes on alcohol or tobacco be reconciled with either the ability-to-pay or the benefit approaches to taxation. If taxes on alcohol and tobacco are imposed to improve community health, then the beneficiaries from these taxes are the persons who do not drink or smoke as a result of the taxes. Thus the beneficiaries from taxes on alcohol and tobacco do not pay the taxes, and the drinker or smoker who does receives, for the extra taxes she pays, no services from the state that are not equally available to a person who does not drink or smoke.

The most perverse of all sin taxes are those levied on gambling, however. Gambling, like alcohol consumption, was originally thought to be a social evil because of its addictive nature and because of the financial hardship it brought to those families that included an addictive gambler. The social response to the intrafamily externalities caused by gambling was originally, as with alcohol consumption, outright bans of it. Until fairly recently, virtually all forms of gambling were illegal in the United States outside of Nevada. One state after another has introduced gambling, however, until it is now quite widespread in the United States and an important source of revenue in many states other than Nevada. Yet gambling has no adverse effects on the health of the gamblers, and no negative externalities except for the intrafamily financial externalities which were the cause of its originally being banned. By taxing gambling, however, the state reduces the income of gamblers, and thus worsens the only external effect of gambling that could possibly justify its taxation in the first place. Thus, as with taxes on alcohol and tobacco, gambling taxes cannot be reconciled with either the ability-to-pay or the benefit approaches to taxation. Indeed, in the case of gambling taxes, they fall heavily on those with a great inability to pay.

The only normative justification for taxing alcohol, tobacco and gambling that one can give is that they impose less excess burden than other sorts of commodity taxes owing to the highly inelastic nature of their respective demand schedules. But these high inelasticities exist because of the addictive nature of the activities taxed. Thus the very high inelasticities that justify taxing these activities to minimize excess burden imply that the taxes do not significantly deter consumption and thus fail to accomplish their alleged goal of deterrence. The main effect of these sin taxes is merely to transfer consumers' surplus to the state, whereby they admirably accomplish the state's goal of raising revenue – which of course explains why the taxes exist.

Because sin taxes involve no quid pro quo of public service benefits for citizen tax payments, and because they typically are very high percentage multiples of the values of the goods taxed, the incentives to avoid them are quite large. Cross-border shopping in response to tax differentials has been common in both North America and Europe. Since the taxpayer gets nothing in return for the taxes she pays, she has an incentive to avoid all of these taxes. "A race to the bottom" in sin taxes is possible if communities are situated close enough to make cross-border shopping practicable. In a highly mobile world, tax harmonization may be the only way to preserve the revenue which the state gets from these sorts of taxes.

Taxation in Europe and the United States

If governments provided only those goods and services which citizens and businesses demanded, and taxed the beneficiaries of their policies in proportion to the benefits that they receive, one might expect that tax and expenditure patterns would be similar for countries at similar stages of economic development. Such is not the case, however. Government expenditures as a percentage of GDP in the major industrialized countries range from around 30 percent in Australia, Switzerland and the United States to some 50 percent in The Netherlands and Denmark (see Table 13.1).[11] An explanation for these great disparities consistent with the assumption that governments do provide the goods and services that citizens and businesses demand would be that "tastes" for government outputs differ greatly even across countries at similar levels of economic development.

Such an explanation would seem more plausible with respect to the goods and services demanded by individuals than for those demanded by businesses. Businesses in different countries can be expected to have similar wants with respect to governmentally provided infrastructures.[12] If in turn governments finance the goods and services supplied to business by means of benefit taxes, then we should expect similarities across industrialized countries in the treatment of the business sector, even if substantial differences exist in the budget aggregated over the business and private sectors. Such is also not the case, however.

Table 13.1 presents the percentages of total tax revenue accounted for by nine major tax categories in 17 industrial countries. We noted above that proportional taxes on sales and value added would reasonably approximate the magnitude of many of the benefits businesses receive from government services. One might expect, therefore, that countries would rely on these taxes to a similar degree. Sales and value added taxes account for less than 10 percent of total tax revenue in Australia, Switzerland and the United States, however, but over 20 percent in Greece, Ireland and Portugal.

If the benefits from country A's governmental services are roughly proportional to a company's production in A, then two firms with the same levels of production in A should pay the same taxes to the government of A, independent of the fraction of this output that is actually sold in A. The fact that one company exports a larger proportion of its output does not mean that it benefits less from the public services supplied to its factories in A. Under the benefit–tax principle, value added and sales

Table 13.1 Composition of tax receipts for major industrial countries, 1988

Country	Total tax revenue as a percent of GDP	Personal income taxes as a percent of total taxes	Corporate income taxes as a percent of total taxes	Employee social security taxes as a percent of total taxes	Employer social security taxes as a percent of total taxes	Taxes on payroll and workforce	Property taxes	Consumption taxes	
								General	Specific
Australia	30.8	45.9	10.6			5.7	9.8	9.1	14.9
Austria	41.9	22.5	3.2	13.7	16.1	5.8	2.6	20.6	10.1
Belgium	45.1	32.0	6.9	10.7	20.6		2.4	16.2	6.9
Canada	34.0	36.7	8.6	4.6	8.4		9.3	15.5	10.8
Denmark	52.1	51.0	4.4	2.0	0.2	0.3	4.6	19.4	12.3
France	44.4	12.1	5.2	12.5	27.2	1.8	4.8	19.7	8.9
Germany	37.4	28.9	5.3	16.2	19.1		3.1	15.6	8.6
Greece	35.9	13.7	3.9	13.6	14.9	1.1	2.9	25.3	17.9
Ireland	41.5	34.8	3.8	5.1	8.4	1.5	4.0	20.7	19.7
Italy	37.1	26.8	9.4	6.6	23.4	0.5	2.5	15.2	10.5
Luxembourg	42.8	24.4	17.3	10.4	13.6		7.7	14.2	10.4
Netherlands	48.2	20.5	7.3	19.0	16.9		3.5	16.5	7.1
Portugal	34.6			9.4	16.6		1.9	20.4	26.6
Spain	32.8	21.5	6.5	5.9	27.2		4.1	17.1	12.2
Switzerland	32.5	34.2	6.6	10.3	10.1		8.3	9.8	7.8
United Kingdom	37.3	26.6	10.8	8.5	9.5		12.7	16.5	13.1
United States	29.8	34.7	8.4	11.4	17.0		10.3	7.5	7.3

Source: OECD, *Revenue Statistics*, 1965–89, Paris, 1990. As reported in Costello (1993), Table 14.

taxes should be levied in the country of origin and not in the country of purchase, as is the common practice in Europe.

We argued that taxes on corporate profits were difficult to defend under either the benefit approach or as a way of achieving a more equitable distribution of income. This source of tax revenue accounts for as little as 3 percent of total tax revenue in Austria to over 17 percent in Luxembourg.

Taxes on immovable property are a particularly good way of identifying the beneficiaries of the services of local and regional governments, and charging them for these benefits. Within Continental Europe, however, very few countries make use of this attractive source of revenue. The percentages listed in the Property taxes column of Table 13.1 include taxes on inheritances, gifts and overall wealth along with taxes on immovable property. Where the revenue from taxes on immovable property is broken out separately, it constitutes a minuscule fraction of total tax revenue in most of the Continental European countries.[13]

The beneficiaries of highways are particularly easy to identify and tax. In most European countries, however, the revenue raised through taxes on petrol and motor vehicles far exceeds governmental outlays on highways (see Table 13.2).[14] Thus taxes levied on road users in these countries do not merely constitute user fees but are to a significant degree a redistribution from those who drive to other members of the community.[15] Taxes on road users, like taxes on businesses, are not a method for getting those who benefit from a government service to pay for it.

Table 13.2 Tax receipts and expenditures on highways for six European countries

Country	Year	Taxes on Petroleum products (1)	Taxes on Motor vehicles (2)	Expenditures on roads (3)	Expenditures as a fraction of tax revenue (3)/(1+2)
Finland	1993	8404	885	5726	0.616
France	1985	85.2	2.3	13.0	0.149
Germany	1993	56.30	NR	11.03	0.196
Luxembourg	1993	11809	791	7106	0.564
Netherlands	1993	69.9	NR	1.3	0.019
United Kingdom	1992	11156	3132	2804	0.196

Notes: Figures are in millions of local currency. NR = not reported.
Source: IMF (1995).

Conclusions

A person wishing to live in Paris realizes that she must pay rent to live in a Paris apartment. She can avoid the rent only by not living in Paris. A person wishing to live in Paris who wants clean streets, police and fire protection, and the other governmental services that make urban life attractive, realizes that she may have to pay taxes for these services. The Government could ensure that she pays these taxes by making them proportional to the rent she pays or to the size of her apartment. She could then avoid the taxes, again, only by not living in Paris. Of course some people will choose not to live in Paris if its rents get too high, and some may choose not to live there if its taxes get very high. Paris is in competition with other cities in France, Europe and the world for population. Should the Government not use the revenue that it raises from the residents of Paris to provide them with public services, or be grossly inefficient in providing these services, it might find itself losing population to other cities. If governments were to rely on benefit taxes as sources of revenues they would be forced to compete in the provision of these benefits. Reliance on benefit taxes and tax competition is a threat to governments that have not used tax revenue to provide services to the taxpayers or to those governments that have done so inefficiently. We conclude that the increasing mobility of capital and labor, and of consumers and citizens, should not pose a threat to states that rely on benefit taxes to finance the goods and services that they supply and are efficient in supplying these goods and services. Tax competition does not pose a threat to these states, and thus tax harmonization is not required. Harmonization of the reporting and collection of taxes could be required, however. As noted above, some sorts of redistribution programs can benefit all citizens and elicit their support. A wealthy Frenchman may gain satisfaction from seeing the wealthy in France taxed to subsidize the poor. At the same time, however, he might attempt to conceal some of his wealth from the French tax authorities by investing in companies in other countries, opening up bank accounts in other countries, and the like. If personal incomes are to be taxed, then some cooperation among governments in the reporting of incomes may be necessary to ensure that the tax authorities in a given country know what the incomes of its residents are.

If all government services were funded out of benefit taxes, the tax/expenditure policies of the state could in principle win unanimous support. Increasing mobility and tax competition reduce the freedom of the state to tax one group for the benefit of another. Increasing mobility and tax competition thus tend to bring about the same outcomes that one expects under the unanimity rule. The tax and expenditure patterns in Western Europe have evolved in majority rule democracies[16] in which citizens and businesses have historically been quite immobile and tax competition has been absent. Tax and expenditure patterns in Western Europe thus do not conform to what one might expect under benefit taxation but, rather, reflect the rent-seeking pressures from interest groups that one expects under majority rule in a democracy.[17] To change these patterns so that they conform to those that would benefit all citizens and thus could win their support would be an enormous task, for it would involve fundamental changes in the structure of both taxes and expenditures in Europe. No government alone could bring this about, and it is difficult to see how all of the governments together could agree to such radical changes. The easy way out of the dilemma is for all of the governments to agree to stick with the present structure of redistributive taxes and eliminate any competition that jeopardizes this structure. And this is certainly the way that the governments of Europe will choose.

Notes

1. See, for example, Cnossen (1990), Edwards and Keen (1996), Genser and Haufler (1996), Keen (1993) and Oates and Schwab (1988, 1991).
2. This literature can be traced back to Knut Wicksell (1896), who proposed that each expenditure

proposal be coupled to a tax proposal for covering the expenditure. For a review of the ability-to-pay and benefit approaches to taxation see Musgrave (1959, Chs 4, 5).
3. See Musgrave (1959, Ch. 6), Mueller (2003, Chs 7, 8), and references therein.
4. The initial analysis of this sort of redistribution is by Hochman and Rodgers (1969).
5. See Rothschild and Stiglitz (1976).
6. To my knowledge Abba Lerner (1944) was the first to justify an egalitarian distribution of income along these lines. See also Harsanyi (1955, 1977) and Buchanan and Tullock (1962, Ch. 8). John Rawls (1971) rejected the utilitarian calculus implied by this approach but also used uncertainty over future position to justify normatively a considerable degree of redistribution.
7. For example, if companies which ship and make heavy use of the highways tend to have less market power than other companies, a reduction in the output of the heavy users would tend to increase social welfare.
8. See Mueller (2003, pp. 246–7).
9. There are situations in which short-run subsidies to business may be optimal (see Chapter 12, this volume), but no community will survive if it continually charges its citizens higher taxes than other communities that provide their citizens with comparable bundles of public services.
10. Tobacco consumption has recently been alleged to harm non-smokers exposed to "secondary smoke," but even if these allegations prove to be true this externality cannot explain the existence of heavy taxes on tobacco in developed countries, since these taxes long pre-date the perception that smoking could be harmful for non-smokers.

    There has also been much concern about the "externalities" inflicted by drunken drivers in recent years. The proper approach to this externality is not to curtail everyone's consumption of alcohol, however, but to curtail the driving of those who do consume it.
11. The figures in Table 13.1 actually understate the extent of government activities in some countries where other revenue sources, like state-owned companies, are significant.
12. Of course, they also may wish to have tax loopholes, subsidies and other sorts of "corporate welfare," but the provision of these would have to come at the expense of the rest of the community and thus is inconsistent with the assumption that government is advancing the interests of all citizens.
13. Taxes on immovable property constitute between *three and six one-hundredths of 1 percent* of total central government revenues in Austria, Belgium, Denmark and France, for example. No additional taxes on immovable property are levied in Belgium, and in the other three countries the percentages of property tax revenues gathered at the local level are not enough to raise these fractions significantly (IMF, 1995; Costello, 1993).
14. Although data were available for only six countries, tax rates on gasoline are similar across Europe, and so we expect that the figures for other countries would resemble those in Table 13.2. These figures are merely illustrative. They omit outlays on police and perhaps other road traffic related expenditures, and revenue from fines, license fees, tolls, and so on.
15. One could also think of gasoline and motor vehicle taxes as Pigouvian taxes intended to reduce the negative externalities associated with driving. High taxes on gasoline existed in Europe long before concern about the environmental effects of driving was widespread, however, so that this argument fails as a positive explanation for their existence. If one wished to reduce the environmental costs of driving without redistributing income away from road users, revenue raised through Pigouvian taxes would be returned to road users. For example, revenue from gasoline taxes could be used to subsidize the purchase of fuel-efficient cars.
16. Given the de facto importance of consensual decision making in Switzerland, this statement arguably does not apply to this country.
17. On this, see Hettich and Winer (1999).

References

Buchanan, James M. and Gordon Tullock, *The Calculus of Consent, Logical Foundations of Constitutional Democracy*, Ann Arbor: University of Michigan Press, 1962.

Cnossen, Sijbren, "The Case for Tax Diversity in the European Community," *European Economic Review*, **34**, 1990, pp. 471–9.

Costello, Declan, "Public Finances in Federations and Unitary States," in *European Commission*, 1993, pp. 243–64.

Edwards, Jeremy and Michel Keen, "Tax Competition and Leviathan," *European Economic Review*, **40**, 1996, pp. 113–34.

European Commission, *European Economy: The Economics of Community Public Finance*, Report No. 5, Brussels: European Commission, 1993.

Furstenberg, George M. von and Dennis C. Mueller, "The Pareto Optimal Approach to Income Redistribution: A Fiscal Application," *American Economic Review*, **61**, September 1971, pp. 628–37.

Genser, Bernd and Andreas Haufler, "Tax Competition, Tax Coordination and Tax Harmonization: The Effects of EMU," *Empirica*, **23** (1), 1996, pp. 59–89.

Harsanyi, John C., "Cardinal Welfare, Individualistic Ethics, and Interpersonal Comparisons of Utility," *Journal of Political Economy*, **63**, August 1955, pp. 309–21, reprinted in Kenneth J. Arrow and Tibor Scitovsky, *Readings in Welfare Economics*, Homewood, IL: Irwin, 1969, pp. 46–60.

Harsanyi, John C., *Rational Behavior and Bargaining Equilibrium in Games and Social Situations*, Cambridge: Cambridge University Press, 1977.

Hettich, Walter and Stanley L. Winer, *Democratic Choice and Taxation*, Cambridge: Cambridge University Press, 1999.

Hochman, Harold M. and James D. Rodgers, "Pareto Optimal Redistribution," *American Economic Review*, **59**, September 1969, pp. 542–57.

Inman, Robert P. and Daniel L. Rubinfeld, "The Political Economy of Federalism," in Dennis C. Mueller (ed.), *Perspectives on Public Choice*, Cambridge: Cambridge University Press, 1997, pp. 73–105.

IMF (International Monetary Fund), *Government Finance Statistics Yearbook, 1995*, Washington, DC, 1995.

Keen, Michael, "The Welfare Economics of Tax Co-ordination in the European Community: A Survey," *Fiscal Studies*, **14** (2), 1993, pp. 15–36.

Lerner, Abba P., *Economics of Control*, New York: Macmillan, 1944.

Lindahl, Erik, "Just Taxation – A Positive Solution," first published in German, Lund, 1919; English translation in Richard A. Musgrave and Alan T. Peacock (eds), *Classics in the Theory of Public Finance*, 1958, pp. 168–76.

Mueller, Dennis C., *Public Choice III*, Cambridge: Cambridge University Press, 2003.

Musgrave, Richard A., *The Theory of Public Finance*, New York: McGraw-Hill, 1959.

Oates, Wallace E. and Robert M. Schwab, "Economic Competition Among Jurisdictions: Efficiency Enhancing or Distortion Inducing?," *Journal of Public Economics*, **35**, 1988, pp. 333–54.

Oates, Wallace E. and Robert M. Schwab, "The Allocative and Distributive Implications of Local Fiscal Competition," in D. Kenyon and J. Kincaid (eds), *Competition Among States and Local Governments*, Washington, DC: Urban Institute Press, 1991, pp. 127–45.

Rawls, John, *A Theory of Justice*, Cambridge, MA: Harvard University Press, 1971.

Rothschild, Michael and Joseph E. Stiglitz, "Equilibrium in Competitive Insurance Markets," *Quarterly Journal of Economics*, **90**, 1976, pp. 629–50.

Samuelson, Paul, "The Pure Theory of Public Expenditure," *Review of Economics and Statistics*, **36**, November 1954, pp. 386–9; reprinted in Kenneth J. Arrow and Tibor Scitovsky, *Readings in Welfare Economics*, Homewood, IL: Irwin, 1969, pp. 179–82.

Thurow, Lester C., "The Income Distribution as a Pure Public Good," *Quarterly Journal of Economics*, **85**, 1971, pp. 327–36.

Tiebout, Charles M., "A Pure Theory of Local Expenditures," *Journal of Political Economy*, **64**, October 1956, pp. 416–24.

Wicksell, Knut, "A New Principle of Just Taxation," *Finanztheoretische Untersuchungen*, Jena, 1896; reprinted in Richard A. Musgrave and Alan T. Peacock (eds), *Classics in the Theory of Public Finance*, London: Macmillan, 1969, pp. 72–118.

PART IV

COMPETITION POLICY RESPONSES

[14]

International Journal of Industrial Organization
14 (1996) 415–445

ELSEVIER

International Journal of Industrial Organization

Lessons from the United States's antitrust history

Dennis C. Mueller

Department of Economics, University of Vienna, BWZ-Brünner Str.72, Vienna, A-1210, Austria

Received October 1994; final version accepted April 1995

Abstract

The United States's antitrust policy spans more than 100 years. For most of its history the United States has had the toughest antitrust laws and enforcement policies of any country in the world. A shift to a more permissive attitude with regard to antitrust matters has occurred in recent years, however. This paper traces the changes in antitrust policy that have occurred, and the concurrent shifts in thinking among economists on antitrust questions. Following this review, the paper offers a critical appraisal of both the economic underpinning of the new learnings on antitrust matters, and the changes in antitrust policy that have accompanied them. It closes with a discussion of the implications of the analysis for European antitrust (competition) policy.

Keywords: Antritrust policy; Competition policy

JEL classification: L4

1. Introduction

The United States has the longest history of antitrust enforcement in the world, over 100 years now. Over this span, US antitrust policy has waxed and waned in its vigor, but on average the US has had the toughest and most vigorously enforced antitrust statutes in the world. In recent years, the wisdom of this policy has been questioned, the government has taken a

SSDI 0167-7187(95)00490-4

noticeably more circumscribed approach to enforcing the antitrust laws, and the courts have become more lenient in interpreting them.[1]

In this paper, I first trace these developments and try to account for them. After critizing the premises underlying recent antitrust policies in the United States, I suggest improvements in these policies that are consistent with the empirical evidence regarding firm and market performance, and the economic goals of antitrust. In the final Section, I discuss the applicability of the lessons learned from the United States's antitrust experience to Europe. I begin with the period of most vigorous and expansive antitrust enforcement in US history immediately following World War II.

2. The era of vigorous enforcement, 1945–73

After a generation of inconsistent antitrust enforcement and a hiatus during World War II, the post-war era was launched in dramatic fashion with the *ALCOA* (1945) and *American Tobacco*[2] (1946) decisions. In *ALCOA* Judge Learned Hand construed evidence that ALCOA had built capacity ahead of demand and bought up bauxite deposits as an effort by ALCOA to prevent entry. His statement that "no monopolist monopolizes unconscious of what he is doing" intimated that virtually all actions of a monopolist might be construed as monopolizing under the language of Section 2 of the Sherman Act (Stelzer, 1972, p.30). In *American Tobacco*, the court for the first time found companies guilty of conspiring to create a monopoly on the basis of only *circumstantial* evidence that they actually conspired. Consciously parallel actions by oligopolists could be construed as "tacit collusion" and thus conspiracy as defined by Section 1 of the Sherman Act. It seemed that actions arising from "the natural, normal, and intelligent consequences of an oligopolistic market structure" like the normal behavior of monopolists would now be construed as a violation of the Sherman Act (Nicholls, 1949, p.109).

Subsequent decisions (e.g. *Theatre Enterprises*, 1954; *DuPont*, 1956) indicated that the most extreme interpretations of *ALCOA* and *American Tobacco*, and the most dire predictions of economists were ill-founded. Nevertheless, the Department of Justice (DoJ) and the Federal Trade Commission (FTC) continued to press and extend their enforcement

[1] The Clinton Administration moved back toward tougher antitrust policy, but the 1994 congressional elections foretell a quick return of a Republican Administration, and more relaxed antitrust enforcement.

[2] To save space I shall refer only to the defendant in government cases, but to both litigants in private cases. With only a couple of exceptions, edited versions of the decisions can be found in Breit and Elzinga (1989) or in one of the editions of Stelzer cited in the references.

powers. The illegality of tacit collusion was firmly established in important victories for the FTC against companies using the basing point system (*Corn Products Refining*, 1945; *A.E. Staley*, 1945; *Cement Institute*, 1948; *Triangle Conduit & Cable*, 1948). The vulnerability of dominant firms to monopolizing charges was reaffirmed in *United Shoe* (1953) and *Grinnell* (1966). Evidence of predatory intent of a large firm against a small was given heavy weight (*Utah Pie Co.* v. *Continental Baking Co.*, 1966).

Over the course of the 1950s and 1960s, it became evident that under Section 3 of the Clayton Act tying and resale price maintenance agreements would almost always[3] be judged illegal per se, and by 1967 it even appeared that territorial restrictions on distribution would be per se illegal.[4] Exclusive dealing arrangements would be carefully scrutinized, albeit under a rule of reason standard.[5]

But perhaps the most vivid evidence of the enforcement agencies' willingness to test the limits of the law, and the courts' readiness to extend these limits, can be seen in the area of antimerger policy. Armed with a resuscitated Section 7 of the Clayton Act, the definition of anticompetitive effect in mergers was extended from horizontal to vertical acquisitions, and even to encompass conglomerate mergers. The highwater marks in vigorous and successful prosecution were undoubtedly the *Brown Shoe* (1962, horizontal and vertical), *Von's Grocery* (1967, horizontal), and *Procter & Gamble* (1967, conglomerate) cases in which companies with market shares as low as 5% of the national market and 7.5% of a local market were prevented from merging, and in the case of *Procter & Gamble* the perceived existence of *potential* competition sufficed to undo the merger.

3. The attitude of economists

Although objections were raised to particular cases (e.g. Nicholls, 1949; Adelman, 1959a,b), the thinking among industrial organization economists seemed in broad congruence with the intensification of antitrust enforcement after World War II. For example, the *Report of the Attorney General's National Committee to Study the Antitrust Laws* (1955), written by a panel of economists and lawyers that read like a *Who's Who* in industrial organiza-

[3] An exception for tying arrangements was *Jerrold* (1960) a district court decision on a tying arrangement utilized by a small company.

[4] See *Schwinn*, 1967 in Stelzer (1986, pp.479–489) and Preston's (1993) discussion thereof.

[5] With respect to tying arrangements, see *International Salt*, 1947; *American Can*, 1949; *Northern Pacific*, 1958; *Loew's*, 1962; *Fortner*, 1969. With respect to resale price and other manufacturers' restrictions on retailers, see *General Motors*, 1966; *Schwinn*, 1967. Key exclusive dealing cases include *Standard Stations*, 1949. (Note not all of these cases were tried under Section 3 of the Clayton Act.)

tion and antitrust policy, although disagreeing with the court's decisions here and there was largely supportive, even with respect to some of the court's more expansive decisions. Another group of lawyers and economists met for several years during the 1950s in Cambridge, Massachusetts to discuss the antitrust laws. Their thinking was incorporated in Carl Kaysen and Donald Turner's influential *Antitrust Policy* (1959, p. xix). This book stressed the importance of market structure in determining firm conduct and performance, and recommended that antitrust policy focus upon market structure to preserve competition.

Although Kaysen and Turner only directly represented the thinking of the group assembled in Cambridge, their belief in the predominant importance of market structure was widely shared by the profession. No Chicago/Harvard schism on this issue existed at this time. Indeed, George Stigler, the quintessential Chicagoan, succinctly iterated the structure/conduct position in an article entitled "The case against big business" in *Fortune Magazine* in 1952: "an industry that does not have a competitive structure will not have competitive behavior".[6]

4. The new learning and the new institutional economics

4.1. The new learning about monopoly and mergers

As the 1960s wore on, and the Supreme Court endorsed ever bolder attempts by the government to extend the reach of the antitrust laws, dissent by economists began to grow. Responding to Justice Douglas' dismissal in *Procter & Gamble* of "[p]ossible economies ... as a defense to illegality" as defined by Section 7, Oliver Williamson (1968) advocated a welfare-trade-off approach to mergers. Instead of focusing exclusively on their anticompetitive effects, courts were to weigh the anticompetitive effects of mergers against their efficiency gains. Williamson presented some calculations to suggest that even modest cost reductions from mergers would outweigh any accompanying increases in market power.

Williamson's call to consider the possible efficiency effects of mergers resonated with the "new learning" stemming out of Chicago that linked high concentration to greater efficiency. High concentration was the *consequence* of some firms being more efficient than others, and thus having grown to be larger, rather than of large firms colluding to raise prices.[7] In *United States Steel* (1920) Justice McKenna stated that "the law does not make mere size

[6] Quoted in Edward Mason's Preface to *Antitrust Policy*, (1959, p. xviii).

[7] The original statements of the new learning were by Brozen (1971a,b) and Demsetz (1973). Subsequent corroboration was provided by Peltzman (1977) and Carter (1978). The name comes from Goldschmid, Mann and Weston (1974).

an offense or the existence of unexerted power an offense". The new learning carried McKenna's logic a step further and made size a presumption for economic efficiency.

The new learning extended also into the realm of merger policy. Where George Stigler (1950, p.76) once expressed skepticism about whether horizontal mergers in the 1890s and 1920s had produced any efficiency gains, no doubt existed in the new Chicago perspective about the efficiency gains from the mostly diversification acquisitions of the post-World War II period (Brozen, 1982). All markets were presumed to be efficient including the market for corporate control. Incompetent managers or those who might seek to pursue goals that conflicted with efficiency and profit maximization would be quickly weeded out (Manne, 1965). Premia paid for acquired companies measured the efficiency gains from mergers (Mandelker, 1974; Dodd and Ruback, 1977; Jensen and Ruback, 1983). The capital market was so efficient that it told us all we needed to know about mergers. The fact that acquiring firms bid up the price of the companies they bought told us that the mergers generated wealth. The fact that share prices of competing companies did not rise when a merger was announced told us that this wealth was a result of efficiency, and not market power increases (Eckbo, 1983; Stillman, 1983).

4.2. The new institutional economics and antitrust[8]

Where the new learning emphasizes the forces of competition and Darwinian evolution in selecting products and firms, the new institutional economics emphasizes the role these forces play in selecting organizational forms, governance structures, and interfirm contractual relationships (Williamson, 1985, 1989). As with the new learning on market power and mergers, the emphasis of the new institutional economics is on efficiency, in particular, on the transaction cost savings from various institutional and contractual relationships.

The main impact of this literature on antitrust has been in the area of vertical restraints. Although the pioneering contribution was arguably Lester Telser's (1960) discussion of resale price maintenance, most papers have appeared in the last 15 years. One by one long held presumptions of the courts about the anticompetitive effects of resale price maintenance, tie-in sales, and exclusive dealing contracts have been challenged with examples of firms or industries where these contractual relationships are claimed to produce efficiencies.[9] So benign are the effects of these vertical arrangements according to some students of antitrust that they have

[8] The term was coined by Louis De Alessi (1983).

[9] On resale price maintenance see Marvel and McCafferty (1984) and Marvel (1985), on tying arrangements Klein and Saft (1985), and on exclusive dealing Marvel (1982).

advocated not just new thinking about the enforcement of Section 3 of the Clayton Act, but its outright repeal (Posner, 1976; Bork, 1978).[10]

5. Antitrust policy since 1973

Chief Justice Earl Warren, and Justices William O. Douglas and Hugo Black formed the liberal core of the "Warren Court" not only on broad social questions, but also in the area of antitrust. As they left the bench and were replaced by Nixon appointees, the philosophy of the court on antitrust issues changed. I have selected 1973 to mark this change, since a shift is apparent between the *Falstaff Brewing* decision in 1973 blocking Falstaff's acquisition of Narragansett, and the 1974 decision to allow General Dynamics to acquire United Electric Coal Companies. *Falstaff* was written by Justice White with Justices Rehnquist and Stewart in dissent, *General Dynamics* by Stewart with White, Brennan, Douglas, and Marshall in dissent. Toward the middle of the 1970s, the dissenting opinions on antitrust matters of the 60s became those of a majority of the court.

This shift is readily apparent in the "landmark antitrust decisions" assembled in leading anthologies.[11] From 1945 through 1973 the government or the plaintiff in a private antitrust suit won 51 of the 67 cases in the anthologies. After 1973 the government or private plaintiff won only 13 out of 35 times. Although the landmark decisions of this era represent only a small fraction of all cases decided, they are an important bellwether of judicial thinking on antitrust because (1) a much higher fraction are Supreme Court decisions than is true of all judicial decisions, and thus they deserve greater weight in defining judicial thinking on antitrust, and (2) being landmark decisions often of the highest court they indicate where the boundaries of antitrust are being drawn and redrawn. They are treated as landmark decisions because they provide new insight into the courts' thinking on what is and is not an antitrust violation. These figures indicate

[10] Indeed, Posner and Bork would repeal all of the Clayton Act, and Posner would toss in Section 2 of the Sherman Act as well.

[11] The term "landmark decision" is taken from the title of Irwin Stelzer's popular anthology. I have relied on the cases included in its second through seventh editions, which appeared between 1961 and 1986. For more recent cases, I have consulted the second edition of Breit and Elzinga (1989), and the first and second editions of Kwoka and White (1989, 1993). When the same case reached the courts twice (e.g. *Yellow Cab*) I classified the case by the outcome of the second decision. A few cases did not proceed to a final judicial outcome, or were decided on criteria other than antitrust laws, and are ignored.

that in the period 1945–73 the boundaries of antitrust were tested and expanded, while since 1974 the boundaries have largely been contracted.[12]

This shift is also apparent in more complete samples of antitrust cases. In his doctoral dissertation, Stacy Jordan (1992) estimated equations to explain the outcomes in horizontal merger, predation, and tying arrangement cases using a sample of cases from both district and circuit appeals' courts. Since all predation cases in his sample were after 1974, he, not surprisingly, did not find any intertemporal variation in the outcomes of these cases. But in the merger and tying arrangements cases, which extended back into the 1950s, he found a significant negative relationship. The later in the post-World War II period a case was tried, the less likely was a violation to be found.

In part this trend can be explained by the influence of the new learning among economists on the judiciary. Indeed, during this period Henry Manne, then Dean of the Miami University Law School, began organizing retreats at which federal judges were instructed in the new learning by its leading proponents. But a transformation in the thinking of sitting judges does not explain all of the shift. Jordan also found that antitrust violations were significantly more likely to be found in tying arrangement and predation cases by judges appointed by Democratic presidents than by those appointed by a Republican.[13] During the 1970s and 1980s more judges with permissive attitudes on antitrust matters were appointed to the bench.

5.1. Sherman Act Section 2 cases: Monopolization

In one area, developments in economic thinking have had an unmistakable and dramatic effect, and that is in predation cases. In 1975 Areeda and Turner (1975) proposed that the courts abstract from the intertemporal aspects of predation, i.e. the aspects that make it potentially damaging to consumer welfare, and focus entirely upon the happy period for consumers when rivalry between the predating company and its targets is driving prices downward. Areeda and Turner proposed that price must fall below the

[12] One might object that anthologies of landmark decisions incorporate the biases for or against tough antitrust enforcement of the editors. Such biases could explain an unrepresentatively large fraction of government victories or defeats, but could not account for the dramatic *shift* in these fractions that is apparent in the Stelzer and Breit–Elzinga anthologies over the full time period.

[13] In horizontal merger cases the party of the appointing president was not a significant factor. Time and the characteristics of the merging firms and their market were the only significant explanatory variables. As we shall discuss below, political ideology has played a conspicuous role in antimerger policy in defining the Guidelines followed by the antitrust authorities, and through them identifying the cases that will *and will not* be brought.

alleged predator's marginal costs during the period of rivalry for the court to infer an injury to competition. Because marginal costs are difficult to measure, courts would also be allowed to use short run variable costs instead of marginal costs. Given that cost information must come from the company charged with predation, this option further advantages a firm accused of predation, since it can effectively avoid conviction by demonstrating that price was greater than *either* marginal or short-run variable costs.

No article's message has, or ever could, go more quickly from journal page to court opinion than that of Areeda and Turner's "Predatory pricing and related practices under Section 2 of the Sherman Act". In the year of its publication it would be cited in *International Air Industries, Inc. et al.* v. *American Excelsior Company*, to the benefit of the defendant. Within a year it was being cited at the district court level in support of IBM's acquittal of Section 2 charges in the case brought by *California Computer Products*. It would figure to IBM's advantage in all subsequent cases brought by peripheral manufacturers (Brock, 1989). The influence of Areeda and Turner's criteria for predation is succinctly revealed by Circuit Judge Kaufman in *Northeastern Telephone Co.* v. *AT&T* (1981), "Detailed economic analysis of this behavior [predatory pricing] is of comparatively recent vintage, gaining wide recognition only in 1975, with the publication of Areeda and Turner's incisive article" (Breit and Elzinga, 1989, p.329).

Thus, where ALCOA, United Shoe and Grinnell would be found guilty of monopolizing in violation of the antitrust laws in 1953, 1955, and 1966, IBM, Kodak, DuPont and AT&T would be acquitted in the late 1970s and 1980s despite evidence of misconduct at least as strong as that presented in these earlier cases. A noteworthy exception to the blanket immunity of dominant firms from Sherman Act, Section 2 convictions is the government's consent decree with AT&T signed in 1982. Given that AT&T's monopoly power was to an important degree a result of past government regulatory policy, it is not clear whether this consent decree should be treated as a triumph for antitrust enforcement or for the deregulation movement of the 1970s and 1980s.[14] The source and nature of AT&T's monopoly power represent such a "special case", that it is difficult to infer from it what other kinds of dominant firm market power are likely to be challenged by the government, and prohibited by the courts. In this regard, the government's other "big case" of around the same time against IBM involved more conventional antitrust issues. The government's decision to

[14] Noll and Owen (1993) discuss the role of regulation in this case.

drop the case in the early 1980s is therefore a less ambiguous bellwether of governmental antitrust policy in the 1980s.

5.2. Vertical restraints

The shift toward a more permissive antitrust policy is also visible in the area of vertical restraints. Both tying arrangements and resale price maintenance have for some time been regarded as per se illegal by the courts. In *Schwinn* (1967) the Supreme Court added manufacturer imposed territorial restrictions on distributors and retailers to its list of vertical relationships that were per se illegal. A short 10 years later in *Continental T.V.* v. *GTE Sylvania* (1977) the court would reverse *Schwinn* in favor of a rule of reason approach to vertically imposed territorial restrictions, and acquit GTE Sylvania of violating the antitrust laws.

The softening of antitrust enforcement is more conspicuous in the criteria employed by the antitrust agencies when bringing vertical restraints cases than in the opinions of the courts.[15] Although the court came close to reversing its longstanding position on the per se illegality of tie-in sales, when four of the justices urged such a decision on their brothers in *Jefferson Parish Hospital* v. *Hyde* (1984), the court has to date failed to take that next step. Similarly, resale price maintenance (RPM) would appear to remain per se illegal in the eyes of the court (*Monsanto Co.* v. *Spray-Rite Service Corp.*, 1984; Warren-Boulton, 1993). The DoJ has been willing to take the next steps, however. After unsuccessfully intervening on behalf of Monsanto before the Supreme Court in 1984 in an attempt to get the court to reverse itself on the per se illegality of RPM, the DoJ issued a set of Vertical Restraints Guidelines in 1985. In these Guidelines the DoJ indicated that *it* would employ a rule of reason approach to vertical restraints when deciding what cases to bring, even if the courts continued to view certain practices like tie-ins and RPM as per se illegal. Moreover, the DoJ's presumption, in line with the new institutional economics, was that most vertical restraints are efficiency enhancing. So that "the clear implication of the Guidelines was that, after application of [their] tests, very few vertical restraints will merit antitrust challenge" (Preston, 1993, p.324). Not surprisingly, the

[15] *Jefferson Parish Hospital* v. *Hyde* (1984) might also be counted as evidence of the shift in thinking on vertical restraints by the Supreme Court in that the plaintiff lost, and the Court of Appeals decision in favor of the plaintiff on the grounds that tying arrangements are per illegal was overturned. But the case was arguably more about the legality of an exclusive dealing contract than a tie-in sale, and thus consistently tried under the rule of reason approach that has always been applied in exclusive dealing cases. See Lynk (1993).

recent judicial history regarding vertical restraints has been dominated by private suits.[16]

5.3. Mergers

In mergers, the shift to more lax standards can be seen not only in the decisions handed down by the courts but, as with vertical restraints, in the criteria adopted by the DoJ and the FTC for prosecuting cases.

5.3.1. The courts

The shift in judicial thinking, at least at the Supreme Court and FTC occurred in the mid-1970s. We noted at the beginning of this section, the shift in the composition of the court majority between *Falstaff* in 1973, and *General Dynamics* in 1974. In *Falstaff* the court blocked a merger by the large, national brewer Falstaff of Narragansett, a regional brewer with a large (20%) market share in New England. It did so, despite the apparent fact that Falstaff did not contemplate de novo entry into the New England market, because in the words of Justice White's majority opinion, "given [Falstaff's] financial capabilities and conditions in the New England market, it would be reasonable to consider it a potential entrant into that market" (Stelzer, 1986, p.313).

Justice Stewart, who had dissented in *Falstaff* as he had in *Von's Grocery* and so many antitrust cases prior to 1974, would finally in *General Dynamics* get to write the decision for the majority. The liberal quartet of Brennan, Douglas, Marshall, and White would, for the first time, be joined in dissent from the outcome of a major merger case. The same four would no doubt have been again united in dissent in *Marine Bancorporation*, decided in the same year, except that William O. Douglas did not participate in the decision. Justice White wrote the dissenting opinion for the remaining three, in which he complained that the court's majority "erects formidable barriers to the application of the potential-competition doctrine not only in the banking business but in other lines of commerce" (Stelzer, 1986, p.337). The portential for blocking conglomerate mergers had been greatly reduced.

The shift in thinking at the FTC is apparent as early as 1975 in the Commission's decision in *Budd*. Budd, a large manufacturer of auto parts, including bodies, and railroad and transit cars was an obvious potential entrant into the manufacture of truck trailers and containers. Gindy's market shares in these markets fluctuated between 4 and 8%. Nixon

[16] The Clinton Administration abandoned the Guidelines so that, for the time being at least, the US has returned to a tougher approach to vertical restraints.

appointee Engman wrote the opinion for the Commission allowing the merger on the grounds that Gindy was sufficiently small for the merger to qualify as a "toehold entry". Commissioner Paul Rand Dixon, a long time member of the FTC's liberal majority, was left to argue in dissent that it was not.

Yet another example of the radical change in judicial thinking about mergers is presented by the 2d Circuit Court of Appeals 1984 decision in *Waste Management and EMW Ventures*. Where Falstaff would be prevented from acquiring Narragansett in 1973 on the grounds that Falstaff was a potential entrant into Narragansett's market, the *Falstaff* decision would now be used to *allow* Waste Management to acquire EMW despite combined market shares of nearly 50%, which exceeded the prima facie threshold for blocking a merger set down in *Philadelphia National Bank* (1963). The merger was allowed, because the court argued that *Falstaff* obliged it to take into consideration conditions of potential entry, and when it did the merger had no anticompetitive effects. (My point in listing these cases is not to argue that the court or FTC was right in this case or wrong in that one. Rather, I wish to emphasize that the shift in outcomes in the 1970s is to a significant degree a result of the change in compositions of the Supreme Court and the FTC, whatever the merits of the respective cases.)

5.3.2. The antitrust authorities

Von's Grocery induced an agitated response in both the business community and in parts of academia. If two firms with a combined market share of 7.5% in a market with low entry barriers would not be allowed to merge, what firms could? In response to this hue and cry the DoJ for the first time in the 78 years since the passage of the Sherman Act issued a set of Merger Guidelines, which defined the criteria it would follow when deciding whether or not to challenge a proposed merger. They set forth tough standards with heavy emphasis on the structure of the markets involved. For example, in a highly concentrated market ($C_4 \geqslant 0.75$) a firm with a market share of 4% or more would in general be challenged, if it sought to acquire another firm with a market share of 4% or more in the same market. The market shares in *Von's Grocery* would constitute the lower bounds to antitrust enforcement, but only just.[17]

[17] Indeed, since the C_4 in food retailing was undoubtedly less than 0.75, the market shares of Von's and its would-be merger partner Shopping Bag fell below the Guidelines' thresholds. One of the other factors the Guidelines stated would be considered was whether concentration had been increasing. This was true in food retailing in Los Angeles and figured in the court's decision. If given enough weight it could justify suit even under the 1968 Guidelines.

The thinking of the incoming Reagan Administration on antitrust matters was quite different than that of the outgoing Johnson Administration. To clarify exactly what that thinking was it announced a new set of Merger Guidelines in 1982. These Guidelines introduced many additional criteria for judging the anticompetitive effects of mergers, criteria that by and large reduced the likelihood of a challenge. Most conspicuously, they raised the threshold concentration levels. There would be no *Von's Grocery* or *Brown Shoe* under the Reagan Administration.

In 1984 the DoJ issued yet another Merger Guidelines largely to clarify ambiguities in the 1982 Guidelines. The 1984 Guidelines did have one radical departure from their predecessors, however, in the form of an efficiencies defense. Where a merger was expected to result in large economic efficiencies that would clearly outweigh its (nonzero) anticompetitive effects, the merger would go unchallenged. Williamson's (1968) welfare trade-off approach to mergers was to become governmental practice.

This addition to the Guidelines was a radical departure in that the Supreme Court had on several occasions explicitly rejected the suggestion that efficiency gains could offset anticompetitive losses. "Possible economies cannot be used as a defense to illegality. Congress was aware that some mergers which lessen competition may also result in economies but it struck the balance in favor of protecting competition." Congress had had 27 years since William O. Douglas wrote these words in *Procter & Gamble* to correct them, if it favored such a trade-off. That it had not chosen to do so, suggests tacit agreement with Douglas's interpretation. Since no court had overruled Douglas on this issue, one must assume that the law of the land in 1984, as in 1967, was that possible anticompetitive effects and only possible anticompetitive effects are determinate on whether or not a merger should be allowed. The Merger Guidelines of 1984 proposed to establish by executive fiat what neither Congress by legislation nor the Supreme Court by judicial interpretation had deemed to bring about.

To what extent the Reagan Administration actually weighed possible efficiency gains against anticompetitive effects in deciding what mergers to challenge cannot be discerned. What is evident is that mergers were proposed and consummated during the Reagan years that never would have been contemplated under the six previous administrations (e.g. General Electric's acquisition of electronics giant RCA; Standard Oil of California's acquisition of Gulf Oil; Philip Morris's acquisitions of *both* food giants Kraft and General Foods). In many cases, mergers which violated the Merger Guidelines, and presumably could have been prevented, were allowed after allowing spin-offs of the "offending assets" that indicated a likely Section 7 violation (e.g. Texaco's 1984 acquisition of Getty). This accommodating attitude was in stark contrast to previous governmental policy on mergers where, as in *Brown Shoe*, high concentration figures in a couple of cities were used as part of the justification for blocking the entire merger.[18]

In addition to assisting companies circumvent Section 7, when a merger violated the statute, the Reagan Administration on occasion simply turned its back on mergers that clearly violated its Guidelines. Notable examples include LTV's acquisition of Republic Steel in 1984, and Ralston Purina's acquisition of Drake. That the latter *could* have been successfully stopped is revealed by the fact that it *was*, as a private suit (*Tasty Baking Co. and Tastykake* v. *Ralston Purina and Continental Baking*, 1987).[19]

In 1992 the outgoing Bush Administration annunciated still another set of Merger Guidelines. These altered the provisions of the 1982/4 Guidelines only as they apply to horizontal mergers. They did not change the concentration thresholds that would precipitate a challenge, nor did they drop the efficiency defense. Instead, they enumerated the many factors related to market definition and structure and business conduct, which the antitrust authorities would consider beyond concentration and efficiency, before challenging a merger. As of April 1995, these Guidelines continue to inform the US Government's antitrust policy in the area of mergers.

5.4. Sherman Act Section 1 cases

The least visible shift in antitrust policy and standards is in regard to conspiracies to fix prices and quantities. The courts still cast a steely eye on such arrangements (e.g. *State of Arizona* v. *Maricopa County Medical Society*, 1982). But even here, some differences in the direction of making it easier for companies to defend themselves successfully against a Section 1 charge are discernable. Where conspiracies to fix prices have historically been tried under the per se doctrine, and thus have not afforded the defendants much opportunity to justify their agreements, several recent cases have been tried under the rule of reason approach (*National Society of*

[18] Mobil and Marathon Oil's market shares in parts of the Midwest were high enough to constitute a Section 7 violation in the eyes of the District Court in Cleveland. Mobil proposed spinning off some assets in the markets in question, à la Texaco/Getty, but the district court refused to allow this option. Mobil appealed to Washington, and the FTC gave its blessing (Scherer, 1993). Although the merger did not take place, because USS (the former United States Steel, and current USX) stepped in "to rescue" Marathon, this case is interesting because it reveals that the Reagan Administration failed to challenge many mergers that the courts probably would have blocked if given a chance.

[19] The market shares of Drake and Continental's Hostess brand were so clearly above the Merger Guidelines in some of the highly concentrated eastern, metropolitan areas that one can only wonder, as with Mobil and Marathon discussed in the previous footnote, why it was left for private parties to file suit (Breit and Elzinga, 1989, pp.178–179).

Professional Engineers, 1978; *American Society of Authors and Publishers* v. *Columbia Broadcasting System*, 1979; *NCAA* v. *Board of Regents of the University of Oklahoma and University of Georgia Athletic Association*, 1984; *Matsushita Electric Industrial* v. *Zenith Radio Corp.*, 1986).[20]

The second development that is apparent in recent Section 1 cases, as in all other aspects of antitrust enforcement, is that the plaintiff is not the Federal Government, but another company or a state attorney general's office. Whereas 52 of the 67 landmark cases from 1945 through 1973 were brought by the federal government, only 15 of the 35 landmark cases since 1974 were initiated by the federal government. No single comparison illustrates more vividly than this one the weakening of the federal government's antitrust policy. When important cases go to court, the federal government is simply not there.

6. Critique

6.1. Bigness implies efficiency

The original new-learning arguments in favor of a size-efficiency hypothesis were based on often weak, but usually statistically significant, positive correlations between industry concentration and industry profitability. The correlation between a *firm's* profitability and concentration generally pales into insignificance, *or becomes negative and significant*, once both the firm's market share and the concentration levels of its industries are included as explanatory variables.[21]

It is easy to show that a firm with a superior product or lower costs has, ceteris paribus, a higher market share. For example, when firms are quantity setters in a homogeneous product industry, their price–cost margins vary directly with their market shares

$$\frac{P - c_i}{P} = \frac{m_i}{\eta} \tag{1}$$

[20] Even in *Maricopa*, cited above as illustrative of the continuing tradition of treating price fixing agreements as illegal per se, Justice Powell in dissent, with Chief Justice Rehnquist concurring, urged the court to apply the rule of reason.

Although the case involved an alleged conspiracy of Japanese television manufacturers, *Matsushita* was actually tried under the rule of reason as a Section 2, Sherman Act case (see discussion by Schwartzman, 1994).

[21] See Shepherd (1975); Gale and Branch (1982); Ravenscraft (1983); Smirlock, Gilligan and Marshall (1984); Mueller (1986, ch.4).

For an attempt to resurrect the profitability/concentration hypothesis, see Mueller and Sial (1993).

where P is industry price, c_i is firm i's constant marginal cost, m_i its market share, and η is the industry's elasticity of demand. Relationships such as this one explain the willingness of many writers to regard the strong positive correlation between market share and profitability at the firm level as indicative of the greater efficiency of *relatively large* firms (i.e. relative to the size of other firms in their own markets, see Gale and Branch, 1982; Smirlock, Gilligan and Marshall, 1984). More generally, it is tempting to attribute the large size and high profitability of some companies to some sort of Schumpeterian dynamism on their part (Mancke, 1974; Littlechild, 1981). An examination of the persistently profitable firms in the United States reveals several that fit this image (Mueller, 1986, ch.3). In particular, the leading pharmaceutical companies clearly owe their persistent profitability to their ability to develop new drugs, and the monopoly advantage afforded them by patent protection (Comanor, 1986).

A closer look at some of the other persistently profitable firms in the United States reveals that many do not fit the image of the Schumpeterian, innovating company. Black and Decker, Coca-Cola, Gardner Denver, Gerber Products, Hershey Chocolates, Kelloggs, Procter and Gamble, and Wrigley's have been among the persistently most profitable firms from one generation to the next. Their Schumpeterian innovations came in several cases a century or more ago. They owe their persistent profitability to first-mover advantages, and the heavy advertising that maintains the value of their trademarks and the monopoly power that goes with them.[22] Many of the persistently most profitable firms in the United States are more efficient than their rivals in maintaining their brand images, and the extra profits these brands generate.

6.2. *Absolute size and diversification*

Bigness can be measured in two ways: relative to rivals' size *within* a market, i.e. by market share; or as bigness in absolute size. Firms which are not dominant in any one market can be of large absolute size, because they are highly diversified. If growing big is a consequence of greater efficiency, then firms that grow big through diversification have presumably done so to exploit economies of scope or some other diversification related efficiency. At the end of the conglomerate merger wave several hypotheses were advanced to explain these mergers as (successful) attempts to improve efficiency (Weston, 1970; Williamson, 1970; Weston and Mansinghka, 1971).

Evidence that diversification leads to greater efficiency and profitability is,

[22] Persistent profitability is not merely an artifact of a failure to properly adjust capital stocks for intangible advertising and R&D capital. Such adjustments do narrow differences in profitability across firms, but do not eliminate them (Megna and Mueller, 1991).

to say the most for it, mixed. Some of the first studies did find a positive correlation between diversification and profitability, particularly when it was into industries related to a company's main lines of activity (Rhoades, 1973; Berry, 1975, pp.120–125; Carter, 1977; Lecraw, 1984). But others have found either no relationship or a negative relationship between profitability and (broad) diversification (Miller, 1969; Rhoades, 1974; Mueller, 1986, ch.7; Lang and Stulz, 1993).

These findings take on added significance when it is recognized that diversification might not only increase profitability by increasing efficiency, it could also do so by increasing multimarket contact and thereby market power (Scott, 1982, 1993; Evans and Kessides, 1994). The possible link between diversification and enhanced market power points to the necessity of measuring diversification's effect on efficiency directly. Caves and Barton (1990) and Lichtenberg (1992) conducted such a test, and found that the plants of diversified firms had significantly lower productivity levels than did those of undiversified firms.

Relevant also are the results relating total sales (absolute size) to profitability. Absolute size is a consequence of a combination of relative size (market share) and diversification. Even a strong positive relationship could merely be picking up the powerful link between market share and profits that so many have found. But the results for profitability and sales, as for diversification and sales, are again quite weak and ambiguous. A few studies have picked up a positive coefficient of size in a profits equation, but most have not. Outside the United States the correlation is much more likely to be negative than positive (Mueller, 1987, pp.32–33).

These negative findings regarding absolute size, diversification, and efficiency undermine at least one version of the bigness–efficiency hypothesis. That a company is large and diversified does not imply that it produces its products more efficiently than they could be produced by smaller, specialized firms. That a company's managers chose to expand and diversify does not imply that the company would not have been more efficient, and its stockholders better served, had the managers not made this choice.

The negative relationship between efficiency and diversification also undermines a major tenet of the new institutional economics. Oliver Williamson (1985) sees the competitive forces of capitalism forcing firms to adopt ever more efficient organizational structures to economize transaction and decision-making costs. If these forces do shape organizational and institutional structures than firms should only diversify if they become more efficient. That they seem willing to diversify even if they become less efficient suggests that the Darwinian pressures in modern capitalism are not as strong as Williamson presumes, and that managers may pursue goals other than greater profits and efficiency. But these findings regarding growth and diversification have broader implications. If firms sacrifice efficiency for size across markets, perhaps they also do so within markets. A company may dominate its market not because it is more efficient than its rivals, but because its managers sacrifice more profits to obtain a dominant position.

During the 1960s and 1970s a group of five Japanese television manufacturers made strenuous efforts to enter the US television market. To do so, they set their prices in the US far below what they were charging Japanese consumers, and below those of US manufacturers. Over a 16 year period they were able to expand their combined share of the US market from zero to around 25%. Although the Japanese companies were successful in capturing a significant fraction of the US television market, they allegedly lost money in the process.[23]

The fact that they appeared to lose money on their US sales figured in the charge by the US manufacturers that the Japanese companies had colluded and engaged in predatory actions. Relying heavily on John McGee (1958), the court reasoned that it would be irrational for profit maximizing firms to price below their costs in the hopes of becoming dominant for as long as the Japanese firms had been expanding their share of the US market. Since it would be irrational, it was not done. There must be some cost differential to explain the lower prices in the US than in Japan (Elzinga, 1993, suggests distribution costs). This logic seemed so compelling to the court, that it refused to even allow the case to go to trial.

But suppose that the Japanese companies were not maximizing profits. Many students of Japanese business have noted that Japanese managers use considerably lower required return cut-offs than US companies, when choosing investment projects. Hiroyuki Odagiri (1981, 1992) has argued that Japanese corporations are better understood by applying Marris' growth-maximization hypothesis than the standard profits maximization behavioral postulate. Perhaps the Japanese manufacturers were simply making a large investment to extend their television sales "empire" to another continent.

6.3. Nonprice competition and rentseeking

The United States antitrust laws and their enforcement are based on the presumption that all competition is good, and the more competition there is, the better the performance of a market. The rentseeking literature calls this presumption into question, at least as it pertains to nonprice competition. The more firms invest in lobbying, advertising, marketing, and even R&D, the worse off society may be (Hirshleifer, 1971; Tullock, 1974; Posner, 1975; Spence, 1976a,b; Marris and Mueller, 1980).

[23] See Schwartzman (1994), a consultant for the US manufacturers in *Matsushita* v. *Zenith* (1986). Scherer (1994, p.85) shows that the firms may not have sacrificed profits. For an account of the case from the perspective of the Japanese companies, see Elzinga (1993).

The rentseeking literature casts a different light on the bigness–efficiency hypothesis as it manifests itself in the profit–market share relationship. The accounting profits of a firm are calculated net of its rentseeking (rent-preserving) expenditures on lobbyists, advertising, and the like. Other firms also make rentseeking outlays to take away sales from the firms with large market shares. These outlays are part of "the social costs of monopoly", part of the social costs of having some companies earning persistently high profits (Cowling and Mueller, 1978). A policy that maximized the social benefits from competition would weigh these rentseeking costs of monopoly, along with the traditional consumers' surplus costs.

6.4. Merger policy

United States antitrust policy presumes that all competition is price competition, and all firms maximize profits. In an environment that was so ruthlessly competitive that no firm could survive, if it did not slavishly pursue profits, the profits maximization assumption would hold of necessity (Alchian, 1950). But the persistently above normal profits that many US firms earn belies the assumption that Darwinian pressures eliminate all excess profits. The managers of many firms have the discretion to pursue goals other than the single-minded maximization of their companies' profits.

We have already suggested with respect to the inverse relationship between diversification and efficiency that size or growth in size might be one of these goals. Mergers are the fastest way to grow and diversify, and one expects growth-oriented managers to resort to them, unless opportunities for internal expansion are exceptional (Mueller, 1969, 1972). If some managers pursue growth rather than profits through mergers, then one expects no or even an inverse relationship between mergers and changes in profitability, and that is what one observes.[24] I have reviewed this literature on several occasions (Mueller, 1977, 1987, 1995a,b), and shall not take space for an exhaustive review here.

6.4.1. The effects of mergers on profitability

The proper way to measure the effects of mergers on profitability is to compare the weighted average profits of the firms *before* they merge with their profits *afterward*, adjusting for changing economic conditions by using

[24] If some mergers increase profits, and others are for growth alone, then a random sample of mergers contains some that increase profits, and others that do not. Whether the net relationship between profit changes and mergers is positive, zero, or negative depends on the mix of the two types of mergers in the sample. Different samples contain different mixes, and one expects to find all three kinds of results. A finding that mergers *significantly* increase or decrease profitability cannot be used to infer that *all* mergers are consummated with one or the other objective in mind.

a control group of otherwise similar nonmerging firms (Hughes, Mueller and Singh, 1980). Twenty studies drawn from 10 countries over the post-World War II period that follow this methodology have produced mixed findings (Mueller, 1995a).

The most ambitious study in terms of sample size, time span, and care in handling the data was that of Ravenscraft and Scherer (1987) for the US. They concluded unequivocally that the profitability of acquired firms declined after they were acquired. The largest study of mergers in the UK reached the same conclusion (Meeks, 1977). No distinct pattern emerges in the studies from other countries. Profit increases were observed in Canada (Baldwin, 1991) and Japan (Ikeda and Doi, 1983), profit decreases in Holland (Peer, 1980) and Sweden (Ryden and Edberg, 1980). In other countries the differences were generally statistically insignificant.

6.4.2. The effects of mergers on market share and growth

A merger that increases one or both companies' efficiency should lower the price of their products and expand their outputs. Market power increases, in turn, should result in higher prices and reduced outputs. Thus, one can test whether a merger has increased efficiency or market power by testing whether output expands or contracts (Hughes, Mueller and Singh, 1980; Mueller, 1986, ch.9).

Studies of the effects of mergers on the growth rates of merging firms have found either no significant change in growth rates [Australia (McDougall and Round, 1986, pp.157–159), Belgium (Kumps and Wtterwulghe, 1980), France (Jenny and Weber, 1980), Germany (Cable, Palfrey and Runge, 1980), Sweden (Ryden and Edberg, 1980), the United Kingdom (Cosh, Hughes and Singh, 1980), and acquired banks in the United States (Rhoades, 1987)], or a significant decline [Holland (Peer, 1980) and the United States (Mueller, 1980b)].

Goldberg (1973) observed insignificant changes in market shares for 44 advertising intensive firms over an average of 3 1/2 years following the mergers. Mueller (1985; 1986, ch.9) observed significant declines in market shares for a sample of 209 US manufacturing companies over an average of 11 years following the mergers. Baldwin and Gorecki (1990) found significant declines in market shares for plants acquired in horizontal mergers, but no significant changes for plants acquired in other sorts of mergers in Canada, and concluded that horizontal mergers increased market power in Canada. Stewart and Kim (1993) reached the same conclusion with respect to the increase in horizontal merger activity in the US under the Reagan Administration's lax antitrust policies. Thus, no study of the effects of mergers on growth or market shares presented evidence that mergers increased efficiency. Three implied significant reductions in efficiency, and two suggested increases in market power.

6.4.3. The effects of mergers on share prices

A large literature estimates the anticipated effects of mergers by examining the changes in stock prices occurring on and around their announcement (Mueller, 1977, 1987, 1995a,b; Jensen and Ruback, 1983). In virtually every merger the buyer offers a premium for the acquired company's shares to induce its owners to sell. The acquired firm's share prices rise to reflect these premia. The median gain to acquired firm shareholders in 29 studies from various countries was 20.6%.

The typical pattern of share returns for acquiring companies is as follows. Starting anywhere from two to five years prior to a merger the acquiring firm's shares begin to outperform the market. Since it is inconceivable that the market is *reacting* to the effects of a merger several years down the road, any causal linkage between these events must run from outperforming the market to undertaking an acquisition. It is reasonable to assume that growth-oriented managers undertake unprofitable acquisitions more often when their company's profits are abnormally high and their shareholders have enjoyed substantial above market returns. The announcements of mergers, on the other hand, result in quite a mixed pattern of return estimates with the safest conclusion "that for the stockholders of the acquiring firms, 'news' of an acquisition may not be worthwhile news" (Mandelker, 1974, p.321). In the months that follow the shareholders of acquiring firms suffer relative declines in the returns on their shares, declines that continue in some cases for several years after the merger.

The acid test of whether mergers create or destroy wealth is to add up the gains and losses on both sides and see what the total is. Acquiring firms are on average much larger than the companies that they acquire. In my 1980 study (Mueller, 1980b) they were 10 times larger. With this difference in relative sizes the median gain of 0.206 for acquired firm shareholders in the 29 studies is fully offset by a loss of only − 0.021 for acquiring firm shareholders. The median wealth change for acquiring firm shareholders from the time of announcement through the post-announcement period was − 0.031.

6.5. Vertical restraints

All potential "efficiency gains" from vertical restraints come about because a manufacturer is better able to develop and exploit the market power inherent in a downward sloping demand schedule. As such they all involve tradeoffs between the losses of buyers who pay more for a product, and the gains to consumers, who may pay less, and to producers and retailers (Scherer, 1983; Comanor, 1985; Katz, 1989). Both tying and RPM agreements, for example, can allow a manufacturer to price discriminate and thereby increase its profits. Although the sum of consumers' and producers' surplus may be larger under price discrimination, it may not.

Other alleged efficiency gains often take the form of increased advertising and selling expenses incurred by local retailers (Telser, 1960; Marvel and McCafferty, 1984). To interpret this effect as unambiguously efficiency enhancing is to assume that all forms of competition, including nonprice competition, enhance social welfare. But the rentseeking literature calls this assumption into question. A given firm imposes an RPM agreement on its retailers because it believes, correctly let us assume, that this restraint will increase its profits. But if this increase comes about in the context of a system of competition in which other manufacturers are imposing RPM agreements in the same belief, one retailer's advertising and selling outlays may to a considerable degree cancel the others. Each firm's profits may be higher, *given the actions of the other firms and retailers*, but society may be worse off than if there were no restraints on retailers, less retailer sales efforts, and more price competition at the retail level (see survey and discussion of Katz, 1989)

The literature on vertical restraints has evolved by example. Each article develops an argument as to why RPM, a tying arrangement, or some other vertical restriction on competition may be efficiency enhancing in a particular context, and illustrates the argument with a real world example. The very nature of the arguments and the literature's evolution make systematic empirical testing difficult. I know of no large scale empirical study, like the ones we have just reviewed for mergers, of the effects of vertical restraints. A few studies exist of the effects of litigated RPM cases (Overstreet, 1983; Ippolito, 1991; Hersch, 1994). They identify no single motive or effect of RPMs, and at best suggest the desireability of a rule of reason approach to this restrictive practice.

7. Implications for antitrust

The economic logic underlying the traditional approach to antitrust is as simple and appealing as an introductory textbook's discussion of perfect competition. Firms maximize profits and compete by price. Consumers' surplus is maximized when competitors are prevented from colluding, from merging to increase market power, and from adopting other practices that might restrict competition or tend to create a monopoly.

The profits maximization assumption implies that every action by a company can be expected to increase profits by either raising market power and price, or by raising efficiency and lowering costs. If an action cannot be shown to increase market power, i.e. to have an anticompetitive effect, it is assumed to enhance efficiency. The legal maxim "innocent until proven guilty" in antitrust cases places upon the plaintiff, until recently usually the government, the burden of proof that an action has an anticompetitive effect. The courts have gone along with this one-sided focus.

Recent developments in economic thinking have emphasized the potential efficiency gains from practices that may also have anticompetitive consequences. The inherent efficiency of dominant firms, transaction cost efficiency of vertical restraints, the potential efficiency from mergers, and even the potential efficiencies from cartel-like restrictions on prices and quantities have been emphasized (e.g. Dewey, 1979; Bittlingmayer, 1982), and have figured in antitrust cases (*ASCAP*). The result has been that potential efficiencies have been given sufficient weight to allow companies to adopt practices and undertake mergers that would have been prohibited in earlier times, if only their potential anticompetitive effects had been weighed.

The recognition that actions, which potentially injure competition, can also improve efficiency is not the only recent development in economics that is relevant for antitrust policy, however. The rentseeking literature emphasizes that intensified nonprice competition can lower social welfare. The managerial discretion, principal/agent literature points out that managers have discretion to pursue goals other than profits maximization, and thus that every action of managers that does not have a direct anticompetitive effect need not improve efficiency. Empirical findings imply that mergers are often likely to be efficiency reducing, even when they do not lesson competition.

If efficiency is to be put on an equal footing with market power in antitrust matters, an alternative approach to that employed in the United States until now is required. The general approach recommended here is that an action *A* with potential anticompetitive effects shall be presumed to be illegal *unless* the firm or firms involved can demonstrate that action *A* is reasonably likely to generate efficiency gains substantially greater than its anticipated anticompetitive welfare losses. Such an approach would shift the burden of proof from the government to the private sector, and shift the emphasis in antitrust proceedings from a proof of anticompetitive impact to a proof of positive, net social welfare gains from increases in efficiency.[25] Specific language for such legislation might look like the following:

7.1 Sherman Act equivalents

Section 1. Every contract, combination in the form of trust or otherwise, or conspiracy, in restraint of trade or commerce is hereby declared illegal,

[25] Louis Brandeis, the famous American jurist, proposed placing the burden of proof on defendants in rule of reason Sherman Act cases three quarters of a century ago (Freyer, 1992, p.67).

unless it can be demonstrated that the contract, combination, trust, or conspiracy is likely to yield substantial efficiency gains in excess of its anticompctitive effects.

Section 2. Any firm which has remained dominant in a market for a period of 35 years or more shall be presumed to have violated this section of the Pro-efficiency statute, *unless* the firm can demonstrate that it owes its position of dominance to superior efficiency or innovativeness.

7.2. Clayton Act equivalents

Section 3. That it shall be unlawful for any person engaged in commerce to lease or make sale or contract for sale of goods, whether patented or unpatented, or fix a price charged therefor, or discount from, or rebate upon, such price, on condition agreement, or understanding that the lessee or purchaser thereof shall not use or deal in the goods of a competitor or competitors of the lessor, *unless* it can be demonstrated that said practice is likely to yield substantial efficiency gains in excess of its anticompetitive effects.

Section 4. That no corporation with sales greater than $500,000,000 ($100,000,000) measured in 1994 dollars shall acquire, directly or indirectly, the whole or any part of the stock or other share capital, or the assets of another corporation with sales greater than $100,000,000 ($500,000,000) measured in 1994 dollars, *unless* it can be demonstrated that such an acquisition is likely to yield substantial efficiency gains in excess of its anticompetitive effects.

The conspiracy section revives a proposal made by Almarin Phillips (1959). Its language parrots Section 1 of the Sherman Act. The statute would essentially retain the presumptive illegality of price and quantity fixing agreements, but allow them to be defended when they produce substantial efficiency gains.

Section 2 revives a proposal made by Williamson (1972). The issue of what a dominant firm is, like the question of what a monopoly is, would have to be established over time through the judicial process, but I would assume that a market share of at least 50% would be involved. The time span that would precipitate action is obviously somewhat arbitrary. I have chosen a number that is double the life of a patent.

Section 3 would place all vertical restraints on an even footing, banning them all, but allowing rule-of-reason defenses when meaningful efficiency gains can be demonstrated. Section 4 would prohibit large firms from engaging in mergers, again subject to an efficiencies defense.

An obvious potential disadvantage of these proposals is their effect on litigation costs. But litigation costs have already risen in recent years as a result of the interjection of the new learning and new institutionalism into antitrust cases, and the increasingly important role economic analysis plays. Where a tying arrangement might have been expeditiously dispatched a generation ago under the per se doctrine, today the new institutionalism calls upon the court to consider the possible social benefits from such a restraint. Where a merger would have been challenged a generation ago on the basis of a fairly straightforward analysis of the structure of the industry and the proposed merger's impact on that structure, today's Merger Guidelines require the DoJ or FTC to undertake what amounts to a Sherman Act analysis of all relevant factors that might impact the vigor of competition in the market (DoJ, 1993; Mueller, 1993). So elaborate is the list of factors that the Guidelines stipulate as relevant, that a pair of giant firms set upon merging could, no doubt, force whichever antitrust authority that tried to stop them into a protracted proceeding.

Even important Section 1, Sherman Act cases, as already noted, have tended to be tried under the rule of reason standard in recent years. Anyone contemplating bringing suit today under either Section of the Sherman Act should anticipate a long drawn-out affair.

Indeed, so costly have antitrust proceedings become under present standards and interpretations, that a shift in emphasis and burden of proof might actually *reduce* litigation costs. Gone would be the *necessity* to prove a potential anticompetitive effect. If a firm seeking to make an acquisition that falls under the statute could not demonstrate a reasonable likelihood that the merger would result in substantial efficiency gains, the merger would not go forward even if it had no likely effect on competition. Vertical restraints that did not increase efficiency would be prohibited, even when their effect on competition was not obviously negative.

Heavy litigation might be expected in the first few years after such a set of statutes came into effect. Once precedents under the statutes had been established, however, the volume of litigation could be expected to taper off. Once the kinds of evidence the courts would accept to justify a particular action and the kinds they would not accept became clear, firms could make reasoned judgments as to what forms of vertical restraints, cartel arrangements, and mergers would pass muster. Once the initial stock of dominant firm cases had been tried, new dominant firms that meet the statute's criteria would come along only every few years.

Litigation costs in antitrust cases might be further reduced by adopting European-style inquisitorial judicial procedures for these types of cases. Whatever the merits of the British/American adversarial system in other areas, it is particularly ill-suited for expeditiously and correctly deciding antitrust cases. The issues to be resolved often require fairly sophisticated reasoning and careful handling and interpretation of data. A process in which at least one side has a strong incentive and ample opportunity to obfuscate the facts cannot be optimal. Establishing a separate set of courts, with judges trained specifically to deal with antitrust matters and empowered to obtain from both the plaintiff and the defendant those facts that the court deemed relevant could in the long run prove to be a more cost effective way to resolve antitrust cases than the present system in the United States, even under statutes as proposed above.

Changes in the antitrust laws are not the only and perhaps not even the best way to deal with inefficiencies fostered by rentseeking, empire building and the like. Direct restrictions on lobbying and advertising might be implemented, the institutions of corporate control could be strengthened. A comprehensive effort to improve the efficiency of the corporate economy would certainly contemplate policies beyond antitrust reform. Mergers, vertical restraints, and dominant firm actions have traditionally been the purview of antitrust, however. Any effort to reform the corporate sector must consider alterations in these policies.

The new learnings and the Reagan/Bush Administrations' policies engendered the widespread view that antitrust policy is at best irrelevant, at worst a hindrance to economic efficiency. Even Clinton's Administration, although reversing previous policies in some repects, has appeared to share this view in giving so little weight to antitrust. To many students of antitrust in North America, therefore, proposals to toughen antitrust policy will seem anacronistic. Interestingly, the era of toughest antitrust enforcement in the US coincided with what now looks like "the golden age of American capitalism". At a minimum this contemporaneousness should dispel the notion that tough antitrust enforcement and a healthy corporate economy are antithetical. Should the overlap in time not be purely accidental, it would reinforce the case for a renewed vigor in antitrust.

8. Implications for European competition policy

The European Union's (EU) current policies with respect to collusive agreements and vertical restraints already balance anticompetitive and efficiency considerations as proposed here. Although there are many national markets dominated by a single firm, there are few if any *European* markets where such dominance exists. Thus, the EU's competition policy comes close to that proposed in Sections 1 and 3 above, and in the case of Section 2 would not require much if any action at the European level. Moreover, a statute like the proposed Sction 2 might never be required, if Europe had a vigorous antimerger policy as contained in the proposed Section 4. It is in the area of mergers, however, that a strong, European antitrust policy is likely to face its greatest challenge.

In response to competitive pressures many European companies may choose to merge and eliminate competition rather than improve their efficiency and product quality to meet it. Efficiencies will be claimed for horizontal and vertical acquisitions in "troubled industries", and political pressure will mount from individual member countries to allow them. In addition, some members of the Commission may actually welcome cross-national mergers as a way of furthering "economic integration." The EU's regulation for the control of mergers adopted in December 1989 looks a bit like my Section 4, *except* that the threshold in world sales is about 12 times higher than that suggested above. In the five years since the regulation was adopted, *one* merger has been prevented (Schmidt and Binder, 1994). Europe needs both tighter thresholds and tougher enforcement of its antimerger policy, if it is going to protect competitive market structures and avoid efficiency debilitating mergers.

The evidence suggests that many efficiencies claimed for mergers ex ante do not materialize, and unforeseen integration problems often actually worsen efficiency. A European competition policy that erred on the side of preventing mergers between large, reasonably healthy competitors would at worst prohibit a merger in a troubled industry today, and force the merger to be allowed tomorrow under a failing-firm, efficiencies defense. On the plus side it would encourage companies to reorganize and revitalize themselves so that they can survive in a more competitive environment, and would prevent mergers that would actually have *lowered* the efficiency of the merging companies and lessened their ability to compete and survive.

The potential efficiency gains from diversification mergers are especially doubtful, and it is in this area where empire building is most likely to conflict with economic efficiency. A policy that prohibited *all* diversification mergers between large firms, subject to a vigorously enforced efficiencies defense, could do much to preserve healthy, reasonably sized, competitive firms in Europe.

In some ways the EU finds itself in the enviable position of being where the US was a century ago, before the two great merger waves of the 1890s and 1920s created dominate firms and high concentration in many markets, and before the two great merger waves of the 1960s and 1980s created numerous diversified behemoths. It also appears likely to follow the same misguided course that the US did, however, of having a tough anticartel policy and a loose antimerger policy, thereby encouraging firms to achieve by merger what they cannot by contract. A vigorously enforced antimerger policy that allowed only those mergers that promise measurable and substantial efficiency gains is the single most important policy step Europe could take to preserve and intensify competition, and thereby strengthen its economic health over the decades ahead.

Acknowledgements

Financial support for research on this paper from the Ludwig Boltzmann Institut is gratefully acknowledged. Helpful comments on an earlier draft were received from Stephen Martin, Louis Philips and an anonymous referee. F.M. Scherer generously provided copious comments for which I am most grateful.

References

Adelman, M.A., 1959a, A&P: A study in price-cost behavior and public policy (Harvard University Press, Cambridge, MA).

Adelman, M.A., 1959b, Economic aspects of the Bethlehem opinion, Virginia Law Review 45, 684–696.

Alchian, A.A., 1950, Uncertainty, evolution, and economic theory, Journal of Political Economy 58, 211–221.

Areeda, P. and D.F. Turner, 1975, Predatory pricing and related practices under Section 2 of the Sherman Act, Harvard Law Review 88, 697–733.

Baldwin, J., 1991, The dynamics of the competitive process, Mimeo, Queen's University.

Baldwin, J. and P. Gorecki, 1990, Mergers placed in the context of firm turnover, in: Bureau of the Census, 1990 Annual Research Conference Proceedings (US Department of Commerce, Washington, D.C.) 53–73.

Berry, C.H., 1975, Corporate growth and diversification (Princeton University Press, Princeton, NJ).

Bittlingmayer, G., 1982, Decreasing average cost and competition: A new look at the Addyston Pipe case, Journal of Law and Economics 25, 201–229.

Bork, R.H., 1978, The antitrust paradox (Basic Books, New York).

Breit, W. and K.G. Elzinga, 1989, The antitrust casebook, 2nd edn. (Harcourt Brace Jovanovich, Forth Worth).

Brock, G.W., 1989, Dominant firm response to competitive challenge: Peripheral equipment manufacturers' suits against IBM (1979–1983), in: J.E. Kwoka, Jr. and L.J. White, eds., The antitrust revolution (Scott, Forsman, Glenview) 160–183.

Brozen, Y., 1971a, Bain's concentration and rates of return revisited, Journal of Law and Economics 14, 351–369.

Brozen, Y., 1971b, The persistence of 'high rates of return' in high-stable concentration industries, Journal of Law and Economics 14, 501–512.

Brozen, Y., 1982, Concentration, mergers, and public policy (MacMillan, New York).

Cable, J.R., P.R. Palfrey and J.W. Runge, 1980, Federal Republic of Germany, 1964–1974, in: D.C. Mueller, ed., The determinants and effects of mergers: An international comparison (Oelgeschlager, Gunn & Hain, Cambridge, MA) 99–132.

Carter, J.R., 1977, In search of synergy: A structure–performance test, Review of Economics and Statistics 59, 279–289.

Carter, J.R., 1978, Collusion, efficiency and antitrust, Journal of Law and Economics 21, 435–444.

Caves, R.E. and D.R. Barton, 1990, Efficiency in US manufacturing industries (MIT Press, Cambridge, MA).

Comanor, W.S., 1985, Vertical price fixing and market restraints and the new antitrust policy, Harvard Law Review 98, 990–998.

Comanor, W.S., 1986, The political economy of the pharmaceutical industry, Journal of Economic Literature 24, 1178–1217.

Cosh, A., A. Hughes and A. Singh, 1980, The causes and effects of takeovers in the United Kingdom: An empirical investigation for the late 1960s at the microeconomic level, in: D.C. Mueller, ed., The determinants and effects of mergers: An international comparison (Oelgeschlager, Gunn & Hain, Cambridge, MA) 227–270.

Cowling, K. and D.C. Mueller, 1978, The social costs of monopoly, Economic Journal 88, 727–748.

De Alessi, L., 1983, Property rights, transaction costs, and X-efficiency, American Economic Review 73, 64–82.

Demsetz, H., 1973, Industry structure, market rivalry, and public policy, Journal of Law and Economics 16, 1–9.

Department of Justice and Federal Trade Commission, 1993, Horizontal merger guidelines, Review of Industrial Organization 8, 231–256.

Dewey, D.F., 1979, Information, entry and welfare: The case for collusion, American Economic Review 69, 587–594.

Dodd, P. and R. Ruback, 1977, Tender offers and stockholder returns: An empirical analysis, Journal of Financial Economics 5, 351–374.

Eckbo, B.E., 1983, Horizontal mergers, collusion, and stockholder wealth, Journal of Financial Economics 11, 241–273.

Elzinga, K.G., 1993, Collusive predation: Matsushita v. Zenith (1986), in: J.E. Kwoka and L.J. White, eds., The antitrust revolution, 2nd edn. (Scott, Forsman, Glenview) 238–259.

Evans, W.N. and I.N. Kessides, 1994, Living by the 'Golden Rule': Multimarket contact in the US airline industry, Quarterly Journal of Economics 109, 341–366.

Freyer, T., 1992, Regulating big business (Cambridge University Press, Cambridge, MA).

Gale, B.J. and B.S. Branch, 1982, Concentration versus market share: Which determines performance and why does it matter? Antitrust Bulletin 27, 83–106.

Goldberg, L.G., 1973, The effect of conglomerate mergers on competition, Journal of Law and Economics 16, 137–158.

Goldschmid, H.J., H.M. Mann and J.F. Weston, 1974, Industrial concentration: The new learning (Little, Brown, Boston, MA).

Hersch, P.L., 1994, The effects of resale price maintenance on shareholder wealth: The consequences of Schwegmann, Journal of Industrial Economics 42, 205–216.

Hirshleifer, J., 1971, The private and social value of information and the reward to inventive activity, American Economic Review 61, 561–574.

Hughes, A., D.C. Mueller and A. Singh, 1980, Hypotheses about mergers, in: D.C. Mueller, ed., The determinants and effects of mergers: An international comparison (Oelgeschlager, Gunn & Hain, Cambridge, MA) 27–66.

Ikeda, K. and N. Doi, 1983, The performance of merging firms in Japanese manufacturing industry: 1964–75, Journal of Industrial Economics 31, 257–266.

Ippolito, P.M., 1991, Resale price maintenance: Empirical evidence from litigation, Journal of Law and Economics 34, 263–294.

Jenny, F. and A.-P. Weber, 1980, France, 1962–72, in: D.C. Mueller, ed., The determinants and effects of mergers: An international comparison (Oelgeschlager, Gunn & Hain, Cambridge, MA) 133–162.

Jensen, M.C. and R.S. Ruback, 1983, The market for corporate control, Journal of Financial Economics 11, 5–50.

Jordan, S., 1992, Political affiliation, appointing president, and judicial voting behavior, Ph.D. dissertation, University of Maryland.

Katz, M.L., 1989, Vertical contractual relations, in: R. Schmalensee and R.D. Willig, eds., Handbook of industrial organization, Vol.1 (North-Holland, Amsterdam) 655–721.

Kaysen, C. and D.F. Turner, 1959, Antitrust policy (Harvard University Press, Cambridge, MA).

Klein, B. and L.F. Saft, 1985, The law and economics of franchise tying contracts, Journal of Law and Economics 28, 345–361.

Kumps, A.-M. and R. Wtterwulghe, 1980, Belgium, 1962–74, in: D.C. Mueller, ed., The determinants and effects of mergers: An international comparison (Oelgeschlager, Gunn & Hain, Cambridge, MA) 67–97.

Kwoka, J.E., Jr. and L.J. White, 1989, The antitrust revolution (Scott, Forsman, Glenview).
Kwoka, J.E., Jr. and L.J. White, 1993, The antitrust revolution, 2nd edn. (Harper Collins, New York).
Lang, L.H.P. and R.M. Stulz, 1994, Tobin's q, corporate diversification and firm performance, Journal of Political Economy 102, 1248–1280.
Lecraw, D.J., 1984, Diversification strategy and performance, Journal of Industrial Economics 33, 179–198.
Lichtenberg, F., 1992, Industrial de-diversification and its consequences for productivity, Journal of Economic Behavior and Organization 18, 427–438.
Littlechild, S., 1981, Misleading calculations of the social costs of monopoly power, Economic Journal 91, 348–363.
Lynk, W.J., 1993, Tying and exclusive dealing: Jefferson Parish Hospital v. Hyde (1984), in: J.E. Kwoka and L.J. White, eds., The antitrust revolution, 2nd edn. (Scott, Forsman, Glenview) 376–399.
Mancke, R.B., 1974, Causes of interfirm profitability differences: A new interpretation of the evidence, Quarterly Journal of Economics 88, 181–193.
Mandelker, G., 1974, Risk and return: The case of merging firms, Journal of Financial Economics 1, 303–335.
Manne, H.G., 1965, Mergers and the market for corporate control, Journal of Political Economy 73, 110–120.
Marris, R. and D.C. Mueller, 1980, The corporation, competition, and the invisible hand, Journal of Economic Literature 18, 32–63.
Marvel, H.P., 1982, Exclusive dealing, Journal of Law and Economics 25, 1–25.
Marvel, H.P., 1985, The welfare effects of resale price maintenance, Journal of Law and Economics 28, 363–379.
Marvel, H.P. and S. McCafferty, 1984, Resale price maintenance and quality certification, Rand Journal of Economics 15, 346–359.
Mason, E.S., 1959, Preface, in C.Kaysenand, D.F. Turner, xi–xxiii.
McDougall, F.M. and D.K. Round, 1986, The determinants and effects of corporate takeovers in Australia, 1970–1981 (Australian Institute of Management, Victoria).
McGee, J.S., 1958, Predatory price cutting: The Standard Oil (NJ) case, Journal of Law and Economics 1, 137–169.
Meeks, G., 1977, Disappointing marriage: A study of the gains from merger (Cambridge University Press, Cambridge, UK).
Megna, P. and D.C. Mueller, 1991, Profit rates and intangible capital, Review of Economics and Statistics 73, 632–642.
Miller, R.A., 1969, Market structure and industrial performance, relation of profit rates to concentration, advertising intensity, and diversity, Journal of Industrial Economics 17, 104–118.
Mueller, D.C., 1969, A theory of conglomerate mergers, Quarterly Journal of Economics 83, 643–659.
Mueller, D.C., 1972, A life cycle theory of the firm, Journal of Industrial Economics 20, 199–219.
Mueller, D.C., 1977, The effects of conglomerate mergers: A survey of the empirical evidence, Journal of Banking and Finance 1, 315–347.
Mueller, D.C., 1980a, The determinants and effects of mergers: An international comparison (Oelgeschlager, Gunn & Hain, Cambridge, MA).
Mueller, D.C., 1980b, The United States, 1962–1972, in: D.C. Mueller, ed., The determinants and effects of mergers: An international comparison (Oelgeschlager, Gunn & Hain, Cambridge, MA) 271–298.
Mueller, D.C., 1985, Mergers and market share, Review of Economics and Statistics 67, 259–267.

Mueller, D.C., 1986, Profits in the long run (Cambridge University Press, Cambridge, MA).

Mueller, D.C., 1987, The corporation: Growth, diversification, and mergers (Harwood Academic Publishers, London).

Mueller, D.C., 1993, US merger policy and the 1992 merger guidelines, Review of Industrial Organization 8, 151–162.

Mueller, D.C., 1995a, Antimerger policy in the United States: History and lessons, Mimeo, University of Vienna.

Mueller, D.C., 1995b, Mergers: Theory and evidence, in: G. Mussatti, ed., Mergers, markets, and public policy (Kluwer, Dordrecht) forthcoming.

Mueller, W.F. and M.H. Sial, 1993, Cyclical variation in the concentration–profit relationship, Mimeo, University of Wisconsin.

Nicholls, W.H., 1949, The Tobacco Case of 1946, American Economic Review 39, 284–296, reprinted in: R.B. Heflebower and G.W. Stocking, eds., Readings in industrial organization and public policy (Irwin, Homewood, 1958) 105–117.

Noll, R.G. and B.M. Owen, 1993, The anticompetitive uses of regulation: United States v. AT&T (1982), in: J.E. Kwoka and L.J. White, eds., The antitrust revolution, 2nd edn. (Scott, Forsman, Glenview) 328–375.

Odagiri, H., 1981, The theory of growth in a corporate economy: An inquiry into management preference, R&D and economic growth (Cambridge University Press, Cambridge, MA).

Odagiri, H., 1992, Growth through competition, competition through growth: Strategic management and the economy in Japan (Oxford University Press, Oxford).

Overstreet, T.R., 1983, Resale price maintenance: Economic theories and empirical evidence (FTC, Washington, D.C.).

Peer, H., 1980, The Netherlands, 1962–1973, in: D.C. Mueller, ed., The determinants and effects of mergers: An international comparison (Oelgeschlager, Gunn & Hain, Cambridge, MA) 163–191.

Peltzman, S., 1977, The gains and losses from industrial concentration, Journal of Law and Economics 20, 229–263.

Phillips, A., 1959, A critique of the United States experience with the Per Se rule, Journal of Industrial Economics 8, 13–32.

Posner, R.A., 1975, The social cost of monopoly and regulation, Journal of Political Economy 83, 807–827.

Posner, R.A., 1976, Antitrust laws (University of Chicago Press, Chicago, IL).

Preston, L.E., 1993, Territorial restraints: GTE Sylvania (1977), in: J.E. Kwoka and L.J. White, eds., The antitrust revolution, 2nd edn. (Scott, Forsman, Glenview) 311–327.

Ravenscraft, D.J., 1983, Structure-profit relationships at the line of business and industry level, Review of Economics and Statistics 65, 22–31.

Ravenscraft, D.J. and F.M. Scherer, 1987, Mergers, sell-offs and economic efficiency (Brookings Institution, Washington, DC).

Report of the Attorney General's National Committee to study the antitrust laws, 1955 (Government Printing Office, Washington, D.C.).

Rhoades, S.A., 1973, The effect of diversification on industry profit performance in 241 manufacturing industries, Review of Economics and Statistics 55, 146–155.

Rhoades, S.A., 1987, The operating performance of acquired firms in banking, in R.L. Wills, J.A. Caswell, and J.D. Culbertson, eds., Issues after a century of federal competition policy (Lexington Books, Lexington, MA), 277–292.

Rhoades, S.A., 1974, A further evaluation of the effect of diversification on industry profit performance, Review of Economics and Statistics 56, 557–559.

Ryden, B. and J.-O. Edberg, 1980, Large mergers in Sweden, 1962–1976, in: D.C. Mueller, ed., The determinants and effects of mergers: An international comparison (Oelgeschlager, Gunn & Hain, Cambridge, MA) 193–226.

Scherer, F.M., 1981, The economics of vertical restraints, Antitrust Law Journal 53, 687–707.

Scherer, F.M., 1993, Merger in the petroleum industry: The Mobil–Marathon Case (1981), in: J.E. Kwoka and L.J. White, eds., The antitrust revolution, 2nd edn. (Scott, Forsman, Glenview) 20–45.

Scherer, F.M., 1994, Competition policies for an integrated world economy (Brookings Institution, Washington, D.C.).

Schmidt, I. and S. Binder, 1994, Wettbewerbspolitik im internationalen Vergleich (An international comparison of competition policies), Mimeo, Universität Hohenheim, Stuttgart).

Schwartzman, D., 1994, Matsushita v. Zenith: An economic analysis, Review of Industrial Organization 9, 1–23.

Scott, J.T., 1982, Multimarket contact and economic performance, Review of Economics and Statistics 64, 368–375.

Scott, J.T., 1993, Purposive diversification and economic performance (Cambridge University Press, Cambridge, MA).

Shepherd, W.G., 1975, The treatment of market power (Columbia University Press, New York).

Smirlock, M., T. Gilligan and W. Marshall, 1984, Tobin's q and the structure–performance relationship, American Economic Review 74, 1051–1060.

Spence, M., 1976a, Product differentiation and welfare, American Economic Review 66, 407–414.

Spence, M., 1976b, Product selection, fixed costs, and monopolistic competition, Review of Economic Studies 43, 217–235.

Stelzer, I.M., Selected antitrust cases: Landmark decisions, 2nd, 3rd, 4th, 5th, 6th, and 7th edns., 1961, 1966, 1972, 1976, 1981, 1986 (Irwin, Homewood).

Stewart, J.F. and S.-K. Kim, 1993, Mergers and social welfare in US manufacturing 1985–86, Southern Economic Journal 59, 701–720.

Stigler, G.J., 1950, Monopoly and oligopoly by merger, American Economic Review 40, 23–34.

Stillman, R., 1983, Examining antitrust policy towards horizontal mergers, Journal of Financial Economics 11, 225–240.

Telser, L.G., 1960, Why should manufacturers want fair trade?, Journal of Law and Economics 3, 86–105.

Tullock, G., 1974, The welfare costs of tariffs, monopolies, and theft, Western Economic Journal 5, 291–303.

Warren-Boulton, F.R., 1993, Resale price maintenance re-examined: Monsanto v. Spray-Rite (1984), in: J.E. Kwoka and L.J. White, eds., The antitrust revolution, 2nd edn. (Scott, Forsman, Glenview) 400–431.

Weston, J.F., 1970, The nature and significance of conglomerate firms, St. John's Law Review 44, special edition, 66–80.

Weston, J.F. and S.K. Mansinghka, 1971, Tests of the efficiency performance of conglomerate firms, Journal of Finance 26, 919–936.

Williamson, O.E., 1968, Economies as an anti-trust defense: The welfare trade-offs, American Economic Review 58, 18–36; repeated with correction in: C.K. Rowley, ed., 1972, Readings in industrial economics (Macmillan, London).

Williamson, O.E., 1970, Corporate control and business behavior: An inquiry into the effects of organization form on enterprise behavior (Prentice-Hall, Englewood Cliffs, NJ).

Williamson, O.E., 1972, Dominant firms and the monopoly problem: Market failure considerations, Harvard Law Review 85, 1512–1531.

Williamson, O.E., 1985, The economic institutions of capitalism (Free Press, New York).

Williamson, O.E., 1989, Transaction cost economics, in: R. Schmalensee and R. Willig, eds., Handbook of industrial organization, Vol. 1 (North-Holland, Amsterdam) 135–82.

Review of Industrial Organization **12:** 655–685, 1997.

Merger Policy in the United States: A Reconsideration

DENNIS C. MUELLER
University of Vienna, Department of Economics, BWZ-Brünner Strasse 72, A-1210 Vienna, Austria

Abstract. This paper reviews the history of U.S. antimerger policy. This history is divided into three periods: a period in which there was almost no effective antimerger policy at all from 1890 up to 1959, a period of vigorous antimerger policy from 1950 up through 1973, and a period of lax enforcement from 1974 to the present. The paper accounts for these shifts in antimerger policy and discusses their effects. After reviewing the logic and consequences of U.S. antimerger policy, a critique of its premises is offered, particularly as these premises apply to the recent era of lax enforcement. The paper closes with suggestions for an alternative approach to antimerger policy that is consistent with the empirical evidence on why mergers occur and their effects.

Key words: Mergers, antitrust policy.

JEL Classifications: L40, G34.

The merger between Boeing and McDonnell Douglas, announced in the closing days of 1996, will join the last two commercial airplane manufacturers in the United States, two of the last three major manufacturers in the world. As with almost all mergers, there is considerable talk of potential synergies and economies surrounding the merger, and these along with the importance of Boeing as an exporter and McDonnell Douglas as a defense contractor ensure that the merger will not be challenged by the antitrust authorities, despite the obvious grounds for doing so. Indeed, the merger occurs in the midst of the United States's fifth great merger wave, a wave that has seen many mergers between giant firms like Boeing and McDonnell Douglas, a wave that appears likely to surpass its four predecessors in terms of the amount of assets acquired (Shepherd, 1997, p. 154).

These five waves have transformed the structure of American industry over the last century. No sector or major industry has not been impacted by mergers. Almost no firm among the very largest in the economy is not to some extent a product of past mergers. From time to time Congress has become concerned about the number of of mergers taking place. Both the 1914 Clayton Act and the 1950 Celler-Kefauver Amendment to it were passed out of concern that the existing legislation was inadequate for controlling merger activity. Neither succeeded in preventing future merger waves, obviously, although the Celler-Kefauver Amendment did arguably affect the *direction* of merger activity for a time, when not its volume.

Both Theodore Roosevelt and Woodrow Wilson were able to capture the Presidency in part on the basis of their advocacy of tough antitrust policies. Congressman Celler and Senator Kefauver also capitalized on their reputations for tough antitrust policy. But no recent Presidential candidate has made an issue out of antitrust policy, nor does it figure much in Congressional races. Both Congress and the President seem content to leave to the enforcement agencies the defining and redefining of antitrust policy. In the area of mergers, this has resulted in policies which have virtually no effect on the volume of mergers occurring. At the peak of the 1980s' merger wave a dozen or so mergers occurred *each day*, roughly the number of mergers that the Department of Justice challenged each year. Of these it would block one or two a year. The Clinton Administration has been somewhat more aggressive, but it lacks both the resources and the legislative authority to launch a frontal attack on mergers. If the past is prologue, the present wave will subside when the stockmarket boom that feeds it ends, only to resume once stock market activity picks up again. Efforts by the antitrust authorities will prevent a merger here and there, but their impact will be imperceptible in the aggregate statistics.

Perhaps this is all to the good. Many view outcomes from activity in the "market for corporate control" as yet another manifestation of Adam Smith's invisible hand theorem – exchanges of assets that ensure that they are in the hands of the persons most capable of utilizing them. I shall review evidence that draws this view into question, and thus indirectly the policy that allows so many mergers to take place.

I begin, however, with a review of the history of U.S. antimerger policy. This history is divided into three periods: a period in which there was almost no effective antimerger policy at all from 1890 up to 1950, a period of vigorous antimerger policy from 1950 up through 1973, and a period of lax enforcement from 1974 to the present. My objective is to account for these shifts in U.S. antimerger policy, and to discuss their effects. After reviewing the logic and consequences of U.S. antimerger policy, I offer a critique of its premises, particularly as they apply to the recent era of lax enforcement. The paper closes with some suggestions for an alternative approach to antimerger policy that is consistent with the empirical evidence on why mergers occur and their effects. We begin with the period of almost nonexistent antimerger policy over the first 60 years after the Sherman Act was passed.

I. The First 60 Years: Antitrust without an Antimerger Policy

The 1890 Sherman Act was a reaction to the expansion of size and power of large enterprises in the United States, i.e., the rise of the "trust". Ironically, by prohibiting cartels it encouraged firms to combine to avoid the costs of unbriddled competition that were expected to follow the disolution of the cartels, and thus helped precipitate the first great merger wave at the turn of the century.[1] This merger wave was, in

[1] (Bittlingmayer, 1985). Since merger waves also took place in Great Britain and Germany around the turn of the century without the stimulus of new antitrust legislation, the Sherman Act cannot be

comparison to the size of the economy, the biggest wave the United States has ever experienced. It transformed one industry after another into monopolies or near monopolies (Markham, 1955; Nelson, 1959).

The *American Tobacco* and *Standayd Oil of New Jersey* decisions handed down by the Supreme Court in 1911 demonstrated that the Sherman Act could be used to prevent mergers that literally created monopolies. But Congress was also concerned about mergers which created highly concentrated industry structures, although stopping short of resulting in full monopolies. So in 1914 it passed the Clayton Act to lengthen the Sherman Act's reach in blocking mergers and in other areas. Now a merger would be prohibited wherever "the effect of such acquistion may be to substantially lessen competition between the corporation whose stock is . . . acquired and the corporation making the acquisition".

Or so Congress thought. But the Supreme Court thought otherwise, and under the U.S. system of checks and balances it is often what the Supreme Court thinks, that determines policy, not what the Congress thinks. In 1920 the Supreme Court demonstrated that the Sherman Act could not be used to block mergers that fell short of creating monopolies. U.S. Steel had *only* 67 percent of the market at the time that 184 companies were combined to create it, and by 1920 its share of the industry had fallen to 50 percent, not enough to qualify as a monopoly under the Sherman Act. If mergers to create giant companies like U.S. Steel were to be stopped, the Clayton Act would have to be used to do it. But in *Thatcher Mfg.* (1926) and subsequent decisions the Court seized upon the Clayton Act's language prohibiting "stock" acquisitions to effectively repeal the statute. Although the statute could in principle[2] block a merger between Companies A and B, when A chose to buy B's stock, B was free to sell A all of its assets to A and then dissolve itself. If B was not so inclined, A could buy B's stock and use its voting power to force the asset sale. Even though the stock purchase would later prove to be illegal, the Court was willing to let the asset sale stand. Thus, when the stock market boom came in the 1920s and brought with it the country's second great merger wave, the antitrust authorities could only prevent mergers that came close to creating pure monopolies.[3] The result was a merger wave that only created "oligopolies" where the first had created "monopolies" (Stigler, 1950). The further consequence was that after World War II industry concentration levels were far higher than they would have been had the country had an effective merger policy over the previous half

given all of the credit for the first great merger wave in the United States (Hannah, 1974; Tilly, 1982; Chandler, 1990).

[2] In practice the Court interpreted "substantial lessening of competition" in such a way that the Clayton Act would not have been very effective, even if the Court had not emasculated it in the way described in the text.

[3] Evidence that the common impression that mergers come in waves is not an optical illusion is presented by Golbe and White (1993).

century, far higher than seemed necessary to achieve minimum levels of average costs.[4]

II. The Era of Vigorous Antimerger Policy

As the economy's first business cycle upturn began to take hold following World War II, merger activity began to pick up for the first time since the 1929 crash. Sensing another great merger wave in the making, Congress moved to repair the damage done to Section 7 of the Clayton Act by the Supreme Court's decisions from before the war. In 1950 the act was amended to prohibit asset as well as stock purchases that might substantially lessen competition. The "Warren Court" of the 1950s was far more liberal on economic, and most other matters, than the Courts that had effectively repealed Section 7 in the 1920s and 1930s. They read the debates in Congress leading up to the 1950 amendment as demanding a tough antimerger policy that would preserve both competition and the kind of decentralized market structures that foster it. The definition of anticompetitive effect in mergers was extended from horizontal to vertical acquisitions, and even to encompass certain forms of conglomerate mergers. Each successive decision seemed to drop the threshholds of market share and concentration that would lead to a merger's prohibition. The highwater marks in vigorous and successful prosecution were undoubtedly the *Brown Shoe* (1962, horizontal and vertical), *Von's Grocery* (1967, horizontal), and *Procter & Gamble* (1967, conglomerate) cases in which companies with market shares as low as 5% of the national market and 7.5% of a local market were prevented from merging, and in the case of *Procter & Gamble* the perceived existence of *potential* competition sufficed to undo the merger.

III. The New Learning about Mergers

Although objections were raised by economists to particular cases (e.g., Nicholls, 1949; Adelman, 1959a,b), the thinking among industrial organization economists seemed in broad congruence with the intensification of antitrust enforcement after World War II. In their influential *Antitrust Policy* (1959, p. 133), for example, Carl Kaysen and Donald Turner placed great emphasis on the maintenance of competitive market structures, and recommended treating any horizontal merger involving competitors with a combined market share of 20 percent or more as prima facie illegal. Acquisitions involving substantial commerce between two vertically related firms would also be prima facie illegal, if one firm had at least 20 percent of the market. But, as the 1960s wore on, and the Supreme Court continued to endorse ever bolder attempts by the government to extend the reach of the antitrust laws, dissent by economists began to grow. Responding to Justice Douglas' dismissal in

[4] See discussion of effects of mergers and determinants of concentration in Scherer and Ross (1990, Chs. 4 and 5).

Procter & Gamble of "[p]ossible economies . . . as a defense to illegality" as defined by Section 7, Oliver Williamson (1968) advocated a welfare-trade-off approach to mergers. Instead of focusing exclusively on the anticompetitive effects of mergers, the courts were to weigh the anticompetitive effects of mergers against their efficiency gains. Williamson presented some calculations to suggest that even modest cost reductions from mergers would be likely to outweigh any accompanying increases in market power.

Where Williamson recommended a trade-off of possible efficiency gains against monopoly welfare losses from mergers, others stepped forward to argue that there were only efficiency gains to be expected from the kinds of diversification mergers that became popular in the 1960s, and that these were of a type heretofore not understood or appreciated. Manne (1965) hypothesized the existence of a "market for corporate control" in which mergers served the purpose of removing incompetent managers or those who might seek to pursue goals that conflicted with efficiency and profit maximization. Lintner (1971) employed the newly invented CAPM to show how conglomerate mergers would help shareholders spread risks, and achieve other financial market efficiencies. Both Williamson (1970) and Weston (1970) saw conglomerate mergers as creating "internal capital" markets that would allow giant diversified companies to reallocate capital more efficiently than external capital markets did.

These claims of efficiency gains from mergers were often supported with empirical evidence. Weston and Mansinghka (1971) interpreted the increases in profit rates of the conglomerates in the 1960s from significantly below that of the average firm to equality with it, as proof that the conglomerates had successfully followed a policy of "defensive diversification". The early event studies of the 1970s found that acquired firm shareholders made significant gains in mergers, while acquiring firm shareholders did not lose. This finding was often interpreted as confirming Manne's corporate control hypothesis. Acquiring firms were trapped in a bidding war to replace the incompetent managers of the target firms, with the result being that the bulk of the gains went to the target stockholders (Mandelker, 1974; Dodd and Ruback, 1977; Brozen, 1982; Jensen and Ruback, 1983).

IV. Antimerger Policy Since 1973

During the 1970s, a shift to more lax standards of antitrust enforcement can be seen in both the decisions handed down by the courts, and in the criteria adopted by the Department of Justice and the Federal Trade Commission for prosecuting cases.

1. The Courts

Chief Justice Earl Warren, and Justices William O. Douglas and Hugo Black formed the liberal core of the "Warren Court" not only on matters of individual rights and other social questions, but also in the area of antitrust. As they left the bench and were replaced by the Nixon appointees, the philosophy of the court on antitrust issues changed. One cannot pinpoint an exact moment when this change took place, and so I have somewhat arbitrarily settled on the year 1973, since a shift is apparent between the *Falstaff Brewing* decision in 1973 blocking Falstaff's acquisition of Narragansett, and the 1974 decision to allow General Dynamics to acquire United Electric Coal Companies. *Falstaff* was written by Justice White with Justices Rehnquist and Stewart in dissent, *General Dynamics* by Stewart with White, Brennan, Douglas and Marshall in dissent. In *Falstaff* the Court blocked a merger by the large, national brewer Falstaff of Narragansett, a regional brewer with a large (20%) market share in New England. It did so, despite the apparent fact that Falstaff did not contemplate *de novo* entry into the New England market, because in the words of Justice White's majority opinion, "given [Falstaff's] financial capabilities and conditions in the New England market, it would be reasonable to consider it a potential entrant into that market" (Stelzer, 1986, p. 313).

Justice Stewart, who had dissented in *Falstaff* as he had in *Von's Grocery* and so many antitrust cases prior to 1974, would finally in *General Dynamics* get to write the decision for the majority. The liberal quartet of Brennan, Douglas, Marshall and White would, for the first time, be joined in dissent from the outcome of a major merger case. Toward the middle of the 1970s, the dissenting opinions on antitrust matters of the sixties became those of a majority of the court.

The same four would no doubt have been again united in dissent in *Marine Bancorporation* decided in the same year, except that William O. Douglas did not participate in the decision. Justice White wrote the dissenting opinion for the remaining three, in which he complained that the Court's majority

> erects formidable barriers to the application of the potential-competition doctrine not only in the banking business but in other lines of commerce. To show that the potential entrant, waiting in the wings, is exercising a present influence on the market, or that its loss as a *de novo* or toehold entrant may be a substantial injury to competition, it will not be enough to prove ability and willingness to enter, along with the probability, or even certainty, of entry. Nor will it suffice to prove that the potential or actual entrant would be a profitable concern and successfully prevent the major figures in the market from increasing their market shares. The courts must also examine conditions in the market and conclude for themselves that there is a realistic expectation that the new entrant will appropriate for itself a substantial part of the business of the major competitors in the market (Stelzer, 1986, pp. 337–338; footnote omitted).

The shift in thinking at the FTC is apparent as early as 1975 in the Commission's decision in Budd. Budd, a large manufacturer of auto parts, including bodies, and railroad and transit cars was an obvious, potential entrant into the manufacture of truck trailers and containers. Gindy's market shares in these markets fluctuated between 4 and 8 percent. Commissioner Engman, an appointee of Richard Nixon, wrote the opinion for the Commission allowing the merger on the grounds that Gindy was sufficiently small for the merger to qualify as a "toehold entry." Commissioner Paul Rand Dixon, a long time member of the FTC's liberal majority, was left to argue in dissent that it was not.

Yet another example of the radical change in judicial thinking about mergers is presented by the 2d Circuit Court of Appeals 1984 decision in *Waste Management and EMW Ventures*. Where Falstaff would be prevented from acquiring Narragansett in 1973 on the grounds that Falstaff was a potential entrant into Narragansett's market, the *Falstaff* decision would now be used to *allow* Waste Management to acquire EMW despite combined market shares of nearly 50 percent, which exceeded the *prima facie* threshold for blocking a merger set down in *Philadelphia National Bank* (1963). The merger was allowed, because the court argued that *Falstaff* obliged it to take into consideration conditions of potential entry, and when it did the merger had no anticompetitive effects.

2. The Antitrust Authorities

The *Von's Grocery* decision induced an agitated response in both the business community and in parts of the academic community. If two firms with a combined market share of 7.5% in a market with low entry barriers would not be allowed to merge, what firms could? In response to this hue and cry the Department of Justice for the first time in the 78 years since the passage of the Sherman Act issued a set of Merger Guidelines, which defined the criteria it would follow when deciding whether or not to challenge a proposed merger. They set forth tough standards with heavy emphasis on the structure of the markets involved. For example, in a highly concentrated market ($C_4 \geq 0.75$) a firm with a market share of 4% or more would in general be challenged, if it sought to acquire another firm with a market share of 4% or more in the same market. The market shares in *Von's Grocery* would constitute the lower bounds to antitrust enforcement, but only just barely.[5]

Although Richard Nixon's appointees to the bench and the Federal Trade Commission had noticeably different philosophies on antitrust and other matters than the majority of the "Warren Court", the staff appointees to the antitrust division and the FTC did not differ noticeably in ideology or competence from their predecessors. While there were no *Von's Grocery* cases brought under the Nixon and Carter Administrations, the 1968 Merger Guidelines appear to have remained in force until Ronald Reagan's election.

The thinking of the incoming Reagan Administration on antitrust matters was quite different than that of the outgoing Johnson Administration. To clarify just

[5] Indeed, because the C_4 in food retailing was undoubtedly less than 0.75, the market shares of Von's and its would-be merger partner Shopping Bag fell below the Guidelines' thresholds. One of the other factors, the Guidelines stated would be considered, was whether concentration had been increasing in the market. This was true in the food retailing market of Los Angeles, and figured in the Supreme Court's decision. If given enough weight it could justify suit even under the 1968 Guidelines.

exactly what that thinking was it announced a new set of Merger Guidelines in 1982. These Guidelines introduced many additional criteria for judging the anticompetitive effects of mergers, criteria that by and large reduced the likelihood of a challenge. Most conspicuously, they raised the threshold concentration levels. For example, where the 1968 Guidelines set no lower bounds to market concentration as criteria for initiating a challenge, the 1982 Guidelines stated that no horizontal mergers would be challenged in markets with a Herfindahl index of less than 1000, roughly the equivalent of a $C_4 < 0.4$, which is just under the average C_4 for 4-digit SICs in U.S. manufacturing. There would be no *Von's Grocery* or *Brown Shoe* under the Reagan Administration.

In 1984 the Department of Justice issued yet another set of Merger Guidelines, largely intended to clear up some ambiguities in the 1982 Guidelines. The 1984 Guidelines did have one radical departure from their predecessors, however, in the form of an efficiencies defense. Where a merger was expected to result in large economic efficiencies that would clearly outweigh its (nonzero) anticompetitive effects, the merger would go unchallenged. Oliver Williamson's (1968) welfare trade-off approach to mergers was to become governmental practice.

This addition to the Guidelines was a radical departure in that the Supreme Court had on several occasions explicitly rejected the suggestion that efficiency gains could offset anticompetitive losses. "Possible economies cannot be used as a defense to illegality. Congress was aware that some mergers which lessen competition may also result in economies but it struck the balance in favor of protecting competition". Congress had 27 years since William O. Douglas wrote these words in *Procter & Gamble* to correct them, if it favored such a trade-off. That it had not chosen to do so, suggests tacit agreement with Douglas's interpretation. Since no Court had overruled Douglas on this issue, one must assume that the law of the land in 1984, as in 1967, was that possible anticompetitive effects, and only possible anticompetitive effects are determinate on whether or not a merger should be allowed. The Merger Guidelines of 1984 proposed to establish by executive fiat what neither Congress by legislation nor the Supreme Court by judicial interpretation had deemed to bring about.

To what extent the Reagan Administration actually weighed possible efficiency gains against anticompetitive effects in deciding what mergers to challenge cannot be discerned. What is evident is that mergers were proposed and consummated during the Reagan years that companies never would have contemplated proposing under the six previous administrations (e.g., General Electric's acquisition of electronics giant RCA; Standard Oil of California's acquisition of Gulf Oil; Philip Morris's acquisitions of *both* food giants Kraft and General Foods). In many cases, mergers which violated the Merger Guidelines, and presumably could have been prevented using Section 7, were allowed after allowing the merging companies to spin-off the "offending assets" that indicated a likely Section 7 violation (e.g., Texaco's 1984 acquisition of Getty). This accommodating attitude toward mergers was in stark contrast to previous governmental policy on mergers where, as in *Brown*

Shoe, high concentration figures in a couple of cities in which Brown and Kinney operated were used as part of the justification for blocking the entire merger.[6]

In addition to assisting companies to find ways to get around Section 7, when a proposed merger appeared to violate the statute, the Reagan Administration on occasion simply turned its back on several mergers that clearly violated its Merger Guidelines, and could without question have been successfully prosecuted. Notable examples here, include LTV's acquisition of Republic Steel in 1984, and Ralston Purina's acquisition of the Drake division of Bordens. That the latter *could* have been successfully stopped is revealed by the fact that it *was*, as a private suit (*Tasty Baking Co. and Tastykake v. Ralston Purina and Continental Baking*, 1987). [7]

In 1992 the outgoing Bush Administration annunciated still another set of Merger Guidelines. These altered the provisions of the 1982/4 Guidelines only as they apply to horizontal mergers. They did not change the concentration thresholds that would precipitate a challenge, nor did they drop the efficiency defense. Instead, they enumerated the many factors related to market definition and structure and business conduct, which the antitrust authorities would consider beyond concentration and efficiency, before challenging a merger. As of December 1996, these Guidelines purportedly continue to inform the U.S. Government's antitrust policy in the area of mergers

V. Critique

United States antitrust policy and its enforcement is based on the presumption that all forms of competition are price competition, and all firms maximize profits. In an environment that was so ruthlessly competitive that no firm could survive, if it did not slavishly pursue profits, the profits maximization assumption would hold of necessity (Alchian, 1950). But the persistently above normal profits that many U.S. firms earn decade after decade belies the assumption that these companies are subject to sufficiently Darwinian pressures to eliminate all excess profits (Mueller, 1986, 1990). Many managers have the discretion to pursue goals other than the single-minded maximization of their companies' profits. Foremost among these appears to be the growth in size of their firms (Marris, 1964). Mergers are the fastest way to grow and diversify, and one expects growth-oriented managers to

[6] Mobil and Marathon Oil's market shares in parts of the Midwest were high enough to constitute a Section 7 violation in the eyes of the District Court in Cleveland. Mobil proposed spinning off some assets in the markets in question, a la Texaco/Getty, but the district court refused to allow this option. Mobil appealed to Washington, and the FTC gave its blessing (Scherer, 1993). Although the merger did not take place, because USS (the former United States Steel, and current USX) stepped in "to rescue" Marathon, this case is interesting because it reveals that the Reagan Administration failed to challenge many mergers that the courts probably would have blocked if given a chance.

[7] The market shares of Drake and Continental's Hostess brand were so clearly above the Merger Guidelines in some of the highly concentrated eastern, metropolitan areas that one can only wonder, as with Mobil and Marathon discussed in the previous footnote, why it was left for private parties to file suit (Breit and Elzinga, 1989, pp. 178–179).

resort to them, unless their opportunities for internal expansion are exceptional (Mueller, 1969, 1972).

The pattern of merger activity in the United States and the United Kingdom over the past century is inconsistent with the hypothesis that mergers are primarily intended to increase efficiency. In both countries merger activity has been strongly correlated with stock market upswings (Nelson, 1959; Melicher et al., 1983; Geroski, 1984). In a Darwinian environment, the pressure to cut costs should be strongest during an economic downturn, when competition intensifies and prices fall. Yet the sharp drop in share prices that anticipates economic downturns inevitably is accompanied by an even more dramatic decline in merger activity.

The constraint on managers, who pursue growth at the expense of shareholder wealth, is the threat of takeover. This threat is likely to be lowest, when share prices are high. The bulk of mergers occur when stock prices are high and rising, and as we shall see below, acquiring firms tend to outperform the market prior to making their acquisitions. Since strong share performance generally signals higher than normal profits, managers of acquiring firms are likely to have both the resources and the sense of security from takeover to make them willing to undertake acquisitions with dubious prospects.[8]

On a more micro level, if some managers pursue growth rather than profits through mergers, then one might expect to find no or even an inverse relationship between mergers and changes in profitability, and that is what one observes.[9] I have reviewed this literature on several occasions (1977, 1987, 1988, 1992, and 1995), and shall not take space for an exhaustive review here. Very briefly the findings have been as follows:

A. *The Effects of Mergers on Profitability*

The proper way to measure the effects of mergers on profitability is to compute the weighted average profit rate of the merging firms *before* the merger and compare it to the profit rate of the merged company *after* the merger. Since economic conditions may differ after the merger from those that held before in a way that affects the profitability of the merged units, one should also control for this factor by comparing the change in profits of the merged firms with a control group of

[8] The correlation of merger activity and stock market prices is consistent with other hypotheses, e.g., the pursuit of promoters' profits (Markham, 1955), or the exercising of managerial hubris (Roll, 1986). Both of these explanations for mergers are also consistent, however, with the mergers not leading to efficiency gains.

[9] If some mergers increase profits, and others are for growth alone, then a random sample of mergers will contain some made to and presumably which do increase profits, and others which do not. Whether the net relationship between profits changes and mergers is positive, zero, or negative will depend on the mix of the two types of mergers in the sample. Different random samples will contain different mixes, and one should not be surprised to find all three kinds of results. A finding that mergers *significantly* increase or decrease profitability cannot be used to infer that *all* mergers are consummated with one or the other objective in mind. All that one can conclude is that the preponderance of mergers in this particular sample appear to be of this or that type.

Table I. The effects of mergers on profitability

Country	Authors	Time period	Merger sample	Control group	Profitability measure	Profit change relative to control group
United States	Piper and Weiss, 1974	1947–67	102 acquisitions by 30 bank holding companies	None	After-tax earnings per share	≈0
	Conn, 1976	1964–70	28 firms acquired by 4 conglomerates	Base industry acquired firm	After-tax profit/total assets	≤0
	Mueller, 1980b	1962–72	247 manufacturing mergers	Base industries; merging firms, size and industry matched firms	Before-tax profit/assets	≤0
			280 manufacturing firms		After-tax profit/assets	≥0
	Mueller, 1986	1950–72	Merger activity 551 manufacturing firms	Companies in 551 making no acquisitions	After-tax profit/total assets	≤0
	Rhoades, 1987	1968–78	413 acquired banks	3600 non-acquired banks	After-tax profit/assets	≈0
	Ravenscraft and Scherer, 1987	1950–77	5966 acquired manufacturing (lines of business)	Base industry (line of business)	Before-tax profit/total assets	<0
	Healy et al., 1992	1979–84	50 largest mergers	Base industries	Before-tax cash-flow assets	>0
United Kingdom	Singh, 1971	1955–60	77 horizontal mergers	None	Before-tax profit/assets	≈0
					After-tax profit/assets	≈0
	Meeks, 1977	1950–71	1000+ mergers	Base industries	After-tax profit/assets	<0
	Cosh et al., 1980	1967–70	225 manufacturing mergers	Size and industry matched firms	After-tax profit/assets	≥0
					Before-tax profit/assets	
	Kumar, 1985	1967–74	241 mergers	Base industries	After-tax profit/assets	≤0
	Cosh et al., 1985	1972–76	66 mergers	Base industries	After-tax profit-assets	≈0

Table I. Continued

Country	Authors	Time period	Merger sample	Control group	Profitability measure	Profit change relative to control group
Australia	McDougall and Round, 1986	1970–81	88 takeovers	Size and industry matched firms	Before-tax profit/assets	≈0
					After-tax profit/assets	
Belgium	Kumps and Wtterwulghe, 1980	1962–74	21 mergers	Size and industry matched non-merging firms	After-tax profit-assets	≈0
Canada	Baldwin, 1991	1970–79	1575 acquired plants	Nonacquired plants in same industry	Value-added per worker/shipments	≥0
France	Jenny and Weber, 1980	1962–72	40 mergers	Size and industry matched non-merging firms	After-tax profit/assets	≈0
Germany	Cable et al., 1980	1964–74	50 mergers	Size and industry matched non-merging firms	After-tax profit/assets	≈0
Japan	Ikeda and Doi, 1983	1964–75	49 mergers	None	Before-tax profit/assets	>0
The Netherlands	Peer, 1980	1962–73	31 mergers	Size and industry matched non-merging firms	After-tax profit/assets	<0
Sweden	Ryden and Edberg, 1980	1962–76	26 mergers	Size and industry matched non-merging firms	After-tax profit/assets	≈0
				Base industry		≤0

otherwise similar nonmerging firms, or the industry averages of the merging firms (Hughes et al., 1980). Table I summarizes the results from 20 studies drawn from 10 countries over the post-World War II period that generally follow this methodology (a few omit the control groups, or focus on the profitability of only one part of the merging pair).

The most reliable conclusions can be drawn for the United States and the United Kingdom, since there are more studies for these countries and larger sample sizes. Only two studies for the United States found any increase in profits for merging firms, I found an increase in after-tax profits for mergers between 1962 and 1972, but for essentially the same sample of companies, *before*-tax profits fell following the mergers relative to changes in the merging firms' home industries (1980b). Since both market power and efficiency changes should affect before-tax profitability, I concluded that these mergers did not increase both, and at least one probably fell. Healy et al. (1992) found a significant increase in the pre-tax cash flows of the companies involved in the 50 largest mergers between 1979 and 1984 implying that the largest mergers in the U.S. during the early 1980s did increase either the market power or the efficiency of the merging firms.

The most ambitious of all of the studies in terms of sample size, time span, and care in handling the data was that of Ravenscraft and Scherer (1987). They concluded unequivocally that the profitability of acquired firms declined after they were acquired.

The largest study of mergers in the U.K. reached the same conclusion (Meeks, 1977). One study observed profit increases following mergers (Cosh et al., 1980), but the preponderance of evidence for the U.K. as for the U.S. points toward no increase and probably some decline in the profitability of merging firms after they merge.

No distinct pattern emerges in the studies from other countries. Profit increases were observed in Canada (Baldwin, 1991) and Japan (Ikeda and Doi, 1983), profit decreases in Holland (Peer, 1980) and Sweden (Ryden and Edberg, 1980). In all other countries the differences were statistically insignificant. But even if one ignores formal statistical tests and looks just at the pattern of changes, it is difficult to draw a firm conclusion that mergers have *increased* profitability. Where mergers seem to result in increases in one country (e.g., Germany), they result in declines in another (e.g., France).

B. *Effects of Mergers on Market Share, Growth, and Productivity*

A merger that increases one or both joining companies' efficiency should lower the price of their products and lead to an expansion in their output over what would otherwise be expected. Market power increases, in turn, should result in higher prices and reduced outputs. Thus, one can test whether a merger has increased efficiency or market power by testing whether output expands by more or less than one would expect if the two firms had not joined (Hughes et al., 1980; Mueller, 1980a, Ch. 9).

A comparison of market shares before and after a merger controls for changes in economic conditions by using all other firms in the industry as a control group.

Three studies of the effects of mergers on market shares exist. Goldberg (1973) observed insignificant changes in market shares for a sample of 44 advertising intensive firms over an average of 3-1/2 years following the merger. Mueller (1985, 1986, Ch. 9) observed significant declines in market shares for a sample of 209 manufacturing companies over an average of 11 years following the mergers. Baldwin and Gorecki (1990) find significant declines in market shares for plants acquired in horizontal mergers, but no significant changes for plants acquired in other sorts of mergers, and conclude that the results are consistent with the mergers having increased market power. The declines in market share I observed were for both horizontal and nonhorizontal mergers, however, and were too large even for the former to be attributable to the rational exercise of market power. Thus, none of the studies presents evidence that mergers increased efficiency, one implied a significant reduction in efficiency perhaps coupled with an increase in market power, and the third suggested a possible increase in market power. The conclusion that market power had increased and social welfare declined as a result of the Reagan Administration's lax policy toward horizontal mergers was also reached by Stewart and Kim (1993).

No evidence that mergers increase efficiency has been found by examining changes in the growth rates of merging firms using either their industries or matched nonmerging firms as control groups. No significant change in growth rates was observed in studies of Australia (McDougall and Round, 1986, pp. 157–159], Belgium (Kumps and Wtterwulghe, 1980), France (Jenny and Weber, 1980), Germany (Cable et al., 1980), Sweden (Ryden and Edberg, 1980), the United Kingdom (Cosh et al., 1980), and acquired banks in the United States (Rhoades, 1987). Mergers in Holland (Peer, 1980) and the United States (Mueller, 1980b) were followed by significant declines in the growth rates of merging companies.

Both Caves and Barton (1990) and Lichtenberg (1992) have estimated plant productivity to be significantly lower for more diversified firms. This finding is consistent with the results summarized so far suggesting that diversification mergers in the United States have lowered the efficiency of the acquired companies. Lichtenberg and Siegel (1987) challenge the latter conclusion, however, with evidence that changes in plant ownership between 1972 and 1981 were preceded by declines in productivity and followed by increases in productivity. They claim that their evidence indicates that mergers in the 1970s were fundamentally different from those in the 1960s.

They do not distinguish, however, between changes in ownership resulting from a spinoff of part of a continuing firm, and those resulting from the acquisition of an entire firm. The findings of negative effects on efficiency from mergers are based largely on analyses of mergers in the 1950s, 1960s, and early 1970s. Consistent with this view, a large "wave" of spinoffs was observed in the 1970s. Ravenscraft and Scherer (1987, Chs. 5, 6) document that spun off units were performing badly at the time of their sale, and had declining performance leading up to it – the same pattern reported by Lichtenberg and Siegel. What is not apparent is whether the improvements in productivity Lichtenberg and Siegel observed occurred for plants involved in complete mergers and in spinoffs, or just for the latter. If they did apply to full mergers, one would expect the acquired firms to be performing badly, but this generally has not been the case.

C. *The Effects of Mergers on Share Prices*

A large literature estimates the anticipated effects of mergers by examining the changes in stock prices occurring on and around their announcement. Table II summarizes the main findings of 35 studies from different countries and time periods listing their control groups in each case. The returns reported are always presented relative to that of the control group.

In virtually every merger the buyer offers a premium for the acquired company's shares to induce its owners to sell. In the late 1960s these were running at between 15 and 25 percent of the premerger market value of the acquired firm, in the 1980s these rose to between 50 and 100 percent. The acquired firm's share prices rise to reflect these premia. On average mergers are consummated six months after announced. Thus, in a matter of a few months, shareholders of acquired firms earn returns substantially *above* what otherwise would be expected. The median gain to acquired firm shareholders in the studies of Table II, a group heavily weighted toward the mergers in the 1960s, was 20.6 percent.

The dramatic rise in acquired firm share prices occurring at or a month or two before their announcement allows us to identify that short interval as the time when the "market" learns of the mergers. The impact this information has on acquiring company share prices is of conflicting signs, and often statistically insignificant. The median gain to acquiring firm shareholders around the announcement date is 0.001.

This lack of positive response by the market to the announcement that a firm plans to acquire another stands in stark contrast to the performance of the acquiring firms' shares *prior* to the announcement. In 15 of the 16 studies that examined acquiring firm share performance for at least 12 months before the merger announcement, positive cumulative returns were recorded. These run-ups begin as far as 5 or 6 years before the mergers occur, and cumulate to as much as 57 percent more than that of the control group. The median cumulative abnormal gain prior to merger announcements is +13.35 percent.

In stark contrast to the premerger period, acquiring firms are generally found to earn returns substantially *below* the market portfolio, or other control groups over the post-merger period. Of the 26 estimates of returns to acquiring company shareholders for at least 6 months after the announcement, the typical interval between announcement and consummation of a merger in the United States, 19 are negative with a median value of −7.2 percent for all 26.

Thus, the typical pattern of share returns for acquiring companies is as follows: Starting anywhere from two to five years prior to undertaking a merger the acquiring

Table II. Returns to acquiring and acquired firm's shareholders, post-merger returns

Study	Time period (country)	Returns prior to merger announcement acquiring firms	Returns in announcement day (d), month (m), year (y) acquiring firm	Post-merger returns in days (d), months (m), years (y) after merger, acquiring firms	Acquired firms' returns	Sample	Control group
Hogarty, 1970	1953–64 (U.S.A.)			−0.05 (y varies from 1 to 11)		43 nonconglomerates engaged in heavy merger activity	Firms in acquiring company's base industry
Lev and Mandelker, 1972	1952–63 (U.S.A.)	0.135[b] (y = −5, −1)	0.083 (y = 0)	0.056 (y = 1, 5)		69 firms making large acqui-sitions	Nonmerging firms matched by industry and size
Halpern, 1973	1950–65 (U.S.A.)		0.063 (m = −7, 0)[c]		0.304 (m = −7, 0)[c]	78 mergers by nonconglomerates	Market portfolio
Mandelker, 1974	1941–63 (U.S.A.)	0.048[b] (m = −34, −1)	0.003[b] (m = 0, 6)	−0.015[b] (m = 7, 46)	0.120*	241 large mergers	Market portfolio
Ellert, 1976	1950–72 (U.S.A.)	0.233* (m = −100, −1)[c]	−0.018[d]	−0.016 (m = 1, 48)		205 mergers challenged by Justice Dept. or FTC between 1950 and 1972	Market portfolio
Franks et al., 1977	1955–72 (U.K.)	−0.048 (m = −40, −1)	0.001 (m = 0)	−0.014 (m = 1, 2)	0.179 distillenes	70 mergers by brewers and	CAPM (m = −29, +8)

(continued overleaf)

Dodd and Ruback, 1977	1958–78 (U.S.A.)	0.117* (m = −60, −1)	0.028 (m = 0)	−0.059[b] (m = 1, 60)	0.206*	136 tender offers	CAPM (m = −72, −13) (m = +13, +72) (m = +13, +72)
Kummer and Hoffmeister, 1978	1956–74 (U.S.A.)	0.170[b] (m = −40, −1)	0.052[b] (m = 0)	0.006[b] (m = 1, 20)	0.187*	88 cash tender offers	Market portfolio
Langetieg, 1978	1929–69 (U.S.A.)	0.136* (m = −64, −1)	−0.028 (m = 0, 5)	−0.262 (m = 7, 78)	0.128*	149 mergers of all kinds	Market portfolio and industry index
Bradley, 1980	1962–77 (U.S.A.)		0.04* (d = 0, 5)	0.01[b] (d = 6, 40)	0.36* − 0.49*	161 tender offers	Market portfolio
Dodd, 1980	1971–77 (U.S.A.)		−0.011 (d = −1, 0)	−0.072* (d = −10, 140)[f]	0.340*	71 mergers	Market portfolio
Kumps and Wtterwulghe, 1980	1962–74 (Belgium)		−0.047 (y = 0)	−0.014 (y = 1, 3)		26 mergers of all kinds	26 nonmerging firms matched by industry
Jenny and Weber, 1980	1962–72 (France)		0.116* (y = 0)	−0.095[b] (y = 1, 3)		43 mergers of all kinds	43 nonmerging firms matched by size and industry
Ryden and Edberg, 1980	1962–76 (Sweden)		−0.040 (y = 0)	0.011[b] (y = 1, 3)		23 mergers of all kinds	23 nonmerging firms
Cosh et al., 1980	1957–69 (U.K.)	0.069* (y = −5, 1)	0.187* (y = 1)	−0.169 (y = 1, 5)		63 mergers of all kinds	63 nonmerging firms matched by size and industry

Table II. Continued

Study	Time period (country)	Returns prior to merger announcement acquiring firms	Returns in announcement day (d), month (m), year (y) acquiring firm	Post-merger returns in days (d), months (m), years (y) after merger acquiring firms	Acquired firms' returns	Sample	Control group
Mueller, 1980b	1962–72 (U.S.A.)		0.088* (y = 0)	−0.084[b] (y=1, 3)		219 mergers of all kinds	219 nonmerging firms matched by size and industry
Firth, 1980	1969–75 (U.K.)	0.014[b] (m = 48, −1)	−0.063 (m = 0)	0.001[b] (m = 1, 36)	0.363	434 mergers of all kinds	CAPM (m = −48, −13) (m = +13, +36)
Asquith, 1983	1962–72 (U.S.A.)	0.132[b] (d = −480, −1)	0.002 (m = 0)	−0.072* (d = 1, 240)	*0.133*	196 mergers of all kinds	Market portfolio
Asquith et al., 1983	1963–79 (U.S.A.)		0.028* (m = 0)		0.175*	214 early mergers by firms beginning merger programs after 1963	Market portfolio
Bradley et al., 1983	1962–80* (U.S.A.)		0.024* (m = 0)		0.318*	161 successful tender offers	Market portfolio
Malatesta, 1983	1969–74 (U.S.A.)	0.043* (m = −60, −1)	0.009 (m = 0)	−0.079* (m = 1, 12)	0.168*	256 mergers of all kinds (m = 13, 60)	CAPM (m = −62, −13)
Dodds and Quek, 1985	1974–76 (U.K.)		−0.0002 (m = 0)	−0.068 (m = 1, 60)	70 mergers of	Market portfolio all kinds	

(*continued overleaf*)

Eckbo, 1986	1964–83 (Canada)	0.031* (m = −12, −1)	0.012* (m = 0)	0.006* (m = 1, 12)	0.100*	413 targets of all kinds 1683 bidders	CAPM (m = −72, −13) (m = −72, −13) (m = +13, +72)
Varaiya, 1986	1975–83 (U.S.A.)		0.036* (d = −20, 0)	0.008 (d = 1, 100)	0.411	80 mergers and takeovers	CAPM (t = −300, −61)
Magenheim and Mueller, 1988	1976–81 (U.S.A.)	0.184* (m = −24, −4)	−0.003 (m = 0)	−0.422 (m = −3, 36)		78 mergers of all kinds	CAPM (m = −60, −25) (m = −36, −4) (m = −36, −4)
Borg et al., 1989	1919–30 (U.S.A.)	0.169[b] (m = −60, −13)				134 mining and manufacturing mergers	Market portfolio
			−0.006 (m = 0)	−0.225 (m = 1, 36)			CAPM (m = −60, −13)
Franks and Harris, 1989	1955–85 (U.K.)	0.570[b] (m = −71, −12)	0.010* (m = 0)	0.045 (m = 1, 24)	0.297*	1814 targets 1048 bidders	Market portfolio
			0.005[b] (m = 0)	−0.126 (m = 1, 24)			CAPM (−71, −12)

Table II. Continued

Study	Time period (country)	Returns prior to merger announcement acquiring firms	Returns in announcement day (d), month (m), year (y) acquiring firm	Post-merger returns in days (d), months (m), years (y) after merger acquiring firms	Acquired firms' returns	Sample	Control group
Lang et al., 1989	1968–86 (U.S.A.)		−0.001 (d = −5, 5)9		0.416*	79 Tender offers	Market portfolio
Franks et al., 1991	1975–84 (U.S.A.)		−0.010 (d – 5, 5)[g]	−0.040 (m =1, 36)	0.280*	399 mergers	Eight portfolios
Salinger, 1992	1976–78 (U.S.A.)	−0.015 (m = −4, −1)	−0.026* (m = 0)	−0.159 (m = 1, 30)		40 mergers of all kinds	CAPM (−64, −5)
Agrawal et al., 1992	1955–84 (U.S.A.)			−0.103 (m = 1, 60)		1264 mergers and tender offers	Market portfolio
Kang, 1993	1975–88 (U.S.A. and Japan)		0.007 (d = −20, 20) 0.000 (d = −20, 20)		0.124* (d = −20, 20) 0.137* (d = −20, 20)	119 Japenese full or partial mergers 119 US mergers	Market portfolio
Leeth and Borg, 1994	1905–30 (U.S.A.)	0.330* (m = −60, −4)	−0.001 (m = 0)	−0.238* (m = 1, 36)		191 mining and manufacturing	Market portfolio

(*continued overleaf*)

Continued

Smith and Kim (1994)	1980–86 (USA)	0.007 (d = −60, −6)	−0.002* (d = −1, 0)	0.302* (d = −5, 5)	177 Takeover attempts	Market portfolio
Hubbard and Palia (1995)	1985-91 (USA)		−0.004* (d = −4, 4)		354 mergers	Market portfolio

Returns are measured between merging companies' returns and control group returns in all cases. In those studies in which the data were centered around the date of final consummation, the series were displaced backwards by 6 months to allow for the fact that announcements generally precede mergers by 6 months.

* Statistically significant at the 0.05 level or better.

[a] Market portfolio implies the predicted performance given a firm's β if it performed as the market portfolio performs. CAPM predicts firm i's returns using the α and β from $R_{it} - R_{ft} = \alpha_i + \beta_i(R_{mt} - R_{ft}) + \mu_{it}$. If only one time interval was used to estimate all residuals, only one is given. When 3 are given, the residuals prior to announcement are estimated from CAPM estimated over the first interval, the announcement residual from the second interval, and the post-announcement from the third.

[b] Reported data do not allow calculation of statistical significance.

[c] Month 0 in the Ellert study is the month in which a complaint is filed.

[d] Announcement of merger in Ellert study is measured as period from judicial complaint through settlement.

[e] Halpern's figures for acquiring firms are for largest of two companies involved in a merger. Acquired firms' figures are for the smallest of the two merging firms.

[f] Dodd reports figure for 10 days before announcement until 10 days after merger is approved. Calculation based on assumption that there are on average 6 months (26 weeks times 5 working days) between a merger's announcement and its approval.

[g] Returns at announcement measured from 5 days before first bid to 5 days after last bid.

firm begins to outperform the market. Since it is inconceivable that the market is *reacting* to the effects of a merger several years down the road, one must assume that any causal linkage between these events runs from outperforming the market to undertaking an acquisition. It is reasonable to assume that growth-oriented managers would choose to undertake unprofitable acquisitions more often when their company's profits are abnormally high and their shareholders have enjoyed substantial above market returns. The announcements of mergers, on the other hand, result in quite a mixed pattern of return estimates with the safest conclusion perhaps being "that for the stockholders of the acquiring firms, 'news' of an acquisition may not be worthwhile news" (Mandelker, 1974, p. 321). In the months that follow the shareholders of acquiring firms suffer relative declines in the returns on their shares, declines that continue in some cases for several years after the merger.

The acid test of whether mergers create or destroy wealth is to add up the gains and losses on both sides and see what the total is. Since gains are generally measured as a percentage of market value, the results of this calculation are not apparent from the figures reported in Table II. Acquiring firms are on average much larger than the companies that they acquire. In my 1980b study they were 10 times larger. With this difference in relative sizes the median gain of 0.206 for acquired firm shareholders is fully offset by a loss of only −0.021 for the acquiring firm shareholders. If we combine the gains to acquiring firm shareholders at the time of announcement with those over the post-announcement period, the median wealth decline for acquiring firm shareholders in the 26 studies that tracked post-acquisition performance for at least 6 months is −0.061. Only four studies calculate the *net* wealth change from mergers. Two find it to be slightly negative (Firth, 1980; Malatesta, 1983), two slightly positive (Halpern, 1973; Varaiya, 1986).

VI. Implications for Antimerger Policy

The economic logic underlying the traditional approach to antitrust is as simple and appealing as an introductory textbook's discussion of perfect competition. Firms maximize profits and compete by price. Consumers' surplus is maximized when competitors are prevented from colluding, from merging to increase market power, and from adopting other practices that might restrict competition or tend to create a monopoly.

The profit maximization assumption implies that any action a company undertakes can be expected to increase profits by either raising market power and price, or by increasing efficiency and lowering costs. If an action cannot be shown to increase market power, i.e., to have an anticompetitive effect, it is assumed to enhance efficiency.

The legal maxim that an individual is innocent until proven guilty has in antitrust cases placed upon the plaintiff, the burden of proof that an action has an anticompetitive effect. The courts have gone along with this one-sided focus.

Recent developments in economic thinking on antitrust matters have emphasized the potential efficiency gains from practices that may also have anticompetitive consequences. The inherent efficiency of dominant firms, transaction cost efficiency of vertical restraints, the potential efficiency from mergers, and even the potential efficiencies from cartel-like restrictions on prices and quantities have been emphasized by economists (e.g., Dewey, 1979; Bittlingmayer, 1982).[10] The result has been that potential efficiencies have been given sufficient weight to allow companies to adopt practices and undertake mergers that would have been prohibited in earlier times, if their potential anticompetitive effects alone had been weighed.

The recognition that some practices and actions, which potentially injure competition, also have the potential of improving economic efficiency, is not the only recent development in economics that is relevant for antitrust policy, however. The managerial discretion, principal/agent literature points out that managers have discretion to pursue goals other than profits maximization, and thus that every action of managers that does not have a direct anticompetitive effect need not result in an improvement in economic efficiency. The empirical findings on the effects of mergers imply that mergers are actions by managers that are likely to be efficiency reducing, even when they do not worsen competition.

If efficiency is to be put on an equal footing with market power in antitrust matters, an alternative approach to that employed in the United States until now is required. With respect to mergers such an approach might look like the following:

Section 1. That no corporation with a market share greater than 20 (5) percent in any one market shall acquire, directly or indirectly, the whole or any part of the stock or other share capital, or the assets of another corporation with a market share greater than 5 (20) percent in any other market, *unless* it can be demonstrated that such an acquisition is likely to yield substantial efficiency gains in excess of its anticompetitive effects. Penalty: suspension or dissolution of the merger.

Section 2. That no corporation with sales greater than $500,000,000 ($100,000,000) measured in 1997 dollars shall acquire, directly or indirectly, the whole or any part of the stock or other share capital, or the assets of another corporation with sales greater than $100,000,000 ($500,000,000) measured in 1997 dollars, *unless* it can be demonstrated that such an acquisition is likely to yield substantial efficiency gains in excess of its anticompetitive effects. Penalty: suspension or dissolution of the merger.

Section 3. The accounts of any firms, whose merger is subject to Sections 1 or 2, but are allowed to merge on the basis of the efficiency defense, must be reported separately for at least 10 years following the merger.

Section 1 picks up the 20 percent market share figure from Kaysen and Turner, and applies it to all forms of mergers in recognition that even diversification mergers can increase market power, as for example when they lead to high levels of multimarket contact, *and* the firms have substantial shares of some markets (Scott,

[10] Although I have focussed upon U.S. merger policy in this paper, a companion piece (Mueller, 1996) takes up the other aspects of antitrust policy.

1982, 1993). The second section diverts large firms away from using mergers as a means of growth. Section 3 would allow the antitrust authorities and capital markets to monitor a merger's success, thereby placing additional constraints on the acquiring firm's managers. The proposed cut-offs in Sections 1 and 2 are a bit arbitrary, but seem reasonable, given the possibility of an efficiency defense, if one wants a truly effective antimerger policy.

Two main objections can be made against the proposals: (1) their litigation costs would be excessive, and (2) they would interfere unduly with day-to-day managerial decisions.

With respect to the first objection, one must recognize that litigation costs have already risen dramatically in recent years. Where a merger would have been challenged a generation ago on the basis of a fairly straightforward analysis of the structure of the industry and the proposed merger's impact on that structure, today's Merger Guidelines require that the Department of Justice or the FTC undertake what amounts to a Sherman Act analysis of all relevant factors that might impact the vigor of competition in the market (*Guidelines*; Mueller, 1993). So elaborate is the list of factors that the *Guidelines* stipulate as relevant, that a pair of giant firms set upon merging could, no doubt, force whichever antitrust authority that tried to stop them into a protracted proceeding.

Indeed, so costly have antitrust proceedings become under present standards and interpretations, that the shift in burden of proof incorporated in the proposed statutes might actually *reduce* litigation costs.[11] Gone would be the *necessity* to prove a potential anticompetitive effect. If a firm seeking to make an acquisition that falls under the statute could not demonstrate a reasonable likelihood that the merger would result in substantial efficiency gains, the merger would not go forward even if it had no likely effect on competition. Heavy litigation might be expected in the first few years after such a set of statutes came into effect. Once precedents under the statutes had been established, however, the volume of litigation could be expected to taper off. Once the kinds of evidence the courts would accept to justify a merger became clear, firms could make reasoned judgments as to which mergers would pass muster. Claims of future efficiency gains might be substantiated using evidence from past mergers, a possibility facilitated by the proposed Section 3.

As far as interference with managerial decision making goes, one must recognize that mergers are not, or at least need not, be a part of the day-to-day decisions of the managers of large companies. Managers of small firms would not be affected at all, and managers of large ones would be free to invest and grow *internally* as they so chose. Normal business practice requires that managers renew worn out plant and equipment, invest in new product development and the like. It does not *require* them to buy up other firms. When there are substantial efficiency gains to be made from an acquisition, the proposed statutes would allow them to take place.

[11] Donald Dewey (1996) has recently suggested that an efficiencies defense would "greatly simplify" antimerger policy.

Presumably normal business practice includes the monitoring of the past success of major business decisions, like mergers. Section 3, therefore, would not require managers to do anything that they already would not be doing in terms of information gathering, it would only require that this information be shared with the general public.

VII. Institutional Changes

If a congress and president were willing to undertake a major reform in the antimerger statutes, they might also be willing to consider reforming the procedures by which they are administered. Antitrust cases often involve quite technical issues of fact. Under the adversarial system, both sides in a case have the incentive and usually the capacity to distort the facts to their advantage. One side always has an incentive to disguise the truth. The assumption that truth will nevertheless emerge out of this noncooperative game seems problematic for all forms of litigation, and especially so in antitrust matters. A reform that would both improve outcomes and significantly reduce costs of litigation would be to replace the adversarial system of litigation for antitrust matters with a form of the continental European inquisitorial system (Mueller, 1996).

Such a change would be particularly beneficial in dealing with mergers. Under the proposed legislation, an antitrust agency would need to monitor mergers to determine which mergers violated the market share or absolute size threshholds. Merging firms could challenge this determination, but this issue should not be a major component of most proceedings. Once it was decided that a pair of firms needed to provide an efficiency defense to justify merging, the next phase would be for the firms to provide evidence that the merger was likely to produce efficiency increases in excess of its social costs. If the firms' managers expect that the merger will increase efficiency, then this expectation presumably rests on some sort of objective evidence. The proposed legislation would impose the modest burden on the firms of requiring that they share this evidence with the judge. The judge might also ask the antitrust authorities to provide evidence of possible social costs from any anticompetitive effects expected from the merger, rather than relying entirely on the evidence presented by the merging companies.

The advantage of an inquisitorial-type procedure would be that the initiative for gathering the required information would rest with an impartial third party to the case, who could request additional evidence from each side, or call upon expert advice as she so chose. When she thought that she had enough information to reach the correct decision, she could announce her decision and close the case. Thus, in many cases the inquisatorial procedure even coupled with the proposed legislation, would probably greatly *reduce* litigation costs in comparison with an adversarial system in which giant firms, which can write-off litigation costs against their tax obligations, largely dictate the length of antitrust procedures.

The structure of the Federal Trade Commission is well-suited for the administration of the kind of antimerger policy envisaged here, and it would be the obvious location for it. Indeed, a similar idea may have been behind the FTC's creation. It could scruntize all mergers and inform those firms that are thought to be subject to the efficiency defense requirement. Its administrative law judges are specialists in antitrust matters, and under current practice have sole responsibility for the initial FTC decisions, i.e., there is no provision for a trial by jury within the FTC. The proposed procedures would differ from current practices only in so far as the more passive role of the administrative law judge under the adversarial procedures would be replaced by a more active, inquiring role. Both the FTC and the representatives of the companies seeking to merge would be limited after the initial presentation of the efficiencies defense to responding to the law judge's requests for information.

VII. Conclusions

Under present laws and practices, only a handful of the thousands of mergers occurring each year are prevented. Many of these mergers increase the efficiency of the merging companies, and those that do not are often harmless. A substantial proportion of those among the largest firms, however, actually reduce the efficiency of the merging firms destroying portions of their assets and their owners' wealth. If antitrust policy is to play a meaningful role in preventing mergers of this type, a rather radical departure from existing laws and practices regarding mergers is necessary. This paper has proposed such a departure.

Unlike in most other legal areas, or even for that matter in other areas of antitrust, at issue in a proposed merger is not whether the parties *have* broken a law, but whether they *will* break one. No previous actions need to be reversed, no damage needs to be undone. The question is only whether the proposed action is likely to damage social welfare in the future. Up until now this damage has been interpreted exclusively as coming about only through reductions in competition. But more than a 100 years of experience with mergers indicates that the main social cost of many mergers is the damage to the efficiency of the firms themselves brought about by their merging. To protect both competition and economic efficiency a new approach to mergers is required.

It is possible, judging from the available evidence on the effects of mergers, that the US economy would be as or even more efficient today, *if there had been no mergers over the last 50 years*. The proposals made here would prevent mergers that are unlikely to increase efficiency, while allowing those that have the best prospects for increasing efficiency. Both type 1 and type 2 errors would of course be made. But, if more mergers were blocked that would reduce efficiency and social welfare than those that would increase it, there would be a net increase in socal welfare. Having experimented with a lax policy toward mergers for the better part of more than a century now, it seems time for the country to try a more stringent policy. Failure to do so will result in one merger wave following upon another in the future as they have in the past with large *private* gains and losses ensuing, but with no measurable net benefits for society.

References

Adelman, Morris A. (1959a) *A&P: A Study in Price-Cost Behavior and Public Policy.* Cambridge: Harvard University Press.

Adelman, Morris A. (1959b) 'Economic Aspects of the Bethlehem Opinion', *Virginia Law Review*, **45**, 684–696.

Agrawal, Anup, Jeffrey F. Jaffe, and Gershon N. Mandelker (1992) 'The Post-Merger Performance of Acquiring Firms: A Re-examination of an Anomaly', *Journal of Finance*, **47**, 1605–21.

Alchian, Armen A. (1950) 'Uncertainty, Evolution, and Economic Theory', *Journal of Political Economy*, **58**, 211–221.

Asquith, Paul (1983) 'Merger Bids, Uncertainty, and Stockholder Returns', *Journal of Financial Economics*, **11**, 51–83.

Asquith, Paul, Robert F. Bruner, and David W. Mullins, Jr. (1983) 'The Gains to Bidding Firms from Merger', *Journal of Financial Economics*, **11**, 121–139.

Baldwin, John (1991) *The Dynamics of the Competitive Process*, mimeo, Queen's University.

Baldwin, John, and Paul Gorecki (1990) 'Mergers Placed in the Context of Firm Turnover', in Bureau of the Census, *1990 Annual Research Conference, Proceedings*. Washington, D.C.: U.S. Department of Commerce, pp. 53–73.

Bittlingmayer, George (1982) 'Decreasing Average Cost and Competition: A New Look at the Addyston Pipe Case', *Journal of Law and Economics*, **25**, 201–29.

Bittlingmayer, George (1985) 'Did Antitrust Policy Cause the Great Merger Wave?', *Journal of Law and Economics*, **28**, 77–118.

Borg, J. R., M. O. Borg, and J. D. Leeth (1989) 'The Success of Mergers in the 1920s: A Stock Market Appraisal of the Second Merger Wave', *International Journal of Industrial Organization* **7**, 117–31.

Bradley, Michael (1980) 'Interfirm Tender Offers and the Market for Corporate Control', *Journal of Business*, **53**, 345–376.

Bradley, Michael, Anand Desai, and E. Han Kim (1983) 'The Rationale Behind Interfirm Tender Offers: Information or Synergy?' *Journal of Financial Economics*, **11**, 183–206.

Breit, William and Kenneth G. Elzinga (1989) *The Antitrust Casebook*, 2nd ed. Forth Worth: Harcourt Brace Jovanovich.

Brozen, Yale (1982) *Concentration, Mergers, and Public Policy*. New York: MacMillan.

Cable, J. R., J. P. R. Palfrey, and J. W. Runge (1980) 'Federal Republic of Germany, 1964–1974', in D. C. Mueller, ed., *The Determinants and Effects of Mergers: An International Comarison.* Cambridge, Mass.: Oelgeschlager, Gunn & Hain, pp. 99-132.

Caves, Richard E., and David R. Barton (1990) *Efficiency in U.S. Manufacturing Industries*. Cambridge, Mass.: MIT Press.

Chandler, Alfred D., Jr. (1990) *Scale and Scope*. Cambridge: Harvard University Press.

Conn, R.L. (1976) 'The Failing Firm/Industry Doctrines in Conglomerate Mergers', *Journal of Economics*, **24**, 181–187.

Cosh, Andrew, Alan Hughes, and Ajit Singh (1980) 'The Causes and Effects of Takeovers in the United Kingdom: An Empirical Investigation for the Late 1960s at the Microeconomic Level', in D. C. Mueller, ed., *The Determinants and Effects of Mergers: An International Comparison.* Cambridge, Mass.: Oelgeschlager, Gunn & Hain, pp. 227–270.

Cosh, Andrew, Alan Hughes, M. S. Kumar, and Ajit Singh (1985) *Institutional Investment Company Performance and Mergers: Empirical Evidence for the UK*. London: Office of Fair Trading.

Department of Justice and Federal Trade Commission (1993) 'Horizontal Merger Guidelines', *Review of Industrial Organization*, **8**, 231–256.

Dewey, Donald F. (1979) 'Information, Entry and Welfare: The Case for Collusion', *American Economic Review*, **69**, 587–594.

Dewey, Donald F. (1996) 'Merger Policy Greatly Simplified: Building on Keyes', *Review of Industrial Organization*, **11**, 395–400.

Dodd, Peter (1980) 'Merger Proposals, Management Discretion and Stockholder Wealth', *Journal of Financial Economics*, **8**, 105–138.

Dodd, Peter, and Richard Ruback (1977) 'Tender Offers and Stockholder Returns: An Empirical Analysis', *Journal of Financial Economics*, **5**, 351–374.

Dodds, J. C., and J. P. Quek (1985) 'Effect of Mergers on the Share Price Movement of the Acquiring Firms: A UK Study', *Journal of Business Finance and Accounting*, **12**, 285–296.

Eckbo, B. E. (1986) 'Mergers and the Market for Corporate Control: The Canadian Evidence', *Canadian Journal of Economics*, **19**, 236–260.

Ellert, J. C. (1976) 'Mergers, Antitrust Law Enforcement and Stockholder Returns', *Journal of Finance*, **31**, 715–732.

Firth, Michael (1980) 'Takeovers, Shareholder Returns, and the Theory of the Firm', *Quarterly Journal of Economics*, **94**, 315–347.

Franks, J. R., J. E. Broyles, and M. J. Hecht (1977) 'An Industry Study of the Profitability of Mergers in the United Kingdom', *Journal of Finance*, **32**, 1513–1525.

Franks, Julian R., and Robert S. Harris (1989) 'Shareholder Wealth Effects of Corporate Takeovers', *Journal of Financial Economics*, **23**, 225–249.

Franks, Julian, Robert Harris, and Sheridan Titman (1991) 'The Postmerger Share-Price Performance of Acquiring Firms', *Journal of Financial Economics*, **29**, 81–96.

Geroski, Paul A. (1984) On the Relationship Between Aggregate Merger Activity and the Stock Market', *European Economic Review*, **25**, 223–233.

Golbe, Devra L., and Lawrence J. White (1993) 'Catch a Wave: The Time Series Behavior of Mergers', *Review of Economics and Statistics*, **75**, 493–499.

Goldberg, Lawrence G. (1973) 'The Effect of Conglomerate Mergers on Competition', *Journal of Law and Economics*, **16**, 137–158.

Halpern, Paul J. (1973) 'Empirical Estimates of the Amount and Distribution of Gains to Companies in Mergers', *Journal of Business*, **46**, 554–575.

Hannah, Leslie (1974) 'Mergers in British Manufacturing Industry, 1880–1918', *Oxford Economic Papers*, **26**, 1–17.

Healy, Paul M., Krishna G. Palepu, and Richard S. Ruback (1992) 'Does Corporate Performance Improve After Mergers?', *Journal of Financial Economics*, **31**, 135–175.

Hogarty, Thomas F. (1970) 'The Profitability of Corporate Mergers', *Journal of Business*, **43**, 317–327.

Hubbard, R. Glenn, and Darius Palia (1995) 'Benefits of Control, Managerial Ownership, and the Stock Returns of Acquiring Firms', *Rand Journal of Economics*, **26**(4), 782–792.

Hughes, Alan, Dennis C. Mueller, and Ajit Singh (1980a) 'Hypotheses About Mergers', in D. C. Mueller, ed., *The Determinants and Effects of Mergers: An International Comparison*. Cambridge, Mass.: Oelgeschlager, Gunn & Hain, pp. 27–66.

Ikeda, Katsuhiko and Noriyuki Doi (1983) 'The Performance of Merging Firms in Japanese Manufacturing Industry: 1964–75', *Journal of Industrial Economics*, **31**, 257–266.

Jenny, Frédéric and André-Paul Weber (1980) 'France, 1962–72', in D. C. Mueller, ed., *The Determinants and Effects of Mergers: An International Comparison*. Cambridge, Mass.: Oelgeschlager, Gunn & Hain, pp. 133–162.

Jensen, Michael C., and Richard S. Ruback (1983) 'The Market for Corporate Control', *Journal of Financial Economics*, **11**, 5–50.

Kang, Jun-Koo (1993) 'The International Market for Corporate Control. Mergers and Acquisitions of U.S. Firms by Japanese Firms', *Journal of Financial Economics* **34**, 345–371.

Kaysen, Carl, and Donald F. Turner (1959) *Antitrust Policy*. Cambridge: Harvard University Press.

Kumar, M. S. (1985) 'Growth, Acquisition Activity and Firm Size: Evidence from the United Kingdom', *Journal of Industrial Economics*, **XXXIII**, 327–338.

Kummer, D., and R. Hoffmeister (1978) 'Valuation Consequences of Cash Tender Offers', *Journal of Finance* **33**, 505–516.

Kumps, Anne-Marie, and Robert Wtterwulghe (1980) 'Belgium, 1962–74', in D. C. Mueller, ed., *The Determinants and Effects of Mergers: An International Comparison*. Cambridge, Mass.: Oelgeschlager, Gunn & Hain, pp. 67–97.

Lang, Larry, Rene M. Stulz, and Ralph A. Walkling (1989) 'Managerial Performance, Tobin's Q and the Gains from Successful Tender Offers', *Journal of Financial Economics*, **24** 137–154.

Langetieg, T. (1978) 'An Application of a Three-Factor Performance Index to Measure Stockholders Gains from Merger', *Journal of Financial Economics*, **6**, 365–384.

Leeth, John D., and J. Rody Borg (1994) 'The Impact of Mergers on Acquiring Firm Shareholder Wealth: The 1905–1930 Experience', *Empirica*, **21**, 221–244.

Lev, B., and G. Mandelker (1972) 'The Microeconomic Consequences of Corporate Mergers', *Journal of Business*, **45**, 85–104.

Lichtenberg, Frank R. (1992) 'Industrial De-Diversification and Its Consequences for Productivity', *Journal of Economic Behavior and Organization*, **18**, 427–438.

Lichtenberg, Frank R., and Donald Siegel (1987) 'Productivity and Changes in Ownership of Manufacturing Plants', *Brookings Papers on Economic Activity*, 643–673.

Lintner, John (1971) 'Expectations, Mergers and Equilibrium in Purely Competitive Securities Markets', *American Economic Review*, **61**, 101–111.

Magenheim, Ellen, and Dennis C. Mueller (1988) 'On Measuring the Effect of Mergers on Acquiring Firm Shareholders', in Jack Coffee, Louis Lowenstein, and Susan Rose-Ackerman, eds., *Knights, Raiders and Targets*. Oxford: Oxford University Press, pp. 171–193.

Malatesta, Paul H. (1983) 'The Wealth Effect of Merger Activity and the Objective Functions of Merging Firms', *Journal of Financial Economics*, **11**, 155–181.

Mandelker, Gershon (1974) 'Risk and Return: The Case of Merging Firms', *Journal of Financial Economics*, **1**, 303–335.

Manne, Henry G. (1965) 'Mergers and the Market for Corporate Control', *Journal of Political Economy*, **73**, 110–120.

Markham, Jesse W. (1955) 'Survey of the Evidence and Findings on Mergers', *Business Concentration and Price Policy*. New York: National Bureau of Economic Research, pp. 141–182.

Marris, Robin (1964) *The Economic Theory of Managerial Capitalism*. Glencoe: Free Press.

McDougall, Fred M., and Round, David K. (1986) *The Determinants and Effects of Corporate Takeovers in Australia, 1970–1981*. Victoria: Australian Institute of Management.

Meeks, Geoffrey (1977) *Disappointing Marriage: A Study of the Gains From Merger*. Cambridge, U.K.: Cambridge University Press.

Melicher, Ronald W., Johannes Ledolter, and Louis J. D'Antonio (1983) 'A Time Series Analysis of Aggregate Merger Activity', *Review of Economics and Statistics*, **65**, 423–430.

Mueller, Dennis C. (1969) 'A Theory of Conglomerate Mergers', *Quarterly Journal of Economics*, **83**, 643–659.

Mueller, Dennis C. (1972) 'A Life Cycle Theory of the Firm', *Journal of Industrial Economics*, **20**, 199–219.

Mueller, Dennis C. (1977) 'The Effects of Conglomerate Mergers: A Survey of the Empirical Evidence', *Journal of Banking and Finance*, **1**, 315–347.

Mueller, Dennis C. (1980a) *The Determinants and Effects of Mergers: An International Comparison*. Cambridge, Mass.: Oelgeschlager, Gunn & Hain.

Mueller, Dennis C. (1980b) 'The United States, 1962–1972', in D. C. Mueller, ed., *The Determinants and Effects of Mergers: An International Comparison*. Cambridge, Mass.: Oelgeschlager, Gunn & Hain, pp. 271–298.

Mueller, Dennis C. (1980c) 'A Cross-National Comparison of the Results', in D. C. Mueller, ed., *The Determinants and Effects of Mergers: An International Comparison*. Cambridge, Mass.: Oelgeschlager, Gunn & Hain, pp. 299–314.

Mueller, Dennis C. (1985) 'Mergers and Market Share', *Review of Economics and Statistics*, **67**, 259–267.

Mueller, Dennis C. (1986) *Profits in the Long Run*. Cambridge: Cambridge University Press.

Mueller, Dennis C. (1987) *The Corporation: Growth, Diversification, and Mergers*. London: Harwood Academic Publishers, 1987.

Mueller, Dennis C. (1988) 'The Effects of Mergers', in Terry Calvani and John Siegfried, eds., *Economic Analysis and Antitrust Law*. Boston: Little, Brown, and Co., pp. 303–321.

Mueller, Dennis C. (1990) *The Dynamics of Company Profits*. Cambridge: Cambridge University Press.

Mueller, Dennis C. (1992) 'Mergers', *The New Palgrave Dictionary of Money and Finance.* London: Macmillan.

Mueller, Dennis C. (1993) 'U.S. Merger Policy and the 1992 Merger Guidelines', *Review of Industrial Organization*, **8**, 151–162.

Mueller, Dennis C. (1995) 'Mergers: Theory and Evidence', in G. Mussatti, ed., *Mergers, Markets, and Public Policy.* Dordrecht: Kluwer Academic Publishers.

Mueller, Dennis C. (1996) 'Lessons from the United States's Antitrust History', *International Journal of Industrial Organization*, **14**, 415–445.

Nicholls, William H. (1949) 'The Tobacco Case of 1946', *American Economic Review*, **39**, 284–296, reprinted in R. B. Heflebower and G. W. Stocking, eds. (1958) *Readings in Industrial Organization and Public Policy.* Homewood: Irwin, pp. 105–117.

Nelson, Ralph L. (1959) 'Merger Movements in American Industry, 1895–1956', Princeton: Princeton University Press.

Peer, Henk (1980) 'The Netherlands, 1962–1973', in D. C. Mueller, ed., *The Determinants and Effects of Mergers: An International Comparison.* Cambridge, Mass.: Oelgeschlager, Gunn & Hain, pp. 163–191.

Piper, T. F., and S. J. Weiss (1974) 'The Profitability of Multibank Holding Company Acquisitions', *Journal of Finance*, **29**, 163–174.

Ravenscraft, David J., and F. M. Scherer (1987) 'Mergers and Managerial Performance', in John C. Coffee, Jr., Louis Lowenstein, and Susan Rose-Ackerman, eds., *Takeovers and Contests for Corporate Control.* Oxford: Oxford University Press.

Rhoades, Stephen A. (1987) 'The Operating Performances of Acquired Firms in Banking', in R. L. Wills, J. A. Caswell, and J. D. Culbertson, eds., *Issues After a Century of Federal Competition Policy.* Lexington, Mass.: Lexington Books, 1987, pp. 277–292.

Roll, Richard (1986) 'The Hubris Hypothesis of Corporate Takeovers', *Journal of Business*, **59**, 197–216.

Ryden, Bengt, and Jan-Olof Edberg (1980) 'Large Mergers in Sweden, 1962–1976', in D. C. Mueller, ed., *The Determinants and Effects of Mergers: An International Comparison.* Cambridge, Mass.: Oelgeschlager, Gunn & Hain, 193–226.

Salinger, Michael (1992) 'Standard Errors in Event Studies', *Journal of Financial Quantitative Analysis*, **27**, 39–53.

Scherer, F. M., and David Ross (1990) *Industrial Market Structure and Economic Performance*, 3rd ed. Boston: Houghton Mifflin.

Scherer, F. M. (1993) 'Merger in the Petroleum Industry: The *Mobil-Marathon* Case (1981)', in J. E. Kwoka and L. J. White, *The Antitrust Revolution*, 2nd ed. New York: Harper Collins, pp. 20–45.

Scott, John T. (1982) 'Multimarket Contact and Economic Performance', *Review of Economics and Statistics*, **64**, 368–375.

Scott, John T. (1993) *Purposive Diversification and Economic Performance.* Cambridge: Cambridge University Press.

Shepherd, William G. (1997) *The Economics of Industrial Organization*, 4th ed. Upper Saddle River, N.J.: Prentice Hall.

Singh, Ajit (1971) *Take-Overs: Their Relevance to the Stock Market and the Theory of the Firm.* Cambridge: Cambridge University Press.

Smith, Richard L., and Joo-Hyun Kim (1994) The Combined Effects of Free Cash Flow and Financial Slack on Bidder and Target Stock Returns, *Journal of Business*, **67**, 281–310.

Stelzer, Irwin M. (1986) *Selected Antitrust Cases: Landmark Decisions*, 7th ed. Homewood: Irwin.

Stewart, John F., and Sang-Kwon Kim (1993) 'Mergers and Social Welfare in U.S. Manufacturing 1985–86', *Southern Economic Journal*, **59**, 701–720.

Stigler, George J. (1950) Monopoly and Oligopoly by Merger', *American Economic Review*, **40**, 23–34.

Tilly, Richard (1982) 'Mergers, External Growth, and Finance in the Development of Large-Scale Enterprise in Germany, 1880–1913', *Journal of Economic History*, **42**, 629–658.

Varaiya, Nikhil P. (1986) 'The Returns to Bidding Firms and the Gains From Corporate Takeovers: A Reexamination', in A. Chen, ed., *Research in Finance*, **6**, 149–178.

Weston, J. Fred (1970) 'The Nature and Significance of Conglomerate Firms', *St. John's Law Review*, **44**, Spring 1970, special edition, pp. 66–80.
Weston, J. Fred, and S. K. Mansinghka (1971) 'Tests of the Efficiency Performance of Conglomerate Firms', *Journal of Finance*, **26**, 919–936.
Williamson, Oliver E. (1968) 'Economies as an Anti-Trust Defense: The Welfare Trade-Offs', *American Economic Review*, **58**, 18–36 (rptd. with correction in C. K. Rowley, ed., *Readings in Industrial Economics*. London: Macmillan).
Williamson, Oliver E. (1970) *Corporate Control and Business Behavior: An Inquiry Into the Effects of Organization Form on Enterprise Behavior*. Englewood Cliffs, NJ: Prentice-Hall.
Zweifel, Peter, and Roger Zäch (1995) 'A Plea in Favor of a New Anti-Cartel Law in Switzerland', *World Competition*, **18**, 31–36.

[16]

A Global Competition Policy for a Global Economy

Dennis C. Mueller

The growth of world trade since World War II and the decline in restrictions on international trade contained first in the GATT agreements, and now promulgated by the World Trade Organization (WTO), have produced what truly can be called "a global economy." The main targets of GATT and the WTO have been *government* restrictions on trade, however. As these have fallen and trade has expanded, the importance of *private* restrictions on trade has grown. What gain is there to a country that reduces a tariff on a product by 20%, if an export cartel promptly raises the price of the product by 20%?

The European Union recognized that its program of freeing trade across the borders of its member states had to be combined with an effective competition policy, just as the United States eventually recognized that its internal "free trade" policy needed an effective competition (antitrust) policy. An obvious parallel question given the rise of the global economy is whether we now need a global competition policy.

Scherer (1994) has recently answered this question in the affirmative, and proposed the creation of an International Competition Policy Office (ICPO) within the WTO, and a set of policies along with a timetable for implementing them. In this paper I shall not discuss the specific proposals Scherer made nor the exact timetable he proposed. I shall assume that an ICPO has been created, and that it can enforce a set of competition policies that resemble those of the European Union or the U.S. antitrust laws. The questions I wish to consider concern the extent to which the logic underlying national competition policies can

The financial support that the Ludwig Boltzmann Institut provided for this research is gratefully acknowledged.

be extended to defend an international competition policy, and some general issues that arise in the latter context that do not arise under national competition policies. In the first section, I take up the general goals of competition policy. The next four sections discuss the likely need for an international competition policy in each of its four, main traditional areas: collusion, monopolization, vertical restraints, and mergers. Section VI briefly draws some conclusions.

I The Goals of Competition Policy

Bork (1978, pp. 61–66) has argued that the intent of the Sherman Act from its first passage was the promotion of consumer welfare, what we might now express as the maximization of consumers' surplus. More recently, however, Libecap (1992) has claimed that the driving force behind the passage of the Sherman Act was a coalition of businesses hurt by the rise of the great trusts. Regardless of which explanation best accounts for the adoption of the act, it is certainly the case that the issue of whether the antitrust laws *ought* to protect competitors or competition has been long debated in the United States (Bork, 1978, chs. 2, 3, 7). Any international competition policy would also need to resolve this fundamental question if it were to be implemented coherently.

The disappearance of unsuccessful competitors is a normal and healthy characteristic of the competitive process. Any set of policies designed to protect and promote competition will inevitably lead to the disappearance of firms unable to compete in the market. Such disappearances can cause considerable personal hardship, of course, and the state has a legitimate role to play in reducing these hardships. Unemployment insurance is an example of one such policy. Others would include tax deductions for expenses incurred searching for a new job, moving to take up a new job, and so on. Retraining programs and in extreme cases state subsidies for firms in situations in which a firm's departure would impose large losses on a community are still others. A coherent set of policies to promote competition would prohibit all private and governmental actions that harmed the competitive process, while allowing individuals and governments the freedom to mitigate the risks from competition through private and public insurance schemes. The "costs of competition" would be borne by private citizens through their savings and purchases of insurance, or by the taxpayers. They would not be borne by consumers in the form of higher prices to subsidize inefficient firms.[1]

Compared with most other countries, it can be said that U.S. antitrust policy has been geared more closely toward protecting competition than toward protecting competitors. Even in this country, however, exceptions have been made with respect to cartels or workers (labor unions), farmers, oddly enough baseball team owners, and most significantly exporters. In Europe, national policies protect workers and farmers from competition, and EU competition policy exempts small and medium size firms from its anticartel provisions. Many other laws, like those regarding shop opening hours, are clearly intended to protect some groups from competition. The same can be said for most other countries. An international competition policy that sought to protect competition but not competitors would run against the domestic policies of many countries.

Many national policies to protect competitors are harmful to consumers only in the countries implementing them, however. Austrian consumers suffer from high shop prices and inconvenient shopping hours, because of its laws, but these do not affect consumers in other countries. Thus, many domestic policies could be left to stand, and much conflict between ICPO and WTO member governments avoided, if the ICPO's goal were clearly defined as that of promoting *international* competition, and any national policies that harmed only the consumers or taxpayers of the nation implementing them were ignored. A strict interpretation of protecting international competition would logically condemn some worker and farmer cartels, but political prudence would suggest not requiring an ICPO to take on these. With these exceptions, the simplest and easiest goal to defend for an ICPO would be the protection of international competition against those practices by private parties and governments that harm international buyers. These practices can be conveniently grouped into four main categories. I begin with cartel arrangements.

---

[1] In this regard, current European Union policy that forbids member countries and regional governments from subsidizing their local firms is mistaken, and forces these governments to try to protect their firms in other ways that are detrimental to the competitive process. For a discussion of when and why subsidies for firms can be justified, see Mueller (1997b).

II Collusion

No components of the U.S. antitrust laws enjoys broader and more unequivocal support among economists than Section I of the Sherman Act prohibiting collusive agreements. Cartels are such blatant devices to benefit producers at buyers' expense that the courts in the United States have come to regard collusive agreements as *per se* illegal. The plaintiff need not prove that the collusive agreement harms consumers or the competitive process. The mere existence of the agreement suffices to condemn it. Although Article 85 of the Treaty of Rome that defines the European Union's policy with respect to collusion does not impose a *per se* criterion on the Commission, this article has nevertheless been vigorously enforced against collusive agreements, *at least against such agreements between larger companies*. European competition policy, like U.S. antitrust policy from time to time, has failed to condemn collusive practices when they have been adopted by small and medium size firms (George and Jacquemin, 1990, pp. 209–222). Indeed, it explicitly allows for such exemptions (Martin, 1994, p. 555). Since it is difficult to contemplate a meaningful world competition policy that would not include and strictly enforce an anticartel provision, I shall assume that this would be the overriding goal of a global competition policy.

Most obviously an anticartel rule would have to apply to companies based in different countries. But equally obviously, it should also apply to companies based in a single country if their anticompetitive actions harm consumers in other countries. *Thus, all export cartels would have to be challengeable.*

In many cases, international cartels have been aided or even organized by the governments of the main producing nations; the OPEC cartel was perhaps the most dramatic and for a while the most successful of these. Once again, it seems obvious that an agency charged with the task of breaking up international cartels must have the authority to challenge international agreements to set prices, regardless of whether they are initiated by private firms or by the governments of their countries. If an ICPO did not have this power, any private firms that wanted to form a cartel would be able to do so, so long as their government(s) was (were) willing to sponsor the cartel. Such an arrangement, in turn, would favor those countries whose governments are more closely entwined with their "private" sectors, which in general would be the less democratic and less capitalistic countries. Such an arrangement would not encourage developing countries to speed up their adoption of democratic and market institutions. It is difficult to see, therefore, how an international anticartel policy could effectively protect competition if it could not attack both privately and publicly constituted cartels.

III Monopolization

What several autonomous organizations cannot achieve in concert, a single organization can sometimes achieve on its own. A single overwhelmingly dominant firm in a market would almost certainly charge a price far above the potential competitive price, even if it fell short of the pure monopoly price.[2] The mere existence of an overwhelmingly dominant firm in a market would therefore seem to demand intervention in the form of either regulation or dissolution.

Although Learned Hand's decision in *Alcoa* (1945) might be interpreted as declaring the mere existence of overwhelming market dominance as a violation of Section II of the Sherman Act,[3] subsequent court decisions have not condemned the possession of market power per se (e.g., *Berkey Photo Inc. v. Eastman Kodak Company,* 1979). Some *action* by the dominant firm to create or *preserve* market power in a way which is harmful to competition has been demanded. Such reluctance to attack dominant firms can be consistent with the advancement of consumer interests if one assumes that the firm achieved its dominance by superior efficiency or innovative activity (Bork, 1978, pp, 67–69).

The creation of a monopoly through the acquisition of one's competitors is, perhaps, the most transparent act of monopolization that is unlikely to advance consumer interests. Indeed, mergers falling well short of producing a monopoly are likely to run counter to the goal of advancing efficiency and social welfare. These shall be left for Section V, however.

---

2 An exception would be a monopolist in a perfectly contestable market (Baumol, Panzer, and Willig, 1982). Where dominant firms are found, however, their markets do not seem to meet the criteria for perfect contestability.

3 Hand's famous utterance that "no monopolist monopolizes unconscious of what it is doing" would seem to make every conscious action of a monopolist a willful monopolization, and thus be in violation of a literal reading of the statute.

Table 1. Market Shares and Profits of Dominant U.S. Companies

Company	M_{50}	π_{50}	π_{p}	π_{94}
Campbell Soup	63.2	0.05	0.56	0.67
Caterpillar	48.2	0.05	0.72	0.29
Coca Cola	30.2	0.34	0.98	2.24
Gillette	43.4	1.41	1.58	0.85
Hershey Foods	38.1	0.64	0.72	0.63
IBM	47.9	0.01	1.10	−1.40
Kellogg	20.5	0.82	1.20	1.77
Procter & Gamble	29.9	0.37	0.86	0.05
Tecumseh Products	38.7	0.78	0.93	0.39
Wm. Wrigley, Jr.	52.8	0.44	0.63	2.67

Source: Mueller (1986, pp. 34–35; 1997a).

Other than mergers, the most transparent acts of monopolization fall under the heading of *predation*, efforts by a dominant firm to drive its competitors from the market. Such actions are likely to be particularly contentious in an international environment. If a dominant international firm must predate to maintain its position, the targets of its predation will often be competitors in other countries. Natural empathy for the underdog combines with chauvinistic sentiment for domestic over foreign producers to produce a potentially explosive situation. If local competition policy proscribes predation, one can expect considerable pressure on local authorities to try the dominant, international firm. Although it would not be able to dissolve a company outside of its borders, it could presumably introduce fines and proscribe particular actions deemed to be predatory. If many countries initiated actions against the dominant firm, it would find itself embroiled in countless legal struggles which could dissipate its resources and divert its management's attention from the important task of running the company efficiently.

The history of dominant firms in the United States leads one to the following observations: (1) Dominant firms often do charge prices substantially above their marginal and average costs, and thus earn substantially higher profits than other companies. The first column of Table 1, labeled M_{50}, reports the market shares in 1950 for a set of dominant firms in the 1950s and 1960s. Although no single source exists that reports the market shares of these companies in later years, it is known that they maintained or increased their market positions following 1950. Column 3, labeled π_p, lists the long-run projected returns on capital for these companies. These projections were made using data for the 1950–1972 period, and are projections to time equals infinity measured as a deviation from the sample mean. Thus, based on its 1950–1972 profits record, I projected that IBM would earn an after-tax return on its total assets that was 110% greater than that of the average manufacturing firm into the indefinite future.[4] The columns labeled π_{50} and π_{94} list the deviations from the sample mean for returns on capital for these firms in the initial years of the earlier study (1950–1952) and for two recent years (1993–1994). Although IBM lost its dominant position in computers and thus by the 1990s was no longer one of the most profitable U.S. companies, other market leaders like Caterpillar, Campbell Soup, Gillette, and Wm. Wrigley did succeed in maintaining both their positions of market dominance and their high profitability.

Observation number two is that the inordinate profits of dominant firms often lead to efforts by other companies to capture these profits. Observation 3 is that the dominant firm often puts up a fight to avoid losing its market position and the profits that go with it. So it was with IBM in the late 1960s as new entrants into the "peripherals markets" for equipment that attached to computer mainframes brought out clones of IBM products, and sold them at substantial discounts below IBM's prices. IBM responded with vigor, and the peripherals manufacturers were driven from the market into the court room, where they accused IBM of predatory behavior.

Whether one judges IBM to have been guilty of predation or not depends on the definition of predation one adopts, the interpretation one gives to the facts, and perhaps the weight one places on the arguments put forward by the economists IBM hired, versus those of the economists who worked on the government's side (Brock, [1989] 1994; Fisher, McGowan, and Greenwood, 1983). Regardless of how one views the facts and outcomes of the IBM cases, however, one must conclude that such cases raise extremely difficult issues of fact and

[4] The average was based on my sample of 551 manufacturing companies. This sample was drawn from the largest companies in the economy and thus should have approximated the average for all of manufacturing companies fairly closely.

interpretation, and are likely to be particularly difficult to arbitrate in an international context.

IBM was able to win all of the private antitrust suits filed against it, in large part because the courts accepted the definition of predatory action put forward by two law professors hired to testify on IBM's behalf. Areeda and Turner (1975) recommended that a firm be presumed not to have engaged in predatory behavior, so long as it did not charge a price less than either its short-run marginal costs or its short-run average costs. Such a definition of predation places exclusive weight on allowing welfare-enhancing transactions in the short run. While buyers are clearly better off in the short run if dominant firms are allowed to cut their prices below their and their smaller rivals' long-run average costs, buyers may be worse off in the long run if the small firms disappear and the dominant firm returns to a high price/high profit strategy.

The adoption of the Areeda–Turner definition of predation by a global competition policy authority would result in few successful convictions of dominant firms. Countries would see local firms arise and offer cheaper versions of the products sold by giant international companies, and then would have to standby and watch their local heroes driven into oblivion by the international companies. The wisdom of such a lax standard for predation is likely to escape the recognition of the countries whose local firms have departed if the large international firm subsequently chooses to raise its prices. In an international context, therefore, a rather tough attitude toward predatory behavior would seem to be warranted. One such approach has been outlined by Joskow and Klevorick (1979). They would allow firms to be convicted even when they charged prices above their short-run marginal or average costs, so long as these prices were below their long-run average costs and it appeared that the dominant firm was purposefully pursuing a policy of driving its competitors from the market, and that this policy was likely to succeed in both this objective and to result in higher prices in the long run.

The approach to predation advocated by Joskow and Klevorick is more in line with the language of the Sherman Act and its enforcement since 1890 than that of Areeda and Turner. It also probably provides greater scope for conviction. Nevertheless, convictions would likely be rare in an international context. Proving the existence of high entry barriers in a global economy should be more difficult than doing so at the domestic level. Moreover, any future rise to world dominance by a company is likely to be based largely on technological leadership. In such instances a predatory strategy of a dominant firm will typically not be restricted to charging lower prices than its rivals, but will involve combinations of changes in technology, product design, and pricing formula–as was alleged in the cases brought against IBM, and has been alleged against IBM's heir to dominance in computer products, Microsoft.

Gazing forward during the closing days of the Johnson Administration in the late 1960s, one might well have predicted that, left alone, IBM would continue or even extend its dominance over the computer industry, and that only the dissolution of this giant through a successful Sherman Act case would restore competition in this industry. Anyone who made that prediction was proved wrong. IBM missed the onset of the personal computer revolution, and has yet to make up for this mistake. Indeed, one might argue that if the U.S. government had pressed its case against IBM, and won a quick dissolution, one of the ensuing parts of IBM would have probably recognized the potential of the PC, and the antitrust suit would have had the opposite effect of what was intended.[5] Be that as it may, the history of the computer industry suggests that projections of future performance in technologically progressive industries are far more difficult to make than in the soft drinks and chewing gum industries. He who bets on Microsoft being a dominant firm with supernormal profits 25 years from now faces big odds.

This being the case it is tempting to conclude that there would be no need for a global policy with respect to dominant firm predatory practices. The forces of technological change and Schumpeterian competition will suffice to eliminate positions of dominance before the force of a global competition policy could reasonably be expected to have an effect. Such an attitude toward predation would be further justified to the extent that one accepts the argument, put forward by some, that

[5] Comanor and Scherer (1995) have made such an argument with respect to the breakup of Standard Oil of New Jersey's monopoly in 1911. The resulting components proved much more successful at growing and generating profits than did the United States Steel company, which avoided dissolution with a 1920 victory against the government.

predation is seldom a rational policy on the part of a dominant firm.[6] If a dominant firm is unlikely to succeed in maintaining or extending its dominance in a single country, how could it hope to do so across the world?

To ignore predation in a global competition policy would, however, be a mistake for several reasons. (1) Because future dominance in world markets is likely to rest on technological superiority, any firms achieving such dominance can be expected to be based in one of the technologically progressive, highly developed countries. The products it sells will be very highly priced relative to income levels in some developing countries. The incentive for local firms to copy the dominant firm's products, and sell them at a fraction of the price of the foreign firm will be strong. A policy of benign neglect to any attempts by the dominant firm to stomp out such competition is likely to be interpreted as politically motivated. Developing countries would deem global competition policy to be stacked in favor of the global economic powers.

(2) Efforts by local firms to copy the products of a dominant international company often involve infringements on patents and/or trademarks. Both technologically progressive firms and their host countries have a strong incentive to curtail such infringements. Having a strong antimonopoly/antipredation component of a global competition should help in getting the governments of developing countries to police international patent and copyright laws.

(3) The most important reason for having a strong antipredation policy as part of an international competition policy, however, would be that it would allow, *indeed logically compel*, the repeal of all antidumping laws (Scherer, 1994, pp. 78–87). Although the exclusive focus of Areeda and Turner on the short-run pricing behavior of a dominant

[6] See, McGee (1958), Bork (1978, pp. 144–160), and Elzinga ([1989] 1994). These arguments are based on calculations of likely losses in the short run and gains in the long run from predation through price cutting, under the assumption that the dominant firm must reduce its price on all of the units it sells. As already noted, price reductions are typically only part of the predatory policy of a firm that owes its dominance to technological leadership. It also often faces competition in only some of its markets. Substantial losses in these may be a cost effective way to signal to potential entrants into other markets that such entry would be a mistake.

firm cannot be defended, if one wants an effective policy against predation, the intuition behind their proposal–that low prices are *ceteris paribus* to be welcomed–is definitely right. If the dominant firm cannot achieve a monopoly and subsequently raise prices, then consumer welfare is advanced by the competitive struggle between the dominant firm and its rivals. Antidumping cases often resemble predation cases in that they revolve around comparisons of prices and costs. As with predation cases, the basic complaint is that prices are too low. But the goal of international trade and an international competition policy is low prices. Antidumping laws are inevitably intended to protect *competitors* rather than consumers or competition and thus are antithetical to the fundamental goals of free trade and an international competition policy. If this competition policy contained a strong antipredation component, one would be assured that any alleged dumping by foreign firms would benefit domestic consumers in the short run, and would not harm them in the long run. Any harm done to domestic competitors should either be ignored as part of the normal competitive process, or offset by subsidies for the domestic producers (Mueller, 1997b).

IV Vertical Restraints

Various vertical restrictions on trade have been proscribed by both the U.S. antitrust laws and the EU competition policy. A large literature has now evolved that argues that these practices are benign if not beneficial with respect to the competitive process (Bork, 1978, chs. 14, 15, 19, 20; Klein and Saft, 1985; Marvel, 1982; Marvel and McCafferty, 1984, 1985; Warren-Boulton, [1989] 1994), and Posner (1976) and Bork (1978) have, on the basis of this literature, argued that the relevant sections of the Clayton Act should be repealed. I shall not go deeply into this debate, but rather focus on some of the issues that come up in an international context.

A Price Discrimination

A firm that has any market power will maximize its profits by setting prices for its products that satisfy the following equation:

$$(P_i - C_i)/P_i = 1/e_i,$$

where P_i is the price charged for the product, C_i the marginal cost of producing it, and e_i is the price elasticity of the firm's demand schedule for this product. This equation is, of course, the familiar Lerner index of monopoly power with the exception that the elasticity of *the firm's demand schedule* replaces that of the industry's demand schedule. Any firm that possesses some market power and can divide its customers into separate groups and charge them different prices will try to do so if the groups have different demand elasticities or there are different costs in supplying them. Not surprisingly, one finds that price discrimination is ubiquitous, ranging from theaters charging different prices for seats, to liquor companies charging significantly different prices for brands of liquor that have only modest differences in production costs.

International firms with market power can be expected to engage in considerable price discrimination also. Markets are geographically and legally separated, and demand elasticities can be expected to differ greatly across countries with tastes and incomes. The costs of supplying different countries may also differ. One should not be surprised to find large differences in both the prices that international firms charge for their products in different countries, and in their price-cost margins. Differences in price-cost margins would constitute price discrimination under an *economic* definition of this action.

Both U.S. and European competition policies do not employ an economic definition of price discrimination, however, but rather define price discrimination as charging different prices for the same product. In the United States a firm can defend itself against a charge of price discrimination if it can justify its prices on the basis of differences in the costs of supplying the different customers. Experience with the U.S. policy has revealed that it is often very difficult to establish such a cost-based defense.[7]

The cases that have been brought against firms accused of price discrimination either under the 1914 Clayton Act or the 1938 Robinson–Patman Act amendment form the least edifying and least economically defensible chapter in the U.S. antitrust history (Edwards, 1959; Scherer and Ross, 1990, pp. 508–516). In this area of antitrust, more than in any other, the enforcement of the antitrust laws have

[7] The second line of defense, "meeting an equally low price of a competitor," has been the more successful of the two options allowed under the law.

worked to protect competitors rather than competition. Where competition *is* protected by protecting competitors, as in predation cases and mergers, other policies can be effectively employed. A global competition policy should not include special provisions against price discrimination.

B Resale Price Maintenance

It is common practice in many industries for a manufacturer to demand a promise from the retailers selling its product that they charge the price for it set by the manufacturer. Such policies often arise as part of a cartel arrangement among the retailers. Being large in number, they require that someone run the cartel for them. A large manufacturer is an obvious choice. Manufacturers may also stand to benefit from such cartels in that vigorous competition at the retail level sometimes works its way back to the manufacturing level. Retailers complain to the manufacturer that they cannot survive in the face of the competition occurring at the retail level unless the manufacturer cuts its price to the retailer. By fixing the price charged by all of its retailers, the manufacturer averts the possibility that competition at the retail level gets "out of hand" and forces retailers to cut prices.

Since retail price maintenance involves a cartel among retailers, it can in principle be challenged under an anticartel policy. In fact, many countries that have competition policies, like France and Germany, sanction resale price maintenance agreements in some areas, like book sales, and France has recently introduced additional legislation to protect its small retailers from competition from large retailers (*Economist*, 1996). Such measures are obviously harmful to consumers, as is retail price maintenance when it exists to protect retailers from competition (Marvel and McCafferty, 1984, 1985; Warren-Boulton, [1989] 1994). But the costs of these restrictions on competition fall entirely on the consumers of the country that introduces them. They do not directly harm international competition. Any attempts by retailers to form cross-border cartels and to require that resale price maintenance agreements be implemented multinationally should be easy to observe, and could be challenged under the anticartel provisions of a global competition policy. There is no compelling reason for a global competition policy to concern itself with resale price maintenance as such.

C Territorial Restrictions

In addition to setting prices at the retail level to protect its retailers, manufacturers have also placed geographic restrictions on where retailers can locate and even to whom they can sell. Thus, automobile manufacturers have forbidden their Belgium dealers to sell cars to citizens of other European Union countries. As with resale price maintenance, an efficiency rationale can be given for some forms of territorial constraints, but they may also be intended to protect both retailers and manufacturers from competition. Both car manufacturers and their retailers probably have benefited from the higher prices that have existed in some EU countries.

To achieve the benefits of free trade, manufacturers should be allowed to sell their products in different countries without restrictions. These benefits may also be forthcoming if retailers are free to make cross-border sales, and consumers can cross borders to take advantage of lower prices. Territorial restrictions on sales imposed by manufacturers, when defined along national lines, restrict the free flow of goods and services precisely as do restrictions imposed by governments. A competition policy which banned cross-national territorial restrictions by manufacturers would be a natural complement to reductions in tariffs, quotas, and other governmental restrictions on international trade.

D Exclusive Dealing and Tying Agreements

Tying agreements have been most frequently employed as a means for engaging in price discrimination. For example, IBM originally required that users of its computers purchase from IBM the cards used to read in data. By overpricing its cards, IBM was able to charge large users of its computers higher prices than small users. A firm cannot successfully employ a tying arrangement unless it has considerable market power in the tied product's market, otherwise consumers will simply purchase the products of rivals which do not require tie-ins. Thus, these sorts of tying arrangements raise the same issue as other forms of price discrimination raise. For the same reason, they are probably best ignored. None of the other possible anticompetitive effects of tying arrangements arise frequently enough, or have sufficient anticompetitive effects to warrant an ICPO's attention. Tying arrangements can also safely be neglected by such a global competition authority.

Exclusive dealing contracts between manufacturers and retailers are harmful to competition only to the extent that they *foreclose* distribution outlets to new entrants into a market, thereby raising entry barriers. For example, if all existing automobile retailers in a country are contractually tied to particular automobile manufacturers, an automobile manufacturer that wishes to begin selling in this country will not be able to find an existing retailer to handle its cars. It will have to develop its own network of retailers, which raises the cost of its entering this country considerably.

Exclusive dealing arrangements are only profitable for firms that can generate large sales volume through single outlets to allow the retailers to survive by selling only the products of the manufacturer, as for example, automobile and farm machinery manufacturers, petroleum companies, and the like. On an international level, such companies are quite large. In the long run, the costs of running one dealer network are the same as for another. Thus, if it is profitable in the long run for one of these large international firms to enter the market of a particular country, the need to make up front investments to establish a dealer network should not constitute a significant entry barrier. Exclusive dealing arrangements are also not prime candidates for inclusion in a global competition policy.

E Refusals to Deal

In a vertical production chain in which the output of industry *A* is used in the production of *B* which is distributed by firms in *C*, competition can be hurt by a dominant firm in *A* refusing to sell to firms in *B*, and by firms in *C* refusing to buy from *B*. In an international context, these possibilities are of interest if *A*, *B*, and *C* are located in different countries.

In general, a firm is not going to make more profits by *refusing to* sell its product in some countries than by selling it. An upstream firm's refusal to sell to buyers in other countries could only be part of a profit-maximizing strategy, therefore, if the upstream firm was attempting to drive downstream firms out of business and thereby create a monopoly for itself over several parts or all of the vertical chain. Such a strategy would be an obvious attempt to monopolize and could be challenged as predatory behavior. Special rules regarding refusals to sell are not necessary in a global competition policy.

Refusals to *buy* are quite another matter, however. Such actions can create significant barriers to entry in countries where companies adopt refusal-to-deal policies, and thereby constitute a barrier to trade. One example of this would be the refusal of retailers in *C* to handle products from manufacturers in *B*. There are good normal business reasons why some retailers refuse to handle some manufacturers' goods. For example, a retailer that specializes in upmarket cosmetics might refuse to stock cheaper brands out of the belief that its customers would be unlikely to purchase them, and that its image as an upmarket store would be adversely affected if it did sell these products. A refusal by *all* of the retailers in a country to carry the products of a foreign firm is unlikely to be the result of independent, profit-maximizing behavior, assuming of course that the quality and prices of the products would make them competitive in this country. Concerted refusals to deal of this type would seem possible only as part of an agreement that included all retailers and perhaps also domestic manufacturers seeking to avoid competition from foreign producers. Since domestic competition policies will not always proscribe such agreements, and domestic competition policy authorities might for obvious reasons be reluctant to attack them even if they could, such refusals to deal must be subject to challenge by an ICPO. They would certainly fall under an anticartel rule, but might be explicitly prohibited to facilitate the ICPO's ability to challenge them.

An explicit prohibition against refusals to deal could also be used to challenge the policies of single, large monopsonistic buyers, like a country's telephone company, major utilities and railroads, and even the government itself. In these instances, no cartel as such exists, but a *conspiracy* of sorts is suspected between the buyer and the domestic suppliers of competing products. Such conspiracies are equally harmful to competition when they are politically motivated as when they are economically motivated. As with resale price maintenance agreements, the prime losers from these sorts of refusals to deal are the consumers and taxpayers in the country engaged in these practices, however. Unlike international cartels, the adverse effects do not spread across countries. The extent to which a global competition authority should concern itself with refusals to buy depends, therefore, very much on whether its mission is only to protect *international* competition from the practices of international firms, or whether it is also charged with the task of protecting consumers within a country from its domestic firms and even from its own government.[8]

V Mergers

The passage of the Sherman Antitrust Act in 1890 and the subsequent enforcement of its anticartel provisions arguably contributed to the first great merger wave in the United States (Bittlingmayer, 1985). The more stringently cartels are policed, the greater the incentives firms have to merge. An effective global competition policy will need to prevent anticompetitive mergers. In addition to their adverse effects on competition, mergers can harm social welfare by *reducing* the efficiency of the merging firms.[9] Since these two effects of mergers raise somewhat different issues with respect to a global competition policy, I will discuss them separately. I begin with anticompetitive mergers, broken down into the customary three categories of horizontal, vertical, and conglomerate mergers.

A Horizontal Mergers

Just as a cartel among exporters can benefit not only the companies which are members of the cartel, but also their countries of origin, a merger between companies that control a large fraction of a world market can lead to higher prices harming buyers in the importing countries while perhaps benefiting the exporting countries. Any hori-

[8] For a skeptical review of the significance of these sorts of vertical restraints to trade with respect to automobiles and film in Japan, see Scherer (1997).

[9] Although some studies have found small increases in profits for merging firms, most have found that the profits of merging companies either do not change or decline, on average, after the mergers. The significant gains in wealth to shareholders of acquired companies at the time of the mergers are subsequently offset, or more than offset by losses borne by the shareholders of the acquiring companies. The growth rates and market shares of merging firms decline after the mergers. This literature is reviewed in Mueller ([1977] 1991, 1996), Caves (1989), and Ross and Scherer (1990, pp. 167–174).

zontal merger involving companies that account for a large fraction of a world market should be challengeable under a global competition policy. In a recent paper, I have proposed that any domestic merger between a company with 20% or more of a market, and a second firm with 5% or more of the market should be presumed in violation of an antimerger statute, *subject to an efficiency defense* (Mueller, 1996). A reasonable global policy toward mergers would look similar, but would calculate market shares relative to world production.[10] Such a policy would ban all mergers between firms possessing the designated market shares, but would allow them to go forward if the merging firms could demonstrate that the merger promised a net welfare gain because the cost savings due to greater efficiency more than offset any consumer surplus losses from higher prices.

The most obvious efficiency to expect from a horizontal merger is through the realization of scale economies. While such economies might be sufficiently large to justify mergers between companies serving a domestic market, where market shares are measured relative to this market, few if any industries have such gigantic scale economies that they need large shares of world production to obtain minimum efficient size.[11] Thus, few if any horizontal mergers that exceeded the market share limits of the regulation would be likely to present a successful efficiencies defense based on economies of scale if the market shares were measured relative to world production. Although market share thresholds like 20% and 5% are somewhat arbitrary, when measured relative to the size of world markets they certainly do not seem excessive.

A merger that did not pass a market share test like the one above would be expected to have the same adverse effect on world competition when the merging firms are located in the same country as when they are in different countries. Thus, a global competition policy would

[10] In some cases, a domestic market might be so large relative to world production that a purely domestic merger would violate the global standard. A company's world market share should then be calculated as its total sales less its domestic sales divided by world production in this market less domestic production. For companies producing in more than one country, this adjustment could only be made for its largest domestic market.

[11] For evidence of the magnitude of scale economies relative to market sizes, see Scherer et al. (1975).

have to be capable of blocking "domestic" mergers when the merging firms account for sufficiently high shares of world sales. A good example of a merger that might result in a sufficient increase in market power to benefit not only the merging companies, but also their home country, is the recent Boeing/McDonnell–Douglas merger.

B Vertical Mergers

Vertical mergers can have anticompetitive consequences by raising entry barriers into vertically integrated markets. The possibility of achieving such dominance in a world market is unlikely to arise in any industries other than those linked to minerals and other natural resources. An antimerger regulation like the one discussed in the previous subsection would effectively deal with vertical mergers, where the market shares would now pertain to firms vertically linked in a production chain.

C Conglomerate Mergers

Several studies have found that companies that compete against one another in several separate markets tend to have higher profit rates and higher prices than one would predict based on their market shares and industry concentration levels (Scott, 1982, 1993; Evans and Kessides, 1994). *Multimarket contact* appears to facilitate collusion and cooperation between rivals. These results based on diversification within national boundaries imply that international diversification might also have anticompetitive effects if the multinational companies were diversified into similar markets in the same set of countries.

One way to deal with the adverse consequences of multimarket contact would be to treat it as a form of collusion, and challenge it under the regulations dealing with cartel behavior. If, however, multimarket contact only facilitates *tacit* collusion between firms, as the empirical evidence suggests may be true, a global competition policy authority which found a group of multinationals guilty of collusion would have to do so on the basis of evidence suggesting higher prices or price-cost margins in some countries than in others. As discussed in connection with price discrimination, such evidence is costly to come by, and decisions to fine or break up international firms based on such evidence would likely be highly controversial.

A simpler approach would be to prevent multimarket contact from arising in the first place by prohibiting the mergers that bring it about. Such an approach would also be fraught with difficulties, however, if the ICPO had to prove that a particular diversification merger was likely to have substantial anticompetitive effects. For such a demonstration, the ICPO would have to be able to determine the number of markets and countries in which a set of multinationals must jointly compete for multimarket contact to be raised to an undesirable level. Any policy that prevented some companies from undertaking mergers that would "merely" allow them to duplicate the international diversification patterns of their chief rivals would appear arbitrary to the companies prevented from merging, and most likely to the governments of their countries of origin. Such a policy would again be likely to embroil an ICPO in considerable controversy.

An alternative way to prevent those diversification mergers that lead to anticompetitive increases in multimarket contact would be simply to ban all mergers between firms above some absolute size, again subject to an efficiencies defense. I have proposed such a ban as part of a domestic antimerger policy (Mueller, 1996). Since only very large multinationals could achieve significant multimarket contact, a size-related ban would prevent those mergers that were most likely to achieve significant multimarket contact.

Although such a policy would obviously target the mergers of large multinationals, it would not prevent firms from becoming large multinationals *if significant economies can be achieved from running large, diversified international firms*. If significant economies of scope can be achieved, let us say, from jointly producing and marketing cigarettes, beer, coffee, and chocolate, then a firm could achieve these economies through either internal expansion or merger in its domestic market. It would also not be prevented from achieving these economies on an international basis, if it chose to do so by building breweries, chocolate factories, and the like in other countries. It would only be prevented from growing as a multinational by *buying* existing breweries and chocolate manufacturers, *unless* it could demonstrate that such mergers were likely to result in significantly lower costs and prices. If significant economies of scope could be achieved by combining these activities, then the would-be multinational would presumably already be experiencing them in its diversified operations in its home country. All it would have to do to justify a similar international diversification effort would be to show that it had lower costs and prices than its rivals in its home market.

D Efficiency-Reducing Mergers

Efficiency-reducing mergers can occur for a variety of reasons: to fulfill the empire-building desires of managers, to fill the pockets of promoters and speculators, out of managerial hubris, etc. (Markham, 1955; Mueller, [1969] 1991, 1996; Roll, 1986). Even when the speculators and managers gain from the mergers, the shareholders of the acquiring companies lose. Society loses also, because the efforts of managers of acquisition-oriented firms are diverted from creating assets to transferring them, and because the mergers often go awry destroying the assets of once healthy companies. The many studies that find that mergers reduce profits, market shares, and shareholder wealth imply that society would gain from the prevention of these mergers.[12]

A ban of all mergers between firms above some absolute size, subject to an efficiencies defense, would also prevent those efficiency-reducing mergers that occur across borders. These might be many or few, depending on where one drew the size threshold. Should it prove difficult to meet the efficiencies defense, conceivably some mergers that would have been socially beneficial would not occur. But so, too, would many that would have reduced efficiency and harmed most likely those living in the country of the target firm. Given that internal expansion is always an alternative to merger, and one which is *sure to create* assets and jobs in the short run, whereas a merger merely *transfers* assets and jobs in the short run and may or may not create them in the long run, society would not lose from a ban of large international mergers.

VI Conclusions

The challenges in establishing and enforcing a global competition policy are at once considerably greater and smaller than for an individual country. They are greater in that for an individual country the winners and losers from the application of a competition policy are both gen-

[12] See again the references in fn. 9.

erally located within the country. Any protest about the application of the policy by those who are harmed by it will to some extent be drowned out by the applause of the gainers. Politicians can deflect the protests of the losers to some extent by eliciting the support of the gainers. Since the net gains to a community from the enforcement of competition policies are positive in the long run, popular support for such policies may reasonably be expected to develop over time, even though particular policy decisions may become the focus of much controversy.

On the other hand, even within countries, a political imbalance between the gainers and losers from competition policy often exists, because the losers are typically the owners and possibly the employees of companies that are prevented from enjoying the rents engendered by monopolistic practices, while the immediate or ultimate beneficiaries are consumers. Thus, the losses are concentrated upon relatively small and well-organized groups, while the gains are spread widely and thinly over a politically poorly organized group. This political disparity helps explain the strength and venerability of laws and regulations protecting workers and workers' cartels in Europe relative to European competition policies and other forms of consumer protection.

This political disparity is even more pronounced with respect to international trade and competition. In the international arena the gains from anticompetitive policies accrue to firms and workers in one set of countries, the losses they generate fall mainly on those in other countries. Thus, not surprisingly one finds countries like the United States, which has relatively consistently and vigorously enforced a domestic anticartel policy, simultaneously allowing domestic firms to form cartels when the victims are buyers in other countries.

The growth in prosperity that has accompanied the liberalization and expansion of world trade over the last 50 years should be ample proof that "free trade" causes, or at least is compatible with, economic prosperity. As the process of liberalization continues to expand with more countries entering the WTO and additional barriers to trade falling, the need for an effective global competition policy grows. Little is to be gained from falling tariffs if cartels are free to substitute their restrictive practices for those of the state.

Up to the present, states have generally allowed their firms to participate in internationally oriented cartels, often encouraged and supported such participation, and sometimes have even organized and run the cartels. The most conspicuous example of the latter has been, of course, the OPEC cartel. The increases in the price of oil that this cartel brought about in the 1970s helped precipitate a major world recession from which Western Europe arguably has never fully recovered. Billions of dollars of assets were destroyed or failed to be created as unemployment rose and investment fell around the world. The value of the assets destroyed by the cartel was undoubtedly far greater than the participating countries could have destroyed had they gone to war against the rest of the world. So long as countries and companies are free to form cartels and engage in other sorts of anticompetitive practices, the growth in wealth of the nations of the world will be hindered. The most difficult challenge facing a global competition policy is to convince governmental leaders of the advantages of such a policy.

This challenge is made somewhat easier by the fact that the full panoply of competition policies that have been tried and are perhaps warranted in the context of an individual country is not required to preserve competition on a global level. I have identified three major components of such a policy: (1) an anticartel policy that can be applied to international cartels, domestic export and import cartels, and government operated cartels; (2) an antimonopolization policy with effective protection against the predatory practices of internationally dominant firms; and (3) an effective antimerger policy. Although refusals to deal (buy) and cross-national territorial restrictions are likely to involve cartel or monopoly abuses and thus be challengeable under the first two policies, additional regulations might also be useful in these areas.

An anticartel policy would eliminate the most important source of restrictions on trade other than those directly raised by governments. An effective antipredation policy would eliminate the only legitimate reason for concern about *low* import prices, and thus would *allow* the repeal or international prohibition of all antidumping regulations. An effective antimerger policy would prevent all firms from achieving market advantages through merger that they could not achieve through the quality of their products and efficiency of their operations. Until an enforceable global competition policy with these elements exists, global trade can never truly be free, and citizens everywhere will be partially held hostage by those who can manipulate "the terms of trade" to their advantage.

Bibliography

Areeda, P., and D.F. Turner. 1975. "Predatory Pricing and Related Practices Under Section 2 of the Sherman Act." *Harvard Law Review* 88:697–733.

Baumol, W.J., J.C. Panzer, and R.D. Willig. 1982. *Contestable Markets and the Theory of Industry Structure*. New York: Harcourt, Brace, Jovanovich.

Bittlingmayer, G. 1985. "Did Antitrust Policy Cause the Great Merger Wave?" *Journal of Law and Economics* 28:77–118.

Bork, R. 1978. *The Antitrust Paradox*. New York: Basic Books.

Brock, G.W. [1989] 1994. "Dominant Firm Response to Competitive Challenge: Peripheral Equipment Manufacturers' Suits Against IBM (1979–1983)." In: J.E. Kwoka, Jr., and L.J. White (eds.), *The Antitrust Revolution*, pp. 160–182. Glenview, Ill.: Scott, Foresman & Co.

Caves, R.E. 1989. "Mergers, Takeovers and Economic Efficiency: Foresight vs. Hindsight." *International Journal of Industrial Organization* 7:151–174.

Comanor, W.S., and F.M. Scherer. 1995. "Rewriting History: the Early Sherman Act Monopolization Cases." *International Journal of the Economics of Business* 2:263–289.

Economist. April 6, 1996, pp. 81–82.

Edwards, C.D. 1959. *The Price Discrimination Law*. Washington: Brookings Institution.

Elzinga, K.G. [1989] 1994. "Collusive Predation: Matsushita v. Zenith (1986)." In: J.E. Kwoka, Jr., and L.J. White (eds.), *The Antitrust Revolution*, Second Edition, pp. 238–259, Glenview, Ill.: Scott, Foresman & Co.

Evans, W.N., and I.N. Kessides. 1994. "Living by the 'Golden Rule': Multimarket Contact in the US Airline Industry." *Quarterly Journal of Economics* 109:341–366.

Fisher, F.M., J.J. McGowan, and J.E. Greenwood. 1983. *Folded, Spindled, and Multilated: Economic Analysis and U.S. vs. IBM*. Cambridge, Mass.: MIT Press.

George, K., and A. Jacquemin. 1990. "Competition Policy in the European Community." In W.S. Comanor et al. (eds.), *Competition Policy in Europe and North America: Economic Issues and Institutions*, pp. 206–245. Chur: Harwood Academic Publishers.

Joskow, P., and A.K. Klevorick. 1979. "A Framework for Analyzing Predatory Pricing Policy." *Yale Law Journal* 89:213–270.

Klein, B., and L.F. Saft. 1985. "The Law and Economics of Franchise Tying Contracts." *Journal of Law and Economics* 28:345–361.

Libecap, G.D. 1992. "The Rise of the Chicago Packers and the Origins of Meat Inspection and Antitrust." *Economic Inquiry* 30:242–262.

Markham, J.W. 1955. "Survey of the Evidence and Findings on Mergers." In: *Business Concentration and Price Policy*. Princeton: Princeton University Press.

Martin, S. 1994. *Industrial Economics*. Second Edition. Englewood Cliffs, N.J.: Prentice-Hall.

Marvel, H.P. 1982. "Exclusive Dealing." *Journal of Law and Economics* 25:1–25.

Marvel, H.P., and S. McCafferty. 1984. "Resale Price Maintenance and Quality Certification." *Rand Journal of Economics* 15:346–359.

Marvel, H.P., and S. McCafferty. 1985. "The Welfare Effects of Resale Price Maintenance." *Journal of Law and Economics* 28:363–379.

McGee, J.S. 1958. "Predatory Price Cutting: The Standard Oil (N.J.) Case." *Journal of Law and Economics* 1:137–169.

Mueller, D.C. [1969] 1991. "A Theory of Conglomerate Mergers." In: G. Marchildon (ed.), *Mergers and Acquisitions*, pp. 496–512. London: Elgar.

Mueller, D.C. [1977] 1991. "The Effects of Conglomerate Mergers: A Survey of the Empirical Evidence." In: G. Marchildon (ed.), *Mergers and Acquisitions*, pp. 349–381. London: Elgar.

Mueller, D.C. 1986. *Profits in the Long Run*. Cambridge: Cambridge University Press.

Mueller, D.C. 1996. "Antimerger Policy in the United States: History and Lessons." *Empirica* 23:229–253.

Mueller, D.C. 1997a. "First-Mover Advantages and Path Dependence." *International Journal of Industrial Organization* 15:827–850.

Mueller, D.C. 1997b. "The Public Economics of Public Subsidies for Private Firms." Forschungsbericht N. 9713. Vienna: Ludwig Boltzmann Institut.

Posner, R.A. 1976. *Antitrust Law: An Economic Perspective*. Chicago: University of Chicago Press.

Roll, R. 1986. "The Hubris Hypothesis of Corporate Takeovers." *Journal of Business* 59:197–216.

Scherer, F.M. 1994. *Competition Policies for an Integrated World Economy*. Washington, D.C.: Brookings Institution.

Scherer, F.M. 1997. "Retail Distribution Channel Barriers to International Trade." ESRC Working Paper No. 55. Cambridge: University of Cambridge.

Scherer, F.M., A. Beckenstein, E. Kaufer, and R.D. Murphy. 1975. *The Economics of Multi-Plant Operation: An International Comparisons Study*. Cambridge, Mass.: Harvard University Press.

Scherer, F.M., and D. Ross. 1990. *Industrial Market Structure and Economic Performance*. Third Edition. Boston: Houghton Mifflin.

Scott, J.T. 1982. "Multimarket Contact and Economic Performance." *Review of Economics and Statistics* 64:368–375.

Scott, J.T. 1993. *Purposive Diversification and Economic Performance*. Cambridge: Cambridge University Press.

Warren-Boulton, F.R. [1989] 1994. "Resale Price Maintenance Reexamined: Monsanto v. Spray-Rite (1984)." In: J.E. Kwoka, Jr., and L.J. White (eds.), *The Antitrust Revolution*, Second Edition, pp. 400–431. Glenview, Ill.: Scott, Foresman & Co.

Name index

Economists of the Twentieth Century

Monetarism and Macroeconomic Policy
Thomas Mayer

Studies in Fiscal Federalism
Wallace E. Oates

The World Economy in Perspective
Essays in International Trade and European Integration
Herbert Giersch

Towards a New Economics
Critical Essays on Ecology, Distribution and Other Themes
Kenneth E. Boulding

Studies in Positive and Normative Economics
Martin J. Bailey

The Collected Essays of Richard E. Quandt (2 volumes)
Richard E. Quandt

International Trade Theory and Policy
Selected Essays of W. Max Corden
W. Max Corden

Organization and Technology in Capitalist Development
William Lazonick

Studies in Human Capital
Collected Essays of Jacob Mincer, Volume 1
Jacob Mincer

Studies in Labor Supply
Collected Essays of Jacob Mincer, Volume 2
Jacob Mincer

Macroeconomics and Economic Policy
The Selected Essays of Assar Lindbeck
Volume I
Assar Lindbeck

The Welfare State
The Selected Essays of Assar Lindbeck
Volume II
Assar Lindbeck

Classical Economics, Public Expenditure and Growth
Walter Eltis

Money, Interest Rates and Inflation
Frederic S. Mishkin

The Public Choice Approach to Politics
Dennis C. Mueller

The Liberal Economic Order
Volume I Essays on International Economics
Volume II Money, Cycles and Related Themes
Gottfried Haberler
Edited by Anthony Y.C. Koo

Economic Growth and Business Cycles
Prices and the Process of Cyclical Development
Paolo Sylos Labini

International Adjustment, Money and Trade
Theory and Measurement for Economic Policy
Volume I
Herbert G. Grubel

International Capital and Service Flows
Theory and Measurement for Economic Policy
Volume II
Herbert G. Grubel

Unintended Effects of Government Policies
Theory and Measurement for Economic Policy
Volume III
Herbert G. Grubel

The Economics of Competitive Enterprise
Selected Essays of P.W.S. Andrews
Edited by Frederic S. Lee
and Peter E. Earl

The Repressed Economy
Causes, Consequences, Reform
Deepak Lal

Economic Theory and Market Socialism
Selected Essays of Oskar Lange
Edited by Tadeusz Kowalik

Trade, Development and Political Economy
Selected Essays of Ronald Findlay
Ronald Findlay

General Equilibrium Theory
The Collected Essays of Takashi Negishi
Volume I
Takashi Negishi

The History of Economics
The Collected Essays of Takashi Negishi
Volume II
Takashi Negishi

Studies in Econometric Theory
The Collected Essays of Takeshi Amemiya
Takeshi Amemiya

Exchange Rates and the Monetary System
Selected Essays of Peter B. Kenen
Peter B. Kenen

Econometric Methods and Applications
(2 volumes)
G.S. Maddala

National Accounting and Economic Theory
The Collected Papers of Dan Usher, Volume I
Dan Usher

Welfare Economics and Public Finance
The Collected Papers of Dan Usher, Volume II
Dan Usher

Economic Theory and Capitalist Society
The Selected Essays of Shigeto Tsuru, Volume I
Shigeto Tsuru

Methodology, Money and the Firm
The Collected Essays of D.P. O'Brien
(2 volumes)
D.P. O'Brien

Economic Theory and Financial Policy
The Selected Essays of Jacques J. Polak
(2 volumes)
Jacques J. Polak

Sturdy Econometrics
Edward E. Leamer

The Emergence of Economic Ideas
Essays in the History of Economics
Nathan Rosenberg

Productivity Change, Public Goods and Transaction Costs
Essays at the Boundaries of Microeconomics
Yoram Barzel

Reflections on Economic Development
The Selected Essays of Michael P. Todaro
Michael P. Todaro

The Economic Development of Modern Japan
The Selected Essays of Shigeto Tsuru
Volume II
Shigeto Tsuru

Money, Credit and Policy
Allan H. Meltzer

Macroeconomics and Monetary Theory
The Selected Essays of Meghnad Desai
Volume I
Meghnad Desai

Poverty, Famine and Economic Development
The Selected Essays of Meghnad Desai
Volume II
Meghnad Desai

Explaining the Economic Performance of Nations
Essays in Time and Space
Angus Maddison

Economic Doctrine and Method
Selected Papers of R.W. Clower
Robert W. Clower

Economic Theory and Reality
Selected Essays on their Disparities and Reconciliation
Tibor Scitovsky

Doing Economic Research
Essays on the Applied Methodology of Economics
Thomas Mayer

Institutions and Development Strategies
The Selected Essays of Irma Adelman
Volume I
Irma Adelman

Dynamics and Income Distribution
The Selected Essays of Irma Adelman
Volume II
Irma Adelman

The Economics of Growth and Development
Selected Essays of A.P. Thirlwall
A.P. Thirlwall

Theoretical and Applied Econometrics
The Selected Papers of Phoebus J. Dhrymes
Phoebus J. Dhrymes

Innovation, Technology and the Economy
The Selected Essays of Edwin Mansfield
(2 volumes)
Edwin Mansfield

Economic Theory and Policy in Context
The Selected Essays of R.D. Collison Black
R.D. Collison Black

Location Economics
Theoretical Underpinnings and Applications
Melvin L. Greenhut

Spatial Microeconomics
Theoretical Underpinnings and Applications
Melvin L. Greenhut

Capitalism, Socialism and Post-Keynesianism
Selected Essays of G.C. Harcourt
G.C. Harcourt

Time Series Analysis and Macroeconometric Modelling
The Collected Papers of Kenneth F. Wallis
Kenneth F. Wallis

Foundations of Modern Econometrics
The Selected Essays of Ragnar Frisch
(2 volumes)
Edited by Olav Bjerkholt

Growth, the Environment and the Distribution of Incomes
Essays by a Sceptical Optimist
Wilfred Beckerman

The Economics of Environmental Regulation
Wallace E. Oates

Econometrics, Macroeconomics and Economic Policy
Selected Papers of Carl F. Christ
Carl F. Christ

Strategic Approaches to the International Economy
Selected Essays of Koichi Hamada
Koichi Hamada

Economic Analysis and Political Ideology
The Selected Essays of Karl Brunner
Volume One
Edited by Thomas Lys

Growth Theory and Technical Change
The Selected Essays of Ryuzo Sato
Volume One
Ryuzo Sato

Industrialization, Inequality and Economic Growth
Jeffrey G. Williamson

Economic Theory and Public Decisions
Selected Essays of Robert Dorfman
Robert Dorfman

The Logic of Action One
Method, Money, and the Austrian School
Murray N. Rothbard

The Logic of Action Two
Applications and Criticism from the Austrian School
Murray N. Rothbard

Bayesian Analysis in Econometrics and Statistics
The Zellner View and Papers
Arnold Zellner

On the Foundations of Monopolistic Competition and Economic Geography
The Selected Essays of B. Curtis Eaton and Richard G. Lipsey
B. Curtis Eaton and Richard G. Lipsey

Microeconomics, Growth and Political Economy
The Selected Essays of Richard G. Lipsey
Volume One
Richard G. Lipsey

Macroeconomic Theory and Policy
The Selected Essays of Richard G. Lipsey
Volume Two
Richard G. Lipsey

Employment, Labor Unions and Wages
The Collected Essays of Orley Ashenfelter
Volume One
Edited by Kevin F. Hallock

Education, Training and Discrimination
The Collected Essays of Orley Ashenfelter
Volume Two
Edited by Kevin F. Hallock

Economic Institutions and the Demand and Supply of Labour
The Collected Essays of Orley Ashenfelter
Volume Three
Edited by Kevin F. Hallock

Monetary Theory and Monetary Policy
The Selected Essays of Karl Brunner
Volume Two
Edited by Thomas Lys

Macroeconomic Issues from a Keynesian Perspective
Selected Essays of A.P. Thirlwall
Volume Two
A.P. Thirlwall

Money and Macroeconomics
The Selected Essays of David Laidler
David Laidler

The Economics and Politics of Money
The Selected Essays of Alan Walters
Edited by Kent Matthews

Economics and Social Justice
Essays on Power, Labor and Institutional Change
David M. Gordon
Edited by Thomas E. Weisskopf and Samuel Bowles

Practicing Econometrics
Essays in Method and Application
Zvi Griliches

Economics Against the Grain
Volume One
Microeconomics, Industrial Organization and Related Themes
Julian L. Simon

Economics Against the Grain
Volume Two
Population Economics, Natural Resources and Related Themes
Julian L. Simon

Advances in Econometric Theory
The Selected Works of Halbert White
Halbert White

The Economics of Imperfect Knowledge
Collected Papers of G.B. Richardson
G.B. Richardson

Economic Performance and the Theory of the Firm
The Selected Papers of David J. Teece
Volume One
David J. Teece

Strategy, Technology and Public Policy
The Selected Papers of David J. Teece
Volume Two
David J. Teece

The Keynesian Revolution, Then and Now
The Selected Essays of Robert Eisner
Volume One
Robert Eisner

Investment, National Income and Economic Policy
The Selected Essays of Robert Eisner
Volume Two
Robert Eisner

International Trade Opening and the Formation of the Global Economy
Selected Essays of P. J. Lloyd
P. J. Lloyd

Production, Stability and Dynamic Symmetry
The Selected Essays of Ryuzo Sato
Volume Two
Ryuzo Sato

Variants in Economic Theory
Selected Works of Hal R. Varian
Hal R. Varian

Political Economy, Oligopoly and Experimental Games
The Selected Essays of Martin Shubik
Volume One
Martin Shubik

Money and Financial Institutions
A GAME THEORETIC APPROACH
The Selected Essays of Martin Shubik
Volume Two
Martin Shubik

Competition Policy, Domestic and International
F.M. Scherer

Macroeconomic Instability and Coordination
Selected Essays of Axel Leijonhufvud
Axel Leijonhufvud

Economic Thought from Smith to Keynes
The Collected Essays of Takashi Negishi
Volume III
Takashi Negishi

Education Matters
Selected Essays by Alan B. Krueger
Alan B. Krueger

The Economic Structure of the Law
The Collected Economic Esssays of Richard A. Posner
Volume One
Richard A. Posner
Edited by Francesco Parisi

Measurement and Meaning in Economics
The Essential Deirdre McCloskey
Deirdre McCloskey
Edited and introduced by Stephen Thomas Ziliak

The Economics of Private Law
The Collected Economic Esssays of
Richard A. Posner
Volume Two
Richard A. Posner
Edited by Francesco Parisi

The Economics of Public Law
The Collected Economic Esssays of
Richard A. Posner
Volume Three
Richard A. Posner
Edited by Francesco Parisi

Public Economics, Political Processes and Policy Applications
Collected Papers on the Experimental
Foundations of Economics and Political Science
Volume One
Charles R. Plott

Market Institutions and Price Discovery
Collected Papers on the Experimental
Foundations of Economics and Political Science
Volume Two
Charles R. Plott

Information, Finance and General Equilibrium
Collected Papers on the Experimental
Foundations of Economics and Political
Science
Volume Threc
Charles R. Plott

Growth Theory, Nonlinear Dynamics and Economic Modelling
Scientific Essays of William Allen Brock
William Allen Brock
Edited by W. Davis Dechert

Capitalism and Democracy
Challenges and Responses in an Increasingly
Interdependent World
Dennis C. Mueller